Physical Culture and
Sport in Soviet Society

Routledge Research in Sports History

Physical Culture and Sport in Soviet Society

Propaganda, Acculturation, and Transformation in the 1920s and 1930s

Susan Grant

Routledge
Taylor & Francis Group
NEW YORK   LONDON

First published 2013
by Routledge
711 Third Avenue, New York, NY 10017

Simultaneously published in the UK
by Routledge
2 Park Square, Milton Park, Abingdon, Oxon OX14 4RN

*Routledge is an imprint of the Taylor & Francis Group,
an informa business*

Library of Congress Cataloging-in-Publication Data
Grant, Susan.
    Physical culture and sport in Soviet society : propaganda, acculturation,
and transformation in the 1920s and 1930s / Susan Grant.
        p. cm. — (Routledge research in sports history ; 2)
    Includes bibliographical references and index.
    1. Sports and state—Soviet Union—History.   2. Sports administration—
Soviet Union—History.   3. Sports—Social aspects—Soviet Union—
History.   I. Title.
    GV706.35.G7 2012
    796.0947—dc23
    2012004326

ISBN13: 978-0-415-80695-4 (hbk)
ISBN13: 978-0-203-10519-1 (ebk)

Typeset in Sabon
by IBT Global.

Printed and bound in the United States of America on sustainably sourced
paper by IBT Global.

To my family

Contents

Figures

Note on Transliteration and Style

The system of transliteration used here is the Library of Congress system. However, there are some exceptions. Well-known names and places are given in their more familiar English forms, for example, Tomskii appears as Tomsky or Lunacharskii as Lunacharsky. In cases where proper nouns or names begin with "E", I have chosen to spell these as "Ye" for phonetic purposes. Thus, for instance, Ezhov becomes Yezhov.

Almost all of the Russian terms that have been transliterated appear in italics. Some terms that are more familiar, for instance, Komsomol or Dinamo, have not been italicized. I have also chosen not to italicize some frequently used acronyms such as Vsevobuch or Osoaviakhim.

Acknowledgments

This research received generous financial support from a number of different sources including University College Dublin's School of History and Archives which awarded me the Postgraduate Scholarship and Doctoral Scholarship. The Russian–Irish Government Exchange Scholarship provided me with the opportunity to study in the Russian State University of the Humanities, Moscow, where I was able to conduct research in the archives for the academic year 2008–2009. An Irish Research Council for the Humanities and Social Sciences Postdoctoral Fellowship in 2010–2011 meant that I could revise my dissertation for publication and also allowed for further research trips to Russia.

This work could not have been completed without the assistance and patience of a long list of people. Atop this list is my supervisor and mentor, Judith Devlin, who has been an unfailing source of support, encouragement and inspiration. Both her willingness to share her time and knowledge, as well as her wit and good humour, have made researching and writing this project an enjoyable experience. The administrative and academic staff of University College Dublin, especially those in the School of History and Archives and the James Joyce Library, were constantly on hand to assist and provide support. Dr. Catherine Cox and Dr. Paul Rouse from the School of History and Archives provided stimulating and valuable comments on health and sport matters. Geoffrey Roberts, Patryk Babiracki, James Ryan, John Paul Newman, Matthias Neumann, Stephen White, Sarah Badcock, Jeffrey Brooks, and Richard Fraher all read parts of the manuscript at varying levels of completion and offered some very timely, helpful, and encouraging words and suggestions. The support and advice of Angela Byrne, Niamh Reilly, Gleb Albert, Steven Jug, Pia Koivunen, Alex Titov, Alistair Wright, and countless others helped me immensely. My thanks also to other friends and colleagues met at conferences or in archives who have helped shape this manuscript in some form or another. The Study Group for the Russian Revolution, especially Christopher Read and Anthony Heywood, have been a source of great support and their kind words, encouragement, and advice have been invaluable.

In Moscow, the Gorky Literary Institute provided a comfortable and congenial environment in which to work. The advice, help and generosity of Dr. Ekaterina Eduardovna Iurchik in particular is much appreciated. The administrative staff and teachers in both the Gorky Literary Institute and the Russian State University of the Humanities were always kind and attentive. The same can be said of the helpful and welcoming staff of the Moscow and Penza archives and libraries. My friend Svetlana Maximenko, her family, and her friends have always provided me, often quite literally, with a home away from home. Olga Kleshaeva has also been a constant Moscow companion and her family and friends in Penza provided me with a warm welcome, taking a keen interest in my work and in showing me the provincial Russian way of life.

For all of their patience and assistance in the production of this book, I thank my editor Max Novick, as well as Jennifer Morrow, Eleanor Chan, and Susan Certo.

Finally, this book would not have been possible without the support of my family. My husband, Shane, is a constant source of support and endures my frequent and sometimes lengthy absences without (much) complaint. My parents, my brother Richard, and Shane's parents have also been instrumental in helping me to complete this project, always on hand to help out whenever necessary. This book is dedicated to them.

Portions of this work have appeared in other publications, and I thank these journals for allowing me to reprint sections of my following articles:

"The Politics of Physical Culture in the 1920s", *Slavonic and East European Review* 89, no. 3 (July 2011): 494–515

"The Fizkul'tura Generation: Modernizing Lifestyles in Early Soviet Russia", *The Soviet and Post-Soviet Review* 37, no. 2 (2010): 142–165

"The Collective Agitation of Arms and Legs: Revolutionizing Physical Culture Organization 1924–1934", *Revolutionary Russia* (2010): 93–113.

Introduction

This is a history of early Soviet physical culture and sport that, by tracing developments in the world of physical culture and sport during a formative and revolutionary period, encounters myriad broader developments within Soviet society, culture, and politics. A study of physical culture provides historians of Soviet Russia with an important prism through which to view these broader transitions and developments while simultaneously proving a worthy subject of study in and of itself. Leading scholars in the field of sports studies, such as Jennifer Hargreaves, have in the past rightly argued that the social significance of sport has been seriously underestimated with a failure "to trace connections between sport, power, domination and political control".[1] This has since changed, and as Jeffrey Hill has demonstrated in relation to British sport and Barbara Keys in relation to the US and elsewhere, sport has had an immense impact on society, culture, and indeed politics.[2] In the Soviet Union the social significance of sport was never underestimated, with physical culture closely linked to power and politics from the outset. This significance of physical culture and sport within a wider social, cultural, and political framework has indeed been acknowledged and reflected in recent studies on Soviet history.[3]

Before going any further, it is first necessary to distinguish between physical culture and sport. Physical culture in the Soviet Union, by definition, was much broader than simply sport and exercise. It in fact covered a wide spectrum ranging from hygiene and health issues to sports, defence interests, labour concerns, leisure, education, and general cultural enlightenment. This broader interpretation of physical culture is what Commissar for Health and Chairperson of the Supreme Council of Physical Culture Nikolai Semashko attempted to convey and is what I want to investigate here. A narrower examination would fail to reflect the wide-ranging impact and functions of physical culture. Semashko was at pains to point out that his key phrase of physical culture "twenty-four hours a day" in actuality incorporated work, sleep, and rest (preferably eight hours of each) and not twenty-four hours of serious physical exercise. Following Semashko's call for a broader interpretation of physical culture, I have duly set out to examine physical culture from a mutli-faceted perspective assessing the roles, efficacy, and impact in each of its many spheres. What becomes apparent is that physical culture was in many ways a lifestyle, an attitude, and a mode of behaviour. It was designed to propel backward Russia into modernity, or at least put her on a par with health and hygiene standards in other European countries. Indeed, with Semashko in charge, the ideology of physical culture became increasingly intertwined with the larger public health issues of social hygiene and prophylaxis.[4]

Catriona Kelly and David Shepherd in their seminal *Constructing Russian Culture* discuss "programmes for identity" with physical culture one such programme. It is this notion of physical culture as a programme for identity that perhaps comes closest to explaining this work. Physical culture was certainly viewed as a programme, a multifunctional and flexible programme that could be used in all manner of ways. The ideology of physical culture, I argue, was frequently adapted to suit the changing needs of society and politics, to meet whatever form of identity the authorities saw fit to project at any given time. In terms of identity, my examination of physical culture in the 1920s and 1930s reflects an ongoing process of, to use Sheila Fitzpatrick's phrase, "identity-moulding", whereby physical culture propaganda, social organizations, educational institutes etc. were deployed by the state to draw people towards practicing "Soviet" physical culture and ipso facto adopting a socialist lifestyle.[5] My primary interest, however, is not in exploring per se Soviet identity or identification, ideology, or image; rather, the objective of this study is an analysis of Soviet physical culture as a subject in its own right.[6] Issues of identity, modernization, ideology, and transformation are what emerge from this study—these are the processes and subtexts that are interwoven within the broader physical culture narrative.

I share the view of Kelly and Shepherd, who argue that it was much easier for leaders and dominant social groups to "manufacture 'blueprints for identity' than to 'engineer human souls' in the envisaged manner".[7] Practical problems continually dictated the successful implementation of any programmes. It was easier to simply disseminate the ideology of physical culture—that is, the potential power of participation in physical culture and sport to impart physical and mental transformation—rather than tackle directly practical issues that could not be immediately resolved owing to economic circumstances. Consequently it was the ideology of physical culture that was repeatedly called upon throughout the 1920s and 1930s, petitioning citizens with a message that sought to instruct and inspire. It became an integral part of the socialist educational ethos of community building and nation building. As a programme for identity physical culture had the potential of near mass appeal and as a result represented a symbol of national unity. Of course "physical culture" was not a uniquely Soviet concept, but the Soviet understanding of physical culture did elevate physical culture beyond the valuation by many other countries in its importance and breadth. In its Soviet interpretation physical culture meant many different things for many different people, and it was precisely this nebulous quality and the lack of a singular direction which often led to complications when it came to the practice of physical culture. On the other hand, this same nebulous quality meant that physical culture could be reinvented, reformulated, or reorganized to suit the changing needs of the state and the individual.

If taken as a larger, theoretical concept in itself then, I contend that physical culture was an important part of the overall struggle to impose socialist ideals on Soviet society, but especially in the form of *vospitanie* and *kul'turnost'*—two of the essential prerequisites of the modern Soviet state and later the New Soviet Person.[8] In this sense the four-level scheme of acculturation forwarded by Régine Robin is useful in understanding the various elements at work in the attempted process of making the Soviet Union a formidable, united, and cultured state. Firstly, access to knowledge and learning—what Robin calls the cognitive level—was critical for social integration.[9] After this came the axiological level—values, ideology, or agitiation and propaganda—which introduced a new discourse and instilled Bolshevik values. The third level described by Robin is the symbolic. This referred to new holidays, new songs, new heroes; included both the everyday and the ceremonial; and "strived to create a new social imaginary".[10] The final level, and as Robin admits, perhaps the most subtle, was that of the "new social codes, new practices and new behaviour which characterized relations between classes and social groups, men and women, the old and the young, children and parents, individuals and families" and which "characterized the attitudes toward sexuality, dietary codes, forms of sociability". The development of physical culture in the early Soviet period reflects this four-level categorization of Soviet socialization: education, discourse, symbolism, and practices were all key features of physical culture. Their application to physical culture (in the form of health, sanitation, hygiene, sport, exercise, dress) can also be interpreted as a form of discourse on Soviet culture and society. Omitted in Robin's hypothesis is organization, which introduced political interpretations of and attitudes to physical culture and how it should be applied to Soviet society. Organization was integral to Bolshevik power and this is amply reflected in a study of physical culture. Whether in the higher state organs or on a lower, local level, those involved in the organization of physical culture sought to implement socialist values through an organized, state-controlled system of physical culture and later sport.

The work of those historians who have already ventured into the realm of Soviet sports history have been of great benefit to this project. The most comprehensive Russian and Soviet publications on physical culture and sport include works by V. V. Stolbov, F. I. Samoukov, F. D. Sinitsyn, and S. L. Aksel'rod.[11] Many of the Soviet sources in this area function as useful background narratives, but display symptoms of Soviet ideological constrictions, with Soviet physical culture viewed as "good" and western sport viewed as inherently "bad". Take for example Aksel'rod's work, which describes sport in the west, but particularly in the United States, as being used to "stupefy the population", to "arouse base instincts amongst competitors and spectators", and to train young people as "lifeless, unthinking cannon fodder".[12] Gaining an objective view from such works thus proves difficult. Furthermore, those publishing on physical culture in the Soviet Union more often than not had close connections to its organization and or dissemination. For instance, both Samoukov and also I. G. Chudinov[13] were members of the History and Organization Faculty of Physical Culture in the Moscow Institute of Physical Culture, and so were unlikely candidates for a neutral treatment of physical culture, no doubt being obliged to toe the party line and provide the "accepted", ideologically correct history of Soviet physical culture.[14] Modern Russian works on physical culture, such as those by Stolbov and Goloshchapov, are once again not especially analytical but rather explanatory reference works specifically designed as textbooks for Russian students of physical culture and sport.[15]

Some of the most significant English-language works in relation to Soviet physical culture and sport have been produced by James Riordan.[16] *Sport in Soviet Society*, Riordan's major work on sport, was written in 1978 and provides a strong narrative history of sport, beginning with the origins of Soviet sport in the 1860s and tracing its ideological roots and history until the 1970s. In such a broad historical account there are key issues that, while noted, are not explored in any great detail. These include gender and the role of women in Soviet sport, peasant attitudes to physical culture, or even the internal faction-fighting in the Supreme Council during the 1920s. Similar to Riordan in style and content, Henry Morton's excellent *Soviet Sport: A Mirror of Soviet Society* offers a comprehensive account of Soviet sport and physical culture.[17] Also like Riordan, Morton traces the history of sport and physical culture from its origins to its contemporary condition (in his case, the 1960s). Morton too relies heavily on the existing Soviet sources, authors such as F. I. Samoukov, F. D. Sinitsyn, or S. L. Aksel'rod, and his study functions predominantly as an overview of sport and physical culture. One of the more recent contributions to the field of Soviet sports history is Mike O'Mahony's 2006 work, *Sport in the USSR. Physical Culture—Visual Culture*.[18] This offers an excellent overview of the interconnecting worlds of physical culture and art. O'Mahony provides interesting perspectives on the subject of physical culture in Soviet art and sculpture, effectively drawing on his expert knowledge of art and painting techniques to lend a fresh and insightful analysis to the *fizkul'tura* theme. His assessments of the 1927 novel *Envy* by Yuri Olesha, his analysis of works of art by Aleksandr Deineka and Aleksandr Samokhvalov, and his chapter on the Moscow metro reinforce the image of the special role of sport and physical culture in the Soviet Union as the principal producers of visual culture. Another recent author to realize the relevance and significance of a study of sport is Australian Barbara Keys.[19] In her exceptional *Globalizing Sport: National Rivalry and International Community in the 1930s*, she takes a more international perspective and argues that sport was the only real link with the west once Stalin was securely ensconced in power. She contends that, in spite of the early years of experimentation (attempting to formulate "proletarian" sport), this eventually did not work and so the Soviet state effectively reneged on its earlier principles to adopt a western style sports system. Although Keys utilizes archival files, a thorough evaluation of physical culture in the 1920s and 1930s in the Soviet Union is beyond the remit of this valuable and enlightening study.

Taking another angle on physical culture and sport, Robert Edelman offers a comprehensive analysis of the public's consumption of sport, dealing with spectatorship rather than participation.[20] In particular he deals with the difficulties of the state in trying to control sport and spectators. While parades and mass displays could be tightly controlled and orchestrated, popular sports, especially football, proved to be quite problematic because sport is, Edelman observes, "relatively autonomous and cannot be completely controlled".[21] Edelman devotes considerable attention to football—the most popular spectator sport of the 1920s and 1930s—and examines hooliganism and hierarchies within the sport. His analysis raises important parallels between developments in sport, particularly football, and in Soviet society as a whole. The creation of a privileged stratum of society—the *nomenklatura*, the *Stakhanovites*, the sports star—emerged as a feature of Soviet life in the 1930s. Edelman successfully captures this development through his assessment of football. Another valuable work dealing with physical culture is Stefan Plaggenborg's *Revolutionskultur (Revolution and Culture)*.[22] His study veers away from the broader trajectories of old and treads a relatively new path in physical culture literature. Plaggenborg examines Soviet culture between the revolutions, looking at the re-organization of people and minds, eugenics, hygiene, and science. Unfortunately, the work is thwarted somewhat by the lack of archival exploration, and again, physical culture is but one chapter in a broader cultural study.

The most recent contribution to the field of Soviet sport and physical culture is a volume edited by Nikolaus Katzer, Sandra Budy, Alexandra Köhring, and Manfred Zeller.[23] This superb volume, seeking to provide a much-needed social history of Soviet physical culture and sport, draws together a wide range of scholarship on Soviet physical culture, with essays on inter alia gender, science, the press, and architecture. My own work aims to build upon this excellent collection, with a firm concentration on integrating the social, cultural, and political processes underway in the 1920s and 1930s. Katzer notes that the chapters in *Euphoria and Exhaustion* ascribe "to sport not only disciplinary and integrating but also destabilizing and subversive functions".[24] Some of these elements were already apparent in the early years of Soviet physical culture and sport and are analyzed here. Physical culture and sport represented a clear site of contestation, one where competing and changing ideologies continually came into conflict, and where those attempting to disseminate ideology encountered all manner of challenges to order and authority.

This study is also informed by the work of scholars such as Frances Lee Bernstein, Tricia Starks, and in particular Karen Petrone.[25] Petrone's *Life Has Become More Joyous, Comrades* provides us with a much-needed study of Soviet celebrations. She recognizes the important role of celebrations and physical culture parades in Soviet society, for both citizens and state. Forming a part of this celebration discourse are the concepts of "bodily hierarchies" and "body and nation", which, in Petrone's view, raise the issue of the selection, appearance, and condition of individuals as a reflection of the state.[26] Frances Bernstein and Tricia Starks also deal with physical culture matters, although in their work the focus is primarily on health and hygiene. An overall review of the literature reveals that a modern integrated social, cultural, and political analysis of the contribution of sports and physical culture to the formation of the early Soviet state and society has hitherto been lacking.

The structure of the book is more thematic than chronological, with all chapters dealing with both the 1920s and 1930s. There is at times considerable overlap between the chapters, symptomatic of the fact that physical culture cannot be neatly divided into tidy, mutually exclusive categories. The first chapter explores the culture of the body and the origins of physical culture in Europe and also serves to introduce in a general, comparative context themes that will be analyzed in later chapters. It assesses the ideological and intellectual roots of Soviet physical culture and maps the development of these into the 1930s. Chapter 2 then traces the organizational development of physical culture after the Bolshevik Revolution, allowing for a more narrow discussion of the organization of physical culture and sport during the 1920s and 1930s by assessing the impact and significance of the many structural and personnel changes that occurred. The next three chapters discuss in particular the discourse and practice of physical culture. Those responsible for overseeing the development and promotion of physical culture targeted particular groups within society, with frequent propaganda campaigns conducted to draw young people, women, peasants and national minorities more closely towards Soviet power.[27] All of the various campaigns, drives, and programmes directed at youth, women, peasants, and national minorities were part of what Aaron B. Retish has called "big tent Bolshevism"— using cultural and modernization programmes to gain the consent of the population.[28] Chapter 3 focuses on how propaganda was directed towards young people and then assesses, largely through an analysis of education, how the ideology of physical culture could be applied to really instruct and reform young people. The sexuality, psychology, and private lives of young people were popular topics of discussion during the 1920s in particular, and those involved in physical culture played their role in the debate.

The fourth chapter takes women as its subject and shows how physical culture was deployed to help raise their political, social, and cultural levels. The image and role of women during the 1920s and 1930s received considerable attention, and these concerns with how women looked and behaved were clearly reflected in physical culture. Chapter 5 tackles those living in rural areas, that is, both peasants and national minorities, demographics generally thought to be benighted. This chapter examines attempts made by all of those involved in physical culture to draw these communities closer to the socialist way of life. The many and varied propaganda and agitation methods used to attract peasants and national minorities towards physical culture are analyzed here. The next chapter, Chapter 6, is concerned with the visual imagery of physical culture and sport, concentrating especially on spartakiads and parades as the two most important symbols of physical culture—and Stalinist culture—in the late 1920s and 1930s. Finally, Chapter 7 explores the "realities" of mass participation in physical culture. It examines the nature of the new Soviet citizen, the notion of a "cultured leisure", and how physical culture came to be re-defined in the wake of the Stalin Constitution and changing social trends. All of these chapters have the common premise that the ideology of physical culture and later sport was harnessed to convey socialist principles, drawing on a vast and diverse array of symbols to impart a sense of a national, Soviet identity. As Stalinist power sought to create the perfect society, physical culture—with its potential to inspire both physical and mental transformation—became an even more valuable means of legitimizing and promoting the regime as well as a new means of popularizing state policies.

When discussing the ideology of physical culture as well as issues of identity building it is necessary to elucidate further the meaning of and differentiation between agitation and propaganda (agitprop). Agitprop was an integral part of Soviet life as the regime sought to legitimize itself and gain support and popularity, but in its Soviet context agitprop was not a pejorative concept.[29] It was not a covert campaign of indoctrination but rather a highly publicized and orchestrated effort applied in a generally positive sense to achieve ostensibly positive results. Propaganda was used by the Bolsheviks as an explicit means of educating Soviet citizens in socialist principles and winning their support. Lenin explained that "the propagandist operates chiefly by means of the *printed* word; the agitator by means of the *spoken* word", while Georgi Plekhanov observed that propaganda "would lose all historical meaning if it were not accompanied by agitation".[30] According to Commissar for Enlightenment, Anatoly Lunacharsky, agitation could be distinguished from "cold, objective propaganda . . . by the fact that it excites the feelings of the audience and readers and has a direct influence on their will".[31] As Peter Kenez comments, propaganda appealed to both the mind and the emotions.[32] More recently Matthew Lenoe has added that agitation, appealing to the masses' emotions, and propaganda, dealing with more complex explanations, "represented two poles of the Bolsheviks' relationship with 'the people'".[33] Whether using agitprop campaigns for increasing literacy levels or improving health and hygiene, agitprop was an ubiquitous feature of the Soviet regime. For the purpose of propaganda, physical culture, and sport—readily identifiable forms of pleasure, emotion, physical expression, and community—were types of culture that could (in theory at least) be easily harnessed to convey new socialist principles to the wider public.

My research is based predominantly on material from Russian archives and contemporary magazines, journals, and newspapers. Archives consulted include RGASPI (Russian State Archive of Social and Political History) where I worked on files relating to the Sportintern or Red Sport International and the party. The Komsomol archive (also under RGASPI) was consulted for the Komsomol material. GARF (State Archive of the Russian Federation) was used for the files on the All-Union Central Council of Trade Unions, the Supreme Council of Physical Culture, and the Ministry of Enlightenment. Unfortunately many of the Physical Culture Committee's secret files were burned following the German invasion of 1941. As Barbara Keys comments in relation to this, it is therefore "difficult to elucidate sport-related decision-making at the highest levels of party and state".[34] The Russian State Military Archive (RGVA) was useful for files on Osoaviakhim and physical culture in the Red Army. Of the Moscow archives, TsAOPIM (Central Archive of Social-Political History of Moscow) and TsGAMO (Central State Archive of Moscow Region) yielded information relating in particular to physical culture parades, parks of culture and rest, and also voluntary societies. The State Archive of Penza Province (GAPO) provided useful information on developments outside Moscow and on how policies were transmitted to the local councils of physical culture. Apart from the archives, the Russian State Library (including its dissertation and newspaper departments in Khimki), the Russian Public Historical Library, and INION-RAN proved invaluable for accessing the physical culture publications as well as other primary and secondary material.

In terms of print media, physical culture publications really only took shape after 1924. Prior to that, publications had either been non-existent or short-lived and sporadic. Following the inception of the Supreme Council of Physical Culture in the summer of 1923, there was a greater push towards establishing sports and physical culture publications. As with other media and publications, physical culture and sport periodicals adopted the party line and repeated the main themes of party and Supreme Council conferences, protocols, and resolutions. Of course the problem with a study of the Soviet press lies in separating rhetoric from reality, particularly in relation to individual contributions. There is no real way of ascertaining whether contributions were doctored or genuine accounts, and this murky area must therefore be borne in mind when assessing popular attitudes to physical culture. Similar caution applies to statistics. Whether published or archival, the reliability of facts and figures supplied by the localities to the Supreme

Council of Physical Culture cannot be taken at face value as being accurate. However, in many cases the unimpressive picture of physical culture portrayed by these statistics suggests that they were not purposely inflated to bolster the reputation of local councils. Perhaps they were even deflated to win additional financial support. Overall, either in personal accounts or statistics, or whether in the press or archives, there do not appear to have been any explicit attempts to conceal problems or shortcomings in physical culture, leading to the impression that expressions of praise and satisfaction were equally genuine. It could be considered that, particularly in the 1920s, both the positive and negative found their voice.

1 Culture of the Body

The roots of modern physical culture lay in the early nineteenth century when defeat at the hands of Napoleon Bonaparte inspired a movement in exercise and fitness in the German states. At the same time the Scandinavian nations also developed an interest in gymnastics, borne out of the Age of Enlightenment's concern with rationality and order. In Germany Friedrich Ludwig Jahn was responsible for pioneering the *Turnen* gymnastics, exercises that were not "geared towards competition, but to personal improvement, skills . . . like climbing, fencing . . . swimming, horseback riding".[1] As Michael Anton Budd notes in his work on physical culture, the more important long-term role of German gymnastics "was found in its emphasis on bodily beauty, tightly connected to physical prowess".[2] These aspects of bodily beauty and physical prowess were particularly salient in Germany, Italy, and the Soviet Union in the 1920s and 1930s as the political regimes of these countries attributed even greater symbolism and significance to the physical body. In the nineteenth century these and other countries had been inspired by gymnastics, and soon physical culture as a means of responding to problems associated with industrialization and urbanization had become part of a larger desire to improve personal hygiene, diet, and clothing. In Germany groups such as the *Lebensreform* and *Wandervogel* surfaced as a reaction to modernization and its unhealthy associations with poor sanitation, materialism, and other negative manifestations.[3] Similar movements emerged in other countries. In the 1860s in Britain, for instance, an organization known as the New Athleticism aimed to utilize the positive effects of sport, with its objectives of "instilling character and bridging class differences, [and] emphasis on teamwork, manliness and modesty".[4] The National Physical Recreation Society was another endeavour that drew inspiration from the German gymnastics movement and it "formed crucial links between old-style rational recreation, military concerns and the coming wave of commercial fitness".[5] Towards the close of the century the desire to improve one's health and physical strength through sport and exercise had grown steadily. As this chapter shows, the origins of Soviet physical culture could be traced back to nineteenth-century developments in Europe and linked to parallel developments in other countries.

In the Russian empire sport and physical culture were still very much for the elite only. By the turn of the century the leisure societies of St. Petersburg and Moscow were largely exclusive collectives for the wealthy, although some philanthropists with a commitment to physical education did aspire to promote exercise and a healthy lifestyle to a wider audience.[6] Since the late nineteenth century, sports such as yachting, rowing, and cycling had become increasingly popular with an estimated forty yachting and cycling clubs in Russia by 1892.[7] This pattern of elitist sport and elitist dominance in sport, at least in its organization, was reflected in other countries, for instance, in Britain, where in spite of some efforts to the contrary, it was again the upper and middle classes who shaped the "development of amateur and professional sport" and who "reconfigured sporting practices into a recognizable form".[8] As for the emergence of physical culture more specifically, throughout most of the nineteenth century the lines between sport and physical culture had been somewhat blurred, and it was only at the end of the century that distinct differences began to be drawn between sport and physical culture, with the latter term beginning to be used with much more frequency. During the 1890s the terminological and conceptual definition of physical culture finally emerged. The term itself, according to Budd, "implied an ideological and commercial cultivating of the body", but "as an ideologically defined and growing commercial movement it did not last much beyond the First World War".[9] This early form of physical culture, its popularity, and its promotion can generally be ascribed to the East Prussian bodybuilder Eugen Sandow, whose magazines, books, and performances did much to publicize physical culture from the late nineteenth century right up until the outbreak of war and served to link this period of physical culture with the cult of the body.

By the start of the twentieth century there was a general trend in Europe for the original values and ideas associated with early German gymnastics to be supplemented and in some cases replaced by a keen interest in physiology. This occurred in Denmark, for example, when Swedish gymnastics replaced German gymnastics in Danish schools and when the emphasis was more firmly placed on discipline and control.[10] In fin-de-siècle France changes in the approach and understanding of physical education were also underway, as "hygienist attention gradually turned to . . . the functioning of the body rather than its forms and appearance".[11] In Russia at the turn of the century the functioning of physical education was receiving some attention, with German and Swedish gymnastics as well as the Czech Sokol[12] system dominating the physical education scene. It was a combination of these three systems which had a lasting influence on the development of physical culture within Russia and later the Soviet Union. Reflecting the rising interest in physical culture and physical education, Russian scientists had by this time begun to turn their attention to developing theories for the correct practice of physical exercise. The pioneers in the development of a Russian form of physical culture were Pyotr Lesgaft (1837–1909) and later

Ivan Pavlov (1849–1936). Lesgaft championed the importance of health and hygiene, activities that incorporated the use of fresh air and water, and also advocated female participation in sports. Pavlov, meanwhile, situated physical education more precisely within a "general theory of physiology".[13] The journals, their contributors, and the leading theorists of the 1920s that were committed to the development of a Soviet form of physical culture repeatedly drew on the theories of the German, Swedish, and Sokol systems. The influence of these schools, as well as the ideas of Lesgaft, Pavlov, and others, fundamentally shaped the development of a "new" Soviet form of physical culture.

It is quite clear that the theories of the 1920s, and indeed that decade's general concern with health, did not rise independently of the past but in fact were strongly attached to the growing popularity of sport and physical culture preceding the First World War and revolution. Sport, leisure and physical culture had already been a feature of Russian society, and while leisure pursuits such as hunting or yachting had traditionally attracted the Russian aristocracy, by the dawn of the twentieth century the demands of industrialization and concerns for better health meant that support for the broader uses of physical culture was increasing. Even by the 1890s amateur sports societies had been set up across the empire, especially in urban centres.[14] Louise McReynolds attributes the success of the early movement in sport to three figures: Count G. I. Ribop'er, Dr. V.F. Kraevskii, and I. V. Lebedev. In their attitudes to sports these three figures foreshadowed the later Proletkul'tist disdain for competition and were responsible for the "emergence of a widespread cult of the body".[15] The wrestler Lebedev was a particularly new breed, born of that age. He came from humble origins and managed to popularize bodybuilding in Russia, no doubt aided by the European-wide craze largely instigated by that other figure who defined pre-war bodybuilding, Eugen Sandow. Lebedev also brought the image of the traditional "strongman" peasant to public attention, an image that will be revisited later in Chapter 5's discussion of peasant physical culture. Of course the rise of these figures would not have occurred so easily had it not been for the increasing public appetite for sports. As McReynolds notes, societies across Russia "virtually exploded after the 1905 Revolution, when many Russians felt newly empowered".[16] These Russians were those who were based in the larger industrial cities and who were coming into closer contact with different forms of culture and politics.

It was about this time in Russia when factories began to establish their own sports societies, and less elite sports such as football began to gain the attention of urban workers. These young workers, by participating in new, modern games such as football, were asserting a new urban identity and mentality.[17] Robert Edelman has argued that for Russian men of all social backgrounds, "sport was a way of accepting modernity".[18] Soon the recreational values of cycling, yachting, and other pursuits became largely superfluous and were overtaken by the needs of a society that was turning towards modes of discipline and defence. The "masculinization of industrialization" had emerged and required a "strong body on the factory floor and [an] agile mind . . . in the office".[19] The Russo-Japanese war highlighted the need for physical preparedness even further, with Russian military defeat raising serious questions over the training of the Russian Imperial army. The repercussions of the war reverberated even beyond Russia. In 1904 the war initiated a wave of interest in physical culture in Britain and its colonies, with fitness publications, instructional pamphlets, and organizations in high demand.[20] This demand was repeated ten years later. In fact, so important was the image of physical strength that King George V appointed Sandow as his official physical culture trainer, as the desire for a strong body became ever more important. By the eve of the First World War, physical culture across Europe "both reflected and capitalized upon the changing value and broadening scope of the image and spectacle in modern life".[21] The optimism of these years and the hope placed in modernity were however soon shattered by the events of war in the trenches and the broken dreams of a generation of young people.

When war broke out in Europe it was naturally the strongest and fittest who were first sent to the front. Sportsmen and physical culture enthusiasts were at the head of the volunteer line, and physical culture became instrumental in promoting a healthy regime among young men, encouraging them to prepare physically and mentally for the battlefield. This was the same in Russia as those who had been active in physical culture and sport were also sent to the front to fight.[22] In many cases this had the adverse effect of leaving clubs without members, forcing some to close as a consequence.[23] In Russia the war effort was all pervasive, so much so that Aaron B. Retish goes so far as to say that the "[s]tate and military practices during the war extended the government domain into the home and even into the soul".[24] Very few escaped the total mobilization and militarization of these years. Over 15 million men served during the three and a quarter years of Russian involvement in the war, with some 5 million men captured and 2 million dead as a result of wounds or disease.[25] As other European countries fighting in the war were quickly realizing however, the civilian population was largely physically unprepared for war, with an absence of adequate state support for the infrastructure, organization, and training of young men. After some late and lacklustre attempts had been made to establish such a sports infrastructure in Russia in 1912, an *Announcement on the Mobilization of Sport* three years later sought to bridge the gap between the civilian and the military by placing military and civilian sports personnel alongside one another to produce a better quality fighting machine.[26] The effort turned out to be futile, for the Bolsheviks were soon in control and sports organization was directed towards revolutionary tasks. Yet the fusion between the military and civilian outlasted the Imperial war effort, with the war having "produced a specific civilian-military hybrid", a result of the "particular historical conjuncture out of which the

Soviet state emerged".[27] Thus Russian and Soviet civilians effectively continued to live in a world dominated by some form of constant mobilization and militancy.

With revolution and then civil war following quickly on the heels of the First World War, one is faced with the difficult task of how to assess the impact of the war on Russia. Recent works by Joshua Sanborn and Peter Holquist have emphasized the importance of viewing this period 1914–1921 as a "continuum of crisis".[28] According to Peter Holquist, the narrative of revolution—the firm belief that a new order was being created and society transformed—meant that the Russian Revolution "became uncoupled from the wartime crisis out of which it had emerged" with war and revolution constituting "points along a common continuum".[29] In terms of physical culture, the revolution resulted in no major changes of organizational principle and the developments of the preceding decades were not radically overhauled within the space of a few years. Training loyal and physically tough soldiers remained the primary goal of sports and physical culture before, during and immediately after the revolution. As the next chapter explains, Vsevobuch (*Vseobshchee Voennoe Obuchenie* or the Central Agency for Universal Military Training) was a new organization set up in 1917. This basically had the same goals of military training and preparation that were present under Tsarism and aside from the establishment of this organization physical culture and sports discourse essentially remained unchanged until the early 1920s. In this regard physical culture in Russia represented a continuum between the years 1912 and 1922, when militarism and paramilitarism dominated. It was also broadly in line with physical culture rhetoric in other European states at this time, and its general shift towards health and hygiene concerns—the desire to revitalize and remake society—at the beginning of the 1920s was again reflective of wider international attitudes towards physical culture and was also an extension of earlier, pre-war efforts to reform the individual through involvement in physical culture.

POST-WAR ATTITUDES TO THE BODY

According to Budd, the immediate post-war period was a time of "unprecedented flux for physical culture" which witnessed changes in how physical culture was both perceived and conducted.[30] This was the case in Russia by the early 1920s and was not just the result of war, but also of revolution. The horrors of war had not lessened the interest in physical culture but rather changed how physical culture was viewed. The inter-war years saw a general worldwide rise in interest in physical culture matters, with different countries seeing physical culture and sports as advantageous for different purposes. For instance, in France physical culture for women stood for "personal hygiene, deportment, exercise, and beauty regimens"[31] while for French men it was part of a larger project of recovery and recuperation following the First World War. In Britain a physical culture movement was also underway, aiming to improve overall fitness and reinforce patriotic values. Many of these movements had their origins in the mid to late nineteenth century, reflecting concerns with low birth rates and the desire to improve health and hygiene. All of these issues were multiplied tenfold following war, when an entire generation of men had been lost. Britain, France, Germany, Russia, and other countries underwent both a crisis of masculinity and a crisis of femininity, to differing degrees. As Ina Zweiniger-Bargielowska states in relation to Britain, "[i]n the wake of the carnage and mutilation of the First World War, the physical culture movement provided a site for the reconstruction of the male body".[32] The rehabilitative powers of physical culture were here recognized and applied to help rebuild the broken male body. In Britain, where the cult of the body had enjoyed so much attention in the pre-war years, the impact of the war meant that the body "began to be concealed again" as physical culture focused on fitness and health rather than on physical strength and masculinity; meanwhile, by the 1920s the "locus of an aestheticized body culture had returned to its earlier home in Germany".[33] As one German contemporary wrote, sport and physical culture were the "symptoms of a new way of life characteristic of the post-war population" where "Bolshevism, fascism, sports, body culture, and the New Objectivity [were] all interrelated".[34]

The rehabilitative aspects of sport and physical culture were not the only influences that were widely recognized after the war, and men were not the sole bearers of societal change in the inter-war years. The war had also impacted upon the lives of women. By the 1920s physical culture was added to the list of activities that witnessed an unprecedented rise in female participation, a rise that was precipitated by both necessity and desire. In Weimar Germany the earlier attractions of German *Kulturbewegung* were now extended to incorporate a wider number of women from different backgrounds and a wider set of cultural norms.[35] Female interest in physical culture increased considerably, but this interest in conjunction with the "women issue"—women entering previously male-dominated fields—led to problems in the definition of femininity.[36] Similar patterns were evident in Russia, though with some pronounced differences. While during the war the remote Russian village witnessed the increased presence of women in public life, afterwards rural women returned to the home where the Bolsheviks placed "class considerations above gender".[37] Following the civil war, "a number of concurrent crises" occurred for women, particularly urban women, as employment and social welfare "came under attack" when the Bolsheviks introduced new policies.[38] Contemporary attitudes to women and Bolshevik attempts to deploy physical culture as a means of making women into "better citizens" are explored in detail in the chapter on women. Analysis of how the state directed physical culture at women reveals how body symbolism was a constant feature under socialism, with image and propaganda especially prevalent in drawing women closer to political and cultural discourses. Changing attitudes under Stalinism further underlined the importance of physical culture in constructing identity and as an additional means of performing and representing the new, Soviet way of life.

The power of physical culture to influence an individual or to reinforce certain political or social values was not limited to the Soviet Union or Europe. Global in nature, physical culture and sport were malleable forces that could be developed in numerous ways and by any nation. Physical culture therefore had an international presence beyond Europe, even enjoying some popularity in North and South America, the British colonies, and elsewhere at the end of the nineteenth century. However, it was not until after the war that sport and physical culture really became internationally renowned and assumed a wider public and political consciousness.[39] After Atatürk's rise to power physical culture and sport in Turkey represented "the hope of achieving economic, cultural, even civilizing progress . . . and the recovery of the Turkish people".[40] In China, Andrew Morris notes that "[t]he values of a fit body and strong nation took hold easily during the Republican period, as patriotic China searched for anything that could finally make China the equal of the hated and envied imperialist powers".[41] As Gerard Taylor notes in relation to North and South America, "[p]hysical culture was a growth area in the 1920s, the decade in which Charles Atlas became the saviour of every American kid" and "was also something practiced by members of the Brazilian elite and educated classes".[42] In the 1930s physical culture in Brazil came to mean "clean living, avoidance of alcohol and tobacco, and martial practices".[43] It was not until the late 1930s however, following the impressive performance of Germany at the Berlin Olympics in 1936, that both European and American (South and North) governments, though eschewing militaristic elements, pushed for more sponsorship of nationwide physical fitness campaigns.[44] In this sense both Nazi Germany and the Soviet Union, in their early attempts to control physical culture and sport, had been unique in subscribing to state organized propaganda campaigns for widespread participation in physical culture and sport.[45]

RE-IMAGINING THE PHYSICAL BODY

With their emphasis on youth and body culture, it is no coincidence that the "totalitarian" states of Germany, Italy, and the Soviet Union have traditionally been compared to one another.[46] Under National Socialism, modern forms of physical culture were expressed through organizations such as *Kraft durch Freude* (Strength through Joy) which promoted mass state-sponsored leisure, while more generally sport and *Körperkultur* (body culture) were major components of the National Socialist ethos. Whereas the

Soviet system combined sports with political socialization and education, in Germany masculinity, machismo, and a more overt display of the body and sexuality were prevalent. Female athletes assumed much more prominence in the Soviet Union and considerably less emphasis was attached to the naked male form. Also, in Germany, there was strict sex segregation with boys only in the Hitler Youth and girls in the *Bund Deutscher Mädel* (League of German Girls). This segregation—largely inspired by biomedical attitudes and discrimination against women—harmed the Hitler Youth, in many ways leading to the formation of rival youth groups.[47] On the other hand, the Soviet monopoly of youth allowed, in fact encouraged, boys and girls to mix together. In spite of Soviet–German differences, the underlying overall objectives of the two regimes were remarkably similar—both sought to motivate collective spirit towards achieving the goals of the state. In his examination of the Hitler Youth, H. W. Koch,[48] a former member of the organization, asserted that Hitler strongly endorsed the role of physical education above all else, commenting that "the *Völkish* state has to adjust its educational work not merely to the indoctrination of knowledge but in the first place to the production of bodies physically sound to the very core".[49] As one young *Bund Deutscher Mädel* leader commented, the Hitler Youth was "institutionalized", and the leaders were "so drilled" that they "created a style of their own as 'managers'" and were "driven from one activity to the next".[50] The National Socialist philosophy in this regard was that, in order for the younger generation to succeed, it would have to be physically fit and hardened—only with this would come emotional and mental strength, will, and determination. Despite their vast differences, Communism and National Socialism were similar in that they both sought to create a new society based on ideology. These "new" societies were then subjected to elements of experimentation and repression as well as promotion and advancement. Both states' attempts to "perfect" and "modernize" their respective societies have led to some arguing that the crimes committed by Nazism and Stalinism were "the legitimate offspring of the modern spirit, of that urge to assist and speed up the progress of mankind toward perfection" with the hopes that were pinned on scientific and industrial progression all-important to their social engineering projects.[51] The means used in achieving the objectives of their various projects were not always the same however, and as Daniel Beer cautions in the Soviet case, modern social knowledge is in and of itself not sufficient in explaining Stalinist repression, for this had its intellectual roots in pre-1917 Russia.

In its high regard for body culture, the Soviet Union also had much in common with Fascist Italy. Indeed, right across Europe interest was rising in the physical form and how this reflected political and national virility. In her work on Italian fascism and women in sport, Gigliola Gori has noted how the Fascist plan to "transform Italians . . . into a chosen race of strong 'new men'" was an inspiration to Hitler.[52] In the Soviet Union too a massive campaign of redefining citizenship and identity was underway, with an emphasis on political loyalty, physical strength, and active participation in the new society. Victoria De Grazia's *Culture of Consent* argues that Italian leisure, sport, film, and theatre were all directed at showing how the state improved the quality of life of its citizens thus helping to generate mass acceptance of the regime.[53] The low birth rate led to incentives for larger families, a clampdown on abortions, and even taxes on bachelor-hood—developments not too dissimilar to its communist counterpart of the 1930s. The importance of the trade unions in Italy is also noteworthy, with workers' recreation and leisure time closely associated with their job and trade union. Work and social life were consequently very much inter-twined because of the trade unions and, as De Grazia shows, the quality of one's leisure depended upon where one worked—also a feature of sport in Soviet society. A major difference between Italy and the Soviet Union, how-ever, was that these recreational clubs co-existed with non–state-run clubs, such as those organized by religious orders. In the Soviet Union, all youth and work clubs were organized by party-state organizations. Moreover, ideological attitudes to women diverged considerably, with Italy (more like Germany) generally unsupportive of active female participation in sport. Under fascism women were considered to be inferior to men, as the cult of masculinity overtook any efforts to promote female emancipation.[54] None-theless, on the surface, clear parallels existed between the Soviet and Italian ethos of sport. Some of the statements from the Italian Olympic Commit-tee (CONI) on *dopolavoro*[55] sports could just as easily have been made by the Supreme Council of Physical Culture on the Soviet physical culture clubs. For instance, CONI stated that *dopolavoro* sports were to "teach the working masses in a practical way that . . . they can better their physical condition, strengthen and invigorate themselves, build up their resistance to disease . . . and ready themselves for the fatigue of work" and that "the ideal *dopolavorista sportivo* was indeed the disciplined mass man: not overtly competitive, yet with a well-developed self-confidence and a sense of 'fair-play', 'fit', and 'virile', with a profound sense of team spirit".[56] These comments were perfectly transposable to the Soviet outlook on sports and physical culture. Soviet physical culture was part of the larger, interna-tional concern for raising health and fitness standards as well as improving military preparedness. At the same time there were also key differences that separated one country's relations to physical culture from another, with dif-ferent ideological and national differences influencing state attitudes.

The era and ethos of body culture, now associated so firmly with images from Nazi Germany, Fascist Italy, and Soviet Russia, were not entirely state directed, however, nor were they necessarily concomitant with the rise of ideologies. Many men and women had indeed long subscribed to public images of desirable body shapes or fashions and sought to effect changes in their own behaviour to emulate these. According to Margaret Lowe, the concept of a "body image" emerged between 1870 and 1930, with the actual term itself first appearing in America in 1930.[57] As Lowe argues, the concept came to be of considerable significance to American women, with "the potential to determine psychological and social self-definition".[58] In 1920s America female college students were conscious of their body shape, wearing clothes and hairstyles that would make them appear attractive to the opposite sex, using their bodies to "explore . . . [the] new landscape".[59] They also attended social events (including sports events) where they could mix in the company of potential suitors who would win them social admiration among their peers.[60] By becoming increasingly integral components of individual and collective identity building, clothing and body image came to be recognized as important social and political tools. As Tammy Proctor has observed, "[c]lothing expresses multiple meanings for both wearers and viewers, simultaneously empowering an individual or group with a sense of identity and dividing people according to status".[61] The opportunity to exploit and politicize this rising body image fetish of the 1920s and 1930s was not missed by the European fascist states, which in the Italian case endeavoured to "construct and define citizenship" through the donning of the black shirt, thereby connecting the "body natural and the body politic".[62] Likewise in Soviet Russia, physical culture, sports activities, and fashions came to reflect the changing goals of the state and what was required of the new Soviet citizen. At the same time this Soviet citizen also had an interest in how fashions, body image, and physical culture could be explored in order to promote their own personal agendas.

Just as Lowe persuasively argues that in the case of America the concept of body image did not only emerge during the inter-war period, the same can be argued in the case of Russia. Christine Ruane has demonstrated the significance of clothing in Imperial Russia, where emancipated peasants began to "craft their own identities" by "buying ready-to-wear garments and accessories".[63] This notion is also expressed in the work of N. N. Kozlova, where, through her analysis of personal documents in the 1920s and 1930s, she contended that "former peasants literally assumed a new identity [and] . . . transformed their body practices".[64] She also observed that "youth and the fit body—their basic capital, was a means of converting this capital [their bodies] into social and cultural capital".[65] The Bolsheviks, intent on the notion of identity building, realized early on the potential impact of clothing and body image. Consequently in the early years of Bolshevik power wearing "bourgeois" or military style clothes said much about one's political allegiance. Fashion became an important political statement. This did not just apply to the young, to women, or to city dwellers. Urban and rural styles of dress, as well as clothes worn by national minorities, came to denote political, social, and cultural affiliations. Reactions to sports attire make it clear that local mores on clothing and culture dictated the implementation and progression of Soviet policies. This was particularly so in the national republics, where the issue of dress and identity was unquestionably a matter of great significance and the "intrusion" of Soviet forms of physical culture seemed alien to locals.

This latter function of body image is closely associated with ethnic identity. The role of sport in ethnic politics has been the subject of considerable study, and, as Allen Guttmann surmises, can be broken down into two overarching variants. The first of these is the "analysis of modern sports as a means for an ethnic minority to participate in the larger society while simultaneously maintaining its sense of a separate ethnic identity", while the second is the "variation by gender in the rate that modern sports are adopted by ethnic minorities" with female members of minorities generally slow to "abandon traditional recreations and adopt modern sports".[66] Beginning with the second variant, this holds true in the Soviet case, though not just in to relation to national minorities. Women in general were slow to welcome Soviet culture and sports, with ambivalence and hostility often to be found among peasant and national minority women. Perhaps because women were "slow to adopt modern sports" physical culture authorities within the Soviet Union were especially keen to win their approval and participation.[67] In the case of Muslim women, the veil and clothing play an important role in asserting Islamic identity, with the female body an ongoing site of contestation. Jennifer Hargreaves, who has addressed this issue, notes that, depending on context, Muslim women "consciously and unconsciously manipulate religious beliefs to negotiate their gender roles and the contradictions between tradition and modernity in sport".[68] National minority women in the Soviet Union had to cope with juggling a number of conflicting identities, identities that were frequently expressed through the politics of the body.

Guttmann's first variant reflects the Soviet policy of *korenizatisya* or indigenization, a Soviet policy originally designed to promote communists from local ethnic minorities.[69] Local officials could simultaneously participate in traditional games and Soviet physical culture, as Chapter 4 will explore in more detail. Replicating standards of physical culture seen in Moscow or Leningrad was not as straightforward in Georgia or Uzbekistan, however, and clothing and body image played a role in determining local attitudes to physical culture. Ethnic concerns could be somewhat alleviated by undertaking small adjustments in sartorial styles in order to make Soviet physical culture become more acceptable. This was shown to be the case when 160 *Adzhars*, when wearing clothes in which they felt comfortable, had within a year joined the physical culture organization, as opposed to none at all the previous year.[70] This was a cultural compromise where national minority participation in physical culture increased, but was done so on their terms. Policies towards national minorities, women, and others show that body image and its symbolic importance were not overlooked by the Bolsheviks but were incorporated into Soviet norms on culture and behaviour.

BODIES AND MINDS

Recent scholarship, in seeking to understand the myriad processes underway in the late nineteenth and early twentieth centuries, has recognized the important forces of science and medicine in political and social thinking. This was not just a Russian but also a European-wide development. Martin Conway and Robert Gerwarth note in their volume on twentieth-century political violence that "the ideal of a purified and healthy community formed an ubiquitous element in the way in which Europeans interpreted the world around them".[71] Conway and Gerwarth link this "way of thinking" to long-held notions of purging communities and establishing local harmony. When applied in practice, the full thrust of these "ways of thinking" differed considerably, with varying, and often violent, consequences. In Russia the achievement of a purified and healthy community was undoubtedly a major goal and in an effort to achieve this goal the Bolsheviks turned to medicine to "regulate questions with a moral or aesthetic component, such as sexuality, criminality, and the health and fitness of future generations".[72] In creating the New Man scientific medicine/medical science were explored and used in a "utopian and pragmatic" manner in order to penetrate "all sorts of spaces and endeavours: attempts to make humanity better, by making us healthier, fitter, saner, and more sober".[73] As Lenin's electrification campaign sought to demonstrate a commitment to using modern technology to improve the lives of ordinary citizens, so science and medicine could also be applied to wider communities to show a commitment to improving collective physical and mental health. All of these projects, as Alexander Genis has suggested, had a purpose that was "demonstrable and verifiable" as it searched for the "geometry capable of controlling the turbulent element of the masses".[74]

The mental as well as physical devastation wrought by the hardship and trauma of the years 1914–1921 drew attention to the importance of mental preparation and conditioning, which also came under the purview of "physical" culture. Once again, this concern with the mind cannot be attributed directly to the war or its consequences, for it was already present in the nineteenth century. Instead, the events of war served to politicize psychology during the inter-war years, bringing both physical and mental culture to the forefront of the so-called totalitarian regimes. The modernist period in Russia produced and heightened an interest in the New Man and in the psychology that continued throughout the Soviet era, in one form or another. Even Soviet "pedagogy"—the study of children and childhood—had its beginnings in the modernism of the late nineteenth and early twentieth centuries, where man was seen as "submerged in culture and formed under the purposive impact of environment, society, and science".[75] The ideology of physical culture, with its heavy emphasis on symbolism, personal development, and transformation, reflected earlier discussions in Russia but now transposed them to suit political ends. To this effect the line between culture, science, and politics under the Bolsheviks often became blurred, with Vladimir Lenin, Maksim Gorky, Aleksandr Bogdanov, Ivan Pavlov, and others all working towards constructing a new political, social, cultural, and physical body. Bogdanov, founder of the Proletkul't movement, was especially important in connecting theories of scientific medicine to political culture. Linking Bogdanov's work back to Russian Darwinists Ivan Sechenov (1829–1905), Vladimir Bekhterev (1857–1927), and Ivan Pavlov, Pat Simpson contends that Bogdanov viewed psychology as the "link between the biological and the social that held the key to understanding adaptive evolution".[76] Although a controversial figure, Bogdanov and ideas associated with him were particularly influential during the initial years of Bolshevik power.

By the early 1920s disciplines such as psychology and pedagogy had thus become intricately connected to physical culture, with exercise, clean living, and sport often just a conduit to the more important task of participating fully in socialist life. Active participation in or observance of physical culture were not sufficient in and of themselves; rather physical culture had to be conducted in the communist spirit with complete socialist consciousness and mental commitment to the cause of the Soviet state. For the Bolsheviks the body was not just an empty vessel, but rather a physical entity to be preened and perfected. It was viewed as a rich symbolic bearer of political policy and ideological destiny. The Bolsheviks understood and capitalized on the culture of the body and mobilized the population to perform and portray socialism on an everyday basis, as Régine Robin's scheme of acculturation indicates. Workers, women, national minorities, children—everyone at some point was encouraged to become a participant in the effort to construct communism through their physical and emotional involvement in inter alia agitation campaigns, shock-work, Pioneer activities, festivals, and later parades. According to official rhetoric, social and individual betterment were possible only through total immersion in socialist life. Nadezhda Krupskaya succinctly summarized these aspects when writing, "In what a communist ought to be like", observing that "a communist is, first and foremost, *a person involved in society*, with strongly developed social instincts".[77] Each person was being assigned some sort of an ethical and moral responsibility with individual involvement in political, cultural, and social life instrumental to the collective well-being of society.

In the Soviet context the party's desire to improve health and involve ordinary people in the political, cultural, and social work of the state while at the same time directing and influencing people's ethical and moral behaviour were closely bound up with Soviet notions of the New Man.[78] The inspiration behind the New Man was in large part derived from the character of Rakhmetov from Nikolai Chernyshevsky's nineteenth-century novel *What Is to Be Done?* (*Chto delat'?*) Rakhmetov was the figure which every Soviet citizen was encouraged to emulate, his austere lifestyle suited to the revolutionary new person of the 1920s.[79] He forsook the pleasures of life (except smoking cigars, his sole vice) and resolved to live "according to convictions and not personal desires" so that "man in general" could be happy.[80] In order to transform his body, Rakhmetov devoted himself to building up his physical strength, "took up gymnastics with considerable dedication", and "put himself on a boxer's diet".[81] The utopian ideas associated with the novel rippled throughout early twentieth-century Russia, inspiring in particular Lenin (with his penchant for gymnastics). Its influence was not limited to politics or literature, for artists such as El Lissitzky encapsulated the new, disciplined form in works such as *The New Man* (1923) while Kazimir Malevich explored the changing "new body".[82]

In discussing the ideology of physical culture and the creation of the New Man, Lev Trotsky, generally critical of the avant-garde's over-indulgence in Futurism, could not refrain from discussing the "evolution of a 'new will-power', 'courage', 'speed' and 'precision'".[83] Bodily discipline and a desire to shape and assert control over one's physical self was attractive at a time when strong workers were needed to rebuild civil society. Responsibility for achieving much of this was placed on the physical culture organizations. When speaking at the congress of physical culture councils in 1924, Trotsky spoke of the "future person" who would look back on the past and "with gratitude recall the work done by the organizations of physical culture", which had prepared for and precipitated the arrival of this future person.[84] The desire for improvement formed part of the ideology of physical culture which, although stretching across a range of different disciplines, had the common objective of stabilizing society by encouraging people to work on themselves to become fitter, stronger and healthier. Pat Simpson maintains that "notions of 'conditioning', changed environment and body discipline deriving from Russian Darwinism and Chernyshevsky's model of the New Person . . . seemed to underpin major areas of body discipline promoted by the party and state" relating "to the redefinition of leisure as physical culture".[85]

During a time of profound austerity, "leisure" was replaced by physical culture in the years after the revolution and civil war as attention was paid to worker health and well-being. Ailing employees with tired and broken bodies working in unsanitary and often hazardous factory conditions represented the antithesis of the New Man. Action had to be taken. Physical culture offered a potential solution and its merits in this regard were endorsed by Soviet and international scientific opinion. Science—held in such high esteem by the Bolsheviks—seemed to confirm that exercise and gymnastics benefited both the worker and consequently production efficiency. If the authorities were to get the most out of their workers, then physical culture in the workplace was viewed as one clear means of achieving this. These views fitted in well with the ideas of Aleksei Gastev of the Central Institute of Labour whose work was based on the premise that labour could be managed through the efficient organization of workers, with the institute conducting many experiments in order to help train and educate workers to increase labour efficiency.[86]

David L. Hoffmann notes in his study of physical culture and the New Soviet Man that Foucault's anatomo-politics came into play in the state's attitude towards physical culture, with "government and expert intervention to improve people's bodily health for the sake of economic and political power".[87] Hoffmann draws attention to theatre director Vsevolod Meyerhold who sought to mould the new actor by placing him "in an environment in which gymnastics and all forms of sport are both available and compulsory, [so as to] achieve the New Man who is capable of any form of labour".[88] The combination of this type of bio-politics philosophy and the Five Year Plan meant that a rising number of factories were beginning to integrate physical culture into the labour process. In discussing the contributions of Gastev, Meyerhold, and others to the field of Taylorism, Pat Simpson concludes that it was Gastev's "visualizations of the New Person" which ultimately represented the most "ideologically acceptable form, of the evolutionary, Taylorized, conditioned, docile labouring body".[89] State support and funding of Gastev's Institute suggested that the party was committed to applying physical culture methodology and ideology in the factory as an economic and political investment.[90]

BODIES AT WORK

This state commitment indicates that, if the concept of the "New Man" was to take root anywhere, it was most likely to do so in the urban centres, among the working proletariat. This was where Marxist-Leninist theory and Bolshevik ideas on science, medicine, and physical culture could be put into practice. Jochen Hellbeck has correctly pointed out that "no Russian Marxist imagined the road to the New Man separate from the proletariat".[91] In factories across the Soviet Union proletarian bodies were to be at work producing and constructing the socialist world as envisioned by the Bolsheviks. In this sense the factory was a crucial component in the construction of not only the New Man, but also of physical culture. Officially, the aim of the "physical culture of the toilers" was "the perfection of [their] physical development" and "the increase of their vitality and their average length of life".[92] Workers were expected to lead the way and be at the forefront of the race to create a new society. Urban centres, ideally populated by the New Man, were to become cauldrons of frenetic socialist activity and physical culture was one such activity. Inspired by Taylorism and Fordism, as well as the "utopias" of past centuries, factories became the scene of intense examination and experimentation.[93]

In May 1932 Gosplan discussed the issue of introducing physical culture into the labour process.[94] The physical culture institutes in Moscow and Leningrad came to agreements with certain factories to observe physical culture in practice on a trial basis. The scientific research section of the Lesgaft Physical Culture Institute in Leningrad had an arrangement with the factory *Krasnyi Tregol'nik* to investigate the "influence on social health and industrial labour of the workers" after two "physical culture minutes" had been introduced into the labour process as well as the influence of physical culture classes every three days before and after work.[95] Based on results from a previous trial the Leningrad Stalin factory decided to introduce physical culture events into the industrial process in two shops in 1931.[96] In these shops gymnastics were conducted during lunch breaks for both the morning and evening shift-workers.[97] In a letter to all physical culture councils, the All-Union Council of Physical Culture leader, Nikolai Antipov, requested in 1932 that practical research work on physical culture in the labour process be extended.[98] It was now to include sixty factories. Scientific and methodological work appeared to conclusively prove that incorporating elements of physical culture into the workplace did indeed improve the health of the worker and arguably more importantly for the factories, boosted production. The physical culture "minute", physical culture "pause", and morning exercises were all considered crucial stepping stones in raising worker health and discipline. This was where physical culture was deemed essential. By teaching young workers about health and labour as well as "educating them in the correct system of work", standards of industrial labour production could be raised.[99] Many of the "experiments" became standard practice, with some former Soviet citizens today holding fond and, for others, not so fond memories of morning exercises (*zaryadki*) in the workplace.

With workers being most exposed to the ideology of physical culture and sport, it was not surprising that they were among the first to become the athletes and sports achievers featured in the physical culture and sports press. The increased chances of encountering propaganda, joining a factory club or having more resources at their disposal meant that workers were most likely to be leading the charge to improve physical culture and sports standards. Indeed the climax of this close relationship between physical culture and the factory emerged in the mid-1930s with the birth of the voluntary societies, when the workplace was transformed into the scene of intense physical culture and sports campaigns. The GTO (Get Ready for Labour and Defence) and spartakiads intensified inter-factory and inter-city competition as sports grew in significance. In an article the *Serp i Molot* factory's newspaper *Martenovka* referred to the American observer Michael Gold, who stated that the factory was creating "a new human race".[100] Its workers paved the way in physical culture, social work, and shock-work both in industry and elsewhere. In many cases physical culture achievements were now something to boast about, conferring prestige on factory shops and factories in general. Taking direction from socialist realism and new Stalinist trends, by the mid-1930s successful workers came to represent the happy new life in the Soviet Union, with their images projected onto screen and print.

After the Five Year Plan a Stalinist inflection could be profoundly detected in physical culture and body symbolism was again catapulted into the limelight, but this time with new meanings ascribed to it. The "new citizens", having worked so hard for so long, were now ready for display and paraded before the world as evidence of Soviet achievement and prosperity.

The leisure element which had been earlier removed from the ideology of physical culture returned. Standards and expectations changed. Success in industry merited reward and recognition but such "successes" raised the stakes even higher and meant that it was no longer sufficient for people to simply observe or engage in physical development or to participate in sports activities. Now such involvement had to be recorded. Taking the form of film, photograph, or text, individual and collective experiences were carefully preserved. Interviews were conducted and noted. This was not just for posterity, as often the process itself—analysis, questionnaires, and recollections—constructed a dialogue in which workers themselves had to engage. As Hellbeck observes, "[h]istory, literature, and textuality form an inextricable whole, central to the definition of the New Man".[101] A key figure in influencing the direction in which the New Soviet Person was to follow under Stalin was Maksim Gorky. In 1931, and with the support of the party, Gorky set about recording the history of the plants and factories.[102] His literary endeavour was to encapsulate the conditions of life in the factory and the lives of workers, especially those who had recently arrived from the countryside. The project was perfectly timed to coincide with Stalin's desire for a new writing of proletarian history and culture. In preserving the history of the factories, physical culture was included as it provided an important example of the everyday culture of workers' lives.[103] As one worker who was interviewed claimed, "without physical culture I cannot live. It helps me in everything, and most of all in my production work—physical culture has become an inseparable part of my membership, a necessary part of my day, my life".[104] This was the kind of worker required by the Soviet state, the type who worked hard in the factory and then participated in physical culture activities in the club in the evenings, also partaking in factory spartakiads and parades. The merging of individual and Soviet identities had by the 1930s assumed a much more public form, as evidenced through participation in physical culture and sport.

In the 1930s the New Soviet Man and Woman were winning cult-like status of almost superhuman proportions. The New Soviet Person was the ideal to which every Soviet citizen could aspire—strong, healthy, devoted to family and political life, as well as being a shock-worker. The 1930s Soviet New Man was a more cultured and developed version of his 1920s predecessor, and was also to be a more exact embodiment of the ideals of physical culture—he was to be clean and smart, healthy, and politically astute.[105] Even more significant was the development of such facets as endurance, persistence, self-sacrifice, and control over one's emotions. This latter characteristic was deemed particularly essential. The New Soviet Man (and indeed woman) had to learn how to direct his (or her) emotions "in the pursuit of a consciously fixed goal", however, "emotionality is in disfavour . . . if man becomes a victim of it, if his will and consciousness cannot retain control".[106] Mental strength was to be accompanied by physical, with new Soviet citizens to excel in sport. As Riordan notes, physical culture was taken very seriously by the state, with anyone neglecting the physical aspects of their development considered "only half a person, like one who neglects the education of his mind".[107] The ideal man was not complete unless he had sporting prowess and achievements to add to those in other spheres of life. The epitome of sporting achievement and demonstration of self-control and discipline in the Soviet case were the GTO awards, the spartakiads, and the physical culture parades.

For those who subscribed to socialism and the regime, there were advantages. In the 1930s there was what Vera Dunham has called the "Big Deal"—privileges in return for loyalty.[108] This in turn contributed to the formation of an elite, but to become a part of this elite, one had to shape both body and mind. Representing physical capital, Pierre Bourdieu posited that the body was "a bearer of value" and that "management of the body [was] central to the acquisition of status and distinction".[109] A prime example of someone who actively partook in Soviet society and thus to an extent "believed" was Leonid Potemkin, as recounted by Hellbeck. Not of a class-alien background, Potemkin had the opportunity to better himself and achieve upward mobility. However, this desire encountered a setback, in that "his weak body and his inability to cope with the challenges presented by life", meant that he had to continually work on himself, strengthening both his body and his mind so that he would be fit to meet the demands required of the New Soviet Person.[110] His weakened physical state and the physicality of his new job (as a driller at a prospecting site in Sverdlovsk) denied him the energy to join the Komsomol or become socially active.[111] Yet Potemkin's will, determination, and self-training meant that he would succeed in "managing his body" to help shape the outcome of his future. His commitment to self-betterment was fulfilled through hard work and dedication, improving his mind and body and helping him achieve the status of deputy minister of geology of the Russian Soviet Republic. His case exemplifies that those who understood the significance of physical and mental development and directed these towards service to the state would have an opportunity to qualify for the title of New Soviet Person. By recognizing the significance of both body and mind—ubiquitous in the realm of socialist discourse—individuals could assume and display new, Soviet identities.

FROM TSARIST SPORT TO SOVIET PHYSICAL CULTURE

In tracing the origins and background of Soviet physical culture, beginning with its German roots in the nineteenth century, its development under Tsarism, and its early Soviet experience, it seems that the era of "physical culture" lasted roughly seventy years, from the 1860s to the 1930s. Even the war and revolution did not impede the rise of physical culture. Conversely, the war for many revealed the restorative powers of physical culture, with countless countries advocating physical culture and sport to reinvigorate debilitated, diseased, and downtrodden populations. The physical body was still at the fore, and this increasingly came to be associated with the health of one's mind. An individual's physical well-being determined their psychological and emotional state. Exercise and fresh air offered a renewed sense of hope that was recognized by the Soviet authorities. Physical culture was to be introduced in schools, the workplace, clubs, and elsewhere. Within a decade the strength and vitality of the nation indeed appeared to have been restored, with parades and competitions demonstrating the physical health of the Soviet Union. This renewed enthusiasm for physical culture and sport continued throughout the 1930s, but with shades of militarism gradually gaining force until the eclipse of the Second World War once again plunged the world into darkness.

It seems appropriate to conclude this opening chapter with a brief biography of a sportsperson whose career began under Tsarism and ended in the twilight of the Stalin years. Born in the 1890s when physical culture was just being defined, the sportsman Platon Afanas'evich Ippolitov (1893–1951) survived the chaotic years of the early twentieth century and managed to pursue his dreams. For Ippolitov, his sporting career began in 1908 when he entered his first speed-skating contest and was placed fifth. Four years later eighteen-year-old Platon became champion of Russia, a feat he repeated in 1914 and 1916.[112] The record time he achieved in the 5000m in 1916 stood for the next twenty years. That same year he was called to serve in the army, joining the Eleventh Army in the summer of 1917. While in action Ippolitov came under heavy German aerial fire. Resulting from a series of explosions, Ippolitov sustained serious leg injuries and had to endure a lengthy convalescence before he could resume training. By the time Platon Ippolitov returned to competitive skating in 1921, the First World War had ended, the Romanov dynasty had been destroyed, and the Bolsheviks were in power, having achieved victory in the ensuing civil war. For this particular skater, politics did not seem to matter however. Sport was his passion and this he pursued with enormous success, both in Imperial Russia and in the Soviet Union. Throughout the 1920s Ippolitov went on to represent the Soviet Union in international competitions in both skating and cycling. The year 1933 marked the twenty-fifth anniversary since Ippolitov had become Russian champion for the first time. In that period he could count ten skating records and twenty-one cycling records, as well as 269 first places among his achievements.[113] The following year he was one of the first generation of sportspersons to receive the honour of "master of sport". In 1936 the forty-three-year-old broke his own skating record which he had set in 1916. The career of Platon Afanas'evich Ippolitov, sports writer and talented sportsman, had spanned some of the most turbulent years in Russian (and indeed European) history and the most formative years of Soviet physical culture and sport.

Although Ippolitov's sports biography is impressive in and of itself, it does not elucidate the trials of physical culture and sport which developed during the same period. For a deeper understanding of this, one needs to delve into the organizational problems and examine the politics and ideology which shaped the development of physical culture and sports in the early years of the Soviet Union. When the initial utopianism of the revolution collided with the practical realities of government, physical culture and sport—like other social and cultural spheres—had to be brought into line with party ideology and with the demands of establishing Bolshevism in Russia. The next chapter analyses the organization of physical culture, firstly by assessing the political wrangling in the development of physical culture during the NEP (New Economic Policy) period, situating it within the broader political events taking place in higher party circles at the same time, and secondly by continuing beyond the NEP years, tracing the development of the organization and structure of physical culture through an analysis of the changes that took place following Stalin's rise to power.

2 The Genesis and Organization of Soviet *Fizkul'tura*

Whilst improving hygiene, health and defence were the main objectives of physical culture, with the associated projects of body symbolism and physical and psychological rejuvenation commanding much attention, these matters could not be adequately addressed without a solid infrastructural base. In attempting to construct such a base, the question of how to effectively organize physical culture arose. As this chapter shows, this was not an easy task and continued to be the subject of heated debate from the 1920s onwards. There seemed to be no simple way of delegating responsibility among the organizations involved in physical culture or indeed of popularizing the idea of physical culture among the Soviet population. If any progress was to be made in the area of physical culture, the dissemination of its ideals and the success of its practical implementation depended upon proper organization. In examining this aspect of physical culture, another form of body symbolism is encountered—that of the organizational body; constructing, reconstructing, and even deconstructing this body occupied an inordinate amount of time for those charged with leading the organization of physical culture. The sheer volume of literature and time devoted to the organization of physical culture makes this contentious arena a necessary and important part of any analysis of the subject. This chapter assesses the difficult period of the NEP (New Economic Policy), a particularly lean time for anyone involved in physical culture. It then moves on to the 1930s and the structural changes that occurred in that decade, as well as the impact of these changes on physical culture.

When the Bolsheviks came to power in 1917 physical culture was placed under the control of Vsevobuch (*Vseobshchee Voennoe Obuchenie* or the Central Agency for Universal Military Training). Just as the Tsarist regime drafted sportspersons into the war, the Bolsheviks too drew on sport and sportspersons to fight for their cause during the civil war. All youth between the ages of fourteen and eighteen were called upon by the party to go to the sports square and participate in military preparation and reserve training.[1] Fulfilling military requirements and placing physical culture under the control of Vsevobuch defined the initial organization and structure of physical culture. This enabled the Red Army to train civilian youth and prepare them physically and mentally for military action. When, after the civil war, Vsevobuch was considered redundant and hence disbanded, questions over the organization and functions of physical culture began to emerge. In 1922 the All-Russian Union for Red Physical Culture was set up in order to oversee matters. This proved unsuccessful, however, and so the Supreme Council of Physical Culture[2] was "re-created" in 1923, released from subservience to Vsevobuch and instead attached to the Central Executive Committee of the Communist Party.[3] Yet this had only limited authority, an organ installed to simply oversee the distribution of powers and responsibilities between various other organizations[4], but especially between the trade unions and Komsomol, the former which had been gaining in influence.[5]

The specific objectives and responsibilities of the Supreme Council of Physical Culture were discussed at the All-Union Conference of Councils of Physical Culture, which took place 15–19 April 1924 in Moscow and attracted the main protagonists from the worlds of both physical culture and politics: Semashko, Mekhonoshin, Kamenev, Ittin, Zikmund, Kal'pus, Yenukidze, Kalinin, Rykov, Trotsky, Zinoviev, Stalin, and Tomsky.[6] The consensus emerging from the conference was that the fundamental tasks to be dealt with included improving the material base of physical culture, eliminating all bourgeois sports organizations, establishing *fizkul'tura* as a mass popular movement, organizing more coherently the role and function of the physical culture *kruzhok*,[7] as well as defining proletarian sport. A number of key trends were also outlined, and these included developing the body, strengthening work capability, fortifying the growing generations, and improving the general health and well-being of the country.[8] On 13 July 1925 the party issued a resolution seeking to elevate physical culture in its broader social context and bestow upon it greater responsibilities. It was also an attempt to impose increased regulation and define more clearly the role and functions of *fizkul'tura*. The party stance was thus that:

> Physical culture has to be considered not only from the standpoint of physical *vospitanie* and health and as a means of cultural, economic and military preparation of youth (rifle-shooting and other sports), but also as one of the ways of educating the masses (as physical education developed characteristics such as the will, collective habits, endurance, resourcefulness and other valuable qualities) and together with these, it was a means of uniting workers and peasants around the party, councils, and professional organizations through which they could become interested in social-political life.[9]

While this stated nothing especially new, it did reiterate the party view and served to emphasize that physical culture could exert a certain influence in social, cultural, economic, educational, health, and military affairs and represented a key unifying function. This resolution set the basis for the

development of *fizkul'tura* over the next four years (until the party intervention in 1929). It set the ideological tone for physical culture, viewing it
as a means of training, educating, and uniting the "masses", a vital step in
modernizing the nation and laying the foundations for the construction of
the new citizen.

One of the major difficulties afflicting the organization of physical culture during these years was the subdivision of responsibilities between many
different organizations, though most particularly between the Komsomol
and trade unions. With up to fifteen organizations playing a role in the
implementation of physical culture, it was no wonder that there was conflict and confusion. Narkomzdrav, Narkompros, the army, and the Zhenotdel in particular were unsure of their roles and responsibilities in physical
culture, with Zhenotdel representative on the Supreme Council, Maria
Glebova, accusing the Supreme Council of devoting too much attention
to the Komsomol and trade unions as well as itself being in organizational
disarray, an over-bureaucratized and directionless organ.[10] Matveev from
the Komsomol considered that the Supreme Council had "lost almost two
years exclusively on fighting and internal squabbling".[11] All of these organizations were to participate in the development of physical culture but continuously found that they were being sidelined by the Komsomol and trade
unions, with Semashko commenting that the trade unions had become a
"hegemon" in this area.[12] Besides the various organs vying for control there
were manifold other influences on the early development of physical culture. One of these influences was the utopian vision of Bogdanov and the
Proletkul't.[13] The Proletkul't, which held its First All-Russian Conference
in September 1918, embodied many of the revolutionary ideals of the time,
especially the disdain for bourgeois culture.[14] Advocating the principles of
new proletarian culture, the Proletkul't presence in physical culture was
stronger in theory than in practice but nevertheless some Proletkul'tist
ideas managed to inspire the thinking of those involved in physical culture.
In its vision of the socialist utopia, the Proletkul't movement under the Bolsheviks sought to create a new, proletarian physical culture that was free
of bourgeois influences, including competition. Instead, labour gymnastics,
excursions, mass displays, and performances were encouraged. Disparaging bourgeois sports such as football or tennis, the Proletkul'tists went so
far as to invent "new" games or rather put a proletarian spin on existing
games. Some even called for a socialist approach to football, changing the
rules so that the winners would not be judged by goals scored but rather by
the deftness and agility of their players.[15] Although many such utopian elements never really gathered much pace in the practice of physical culture,
some practical elements—excursions and mass displays—did however succeed in becoming a central element of physical culture and sport and were
for example incorporated into the 1928 Spartakiad.

In a similar vein the Hygienist movement had some influence upon physical culture. One of the most high profile Hygienists in physical culture

was rector of the State Institute of Physical Culture and chairman of the NTK (Scientific Technical Committee) A. A. Zikmund. Influential in the 1920s, Zikmund pushed for the application of the Hygienist methodology in physical culture. Hygienists considered the promotion of personal and social health and hygiene through physical culture as the best way of reducing illness and disease and of improving overall standards. New sports and games considered safer and healthier than existing "bourgeois" sports such as football, boxing, or even athletics were advocated. In the end, the debates between competing utopian schools of thought were short-lived. The more moderate "Semashko" line saw that the practical exigencies of physical culture came ahead of the utopian or that the utopian were at least relegated to theoretical discussions rather than mass application.

Aside from the Hygienist groups associated with the state institutes of physical culture, which included medical theoreticians A. A. Zikmund and V. V. Gorinevsky, there were other more important political factions. For example, Semashko, Mekhonoshin, and F. Seniushkin (trade unions) represented one such power bloc, one which reinforced the importance of the trade unions as well as protecting health and military interests in physical culture. The great rival to this group was the Komsomol, with physical culture interests headed by Mil'chakov, Rogov, Matveev, and others. On the fringes of these two groups were the generally unpopular and controversial figures of Aron Ittin (hovering between the two groups) and Nikolai Podvoisky[16] from the Sportintern,[17] who themselves seemed to have been bitter adversaries. Boris Bazhanov, the party representative, appeared to take little or no interest in physical culture whatsoever (which in itself spoke volumes for party interest in physical culture affairs). The two key areas at the root of this conflict within physical culture were the overlapping realms of organization and the "personal question".[18] Those involved in physical culture, but especially the trade unions and Komsomol, were uncertain of their standing in terms of their respective "spheres of influence" and exact tasks. In this the party was blamed for failing to outline specific duties and not issuing any clear directives on physical culture.[19]

The absence of a mediator caused endless problems. Clashes between the power factions were allowed to continue and develop. In 1924 Podvoisky complained about Semashko and Mekhonoshin whom he accused of "inhibiting" him in his physical culture work.[20] He was particularly annoyed with Semashko, who had made some pejorative comments about Podvoisky's organized mass festival by Lenin Hills in an article in *Moscow Workers* (*Rabochei Moskvy*)[21] entitled "Drunken Hills" (*P'yanyie gory*). Podvoisky, who had obviously been very proud of his initiative, took serious issue with Semashko's article.[22] He also claimed the article had been the source of rumours suggesting that Lenin Hills was on the verge of flooding and that Podvoisky had squandered over 20,000 roubles on geological research on the area.[23] This must have been especially unwelcome for Podvoisky, whose labour of love at that time was his work on the project for the construction of the International Red Stadium to be situated by Lenin Hills (a project that was never completed). Semashko expressed his dissatisfaction with Podvoisky a year later in Orgburo discussions where he complained about Podvoisky's penchant for saying "poka" (meaning "not yet" or "by and by") whenever important questions were raised over disagreements.[24] Petty "tit for tat" disputes in the press as well as those conducted behind closed doors led to dissatisfaction within physical culture circles. The failure of two leaders from physical culture's two primary organizations (the Supreme Council and the Sportintern) to remain civil towards one another did not bode well for the movement. Yet what else could be expected when all of this took place in a political atmosphere where personal grievances were freely aired in public and where political "neutrality" was frowned upon.

POLITICAL DEVELOPMENTS

It was also during this time that discussions over the future form and direction of the party were taking place. With Lenin more or less incapacitated the leadership battle had begun and the triumvirate of Stalin, Lev Kamenev, and Grigory Zinoviev had already unofficially formed within the Politburo. Towards the end of 1923 Lev Trotsky had become increasingly marginalized within the party, the triumvirate by this stage extending to a "semerka" including Nikolai Bukharin, Valerian Kuibyshev, Mikhail Tomsky, and Aleksei Rykov.[25] The campaign against Trotsky intensified throughout 1924, with his supporters losing their positions. This was especially prevalent in the military, where many disillusioned Trotsky supporters committed suicide.[26] To a degree the anti-Trotskyism campaign extended into physical culture, where the Hygienists, owing to their ties to Trotsky, were discredited, leading to the virtual disappearance of Hygienist politics as a leading force in Soviet physical culture by the mid to late 1920s.[27] By the time of the thirteenth party congress in May 1924, Trotsky was being accused of factionalism by Zinoviev and Trotskyism subjected to an onslaught of criticism by Stalin, Bukharin, and others. Soon afterwards Zinoviev himself, and then Kamenev, fell out of favour, to be demoted and completely sidelined by 1926.

The disharmony within the party was reflected in the organization of physical culture, and by the mid-1920s the party was forced to intervene. In July 1925, the Central Committee issued a resolution stating that all physical culture work had to exist in connection with the appropriate organizations.[28] This meant that trade union work was directed by the union organs; the Red Army was directed by the appropriate organs of the military department, schools were directed through the organs of Narkompros, and so forth.[29] In relation to the future development of mass physical culture, the resolution stated that the trade unions and Komsomol played an especially important role and therefore more meaning would have to be attached to the formation of their relationship. The Central Committee declared that, in the union clubs, physical culture work had to come under the direct influence of the trade union leadership, with Komsomol participation. In this way the Komsomol could exert its own influence and leadership in the development of physical culture in the trade unions.[30] It was also the Komsomol's responsibility to introduce peasant youth and Pioneers to physical culture. The trade unions meanwhile had to show their full support in attracting active *fizkul'turniki* to the Komsomol. Yet even in spite of party intervention, problems remained.

By 1928 the limited freedoms which some elements of society had enjoyed during the NEP years were curtailed and then completely rescinded as Stalinist mechanisms of power gained force. In physical culture the intense dissatisfaction led to increased pressure for change. The lack of progress, organizational intransigence and personal rivalries meant that control and authority in physical culture were generally weak. Therefore, as a reaction to the continued lack of control by the Supreme Council and the deteriorating relationship between the Komsomol and trade unions, the Central Committee issued a further decree in 1929.[31] This recognized the need to eliminate the lack of coordination in physical culture work, to introduce more planning and organization, to maximize and expand the general scale of physical culture work, to attract the masses to physical culture, and finally to strengthen physical culture work in the villages.[32] Together with these, the party Central Committee considered that, without reinforcing centralized state leadership, on the one hand, and without mass worker participation in physical culture, on the other, the development of the physical culture movement would never truly get underway.[33] With this position more or less echoing the previous resolution of 1925, it remained to be seen whether or not this would suffice. As the 1930s beckoned, major changes were taking place at the top of the physical culture organization.

NEW DIRECTIONS

If the development of physical culture and sport during the NEP period was characterized by inter-organizational disputes and a tension between idealism and practice, then the period of the Five Year Plan and the mid-1930s was characterized by frequent personnel changes and a tension between mass and individual sports. The personalities that dominated physical culture in the 1920s, such as Semashko, were no longer to be found in the leadership repertoire of physical culture and sport in the 1930s. Many indeed later disappeared in the purges. The replacement of Semashko by Nikolai Antipov in 1931 ushered in a new period in physical culture history. This was not signified by the actions of Antipov himself, but rather by the beginning of the period whereby no single individual would have such an important role and influence in the development of physical culture and sport. The leader, in effect, had been superseded by the system. Antipov was chairman for a brief two years and replaced by Vasily Mantsev in 1933. Mantsev also remained in this position for just two years and was replaced by Ivan Kharchenko in 1936. Kharchenko was in charge for just over one year, from June 1936 to August 1937. Following Kharchenko was Elena Knopova who occupied the role for only three months and was replaced by Alexander Zelikov in October 1937. He was then removed in September 1938 and replaced by Vasily Snegov. Almost all of the above were either executed or died in labour camps. The reasons for the removals were all political. The abrupt changes were clearly not in the interests of physical culture and sport and the lack of continuity served only to underline the precarious position of the individual within Soviet society. The agency responsible for physical culture was also subject to reform, with two major organizational and structural changes occurring in 1930 and 1936. On 3 April 1930 the Supreme Council of Physical Culture was replaced by the All-Union Council of Physical Culture and on 21 June 1936 this was replaced by the All-Union Committee on Physical Culture and Sports Affairs (respectively referred to hereafter as simply the All-Union Council and the Physical Culture Committee).

The 1930 restructure essentially called for increased centralization and party control. The party reiterated its concerns about the development of physical culture and urged that "in the interests of constructing socialism" further important work had to be achieved in the area of physical culture.[34] It was repeated that the physical culture movement remained poorly organized and continued to display signs of record-breaking, parallelism and departmental rivalries.[35] Like the other bodies involved in physical culture, it was stated that the party too wanted to see increased organization and planning. It was considered that for the "complete realization of centralized leadership" there had to be planned and controlled work in physical culture by the state organs, the cooperative organizations, the trade unions, Komsomol, voluntary societies, and other social organizations.[36] All of these were urged to become more involved in general cultural-enlightenment work. With the aim of implementing more planning, state leadership and control into physical culture work, the state organs and voluntary societies had to consolidate the position of the Central Executive Committee of the Supreme Council of Physical Culture.[37]

Under this new piece of legislation the Supreme Council's role and responsibilities were revised. It became the All-Union Council of Physical Culture and was set to have more authority and control over physical culture and those involved. The All-Union Council of Physical Culture was now composed of eight people, personally appointed by the Presidium of the Central Executive Committee. The All-Union Council was also composed of representatives from the various republics as well as four representatives from the Revolutionary Military Council, one representative from Narkomtrud, one from Osoaviakhim, two from Dinamo, and finally one from the tourism society.[38] There were to be twenty representatives from the VTsSPS and ten from the Komsomol.[39] The fact that there were twice as many representatives from the trade unions as from the Komsomol was testament to their enhanced stature in physical culture and this re-structuring gave them more authority than the Komsomol. The All-Union Council (though still the "VSFK"), had responsibility for organization, scientific and methodological affairs, sports techniques, provincial physical culture, chess and checkers, external relations, agitprop, physical culture publishing, sports economy, and physical culture work with children.[40] All work by the All-Union Council had to go through its Presidium of nineteen members.[41] According to Henry Morton, this resolution was the result of the "bickering which had held back the development of the sport movement" and a fear that a "Komsomol-inspired organization would fail to fulfil the numerous objectives it [the party] had assigned to sport".[42] It was hoped that this "central agency would give sport the prestige it needed to eliminate internecine organizational warfare" and envisaged assuaging the schisms within the organization.[43] It was not just the re-structuring of the Supreme Council alone however which was designed to effect such changes—as this chapter shows there were other manoeuvres and decisions within physical culture that contributed to changes in the organization of physical culture.

These changes that occurred were the changes which transformed physical culture into the "Soviet" sports system. Events taking place in 1928 such as the International Spartakiad and the physical culture parade had gained much attention for physical culture and sports, but attention did not denote mass enthusiasm and support. Nevertheless, with the potential of physical culture recognized and with the influence of the Five Year Plan, the revisions of the early 1930s were set to witness a new era in physical culture complementing the development of the "New Soviet Person". The 1930s brought a heightened awareness of the importance of physical culture into the public consciousness, with the state and physical culture leadership now seeking to implement a range of measures that would effectively make physical culture another duty of the Soviet citizen, encouraging the individual to partake in the collective drive to attain physical strength and perfection.

TOWARDS MASS PHYSICAL CULTURE
AND SPORT: THE GTO COMPLEX

Part of this drive to attain physical superiority included the introduction of the GTO complex. The GTO (*Gotov k trudu i oborone*) system, a Komsomol influenced idea, was officially established in order to stimulate more interest in physical culture and introduce that structure and direction which was so clearly necessary. It was introduced by the All-Union Council in order to encourage mass involvement in physical culture and to create a population that would have a strong all-round ability in several different types of sport which were largely oriented around labour and defence interests. Successful participants would receive tangible rewards for their achievements in the form of the GTO badges. In order to achieve the GTO norm, a participant had to train for fifteen events and six subjects which covered basic sports such as running and swimming as well as military activities such as shooting and grenade throwing. This was just for the first level which existed from 1931 to 1934. Then a second level was introduced which added an extra three events bringing it to twenty-four in total. The "Be Prepared for Labour and Defence" complex (BGTO) was the equivalent norm for school-age children and Pioneers and was introduced in 1934 with the inclusion of sixteen sports and theoretical subjects to be passed. This was designed to nurture the physical development of young people, help them to study, and encourage group activity amongst their peers. The GTO system thus had three levels, increasing in difficulty, by the mid-1930s. The GTO Level 2 norm was most difficult and numbers passing this level were much smaller than the first level, with those trained in the institutes of physical culture or the military composing the bulk of successful medallists. The system as a whole would appear to have been reasonably successful (yet at the same time plagued by practical problems) and despite several revisions over the years the GTO essentially retained this format until 1988.

The introduction of the GTO complex had wider social and political repercussions than in just physical culture and sport. It was in large part a reaction to successive failures in the organization of physical culture but it was also a reflection of changing emphases of state policy which sought to address labour and defence as its priority, building up a potential army of fit, healthy Soviet citizens. It could further be viewed as part of the general stratification and centralization that accompanied Stalinism, as well as an intrinsic element in modernizing and improving society. The GTO system was an ideal means of incorporating vast sections of the population into systematic physical culture work and motivating them towards actively achieving state goals. The GTO in some respects could therefore be considered a "repackaging" of physical culture and sport, a scheme designed to satisfy the Komsomol and trade unions as well as make sport more comprehensible and attractive to ordinary people.

In spite of the GTO's apparent later popularity and significance, it was initially slow to get off the ground, even in Moscow and Leningrad. At an All-Union Council meeting in 1932 it was reported that the GTO was not practiced on a daily basis and that the trade unions and other organizations undertook no work in this regard.[44] The trade union organizations, Narkompros, and Narkomzdrav were accused of not having issued a single directive on the GTO and the All-Union Council resolution was apparently ignored.[45] It was argued that more needed to be done to promote the system, especially in the summer months. Problems were numerous. These included the poor participation of Osoaviakhim, the Red Army, and

Narkomzdrav in the GTO system; the indifferent attitudes of the trade unions; incorrect directions by the physical culture centres in the conduct of exams; the absence of preparatory study; absence of references to the GTO in the press apart from specialized publications or radio programmes; absence of agitprop campaigns in the workplace; the lack of female participation; a lack of interest in refereeing and examinations; and insufficient participation by students, particularly in the regions.[46] In the view of one commentator, the practical implementation of the complex amongst workers was "random" and "all over the place" (*vkriv' i vkos'*).[47] Ordinary people were also lambasted, with anyone especially talented and able in sport reminded that they should improve their knowledge of the theoretical aspects of physical culture, hence the inclusion of theory as well as practice in the GTO complex.

The regions in particular yielded a number of practical problems for the establishment of GTO rules and standards. In the Kirgiz Republic, for example, where there was high mountainous terrain, GTO organizers had to consult alpinists in order to resolve the issue of how to implement the norm fairly and safely.[48] There were also more fundamental problems with the GTO and GTO officials in the regions and provinces. In the *sovkhozy* in particular GTO instructors lied about their qualifications, exaggerated norm statistics, forged norm cards, and were generally accused of creating an atmosphere of distrust wherein instructors commanded little by way of respect or authority.[49] One of the more amusing cases testifying to the ineptitude of GTO instructors took place on a *sovkhoz* in Odessa Oblast', where three GTO norm achievers could not be awarded their title because the instructor did not know where to find the medals.[50] The many instances of incompetence and a lack of interest in the GTO illustrated the innumerable obstacles still lying before the physical culture leadership.

The introduction of the GTO complex put sport and sporting competition more firmly back on the political agenda. The taboo of the 1920s, when comparisons with bourgeois sport had become increasingly frequent in physical culture discussions and were used to distinguish the positives of socialist sport from the negatives of bourgeois sport, had now largely been lifted. The main argument of the 1920s and even early 1930s was that in the west sport was used to cripple athletes' bodies, for example, by their use of stimulants and doping, that they deployed underhand tactics, glorified the cult of personality, and fostered individualism.[51] On the other hand, socialist sport was not concerned with sport "as an end in itself" but rather with physical preparedness, correct and systematic training, and a healthy, cultured lifestyle.[52] By now the Proletkul't and Hygienist debate had largely dissipated. The cult of personality and obsession with records would very shortly come to dominate Soviet sport, with a strange hybrid of bourgeois sport and Soviet physical culture emerging by the mid-1930s. The principles of Soviet physical culture projected a very much sanitized image of Soviet sport. Soviet sportspersons were, in reality, essentially no different from those in other countries and were far removed from the ideal of the "New Soviet Person". Robert Edelman has made clear the dirty and dangerous character of Soviet sport, especially with regard to sports such as football (with the infamous "soccer hooliganism" already in existence in the 1920s).[53] A further illustration of "un-soviet" sporting behaviour was an incident which took place in Penza in 1927, where two football players were disqualified for two years after violent behaviour in a football match.[54] Many reports were filed, the referee and linesmen were censured (for being unable to implement proper "*vospitanie*"), and there was general unrest as a result of what had occurred. Irrespective of organizational revisions and calls for sports reform, little control could be exercised over the behaviour of players on fields and sports squares across the Union.

With football violence and sporting misbehaviour making Soviet sport appear less than perfect and making the "new" Soviet citizens look distinctly average, the campaign to glorify Soviet sports continued unabated. In spite of the domestic problems being experienced in the organization of physical culture, by the start of the 1930s the Soviet media was able to greatly capitalize on the worldwide depression. The Soviet press depicted the western financial crisis as having a negative impact on sport by curtailing funding and activities. Under such circumstances, it was claimed, most people could not afford to partake in expensive sports or attend events, although this did result in making cheap and accessible sports more popular. Bourgeois sport could not be underestimated however, especially as American Olympic dominance and sporting internationalism grew in the 1930s. As Barbara Keys has shown, the Soviet press warned of the American desire to "spread their own values and ideas" and embark on a "moral crusade to spread peace and democracy" through sport.[55] Not only was the Soviet attitude hostile to the ideology and principles of bourgeois sport, but in their structure and organization bourgeois and proletarian sport also assumed different directions. As with its political structure, Soviet physical culture was highly centralized and controlled, whereas the federal government in the United States took a "hands-off approach", legalized prizefighting, and refrained from intervention.[56] Although the Soviet press tended to denounce "bourgeois" countries and emphasize their differences, there were still commonalities.

In spite of organizational changes at the top in the 1930s, the introduction of the GTO, and various theoretical debates over the nature of sport, certain issues remained unresolved. One of the key issues that needed to be addressed was the increasingly ambiguous position of championism and record-breakers. The fervour for competition and record-breaking unleashed under the Five Year Plan had begun to seep its way into physical culture, creating more problems. The quest to break records was still viewed as bourgeois and at odds with proletarian sport. In relation to the latter debate, the frost had begun to thaw somewhat in 1931, no doubt related to the introduction of the GTO norm. According to one source, record-breakers per se were not targeted as negative influences, but rather they were against a system of physical culture work which focused on producing record-breakers and then rewarding them with salaries and wages.[57] Achievements and successes in competition would not be frowned on as long as the correct "system" was in place. In terms of the system of physical culture, the worry was that specialization, record-breaking, and professionalism would stunt the popular growth of sports and limit participation. The ideal system would marry mass participation with achievement. The GTO system had some inherent contradictions in this regard too. The objective of the GTO was to embrace everyone and every level, eventually raising mass standards of fitness and military preparedness. Its explicit aim was to stimulate mass participation in physical culture and sport. Yet it also harboured an elitist element and fostered championism. This was justified on the grounds that those who reached the level of "champion" could offer an example to others, as well as invest their own knowledge and experience back into physical culture by instructing those in need of training. "Negative" championism was still frowned upon. Antipov commented that a few "champion sportspersons" undervalued the construction of physical culture on the production principle (factory, plant, *kruzhki*) and did not want to abandon their old ways, arguing that "for fifteen years they played one way, so why should they stop this now?"[58] This, he added, was the opinion of certain footballers who continued to play for one organization and work for another, and this, Antipov noted, was anti-social behaviour. Though such "behaviour" was publicly scorned, it was common knowledge that it frequently occurred.

VOLUNTARY SPORTS SOCIETIES

Russian sport today, as well as that of other former Soviet republics, can be recognized in football or hockey by team names such as "Dinamo", "Spartak", or "Lokomotiv". The genesis of these societies lay in the orientation of physical culture and sport around the production principle in 1930.[59] Every trade union was to create its own society which was then to introduce all of its members to physical culture.[60] Factories consequently had greater responsibilities for physical culture, and the factory unions played a leading role in the organization of workers' leisure. So it was that the most important unions or those that had the most number of workers in turn spearheaded the most successful teams. The specified aims of the societies were to promote health and well-being among the workers, improve their work capacity, as well as construct facilities and provide equipment. The societies were assisted financially in achieving these objectives through a variety of means, such as the collection of members' dues, income received through competitions, festivals and other mass events, trade and industrial activities, and from the VTsSPS.[61] Every union member had to pass the GTO, as had family members over eighteen years. Members' rights included voting at meetings, the right to elect and be elected to the leadership organ, the free use of sports facilities and equipment, the right to be in the sports club and school societies, and the right to attend lectures, classes, or competitions. Candidate members (those who usually had not yet passed the GTO norm) had the same rights as full members excluding the right to elect or be elected. For their part, members were obliged to regularly attend *yacheiki* meetings, club activities, and society work; be a shock-worker in industry; attract new members to the society; raise cultural and sports levels; fight against anti-social and anti-physical culture behaviour; have regular health check-ups; observe hygiene standards; and take care of the equipment and facilities belonging to the club.[62] In order to join and be accepted interested workers had to apply to the society *yacheika* at their place of work and complete an application form. Upon payment they would receive their membership card. Under certain circumstances members could be excluded. This occurred if fees went unpaid for a period of three months, if a worker was excluded from the trade unions, committed a crime, or was guilty of anti-social activities.[63]

While the mere mention of creating societies had caused alarm in the 1920s, becoming more fodder for trade union and Komsomol disputes, this was no longer the case in the 1930s. The main difference between the voluntary society debate of 1928 and the eventual creation of the voluntary societies in the mid-1930s was that the 1928 debate had argued for the establishment of a separate society, with no links to the trade unions.[64] The societies of the 1930s were inextricably connected to the internal trade union structure and thus confirmed the pre-eminence of the trade unions in physical culture.[65] As for the Komsomol, the organization encountered difficulties between 1931 and 1936, with falling membership figures, mass expulsions (especially in Leningrad following the Kirov murder in 1934), and trouble regarding "clique building" in Ukraine.[66] So with the voluntary society question seemingly more or less settled by 1935, the main focus of the trade union members was to be the achievement of the GTO norms. Links between the trade unions, labour, physical culture, and shock-work now became even more closely tied. Certain *fizkul'turniki* became distinguished in their factories and places of work for their achievements in both sport and production. At the All-Union Conference on Physical Culture in 1930, Shvernik, head of the trade unions, had stated that the working class, under the leadership of the party and the trade unions, had to conduct shock work, so that "every *fizkul'turnik* was a shock-worker and an active constructor of socialism".[67]

As the final chapter will later demonstrate, the status of the voluntary societies was a significant matter, with the major societies able to attract the most talented sportspersons. Patronage was also a key factor. Dinamo and TsDKA (Central House of the Red Army) were connected to security and defence, Spartak to Komsomol leader Alexander Kosarev, while Zenit[68] (union of workers in military and metal industry) had the support of Nikita Khrushchev and also Lazar Kaganovich. Perhaps the most famous, or more appropriately infamous, patron was Lavrenti Beria. Beria had become honorary head of Dinamo football club in 1936 and had assumed leadership of the secret police in 1939. A football fanatic and former youth player, Beria took a keen interest in Dinamo's progress in the football league and was unimpressed by Spartak successes. In the club life of Zenit, Khrushchev was frequently praised for his interest and involvement in its affairs, as well in the club's very initiation.[69] The attention of Khrushchev, who was then secretary of the Moscow Party Committee, was highly significant for the club. In fact, Khrushchev was accredited as having been a key figure in the overall establishment of the voluntary societies, himself and Lazar Kaganovich having put forward a proposal for the creation of twenty-four such societies in Moscow region. According to Belyakov of the MOSFK (Moscow Regional Physical Culture Council), Khrushchev was very interested in Zenit and physical culture, "carefully following" the progress of two young girls from the *Elektrokombinat* factory in Tiumen, who were both on a skiing expedition. He was said to have inquired about their health and sent telegrams "everyday".[70] Belyakov suggested that the leadership of the organizations in the factory committees and the trade unions take a similar interest in the physical culture movement.[71] The power blocs of the 1920s had clearly shifted. There was now a new posse in physical culture with links that went right to the top of the Soviet political system. Defying these individuals would most likely have weighty consequences.

Regardless of the interest of certain high-ranking party members or influential patronage, the voluntary societies on an everyday level witnessed no substantial improvements. Re-organization did not eliminate the problem of a lack of resources, bureaucracy, or a general lack of interest in sport. Documents from the industrial city of Tula, in European Russia, show the kinds of difficulties experienced by cities and industrial centres outside of Moscow. In one factory the physical culture representative reported that there was some Komsomol support in that Komsomol youth were attracted to the GTO norm but in general Komsomol work was poor.[72] Among the *fizkul'turniki* there was no example of shock-work in industry. A representative from another factory remarked that the physical culture bureau attached to the factory collective had been purged twice that summer and that now physical culture work was apparently better.[73] Meanwhile the trade union factory committee and party organizations were paying more attention to physical culture organization. There had even been an initiative to invite various masters of sport to the factory for consultation, and so, for example, Platon Ippolitov had come to provide advice on skating. Some of the smaller factories struggled to offer their workers adequate facilities, with some reporting that physical culture was limited due to a lack of premises and no financial means to use those belonging to another factory.[74] The sad state of affairs was highlighted by the fact that one factory warehouse only had five players on its hockey team. Two years later and the factories continued to report problems. From factory no. 58 the physical culture representative commented that young people were not interested in physical culture work.[75] He added further that "all members of the society Zenit were members only on paper and members' dues were not paid".[76] Others from the factory noted that the Komsomol was not interested in the work of the societies and that work in general was unplanned with frequent disagreements occurring.[77] Finding representatives with an interest in physical culture often proved difficult. At one factory the Orgburo representative, who was also the trade union representative, was reported as doing "absolutely nothing".[78] Again there were comments that while sports sections did exist, this was only "on paper" and in reality work was weak.[79] The long lists of GTO achievers and voluntary society members were cast into doubt (especially given the evidence that GTO cards and statistics were frequently fabricated). The problems experienced in Tula were not unusual and could be found in other workplaces across the Soviet Union. Getting ordinary people to participate in physical culture and sport, especially outside the major factories and urban centres, proved a constant problem.

TIGHTENING THE REINS OF CONTROL

In the last major organizational re-shuffle for thirteen years, the All-Union Committee for Physical and Sports Affairs was established on 21 June 1936 with Ivan Kharchenko as its chairperson. The official point of this re-shuffle was to increase centralization but it was also a response to other factors, including the introduction of the Stalin Constitution. This time physical culture was brought closer to the party line politically. In a letter to Stalin, Andreev, and Molotov, Komsomol and physical culture leaders Kosarev and Kharchenko outlined the new structure and organization of the All-Union Committee for Physical Culture and Sports Affairs.[80] The structural changes introduced were (once again) designed to "strengthen state control and leadership work in physical culture and sport" and to this end—and this was the difference in comparison with past revisions—it had the "right" of a People's Commissariat.[81] There was another distinct turnabout in this overhaul. In a clear break with past party statements in regard to physical culture and sport, the awarding of prizes and titles to sportspersons was now officially sanctioned.[82] Again, this reflected the change in direction following the Constitution and Stalinist principles of socialism. Yet the most important revision was the decision to confer upon the new body the powers of a People's Commissariat. This meant that physical culture and sports issues had to pass directly to the chairman of the Council of People's Commissars (*Sovnarkom*) who from 1930 to 1941 was Vyacheslav Molotov and from 1941 to 1946, Stalin.

However, this was arguably not so much to do with the best interests of physical culture, as it was stated, but rather with the political hunt for "enemies" that dominated the latter half of the 1930s. Trotskyists, Bukharinists, and spies were reportedly to be found in physical culture, attempting to ensconce themselves in leadership positions.[83] Some of these had already been "uncovered". There were Korytnyi and Nemkovskii from Kiev, Sharoev from Sverdlovsk, as well as others from different parts of the Soviet Union. All of these had apparently managed to get into influential positions in various departments of physical culture organizations and had earned the "blind trust" of the physical culture workers.[84] There was the case of a physical culture instructor who was a "fascist spy". A Donbass worker in the automobile club was revealed as a "contrabandist" and "speculator". A certain Lazutskii, whose father was a "White Army captain living in Paris", was accused of forging documents, destroying GTO norm cards, and conducting absolutely no physical culture work. Why this Lazutskii would go to the trouble of destroying GTO norm cards was not elucidated. Norm cards were hardly politically sensitive documents and destroying them served no apparent purpose, their destruction probably being little more than a nuisance to their holders. Nonetheless, Lazutskii was in fact charged with spreading counter-revolutionary ideas among teachers and students. There were many more besides. Those in possession of German names were in a dangerous position—Schultz, Val'ter, Schutz-Kan, and Shuman were *fizkul'turniki* who were all accused of being German spies. The 1937 campaigns against "enemies of the people" did not necessarily need to legitimize actions—mere suspicion was sufficient grounds for arrest, incarceration, or worse.

The *"chistki"*, referred to by western scholars in the sense of a purge but rather meaning a "cleaning out", were a regular occurrence under the Soviet regime but it was not until the mid to late 1930s when *"chistki"* or purges became synonymous with widespread removals, arrests, and mass murder.[85] The various purges hitherto carried out in physical culture—whether the removal of apparently inept local instructors or the removal of physical culture leaders at the top—had not by any means been infrequent occurrences. There were different types of *chistki*, which as John Arch Getty notes, "had different targets and were conducted by different agencies for different reasons".[86] The year 1937 marked a watershed for the purging of physical culture. Party intentions were made clear to readers of the physical culture press when several pages of leading newspaper *Krasnyi sport* were hijacked to allow extensive coverage of the "anti-Soviet Trotsky centre" or the "trial" of Tukachevsky and others. Fear and suspicion—which had more or less always been present but to varying degrees—escalated and spread throughout Soviet society. The Great Purges, begun in 1937, marked a significant turning point in the unprecedented scale and ferocity of the *chistki*. Physical culture provides ample evidence of this. Whereas in the past many of those purged were simply demoted or removed, in the

Terror arrest and often execution awaited. Among those to meet such a fate in physical culture were the once eminent Antipov, Kharchenko, Ittin, Mekhonoshin, Kal'pus, and others who were all executed in either 1937 or 1938.

John Arch Getty's description of the party before the Second World War as a "certain type of disorganized and cumbersome machine" is apt; the party had some vague notion of where it wanted to go but was being pulled and dragged in different directions as it stumbled onward.[87] Getty even takes this confused bureaucracy, with a complicit Stalin, as grounds for the Great Terror, arguing that "[t]he existence of high-level personal rivalries, disputes over development or modernization plans, powerful and conflicting centrifugal and centripetal forces, and local conflicts made large-scale political violence possible". The aim here is not to discern the origins of the Terror but to place physical culture within the context of the Terror. The picture that emerges is that, unsurprisingly, physical culture and sport were no different from any other sphere of Soviet life during this period, suffering many losses. The fundamental lack of trust between centre and periphery as well as between party and people led to constant personnel changes, removals and eventually, executions. All of these actions—the purging, centralization, repression—were, ostensibly, committed in the name of socialism for the good of the party and society.

It was not only prominent leaders or individuals with an uncertain past who were in danger. Perhaps the most well-known case of the purges within a sporting context was that of the Starostin brothers, in particular Nikolai.[88] In 1937 suspicions spread to envelop famous Soviet footballer Nikolai Starostin and the control he wielded over Spartak. Too much influence in the hands of any one individual was especially dangerous in the late 1930s and the name of Starostin was the type of influential and well-known name that began to attract the interest of the authorities. Although brewing since 1936, the "Starostin affair" became much stormier in September 1937 when the All-Union Committee for Physical Culture and Sport published a resolution in *Pravda* calling for the removal of Nikolai Starostin from his position as representative of the Football Section Committee for his "complete inactivity".[89] In response, the four footballer Starostin brothers (Nikolai, Alexander, Andrei, and Petr) wrote to Kosarev, Stalin, Molotov, and *Sovnarkom* representative Chubar' to clarify the situation and obtain their support. They addressed Kosarev as the "real leader of Soviet physical culture" and no doubt hoped that his close ties to the club would help save the brothers.[90] Their letter to Stalin attributed the increasing negativity towards Spartak and the Starostins personally to "jealousy and dishonesty" following the society's success.[91] Not directly mentioned by the brothers, the "jealousy and dishonesty" accusation was more than likely directed at their great rivals, Dinamo and its sponsor, Beria. The brothers, in keeping with socialist "self-criticism", acknowledged that in the "huge and intensive" work done by Spartak there "may have been mistakes and inaccuracies" and requested that this be investigated. This was all the more necessary as they were personally "unfairly accused of living beyond their means" and importing many goods from abroad.[92] They claimed that the situation was made worse by the behaviour of acting All-Union Committee representative Elena L'vovna Knopova,[93] who they maintained took every opportunity to "terrorize and discredit" them, insinuating that they, Kharchenko, and even all Spartak masters of sport were "enemies of the people".[94]

In an excerpt from their letter to Molotov (from the brothers and Spartak members) they refuted allegations made by the newspaper *Krasnyi sport* and again condemned the *Pravda* article. The *Krasnyi sport* article to which they referred accused them of "making contracts, buying and selling players, corrupting masters of sport, lacking in political-educational work, undervaluing military types of sport and squandering state funds".[95] All of these accusations, they claimed, "did not correspond to the reality". They countered that the work of all voluntary sports societies, as yet conducted by "inexperienced personnel" was bound to have "many mistakes" and that Spartak, like other societies, also had to work without any "clear leadership from the Committee of Physical Culture".[96] The four "crimes" which Nikolai Starostin and others allegedly committed were "living beyond their means, importing a multitude of presents from abroad, receiving an apartment and dacha from Spartak, and for using prizes and awards for special purposes thereby introducing 'bourgeois' elements into sport". They refuted these allegations point by point and argued that they had served the party and the state well in the last fifteen years and had "never compromised the name of Soviet physical culture".[97] The brothers clearly sensed the precarious situation which they were in but attempts to justify their lifestyle and their expenditures on the Paris trip in July 1937 were hardly enough to save them. Mercy was rarely shown in the witch-hunts of late 1930s, when three quarters of a million were executed in 1937 and 1938, many without trial.[98]

In any case, even if the accusations had been true, they were hardly, as Edelman points out, "crimes" in the ordinary sense of the word but only in the Soviet context of the late 1930s. Nikolai's actions—the buying and selling of players and rewarding them—contravened socialist principles but they had also helped make Spartak Moscow the most successful club in the Soviet Union. Moreover, the Starostins were not alone in their involvement in these kinds of activities. The circle of protection in which Starostin had ensconced himself was not quite the fortress he might have hoped for—in 1938 Spartak patron Alexander Kosarev was branded an "enemy of the people" and executed. The terror had permeated all levels of society. The reports by the Starostins and the secret denunciation of the Starostins by Georgii Znamenskii[99] were characteristic of those years—fear and uncertainty were here expressed by both informed and informer. Starostin was under investigation but, as Znamenskii stated, had links to Kosarev, the

NKVD and Moscow police. Znamenskii, the informer with possible links to the NKVD, was unsure of who to trust having being "found out" himself by Starostin. The political intrigues of the upper party echelons repeated themselves throughout the Stalinist bureaucracy and sport was one such bureaucracy. The denunciation also corroborates the view that "the terror was a series of group efforts rather than a matter of one man [Stalin] intimidating everyone else".[100] The wave of executions following the Bukharin and Rykov trial that saw off Kosarev, Yezhov and others did not in the end see the arrest of the Starostin brothers. They were not arrested and sent to labour camps until 1942.[101]

SOVIET SPORT

Ironically, sport had become a matter of state importance, but not in the way that physical culture leaders might have wished. Stalin's rise to power meant a loss of innocence for physical culture, not in the sense that what had been happening previously was pure and untainted, but in that its utopian ideals dissipated and with those vanished many of the figures of the 1920s. Having finally won itself state attention, physical culture and sport became much more visible in Soviet life and indeed Soviet sport became more visible in the international arena. Proletarian ideals were compromised by quests for records and Stalin-inspired socialist competition. Of course it was not Stalin alone who was responsible for this—it owed just as much to the bureaucratic system spawned by him. This system did to a certain extent achieve the mass organization of physical culture through both the implementation of the GTO complex and the establishment of the voluntary sports societies but this entailed sacrificing physical culture for sport. The replacement of one type of system with another did not necessarily solve any problems but rather created a whole set of new ones. Physical culture and sport had in a sense been modernized, but not in the socialist sense initially envisaged by the authorities. At the same time as much of the old guard involved in the leadership of physical culture were being arrested and executed, along with countless others, Soviet citizens were required to don sports costumes, join clubs, and parade across towns and cities of the Soviet Union to visibly prove how "life had become better and merrier". The following chapters demonstrate and reiterate how the difficulties experienced by the higher and middle level organization of physical culture filtered down and impacted on the lives of ordinary people. Whether denied or offered the opportunity to participate in physical culture activities and thus make themselves into "better" Soviet citizens, ordinary people—the all important masses—in many instances made up their own minds on physical culture participation. This was clearly in evidence with regard to young people, the so-called vanguard of the revolution.

3   The Creation of an Ideal Young Citizen

After the civil war and the introduction of the NEP, many young people experienced political and ideological disillusionment which was often heightened by immense social dislocation, poor living standards, serious health problems, and unemployment. This chapter examines how the ideology of physical culture was to be applied to help alleviate the various social problems of illness, depression, and even suicide. It shows how exercise and hygiene were directed at informing and educating young people, with the ideology of physical culture formulated to provide them with a clearly defined programme for assuming the role of new socialist person. The objective of physical culture education and propaganda was to mould young people into healthy, physically strong citizens, and this was frequently accompanied by a moralizing element that sought to influence the sexual and behavioural desires and actions of young people. This was all part of an ever-expanding literature on health, hygiene, and youth behaviour, trying to deal with the "sexual revolution".[1] In the state effort to reach young people, physical culture propaganda campaigns found formal expression in schools and clubs. Schools were to be of particular significance and here physical culture teachers and instructors were to play an important role in educating students in the ways of socialist physical culture. As this chapter shows, implementing the ideology of physical culture was not an easy task, however, and the reaction and attitude to any programmes for acculturation by many young people—such a diverse and disparate group—were not necessarily positive or predictable.

In dealing with young people, problems such as hooliganism and suicide, though not unique features of early Soviet life, certainly became more apparent in the 1920s. In a recent study of ideology and everyday life in the 1920s and 1930s, Natalia Lebina, Pavel Romanov, and Elena Yarskaya-Smirnova referred to the acute social problems with which the young Soviet state had to cope, especially during the NEP years, which experienced a sharp increase in cases of hooliganism.[2] This was predominantly an urban problem and according to Lebina about 17 per cent of the population lived in the cities with the rate of urban crimes and misdemeanours standing at more than 40 per cent.[3] Under such circumstances, it is unsurprising that, as Eric Naiman has noted, the NEP era was a "profoundly *anxious* time".[4] Many people became quickly despondent, a problem exacerbated by the high unemployment levels. Young people who were expected to settle down and start a family instead found themselves trained and educated but with no work. Disillusionment mounted as a sense of betrayal of the revolution's goals took hold among the party's primarily young following.[5] Angry and idle youth soon began to express their discontent in a number of ways including through crime and suicide.

If any one person represented the disillusionment with life it was the poet Sergei Yesenin. His decadent lifestyle epitomized everything the ideology of physical culture opposed. Poems such as "The Taverns of Moscow" and "A Hooligan's Love" reflected Yesenin's own tastes and had earned him quite a reputation and quite a following, especially among young people. Following his suicide in 1925 the party ran a propaganda campaign directed at youth condemning *Yeseninshchina*.[6] His death was shown to be the culmination of excess and bohemianism, his life the story of a young village boy succumbing to the wicked temptations of the city. As Gregory Carleton observes, the *Yeseninshchina* "became an all-purpose epithet, a blend of fact, myth and innuendo that represented the worst of young people's waywardness".[7] It also tarnished all of Yesenin's work with the same pejorative brush and ignored the underlying factors which contributed to Yesenin's and youth's unhappiness. Rather than address these issues, experts played down links between suicide and pessimistic attitudes, claiming, as Kenneth Pinnow observes, that Yesenin's death was "not 'characteristic' of the current time" but rather, "indicative of the mood of writers".[8] Meanwhile, Semashko claimed that Yesenin "suffered from a mental disorder and a general weakness of will".[9] Rather than attribute suicide and other problems such as hooliganism to social or political issues, the individual was instead held directly accountable for his or her failings and weaknesses.

In spite of the existence or non-existence of such failings, from the Bolshevik viewpoint young people still embodied the revolutionary spirit. Great emphasis was consequently placed on educating younger generations in the socialist way and attention turned to the question of *vospitanie*.[10] The debate surrounding the question of *vospitanie* focused on how to correctly bring up new socialist youth and touched upon the issue of the "withering away of the state".[11] Both were contentious matters in the early years of Bolshevik power and received considerable thought and examination, often with radical and unorthodox methods being considered or applied.[12] With children requiring "a uniquely proletarian upbringing", psychologists and pedagogues set about incorporating socialist values into education.[13] The enthusiasm did not last long; radical notions on socialist upbringing faded into the background towards the mid-1920s and especially in the 1930s as Stalin returned to more traditional policies in what Nicholas Timasheff termed the "Great Retreat".[14] By the time Stalin was in power it had been recognized that the "withering away of the state" and its concomitant policy of the "withering away of the family" were impracticable and both concepts disappeared from education and family life. Gaining in popularity though was the idea that a potential marriage between *vospitanie* and *fizkul'tura* could assist in disciplining and controlling young people along socialist lines, helping to transform them into ideal Soviet citizens. Physical culture for its part in *vospitanie* was viewed as an important element in transforming children, helping them to become strong and healthy proletarians as well as offering a possible means of stemming mounting social problems such as drunkenness, hooliganism, and suicide. The terms "young people" and "youth" here refer to children, teenagers, and young adults. All of these age groups were affected by social problems, were generally in education of some sort, and were the primary age group targeted by the ideology of physical culture.

VOSPITANIE, EDUCATION, AND CHILDREN

If the creation of an ideal socialist society was to be created, then it was essential to extend *vospitanie* so that it incorporated the private lives of young people. By doing this efforts could be made to influence and dictate sexual practices among youth. Scientists, pedagogues, pedologists, doctors, and many others clamoured to voice their opinions on how to establish the best environment in which to raise young communists. Physical culture, it was argued, could be used to help establish the "correct social environment" as social factors played a more influential role than biological factors in the sexual *vospitanie* and habits of young people.[15] In regard to youth during the NEP Anne Gorsuch has rightly pointed out that "the family, the neighbourhood and the street remained vital sources of socialization", with the "new mechanisms of socialization through political education and youth clubs" long-term projects.[16] Given the awful conditions of early 1920s, schools—although a longer term project—were still to play a particularly important role in instilling socialist values. While access to school education might not have been possible for all, physical spaces such as schools or clubs were still the most appropriate venues for the organization of proper communist forms of socialization. According to Semashko, schools represented "the *vospitanie* of the future defenders of socialism and socialist revolution".[17] In terms of establishing an organized, coherent "programme for identity" for young people, schools arguably represented the state's best chance of familiarizing youth with new, socialist principles.

The old school system was viewed as having been a particularly bad environment for children, having a deleterious effect on their physical and mental health. There was much debate about how to eliminate masturbation or onanism—"the main scourge of the old schools".[18] The "best, and indeed, only cure" for masturbation was, in Semashko's view, physical culture. In such cases, doctors and specialists had to advise patients to practice sports.[19]

Children were encouraged to wear "free" clothes without any unnecessary pleats or folds and clothes which should not "draw attention to the sexual organs", particularly for girls.[20] Physical culture was endorsed to help educate these young people and to help create the correct social environment through persuading children to adopt a hygiene routine, advising them to wear hygienic clothes, exercise, and perform socio-political activities in their schools and communities.[21] Schools had their important socio-political goals to fulfil and so had to implement the policy of "physical culture twenty-four hours a day". Semashko repeated that exercises, games, and sports were significant not only in developing health, agility, and endurance but also in imbuing a sense of collectivism and solidarity.[22] As if to reinforce the importance of physical culture in school, the monthly journal *Fizkul'tura v shkole* was published in 1930.[23] The journal not only sought to inculcate discipline through exercise and physical culture but also included articles on a wide range of other topics including the differences between socialist and bourgeois sport, anti-religious propaganda, sexual hygiene, and rural education. Teachers, as disseminators of the new values and ideals, were to be literate in the social, cultural, and political debates of the time.

Visual propaganda was also important in depicting a vivid image of how to conduct oneself under the new regime and could be used in schools and clubs. One of the most popular forms of propaganda was the poster, and as Peter Kenez observes, this was the "quintessential form of propaganda" with a message easily understood by "unsophisticated viewers".[24] In schools especially these were to be colourful, interesting, and eye-catching so as to gain the attention of students. To maximize impact they were to be hung on the walls in the physical culture corners (if these existed), recreational areas, or where young people gathered. Posters were also to be used in conjunction with talks and lectures to children on the themes they identified. In cases where *fizkul'tura* posters in schools were produced their thematic scope tended to be quite broad. They ranged from informing students that smoking led to shortened life expectancy, warning students not to spit on the floor or walls, stating that walls were not for graffiti or for throwing rubbish at, and that they should not climb over fences as this could destroy their clothes (there was evidently a delinquency problem here).[25] In this sense physical culture was much more than simply sports or games, it was intended to be a form of *culture*, an effort to inculcate some level of *kul'turnost'* in children and youth. It was an essential part of *vospitanie*, as it sought to "develop social habits and qualities and to address the matter of how comrades conducted themselves".[26] It was part of the overall effort to modernize and develop the Soviet citizen. Posters, exercise drills, talks, living newspapers—all were aimed at both educating and disciplining. These were of course by no means exceptional. Other countries adopted similar approaches and ran similar campaigns. For instance in Germany and America, smoking and the consumption of alcohol were strongly condemned and their harmful effects on health publicized as a deterrent.[27]

Figure 3.1 Anti-smoking physical culture poster. "Khochesh' ran'she umeret'—Kuri bol'she!" (Want to die younger—smoke more!). School physical culture poster from *Fizkul'tura v shkole*, no. 3 (1930): 29. Courtesy of the Russian State Library.

Physical culture authorities were faced with great difficulties if they were going to turn every child into well-behaved and acquiescent young citizens. This was made all the more challenging because often those who were supposed to be directly instilling the new values were themselves guilty of committing the "sins of old". One such problem was faced by local physical culture officials in Saransk, Penza province. During the course of discussions a physical culture official there, Strunikov, had commented on the prevailing perception that the example of instructors could assist physical culture. Strunikov was correct; as conveyors of the physical culture ideology, instructors were to set a good example. However, he noted that, although "*fizkul'turniki* were not allowed to smoke . . . instructors everywhere agitated about this even though they themselves smoked".[28] This kind of situation, he astutely observed, was "not exactly good for the introduction of physical culture to the masses". Another official acknowledged that Strunikov was no doubt correct but reasoned that some instructors were "children of war communism and so have become people with weak nerves and maybe even weak will-power" and that "therefore it is natural if a person finds it very difficult to give up any deep-rooted habits, in particular smoking".[29] According to him it was not especially bad that such instructors "agitated against smoking". The contradiction did not bother some, whose main concern was that the official policy of agitation was being carried out, notwithstanding the example that was actually being set. Of note too is how the local physical culture officials of Penza had come into contact with the social and political issues associated with the NEP, using the current political terminology of "nervousness" and "war communism" to rationalize the daily obstacles that came their way.

The comments expressed by those in Saransk illuminated the wider problem of instructors or teachers. In early Soviet Russia finding good instructors who were both competent at physical culture and equipped to transmit socialist principles seemed elusive. Here and elsewhere we come across instructors who smoked, jeered women, or who were only interested in talented sportspersons and in their own upward social mobility. Educating and helping young people seemed to be the last on their list of priorities. A letter written by one physical culture instructor from Bedno-Demyansk (near Penza), relayed that, after finishing just a month-long physical culture course, he was so immersed in physical culture duties that he was apparently overburdened with work and responsibility.[30] He was unhappy with his salary, found the work to be "too difficult", and so asked to be relieved of his duties. Instead, he wanted to work in one particular seven-year school, and one which already happened to have a physical culture teacher who "practices for six and a half hours a week for one rouble per hour" and also "works as a teacher of German and drawing, so probably manages quite well". In the view of the disgruntled instructor, Nikitin, this "former officer" did not devote sufficient attention to the wide range of physical culture, practicing only "running formations". Nikitin therefore considered that the GSFK should satisfy his request to be the new physical culture instructor in the school. Though not particularly experienced, the forthright and ambitious Nikitin felt himself entitled to better pay and conditions. Rather than having the interests of physical culture or the good of the collective at heart, he was instead driven primarily by a personal desire to improve his own lot. This kind of behaviour was not supposed to be that of the new socialist citizen and was a far cry from the example that was to be set by instructors.

The use of physical culture as a transmitter of socialist values was not always effective. If instructors generally lacked the necessary qualities and commitment to convey state policy, then these very instructors were hardly in a position to offer a good example to young people. While physical culture might have been intended to be deployed as an educating and moralizing tool by the authorities, its message of clean healthy living and morally upright behaviour seems to have been lost on many young people as problems with hooliganism persisted throughout the 1920s. Perhaps, as those in Saransk noted, the hangover of war communism deadened the senses of the young to the new culture, or the wave of social problems during

NEP lingered on and drowned out the voices of physical culture advocates. Whatever the reasons, physical culture ideology was failing to have any influence on young people. There was evidence of further trouble in 1930, the example again from Penza province. According to a local newspaper report, the "latest incident" occurred in the May 1 club where some *fizkul'turniki* in the physical culture *kruzhok* "gave a good thrashing to one of their own members because she was a '*baryshnya*' (daughter of a landowner or gentleman)".[31] The attack was so bad that the victim was hospitalized and a show trial had been organized for those guilty of the assault. It was also reported that in the club M-K Railworkers *fizkul'turniki* "always start fights and are drunk". Finally it was noted that "hooligans who harm work will be driven out from the ranks of the *fizkul'turniki*". The world of physical culture was evidently not immune to the social ills that plagued the NEP years and beyond. The explicit mention of the term "*baryshnya*" suggests that, moreover, the assault referred to previously was not any random attack, for the incident coincided with increased calls for the arrest and punishment of kulaks, which had picked up pace during the class war of the late 1920s. As a so-called "*baryshnya*", the victim would have been an easy target for young, drunken hooligans who more than likely attempted to take the law into their own hands. In relation to *komsomol'tsy* Matthias Neumann has recently argued that while many engaged in wanton acts of hooliganism others, perhaps like those in Penza, were more militant and committed acts of hooliganism in order to enforce their own understanding of the revolution and the new socialist life.[32] In either case, the perpetrators of such crimes still showed that the Soviet citizen that existed in schools and clubs evinced the self-interest and violence that continued to mar the socialist body politic with the ideology of physical culture failing to translate into practice.

Hooliganism was a constant problem during and indeed after NEP. Of course not all youth were hooligans, and naturally some did enjoy participating in Soviet physical culture. One of the determining factors in the success of physical culture was physical space. Schools often appeared to lack resources, while clubs seemed to harbour hooligan elements. A breakthrough of sorts was radio, which transcended physical space. The broadcast of the physical culture programme "Morning Dawn" was by most accounts a particular hit. Intended to be youth friendly and lively, the programme aimed to attract children to physical culture in a short (less then ten minutes) and accessible fashion.[33] The physical culture content was relatively limited given that it was such a short programme, and there were concerns over this. However, the programme did genuinely seem to have a reasonably big youth following. In 1934 the editors had even received over 400 letters from children who had written about their experiences of physical culture and sport. Most children, generally aged about ten years and hailing from all corners of the Soviet Union, wrote about how they practiced physical culture classes to the radio every morning. One Armenian mother wrote to explain that, because the broadcast was of poor quality, her five-and-a-half-year-old son would like to be sent a copy of the exercises. Some children even had their favourite exercises or wanted more challenging ones. Others were so eager to listen to "Morning Dawn" that they requested it be broadcast earlier (at 7.30 instead of 8.00) so that they would not miss the show on their way to school.[34] Exercises were done both collectively in schools as well as at home, with family. Some wrote of how they converted siblings and parents to the ways of physical culture. Parents even wrote to thank the editors after practicing the exercises and following the programme had helped to improve their own health. The editors hoped that all of these letters should be used constructively to help progress physical culture and help greater numbers of children. Here the combination of a relatively new form of technology and physical culture proved to be a successful means of involving Soviet citizens in everyday life, not only encouraging them to identify with the new regime but actually getting them to interact with the state's cultural programmes on a physical and emotional level.

DOWN WITH DEPRESSION AND DELINQUENCY!

> Don't smoke, don't drink spirits,
> Friends, for amusement,
> Don't flirt:
> It's all poisonous.

'*Chastushki*[35] instruktorskie'.[36]

One of the more popular social venues for young Soviet people was clubs and here physical culture themes again cropped up, exhorting the value of practicing sports and exercise. Agitation plays were a means of (relatively) subtly articulating this message, instructing and informing audiences on socialist life and behaviour. Agitation plays (*agitki*) had been quite successfully used during the civil war to draw public attention to social and political problems as well as to popularize the Bolshevik cause. These plays were very short—usually one or two acts—and used caricatures and stereotypes to emphasize the "virtues" of Bolshevism over the "vices" of Bolshevik opponents.[37] During NEP agitation theatre developed into what Lynn Mally calls "theatre of small forms" which in fact retained many of the characteristics of *agitka* theatre but which now "intended to be engaging", including skits using "humour and buffoonery", with some groups "employing elements of NEP culture in order to interest viewers".[38] Very often the themes of such plays included physical culture and sport, and were intended to be performed in worker and youth clubs, appearing for instance in many of the plays published in the trade union magazine *Materialy dlya klubnoi stseny* (*Material for the Club Stage*). The aim of the magazine, according to its editors, was to provide clubs and red corners with a repertoire of "high quality art and ideology", which, it was acknowledged, was hard to find.[39]

These plays depicted those involved in physical culture as representatives of the new socialist way of life—the new generation. Agitation and propaganda showed the audience that they, ordinary people, could be active participants in the socialist life through everyday activities such as physical culture. Both the plays and *chastushki* were designed to entertain but also to educate by disseminating state policy. The performance aspect was particularly effective and popular, not only telling but actually showing the audience how to live. In this regard both *chastushki* and plays were often written with the local club stage in mind. The themes of the plays and *chastushki* featured here were consistent with the social obstacles faced by many young people. For some of those young people who believed in communism and carried out these kinds of propaganda campaigns, the act of trying to teach others was often, as Neumann argues, a "two-way process", a means of "first and foremost reinforcing their own beliefs".[40] As for physical culture and sport's role in this type of theatre, its mere presence signifies its importance as a feature of social life and its relevance in projecting positive images of progressive and responsive youth. Agitprop thus functioned as a sort of guidebook with instructions on how to overcome these obstacles. The problem with this type of agitprop in the 1920s was that it could not be completely controlled and as Lynn Mally comments, "[S]cripts were prepared and altered at the performance site by individual instructors and the actors themselves".[41]

In the play "Konkurs na luchshego strelka" ("Competition for the Best Rifle-Shooter") by Evgenii Pavlov, *komsomol'tsy* and the sports square dominate proceedings.[42] Readers or viewers are thus instantly confronted with sport and youth. Key messages in this play are those of the struggle between young and old and between progress and bureaucracy. The opening scene features young Tosha and Gosha in the firing range, with Tosha—a first-class rifle master—showing Gosha how to use the rifle correctly. Tosha assumes the role of model *komsomolka*, constantly correcting Gosha and reminding him of the responsibilities of the *komsomol'tsy*. Tosha and Gosha, having "come straight from work", are in the firing range before it has opened and are thus scolded by the caretaker. Hunting them away, the caretaker curses "champions" and their eagerness for training practice. He was here fulfilling the stereotypical role of the older generation who could not understand young people or physical culture. When another character—Tonya, the secretary of the shooting *kruzhok*—enters, she also encounters resistance and inflexibility from the caretaker who is depicted as caring only for order and bureaucracy. Here, the caretaker represented another stereotype—the overly zealous bureaucrat or apparatchik whose love of order and procedure inhibited practical progress. Yet with classes in the range soon starting Tonya gets her way and the caretaker leaves, again cursing the champions.

In another play, this one from the TRAM[43] repertoire, the club and sports hall are once again the scenes of physical culture. "Klesh zadum-chivyii" ("The Thoughtful Dandy") centres on love and marriage within the Komsomol and includes a scene where two Komsomol factory secre-taries instruct a group of textile and metalworkers in physical culture.[44] With the workers running about and performing exercises to music, the play portrays physical culture as being a vital part of everyday factory life. These pieces of agitprop portray youth at the helm of Soviet life, propelling socialism forward. Their two most likely hurdles—older gen-erations and bureaucracy—are eventually overcome by determination and enthusiasm. In a TRAM meeting following a 1931 performance of "Klesh zadumchivyii", one representative argued that it should no longer be per-formed because it took place "outside of a specific factory or a specific city" and so "did not address concrete, specific, problems".[45] By the 1930s it was proving increasingly difficult for TRAM and other agitprop the-atre groups to satisfy audiences and find an acceptable balance between humour and seriousness.

Incorporating more humour was the comedy "Bumazhka" ("The Note") by A. Larskii, where the "smart and impudent" Vasya Kuritsyn attempts to get "protection" by trying to convince various characters to satisfy his demands.[46] In the first scene he tries to persuade a distant relative that he is obliged "by blood" to assist him. In the second scene, having been sent to the representative of the local committee, Kuritsyn tries to impress by emphasizing his proletarian credentials. He pretends to be the son of a peasant mother and worker father and claims to have written a book on Soviet economic achievements in international politics published by Narkompros with an introduction written by none other than Lunacha-rsky. Suitably impressed, the representative sends Kuritisyn along to the appropriate official, who he describes to Kuritsyn as being "crazy about physical culture" (*bez uma ot nee*). Kuritsyn accordingly assumes the role of *fizkul'turnik*, running and jumping about before the official and inquir-ing about his training regime. Using all the politically correct slogans he can muster, Kuritsyn says how he believes that in a healthy body lies a healthy soul and that only physical culture will lead to a bright future. This time masquerading as a boxing trainer (though claiming to be active in athletics and football also) he invites the official to train with him. When the official offers to pay for the instruction, Kuritsyn is disgusted, replying, "Money! For pure physical culture—money? You clearly don't know me: I practice physical culture for the love of art, not money".[47] However, the official also refuses to sign anything as he is against protection and again sends Kuritsyn on his way. The play is a parody of the type of person who takes advantage of whatever means possible to suit their own ends. Kurit-syn does not value physical culture and was mocking the representative who was genuinely interested in physical culture. Kuritsyn's behaviour was no doubt entertaining from an audience's perspective, but the successive refusals of the other characters to succumb to his charms was to show that adhering to socialist principles would overcome the "self-seeking tendencies" of others (here exemplified by Kuritsyn). Occupying an important role in agitprop theatre, physical culture was once again used (albeit in a different context) to highlight the various and important facets of socialist life and socialist principles. In spite of their political messages, these plays were humorous and not intended to be taken too seriously. However, this was not always the case. In an early 1930s staging of Nikolai Gogol's *The Inspector General* (where the character of Khlestakov is not entirely dissimilar to Kuritsyn), one critic took offence "because the theatre dared to draw parallels with the Soviet bureaucracy".[48]

The sketch "V poryadke samokritiki" ("Correct Self-Criticism") by Gr. Gradov was another piece of agitprop theatre which again demonstrated the extent to which the language and ideals of Soviet political ritual and in particular of physical culture had entered into everyday life, even if, as references to "self-criticism" suggest, not always in a way the authorities devised.[49] Here in the second "picture" the young characters Olya and Petya (aged eighteen and fourteen years, respectively) play ping-pong on their dining table in their apartment, with a smaller table located to the side of the stage. When their father returns home from work in the factory, he surveys the scene before him in astonishment, wondering where on earth he would dine. When told to dine on the smaller table ("in line with self-criticism"), the father is not pleased. Little Petya elaborates, telling his father that it would be more "rational" for them (Petya, Olya, and their mother) to remain at the bigger table while he could dine at the smaller one. After all, Olya adds, sport is the "guarantor of health".[50] Angry, their father turns to his wife to see what is to become of his dinner. However, she replies that there will be none. Becoming more frustrated, the father asks what all of this was supposed to mean. The mother begins to answer: "It's in line with . . . in line with (turning to Petya) what's it in line with?" To which Petya replies "self-criticism".

A first glance here shows how physical culture was used to demonstrate political policies and how they were to be understood by people in an everyday sense—whether these interpretations were correct or incorrect. The sketch emphasized that Petya and Olya, as the youngest members of the household, were most receptive and most adaptable to the policy of "self-criticism" and understood the value of not just physical culture and sport but also politics in a wider, practical sense. As Victoria Bonnell contends in relation to Soviet posters of idealized peasant women, the purpose of such constructed forms of propaganda was not to reflect a realistic image but rather to "invoke" and become a "vehicle for anticipating and achieving the future".[51] Yet the play was also a parody of party slogans and the difficulties of practically implementing them. The audience more than likely recognized that young people trying to emulate Petya and Olya in real life would in all probability have received a quick rebuke from their father.[52] Nonetheless, the humour here lies in the reversal of traditional family roles and the inversion of power and authority from the father to the children. The balance between entertainment and education was proving to be a challenge. The political overtones which characterized this type of theatre made it difficult for theatre groups to perform before a mixed audience where some were steadfast supporters of the regime and some were just there for entertainment.

The other popular form of agitprop directed at youth was the *chastushka*, a lyrical song or poem that captured the social mores of the rural populace. With just over half the population in the countryside under twenty years of age, this was a very significant target audience indeed.[53] The *chastushki* that follow here are official, prescriptive *chastushki* that were either invented or adapted by the Komsomol and disseminated by Komsomol publications, Komsomol clubs, the People's House (*nardom*), or rural clubs. It was hoped that city dwellers visiting the countryside would help spread these *chastushki* among the locals.[54] That these were not the traditional folk art form composed by the peasants is not reason enough to disregard their significance or to suppose that they had no place in peasant life—as Isabel Tirado observes, "[a] singer might have heard a Komsomol *chastushka* or seen it in published form, but she might have only used the part that suited her and tailored it to her needs".[55] She adds that the Komsomol was vital in "developing political views among the young" and was "on a par with the Red Army in importance", second only to the schools.[56] These *chastushki* thus made a significant contribution to the broader agitprop campaigns used to motivate young people, peasants, women, and the population in general. Alongside other forms of agitprop such as theatre and wall-newspapers, *chastushki* proved a cost-effective and accessible means of educating the masses in the new political discourse.

A *chastushka* from 1927 provides a useful illustration of how young people were expected to embody the new ideology and promulgate it in an everyday sense. By their very behaviour and commitment to the new regime young people were to demonstrate the benefits of socialism and educate others, especially the older generations. In this *chastushka* an "old man" describes the "shocking" scene he encounters one day when walking down a Moscow street.[57] He is paralyzed by fear when confronted by a youth wearing only "some type of underwear". Fearing this person might attack him, he considers running away quickly. Yet it is too late as the youth is before him. The old man closes his eyes and covers his ears. Nothing happens. The youth does not bite or choke him (as the man had expected), but rather talks to him about health and *fizkul'tura*. The young person invites the old man to the *kruzhok*, where "all the lads were in some kind of shorts/jumping/waving their hands/exercising" and enjoying the sunshine. In response, the old man says to the boy: "It's a pity, son/They are tormenting you here/You'll probably be sick after a whole day". However, the boy admonishes the old man, replying, "No/Comrade grandpa!/What's wrong with you?/We're as healthy as bulls here". He then asks the man to discard his "cheap" clothes and enjoy the sunshine. The old man claims that he is converted. He tells his audience that he is not lazy—he now practices physical culture everyday. He adds that he consequently has fine hearing, a "strong belly", sharp eyesight, has become very healthy and can do the work of two people. The *chastushka* continues with the old man noting that "a healthy body means a healthy soul", saying, "I confess, now, friends: You need to practice physical culture". At the end of the *chastushka* the audience are informed that, in order to prepare for labour and defence, they have to strengthen their bodies. Anyone who does not do this and who does not practice physical culture is a "*sovdurak*" or a fool.

This *chastushka* first of all showed how alien a concept physical culture was for older generations. It contrasted the old way of life (scepticism, conservatism) symbolized by the old man with the new, modern way of life, as represented by the youth. The old man figure featured here was won over however and he was able to show that following the new way of life was in one's own personal interests and the state's—he was now active and healthy and thus a valuable worker and asset to society. Also, the "encounter" described by the old man character highlighted the tensions between young and old, but the old man's conversion to *fizkul'tura* demonstrated that a little education and understanding was all that was needed in order to change. Significantly here this change was initiated by youth—it was the young boy who approached the old man. This *chastushka* therefore had an arguably even more important message for young people than for an older audience. As the revolution and the Bolsheviks were closely aligned with youth, young people were called upon to lead and direct the older generations in the new way of life. For their part, older workers and peasants were asked not to resent or suspect the young but to listen to them and impart their knowledge. These attitudes were particularly prominent in industry and labour, as well as in physical culture. However, just like the other physical culture propaganda, the image created by this *chastushka* is also idealistic. In reality young people in the *kruzhok*—as seen already—could just as often be found smoking, drinking or looking for girls than preaching the benefits of physical culture to older people whom they encountered on the streets of Moscow, or anywhere else.

By the first Five Year Plan shock-work had come to dominate the direction and style of theatre as the concept of the agitprop brigade gained in importance. In theatre small groups of amateur theatre enthusiasts who had strong political messages to communicate "hunted down viewers" and "took their works to the countryside".[58] According to Mally, the agitprop brigades "saw themselves as conduits for government programmes, interpreters who transformed the bureaucratic jargon of state initiatives into a language that average people could understand".[59] These brigades consisted mainly of young people who sought to spread ideas of industrialization and collectivization. They used an assortment of material to convey these ideas and messages, ranging from newspapers to speeches. As Mally observes, if these brigades did not have the "skill or confidence to shape their own work from scratch, they could turn to outlines and examples published in the trade union or Komsomol press, which they were encouraged to use for their own purposes". These included the types of plays examined above which provided a clear model for brigades seeking to adapt material. Some of those who composed these plays, such as Aleksei Arbuzov, drew on the works of Mayakovsky, Demyan Bednyi, and others, as well as political speeches by Lenin and Stalin.[60] Mally's work shows that plays and *chastushki* were open to wide and varied interpretations, whatever their content and the desired outcomes. Physical culture was no different, and the agitprop employed to convey important messages relating to politics or physical culture may not necessarily have gone according to plan. All the same, the fact that physical culture was in any case the subject of such plays and other propaganda was a positive development in putting physical culture into the public domain.

PHYSICAL CULTURE, SCHOOLS, AND PUPILS

Besides clubs, another means of propagating physical culture and educating young people in the correct practice of physical culture was in the schools. Although this might initially seem to have been the most direct route in reaching out to the young masses, this was not quite so, particularly because of the low status attached to physical education as a school subject and the fact that it was only a minor subject (alongside art and singing). In addition there were the usual problems with lack of facilities and resources. Notwithstanding the promotion of physical culture by Semashko and the Supreme Council, the division of responsibilities between the various organs and organizations meant that physical education was overlooked. Physical education as a compulsory subject was not introduced in schools and colleges until the late 1920s, as during the earlier part of that decade it assumed the form of health and hygiene studies which were "seen in their relation to a factory, a market, a bakery and so on".[61] James Riordan, while acknowledging that some sort of physical culture was included in the general syllabus of 1927–1929, considers that "it was not until 1929 that physical culture actually became a compulsory subject in schools and colleges".[62] Meanwhile, in his work on physical culture, Goloshchapov contends that Narkompros had introduced a proper, obligatory syllabus in 1927, with a compulsory three hours a week for Level 1 schools (four-year schools for younger ages) and two hours a week for Level 2 schools (ten years education).[63] Preceding the introduction of a compulsory syllabus in schools, it was up to each individual educational institute to adopt its own programme for physical culture.[64] Guidelines were issued by the State Institute of Physical Culture (drafted by Zikmund), and these educational institutes had a certain number of hours for physical culture classes allocated to them.[65] Yet these were often not followed, and in some cases the hours were curtailed. For instance, in Ukraine in 1932 Narkompros cut back the mandatory three hours of physical culture classes to a paltry one hour in a ten-day period.[66] This was blamed on a number of issues such as the "under-appreciation" of physical culture education by Narkompros and the educational institutes.[67] This was why, it was concluded, physical culture had still not "received any legal rights" in the VUZy, technical colleges and *rabfaki*.[68] Further problems afflicted physical culture when Narkomfin intervened and cut the number of annual physical culture hours being conducted in VUZy (which Antipov claimed to be completely illegal).[69]

According to the Central Statistics Office, the Soviet Union had a total number of 95,696 educational institutes in 1924.[70] Yet out of this number physical culture was practiced in only 823 schools with just over half of these schoolchildren (54 per cent or 319,000) participating in physical culture.[71] Even this figure is surprising given the deplorable conditions of the 1920s and it is likely that the standard of any physical culture education was quite low. With inadequate buildings, the poor health of pupils, curtailed academic hours, and seemingly ever-changing curricula, one wonders if physical culture classes were indeed ever carried out in the 1920s.[72] The Five Year Plan seemed to have had minimal impact on physical culture education, with schools in the 1930s appearing to be in only a marginally better position than in the 1920s and with poor conditions still widespread. One Moscow school did not receive a pair of slippers, a vest, or shorts, despite rumours that the Moscow Provincial Physical Culture Council was supposed to be allocating 25 per cent provisions of inventory to schools. The physical culture instructor in this particular school had to conduct lessons wearing "whatever footwear he arrived to work in".[73] There was also great difficulty in the actual production of equipment for children, as factories did not seem to produce skis, skates, boots, discs, or hammers for children.[74] Statistical information, based on questionnaires, shows that schools in the 1930s still lacked premises and equipment for the practice of physical culture. Where these did exist, then repairs had not been carried out, there were not enough instructors, or sports halls were not suitable for other reasons (some were used for storage or, more commonly, were too cold in winter). Students of one school from Leningrad's Ostrovskogo district practiced physical culture on a parquet floor that was in need of repair while the 900 students of another Leningrad school had to practice physical culture in a recreational hall that also housed the school cafeteria.[75] It was not the case that older schools were the only casualties of inattention to physical culture premises. In 1928 a "huge new school" had been built in Leningrad's Kirovskii district but no sports hall or showers had been built and its floors were already "dangerous and in need of repair". [76] Over 60 per cent of schools in Leningrad did not have special physical culture halls. [77] From a total of twenty-three schools in the Vologarskii district of Leningrad, only five were ready for "planned, systematic lessons" by 18 September 1932. [78] In Leningrad province clothing provisions (slippers, shorts, vests) for children in schools was actually better than in Moscow. [79] In 1932 in Moscow's Zamoskvoretskii district six out of eighteen schools had satisfactory premises for physical culture, though one of these was adapted from a cinema theatre and the other from shower rooms located under an office. [80] The Stalin district in Moscow fared even worse, with only three of twenty schools claiming access to physical culture premises.

Schools were also found to neglect children's work when it came to matters of physical culture because those charged with responsibility for this task found that they were often alone and unsupported. [81] In the Stalin-skii district of Moscow a 1932 study of twenty-five schools showed that there were seventeen physical culture teachers with higher education, seven with middle level education, and three with some course preparation. [82] Of the forty-eight physical culture teachers in the schools of Moscow's Krasno-Presnenskii district only eight had higher education, thirty-one had achieved mid-level education, and nine had received some course preparation. [83] The overall quality of teaching was quite low, and in many cases teachers specialized in other subjects. Schools sometimes did not subscribe to any physical culture literature and did not adhere to study plans. [84] Unsurprisingly the situation was much worse outside of Moscow and Leningrad, where under-qualified and overworked instructors in schools were commonplace in both urban and rural areas. In parts of the Central Black Earth region (an industrially rich area with fertile soil that included the provinces of Voronezh, Tambov, Kursk, Lipetsk, Belgorod, and Oryol) the lack of resources and poor conditions in schools meant that the quality of teaching was even lower. Rural areas and the national republics struggled to provide students with access to physical culture. This was particularly evident in the latter, where in the whole of the Buryat-Mongolian republic, there were only eight physical culture teachers, and none of these were from the local nationalities. [85] This was actually in spite of the official policy of attracting more national minority instructors to physical culture. [86]

By the late 1930s the situation in schools was not much better, with the lack of adequate facilities continuing to be a major obstacle to progress. In Moscow's Fruzenskii district in 1937 fifty schools had just five sports halls with thirty-six schools using corridors to teach physical culture. [87] In 1939 middle school No. 52 in the same district had a physical culture hall that was dirty and which had a broken window, the result of vandalism by passing children from the street outside (an ironic reiteration of the failings of *vospitanie*). [88] In a school just built in 1936, physical culture classes again took place in a corridor. While architectural designs for clubs and physical culture had been espoused since the 1920s, the regular construction of physical culture facilities in schools, even in Moscow, was still being overlooked in the late 1930s.[89] With the physical space for physical culture largely absent, and with a lack of teaching quality, it is consequently of no surprise that, when assessing the "physical culture *vospitanie* among Moscow schoolchildren", an internal memorandum by the All-Union Committee for Physical Culture and Sport found that many students did not attend classes. [90] Indeed the very reason given for non-attendance was the poor state of premises, which in some cases were so bad that classes had actually been stopped altogether. Where physical culture instruction was satisfactory there was allegedly 100 per cent attendance.[91] Evidently children and young people either did not want to waste their time attending classes taught by poorly qualified teachers and those conducted in below-standard facilities, or else they simply used these poor conditions as an excuse to refrain from participating in physical culture activities. The latter was just as likely as young people often found the obligatory military exercises and physical culture education boring.[92] There was no escaping the fact that physical culture work among young people in school was not really being implemented at all.

While physical culture parades and festivals of the 1930s showed costumed youth demonstrating their talent and commitment to physical culture, this image did not correlate to physical culture education in school. Even as late as 1939 there were reports of a lack of physical culture teachers and of problems with teacher turnover. The reason given for this problem was that school directors did not show sufficient opposition to physical culture teachers leaving schools without valid reasons. The director of one Moscow school apparently "reflected the mood of many directors" when she stated to the inspector of the All-Union Committee for Physical Culture and Sport that "we would be delighted for the physical culture teachers to leave primary schools because then we would have additional classes in maths and Russian".[93] Signs of an anti-physical culture mood among school leaders again surfaced when the director of another Moscow school changed the physical culture classes of eighth and ninth grades to Russian, despite "the presence of a physical culture teacher and hall".[94] In the 1930s school directors, under pressure to achieve in other subject areas, appeared quite content to sacrifice physical culture. For physical culture teachers working in schools with a lack of facilities, lack of equipment and evidently with hostile school directors, working in education seemed not at all congenial. Under such circumstances it was argued that physical culture teachers struggled to make it to the end of the school year. Even those teachers who were experienced and committed were sometimes driven to seek work in other areas.[95]

It was not only general education schools that neglected physical culture, for even schools specializing in physical culture were beset by numerous problems. One such school, the Novosibirsk technical secondary school, had a hall that measured just 3x20m and in winter was so cold that students had to train in a neighbouring factory sports hall.[96] Student stipends were often delayed by five to six days and the school had no showers. Its students, understandably, were not pleased. Some noted that work there was poor with timetables posted "barely an hour before classes begin", with students left short "many hours" in different disciplines.[97] Teachers also came in for criticism. Some students claimed that one lecturer was "rude" and that during exercises he "taunted and jeered" students, saying to them that they should have been better qualified when arriving at the school. Their hygiene teacher apparently read the course "for himself" alone, as the students "did not understand him", and moreover he was "not interested" whether the students understood him or not. Finally, students told the inspector, neither the school director nor the head-teacher were "interested in a credible course".[98] One student, Dolkova, complained to the inspector that slippers or correct attire were not provided and students arriving barefoot to class were forbidden to train by their teachers. This farcical situation seemed all the more ludicrous when Dolkova added that money collected from the students by the director to pay for gym clothes had been returned to them.[99] In this case a school explicitly set up to cater for physical culture among young people effectively failed these very young people.

All of this suggests that the interests of young people were in fact neglected by the education system, at least where physical culture was concerned. If better standards for physical culture education had been in place it would seem that young people might have participated. The problem was that the system itself could not provide for its young people. Nor did it seem to have any control over how schools approached the teaching of physical culture. When it came to physical culture, other subjects, in spite of physical culture having its place on the curriculum, were sometimes deemed by the schools themselves to be more important and worthy of increased attention. Consequently those young people who genuinely were interested in physical culture were more likely to participate in clubs via the Komsomol than in schools. Clubs, supported by the Komsomol and trade unions, were often in a better financial position than schools and in these there were elements of entertainment as well as education.[100] A club that had been set up with the specified aim of catering to Pioneers and schoolchildren interested in physical culture enjoyed great success. This sports club, organized with permission from Kosarev and Antipov, had three sections including gymnastics, swimming, and volleyball.[101] It had already attracted some 250 children and was struggling to cope with the large numbers hoping to join. Aforementioned school directors might have been interested to learn that club members supposedly recorded improved discipline and academic performance in school. Its success had also spread beyond the district, as its leaders had recently received a letter from a school in Sabaevo, Mordovskii Autonomous region (located near Penza in south-east Russia) requesting help and advice on how to organize physical culture.[102] The setting up of this club showed above all a victory for the genuine interest of young people in sport.

SEXUALITY, PSYCHOLOGY, AND YOUNG ADULTS

Scientific and medical experts did not just focus their attention on the sexual upbringing of young children or on implementing changes in a school environment. The private lives of teenagers and young adults were of interest too, and once again active involvement in physical culture was seen as the best, most healthy lifestyle for this age group. In dealing with the issues faced by young adults, *fizkul'tura* touched upon debates over the family, marriage, sexuality, and the relationship between men and women. Sexual mores were high on the agenda in early Soviet Russia, and as Sheila Fitzpatrick notes, the "sex problem" was one which also preoccupied students throughout the 1920s.[103] The problem arose because students (and the population in general) received "contradictory signals on how to behave"—one advocating sexual liberation and the other sexual restraint.[104] These attitudes were reinforced by the social policies pursued by the state and the ideology of certain figures such as Alexandra Kollontai.[105] Those involved in physical culture frequently contributed to the ever-expanding literature on sexuality. B. A. Ivanovsky[106] from the Institute of Physical Culture considered that the sexual question in contemporary society was "abnormal".[107] Physical culture, however, could help cure society of its ills because it was a "wonderful and healthy form of rest and relaxation; it strengthened the body and mind and developed skills such as mastery of oneself". [108] Rather than loiter about drinking vodka or beer, *fizkul'turniki* engaged in sports and other, healthy activities. In this way, it served as a "necessary diversion from sexual and emotional experiences".[109]

Ivanovsky also argued that sexual relations actually weakened muscle strength. He noted that sportsmen were aware of this and consequently abstained from sex when competing in events. He provided the example of a weightlifter who, after sex, lifted a quarter or a third less than he could beforehand. Another advantage of physical culture and sport, in Ivanovsky's view, was that it afforded men and women the opportunity to see one another's bodies more freely. As a result men would not become so "excited" at the sight of the naked female form. It would be even more useful if these habits could be developed at an early stage, among boys and girls. This would eliminate the experience of seeing each other as "objects of desire" and instead encourage the view that that they were no more than comrades and co-workers. He referred to a questionnaire conducted in 1924 by Dr. Iu. I. Pinus[110] in Stalingrad where 32 per cent of those aged seventeen years already had an active sex life. This figure was only 12.5 per cent for *fizkul'turniki*. For eighteen year olds, the figure was 52 per cent (non-*fizkul'turniki*) and 33 per cent (*fizkul'turniki*). Referring to the survey

Dr. Pinus commented that "such early commencement of sexual relations is undoubtedly one of the main causes of the high percentage of psychoneurosis and neuropathy among teenagers".[111] In such instances, he continued, physical culture was the perfect means of sublimating sexual energy. He considered the survey as evidence that physical culture diverted teenagers from sexual relations and that therefore, physical exercises should be used in sublimating sexual energy.

While it remains unclear whether or not this Stalingrad study was typical of all Komsomol or physical culture students, there is further evidence to suggest that such surveys were certainly not an uncommon occurrence. A questionnaire among *fabzavuchei* (factory and works' students) in Leningrad showed that, on average, *fizkul'turniki* became sexually active a year and a half later than those not involved in physical culture.[112] It is unsurprising, in light of these surveys and the increasing concern for the implications of sexual freedoms on society, that *fizkul'tura* came to be considered an ideal means of integrating the communist ideals of restraint in society. While sexual prowess was once held as an indicator of machismo and strength, the opposite standpoint soon prevailed. Ivanovsky's claims that *fizkul'tura* in fact strengthened muscle mass and the general scramble of the health and hygiene ideologues to promote *fizkul'tura* as a healthy and beneficial substitute for sexual licentiousness as well as other social ills could be in some respects viewed as a response to these apparently widespread fears.

PHYSICAL CULTURE, HEALTH, AND THE RED ARMY

If the Soviet Union was to live up to its image as a young, strong, and dynamic nation, then clinics full of patients with "pyschoneurosis and neuropathy" were unacceptable.[113] So as a part of the new psychology attached to *fizkul'tura*—using it to encourage feelings of collectivism and foster positive emotions and attitudes towards society as well as sublimate sexual energy—the development and significance of physical culture assumed a new dimension. There was evidence to suggest that physical culture had the power to transform individuals, not just physically but also emotionally and psychologically, bestowing a sense of belonging and satisfaction on its participants.[114] This power was acknowledged by the state, which sensed that physical culture had positive effects that could be used to its advantage in a variety of ways. One such way was in combating problems of nervousness and suicide. Suicide was especially prevalent during and after the NEP years, when a "wave of suicides . . . [swept] the ranks of youth".[115] The toll of years of struggle, revolution, civil war, and the transition to peacetime life was said to have been too great for some, while for others, factors such as the *Yeseninshchina* were blamed. As the aftermath of Yesenin's suicide showed, there was a clamour to disassociate suicide from current state policies but, as Kenneth Pinnow argues, suicide was still viewed as a "social" illness and was considered a reflection of the health of society.[116]

An area where suicide was a particular concern for the authorities was in the Red Army. Problems in the military reflected those affecting society, where the army was "a copy of society and suffers from all its diseases, usually at a higher temperature".[117] Creating a modern, well-drilled fighting machine was highly dependent upon the health and fitness of troops. Mentally and emotionally sound, physically strong, and loyal soldiers were paramount to the realization of the Soviet modernization project. However, the environment in which army recruits operated impeded their mental and physical development. Conditions in the army were not exactly in line with the physical culture lifestyle. New recruits experienced fatigue as a result of their winter studies, the exhausting work in building and equipping their barracks, and their preparations for their impending departure to the camps.[118] Winter was especially burdensome as recruits lived in insufficiently equipped barracks, received no holidays, and experienced additional wintertime expenses. The number of suicides in spring was still relatively high and blamed on continued labour in constructing and equipping camps, increased study, fieldwork, and homesickness related to these activities. The slight decrease in the suicide rate in this period was attributed to the forthcoming summer season and the prevalence of more comfortable living and working conditions associated with spring.[119]

The reasons for suicide in the Red Army were mainly filed under the category of "unexplained and unknown".[120] In the cases where reasons for suicides were known, the main cause was "moral oppression and fear of responsibility for crimes committed".[121] The highest number of reported suicides fell under the category of nervousness and exhaustion, the social plague from which not even the military could escape and which was often attributed to years of stress, hardship, and deprivation during the revolution and civil war. Compared with suicides in the Imperial Army, Red Army suicides were certainly a cause for concern. According to the statistics the only year in which the rate of suicides was higher in the Tsarist army than in the Red Army was 1912.[122] One of the explanations forwarded for the suicide increase in the Red Army was the First World War, civil war, and the famine. Yet another explanation for the rise would be nervous exhaustion and political discontent associated with NEP policies. An example of a suicide in many ways attributable to nervous exhaustion was that of Comrade Parsh, a twenty-three-year-old peasant soldier, who left behind a suicide note and whose case has been examined in the work of Mark von Hagen.[123] Comrade Parsh committed suicide in the summer of 1929 and wrote the letter before fatally shooting himself. The main reason he cited for his suicide was his despair at not being accepted into a higher military school and hence hopelessness for his future. This was compounded by the fact that he was due to be released in the coming weeks and had been unable to secure employment. His situation was made all the more untenable because of his low social origin—he was a *batrak*. Apart from the circumstances cited for his suicide, he apportioned blame to psychological issues—"it was my own nervous condition that drove me to this incident".[124] The nervous exhaustion afflicting Parsh arose out of anxieties experienced as his term of duty drew to a close.[125] There is no doubting that similar cases of nervous exhaustion, disillusionment and anxiety over the future were experienced by many, whether lowly *batrak* peasants, senior ranking soldiers, or just workers.

What was clear was that action needed to be taken. As Mark Von Hagen comments, the "suicides, troubled domestic lives, drunkenness, careerism, unbridled self-interest—eroded any sense of solidarity among the army's elites and their authority in the eyes of the soldiers".[126] In addressing some of these issues, the military report concluded that the material conditions of army life should be improved and that life outside their military service should be better organized. Other measures included mobilizing social opinion against suicide and organizing sanitary education and propaganda advocating a new lifestyle and improving the relevant services, especially in regional areas.[127] This was also where *fizkul'tura* propaganda and its "new psychology" could be of use. In order to deal with issues leading to suicide, physical culture could form a practical means of raising solidarity among the troops. While not wanting to over-emphasize the significance of physical culture as a major factor in the military's response to dealing with suicide (or indeed in suicide in general) it must nonetheless be considered as a factor in dealing with the matter. Physical culture was an inseparable part of Red Army work and was considered a vital element in raising fitness and hygiene levels among the military, and the military in turn disseminated physical culture propaganda in society through training programmes and instruction. Indeed, having reviewed questionnaires of *fizkul'turniki* in club *kruzhki*, the primary point of sustained contact with and training for young men involved in physical culture was through army service.

DAZED AND CONFUSED

The Soviet state paid a great deal of attention to its young people. For those dealing with issues of disease, disillusionment, and depression in the 1920s and 1930s, physical culture agitprop and education was considered fundamental in addressing these problems. Informing young people through school education, the press, clubs, and other means was vital in propagandizing correct modes of behaviour and agitating youth to adopt a new, healthier lifestyle. By constantly subjecting young people to state propaganda and by introducing them to socialist values, for example, through physical culture, it was hoped that young people would not be drawn towards any "counter-revolutionary" influences but would in fact become strong, healthy, and loyal party cohorts, as the writings of Semashko, Ivanovsky, and others demonstrated. It is clear that physical culture was one way in which the Bolsheviks attempted to "cultivate a new culture" with which youth could identify.[128] However, the reality was of course somewhat different as it proved exceedingly difficult, sometimes impossible, to regulate and monitor the actions, thoughts, and emotions of any Soviet citizen, let alone young people. Moreover, in spite of the propaganda, there was no guarantee that the "intended audience" was even listening.[129] Young people, particularly adolescents, were at a stage in their lives when they were already faced with a number of competing identities, with parental and peer influences strongly dictating lifestyle choices and behaviour. With strong political, economic, and cultural pressures added to this confusing mix, it is hardly surprising that meanings often got lost and misinterpreted along the way.

4 The Quest for an Enlightened Female Citizen

If young people were considered propitious targets of physical culture propaganda, then so too were women, with the "woman question" frequently debated and the female body a site of considerable contestation. Indeed, once the Bolsheviks were in power legislation was introduced which directly touched upon the female body and women. Easy divorce and abortion were legalized, with the 1918 Family Code setting the marriage age at sixteen for women and eighteen for men.[1] The radical changes did not have a positive outcome however. The disarray unleashed by the 1918 code was clearly illustrated when one considers that by the mid-1920s the Soviet Union could claim to have had the highest divorce rate in the world. Adding to the social disorder was that during these years abortion was one of the primary means of contraception.[2] The upshot of this was that by the mid to late 1920s there was serious concern about the effects of multiple abortions on women's health, and in particular surrounding those abortions carried out by unqualified peasant women. This problem was so grave that the "*Besedy Vracha*" or "Doctor's Talk" section of *Krest'yanka* regularly featured articles urging women to consult a doctor when pregnant so as to avoid unnecessary or mal-practiced abortions, miscarriages, home births, or possible complications following childbirth.[3] As a reaction to social conditions, propaganda directed at women was most often educational and dealt with health issues. In her study on women, Mary Buckley contends that basic hygiene was "more important than political enlightenment".[4] Physical culture propaganda supported this viewpoint, with full political enlightenment unattainable without first refashioning oneself into a more roundly developed and cultured citizen. Physical culture was seen as an aid to modernizing and educating women, explaining basic sanitary and hygiene issues and ensuring that they were physically capable of taking on the new role which the revolution had assigned to them.

Bolshevik proclamations of female emancipation and equality between the sexes had yet to be realized in physical culture, as elsewhere. Women were very much underrepresented in physical culture and according to official Komsomol statistics the number of women participating in *fizkul'tura* in 1924 stood at 207,962 (33 per cent).[5] Even when it came to "showcase" events such as parades, women were still found lacking, with insufficient training showing them up on the day.[6] Supreme Council of Physical Culture representative Dmitri Yeshchin encouraged women to become more involved in physical culture, suggesting that more excursions and festivals be organized for women only.[7] He criticized the Zhenotdel for its lack of interest in drawing women towards physical culture. He wondered why, if it was interested in the socio-political and cultural interests of women, had it not become more supportive of women and physical culture? After all, he added, physical culture was one of the main factors in the general system of cultural and social education. The Zhenotdel responded with its own criticisms. In Orgburo discussions Zhenotdel representative, Maria Glebova, was fiercely critical of the Supreme Council of Physical Culture and claimed that it virtually boycotted the Zhenotdel.[8] She noted that the Zhenotdel was "generally against the VSFK" as it never consulted the Zhenotdel and, moreover, its structure was "completely incomprehensible". The Zhenotdel, Glebova maintained, considered that women did not participate in physical culture and those women who did were either white-collar workers, teenage daughters of "specialists", or the bourgeoisie.[9]

In promoting greater female involvement in physical culture, propaganda campaigns were increased and organizations urged to implement policies more vigorously. The propaganda examined here was designed to lure more women into engaging with physical culture, with the press and *chastushki* acting as a cost-effective and popular means of reaching as wide a female audience as possible. Even publications directed at women such as *Rabotnitsa* and *Krest'yanka* occasionally dealt with physical culture matters, demonstrating to their respective audiences how physical culture and sport could be used to their advantage and how they could become involved in physical culture activities. As one female authority on women and sport noted, physical culture for women merited more attention and action as it was instrumental in fighting degeneration, in helping women become mothers, and in building the new life in Soviet society.[10] Propaganda was needed in order to popularize female participation in physical culture and draw attention to its benefits. This chapter assesses the various ways in which the physical culture leadership and the state sought to mobilize women around physical culture. It returns to some of the earlier debates outlined in the first chapter by exploring in detail issues of body shape and body image, as the Bolsheviks attempted to introduce women to the new social codes and practices referred to by Régine Robin.

IN THE EYE OF THE BEHOLDER: MEDICAL AND SCIENTIFIC VIEWS OF WOMEN AND *FIZKUL'TURA*

Given the social climate of the 1920s, it is unsurprising that much of the propaganda surrounding physical culture was directed towards women in their capacity as mothers. This was not only due to the problems surrounding abortion and divorce but also arose from the demographic dominance of women and young people and the social significance of these two groups. The state focused on women and children because they were crucial contributors to the future of the socialist state. Mothers had the important role of raising communist children, and it was imperative that this function be fulfilled according to socialist ideals. Included in this was physical culture. It was considered that in the earliest years of a child's life the influence of the mother, especially as educator, was fundamental.[11]

In view of their important role women's bodies and their functions in society were widely discussed by the medical and scientific communities.[12] Dr. Nikolai Danilovich Korolev, a Leningrad-based doctor who specialized in the physical development of women, analyzed the female form and function in several articles that appeared in physical culture publications.[13] He argued that women's relationship to physical education could be divided into two sections: the first was the historical place of women, and the second was the biological role of women.[14] Writing in 1924, Korolev discussed the "complete and unconditional emancipation" of women following the revolution and how they were now viewed as being on an equal playing-field as men. The new woman, like her male counterpart, was strong, healthy, and cultured. She was also considered representative of nature and could cultivate and use physical culture to assist in finding her true and ideal physical form. Physical culture, Korolev argued, would help liberate woman from conventional views and traditional associations, releasing her into the free socialist world. Korolev stated that there were two laws and covenants of nature.[15] The first of these was the will and desire to live, and the second was the will and desire to create life. With regard to the latter, Korolev claimed that men and women were diametrically opposed to one another—men were solely interested in external, physical pleasure; women were not so much interested in the sexual act, approaching it more like "gynaecologists".[16] This observation was, Korolev noted, based on twenty years of scientific research conducted through questionnaires of several thousand women. Men focused their energies primarily on physicality, while women were of a more "psycho-physical" nature. This, in Korolev's view, was the great schism between the sexes.

He noted that the woman underwent astounding physical changes during pregnancy as she went on to fulfil her natural role as the creator of life. While the mother was engaged in bringing up her child, the father was expected to exude patience and self-sacrifice as this was considered beyond his strength and ability. Korolev contended that women had a "sacrificial" role and men an "exploitative" role. Culture, he maintained, had given man the opportunity to sublimate his energy only to correct a mistake of nature, and that man, in his greatest creative act, was doomed to occupy this exploitative role. Owing to their important role, the health of women was considered extremely significant. He stated that an unhealthy girl meant an unhealthy mother which in turn meant an unhealthy civilization. Therefore the physical education, hygiene, and health of the new, modern woman were essential. The reality of course was somewhat different, and Korolev's glorification of the pregnant female body was not universally shared. Some pregnant women who heeded medical advice by participating in physical culture were often ridiculed. As another specialist on women in physical culture, Irina Pellinger, commented, pregnant women gave up going to the clubs not just because the exercises became too strenuous for them, but more so because they were subject to vulgar comments and remarks from the young male club members regarding their changing figures.[17]

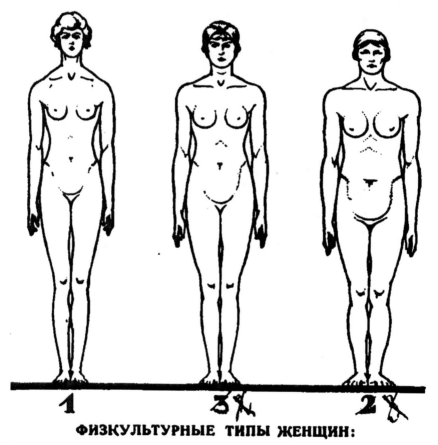

ФИЗКУЛЬТУРНЫЕ ТИПЫ ЖЕНЩИН:

Figure 4.1 Female body shapes. Dr. Korolev's "Fizkul'turnye tipy zhenshchin" ("Physical culture types of women"), *IFK*, no. 1 (1926): 2. Courtesy of the Russian State Library.

The female figure was also of interest to Dr. Korolev. According to him, there were three categories of female shapes. The first was poorly developed, with a long neck, narrow, sloping shoulders, a short torso, narrow pelvis, and skinny legs with little muscular development.[18] This type of woman found in pre-revolutionary times was the "female lover". The principal task of her physical education centred on making her more attractive to men. This focused on her bodily form becoming more "plastic", ensuring her movements were "beautiful", and in developing "aesthetic" feelings. The figure in the second category was akin to the male shape, and was well-developed—she had a short neck, over-developed waist, prominent pelvis, long torso, and short legs. In Tsarist times this type of woman was typically the housewife found among the peasantry. She often undertook the work of men in the home or in the fields. She was analogous to a domestic machine and treated as such. The final category of figure struck a balance between the first and second types, and was the ideal shape—not as physically weak as the first but not as overtly strong as the second. This was the shape of the new socialist woman and *fizkul'turnitsa*, in Korolev's view. He envisioned this woman as well-developed, healthy and strong, joyous, and immune to sickness as well as representing the ideal physical candidate for motherhood. Just what the women who had the misfortune to fall into the first and second categories could do to overcome the cruel blow that genetics had dealt them, Korolev failed to elaborate upon. Perhaps it was assumed that participating in physical culture and sports would make some strides in developing this ideal body shape.

Korolev's views of the emancipated Soviet woman still placed her in the home, looking after her children. Moreover, his depiction of them as procreators demoted women even further by relating their own health and needs as being important solely in terms of giving birth to new generations.[19] So while the state espoused female emancipation and equality between the sexes, women's liberation was in fact ostensibly undermined and inhibited by the alleged physical, emotional, and psychological disposition of women themselves. Korolev's writings carried weight. He was a respected doctor with some influence, as well as author of several publications on women and health.[20] He was in charge of the Petrograd Women's Anthropological Centre "Spartak" and was involved in the Leningrad publishing union of physical culture. At the First All-Union Conference of Scientific Workers in Physical Culture in 1925, he delivered a paper on "The Tasks, Plans, Programmes and Norms of Women's Physical Culture".[21] Furthermore, his texts were recommended by *Fizkul'tura v nauchno-prakticheskom osveshchenii*, a collection of works published by the Central State Institute of Physical Culture under Narkomzdrav. With a foreword by Semashko and with Rector Zikmund and Professor V. V. Gorinevsky as editors, this was quite a prestigious and important publication. In relation to physical culture methodology, Korolev's *Osnovy fizicheskoi kul'tury muzhiny i zhenshchiny* was recommended for mass readership, while this and his *Kratkoe*

Figure 4.2 The "bourgeois" woman: "Fizkul'turnitsy sovetskoi strany", *Smena*, no. 5 (1929): 6. Courtesy of the Russian State Library.

rukovodstvo po fizicheskoi kul'ture zhenshchiny were highly recommended for physical culture teachers wanting to gain an understanding of physical culture and women.[22]

Korolev's views, while striking a blow for female emancipation, were nonetheless consistent with medical views held in other European countries. Ríona Nic Congáil has drawn similar conclusions relating to Irish attitudes to women in sport, albeit in the 1930s, a later date than in the Soviet case. The camogie enthusiast Agnes O'Farrelly, she noted, claimed that "Camogie players would be better women and better mothers of their race because of this game", a view which she backed up with the views of a leading gynaecologist.[23] As Nic Congáil argues, "O'Farrelly's intention in this instance was to highlight a medical view which endorsed sport for women; however, in her statement she unwittingly reduced women to the subordinate domestic sphere in what was deemed to be their primary role as mothers".[24] In both France and Germany, physical culture for women focused on female reproduction and the doubts of the usually male medical experts about the ability of women to engage in any sort of physical activity beyond basic gymnastics. Anything more vigorous would damage the uterus, make childbirth more difficult, or damage the health of both the unborn child and the mother. As Gertrud Pfister explains, the German gynaecologist Dr. Hugo Sellheim even contended that women's sports led to "the wanton destruction of a part of their femininity".[25] In interwar France, attitudes were mixed, and despite some efforts to encourage sport amongst women, public opinion was still slow to move in favour of strenuous exercise, with one Catholic newspaper in 1934 reporting that the female's "special functions . . . are incompatible with intense muscular efforts".[26] Italian women under the fascist regime were considered inferior to their male counterparts and female participation in sport was for the most part frowned upon by the Catholic Church. As Gigliola Gori observes, women were "exhorted to concentrate on housework and to bear numerous children".[27] In the United States and Britain sport, in large thanks to the school and college systems, was popular among women and more widely accepted.[28] While Korolev's article and other writings showed that women in the Soviet Union were still largely associated with their role as "reproducers", there were clear differences with some of their European counterparts. From the outset Soviet official attitudes were generally much less discriminatory than those in some other European countries and medical experts, while still stereotyping women as mothers, did not discourage women from engaging in sports activities. On the contrary, women and girls of all ages were in fact encouraged to become much more active. In the 1920s and 1930s Soviet attitudes to women in sport were, if anything, more closely related to American views of women in sport rather than those held in continental Europe.

This willingness to support women in sport raised a number of biological and physiological issues, particularly concerning the standardized ideal of the "Soviet" woman. When competition was eventually permitted and the GTO introduced, all sorts of practical problems arose, especially in regard to the national republics. Those in charge of drawing up the rules in 1938 were unsure of how a girl from the Russian Republic could be compared to a girl from some of the national republics, where "a sixteen year old is already an adult woman".[29] As a result, the age gradation for the BGTO standard for women in the national republics was to be lowered, though it would be "smoothed out" in later years. The main problem appeared to have arisen from past confusion regarding the national republics and the "early biological advancement towards fulfilling norms" by some girls despite these girls "having the same conditions of schooling as, say, a girl from Tula".[30] It was suggested that some of the GTO norms might also be lowered in respect to the nationalities. Certain exercises could be introduced perhaps, as a compromise, but generally GTO planners had to tread carefully when it came to questions of a woman's "biological inferiority"; it was recalled that a representative from Kazakhstan at the All-Union Council of Physical Culture presidium meeting caused a "big scandal" when he claimed that Kazakh women were not able to run as fast as Russian women "as their legs were shorter".[31] Those involved in developing the GTO norm in the late 1930s were acutely aware of the complications involving women in physical culture and of the need to allow women to pass the norm but without "offending" (*obizhat'*) them.[32] By this stage the predominantly male organizers acknowledged that the issue of women in sport was a delicate one and one which had to be approached with some care and consideration. Several years of experience in dealing with women involved in sports and physical culture had proven that these women were not bodies detached from minds (as Korolev's theories at times implied) but active, able athletes and individuals.

EDUCATION AND MOBILIZATION

Educating women in the ways of physical culture assumed a number of forms. *Fizkul'tura* periodicals as well as magazines specifically targeting the female peasant population such as *Krest'yanka* consistently urged women in the villages to change their ways and adopt "new" habits. These ranged from themes such as cooking, child-rearing, and giving birth, to washing and pastimes such as sewing. Meanwhile, *Rabotnitsa* encouraged older female workers to become more involved in physical culture and tried to impress upon readers that it was good for their health and physical appearance.[33] These messages were also frequently voiced through the medium of *chastushki* , which were a particularly useful form in communicating to the female population, as they were traditionally composed and sung by women.[34] The following *chastushki* were part of the Komsomol brochure of official *chastushki* to be distributed and so were part of the official discourse. It was through these means of propaganda that the party strove to mobilize public opinion and influence the "masses". Unfortunately, there is no real way of ascertaining how widespread or popular these particular *chastushki* were, but given that Komsomol and trade union agitprop workers used such material, it is reasonable to assume that they found an audience in clubs and village reading-rooms. By disseminating this kind of material it was hoped that women would become more open and involved in socialist activities.

In *Fizkul'turnye provody* by Demyan Bednyi,[35] the scene is set in the physical culture *kruzhok*, where a *fizkul'turnitsa* called Masha tries to convince doubters of the merits of *fizkul'tura*.[36] Masha's mother and the peasant women question why she needs to be strong and agile, noting that it would be more beneficial for her to quickly get married. Masha is not convinced, arguing that if everyone were to live as they were, then all would die of dirt and disease. She criticizes these peasant women for living under damp walls and ceilings (breeding grounds for malaria and typhus) as well as for allowing the children to sleep on dirty floors and haystacks (*spyat detishki na polu/V gryaznom sene*). Instead, they should be taught hygiene in the physical culture *kruzhok* (*Nauchus' v fizkul'tkruzhke/Gigiene*). Following Masha's harangue, the stage directions refer to her relatives, who, having at first listened disbelievingly, in the end are converted and exit singing the final few words uttered by Masha. As with *chastushki* in general, the message was direct and simple. Here, the moral of the story was that *fizkul'tura* represented the way forward. The peasant-women should not shun other women for wanting to embrace physical culture. These women were in fact right and wanted to lead the peasants out of the dirty and disease-ridden world they inhabited. The peasant women depicted reflected the communist view that they were the "darkest", most "backward" layer of the Russian population who needed a "fundamental change in their outlook and values".[37] If Masha's example was followed and physical culture was widely accepted, then these "dark" women would be taking active steps towards improving their personal and social position.

Another *chastushka* directed towards women and applicable to either urban or rural women was *Zhenotdel'skie fizkul't-chastushki*, which advocated adopting the new *fizkul'tura* lifestyle. In this *chastushka* the already-converted preach the advantages and hallmarks of being a *fizkul'turnitsa*. She is wise and sensible, not wearing lipstick, make-up, or any jewellery (*Ya postupaiu vo vsem premudro:/Gub'ev ne mazhu, ne syplius' pudroi*) (*Kolets ne nosim i ni serezhek/I kirpichom ne mazhem rozhi*). These women are also somewhat politically astute, declaring, "Down with the bourgeoisie and fashionistas—we're for the peasants and the workers", and eschewed any exterior manifestations of these types of people, such as dress-coats or cuffs (*Doloi meshchanok, burzhuek, modnits—/My za krest'yanok i za rabotnits*) (*Kto nosit fraki i manzhety, /Te dlya liubvi nam ne siuzhety*). In contrast to the "superficiality" of the bourgeoisie, *fizkul'turniki* value friends and family, preferring to wear a simple pair of shorts (*Nash vkus inoi, v drugom, brat, rode:/My liubim tekh, v trusakh kto khodit*). One of the women comments that her loved one (presumably in his shorts) appears "almost naked" and they then play basketball together (*Moi mil gulyaet pochti chto golym,/My zanyalis' s nim basketbolom*). This last comment is significant in that it portrays men and women in harmony together. There was no mention throughout of physical attraction; the mood depicted was rather one of compatibility and mutual respect. The verse then ends, with the protagonists calling on the peasant women and others to go to the sports-square (*Poidem, bab'e, poidem, rebyatki,/Zaimemsya vse na sport-ploshchadke*). Both of these *chastushki* appealed to two segments in particular within society—the young and the upwardly socially mobile (who were anyhow often interchangeable). While the first *chastushka* was more instructive, encouraging rural women to look upon physical culture as positive and progressive, the second portrayed women involved in physical culture as confident, cultured, and in control. This was the archetypal Soviet woman portrayed by the state.

The final *chastushka* geared towards women and *fizkul'tura* was similar to the first two. In the third, *Chastushki zhenskie*, a woman tells of how she became enlightened by *fizkul'tura*. The opening stanza unambiguously states her break with the past through her involvement in physical culture: "I don't want to be as before,/A dark fool,/I have started to practice/Physical culture" (*Ne khochu ya byt', kak ran'she,/Temnoi duroiu,/Zanimat'sya ya nachnu/Fizkul'turoiu*). Even though her mother sends her to the church to pray, she forsakes the church for the sports-square (*A ya sportom zanimalas'/na platsu do nochki*). She then speaks of the factory sports' club where the clever women need muscles to work (*V sport-yacheiku na zavode/Ne idet lish' dura,/Dlya raboty nam nuzhna/V-vvo muskulatura*). In spite of the physical exertions in gymnastics, including such ailments as an aching neck, arms, and waist (*Kak prodelala na nikh/Sal'tomortale ya,/Bolit sheya, bolyat ruki,/Bolit taliya*), this woman nonetheless loves it and continues to practice physical culture "day and night" (*Do gimnastiki uzh bol'no/ Ya okhochaya,/Zanimalas' by fizkul'tom/Dni i nochi ya*). Adhering to the physical culture lifestyle, she no longer smokes or drinks alcohol and can "unsettle a boxer" (*Ya niskol' vina ne vyp'iu,/Broshu kurevo,/iz milogo boksom vyb'iu/ Vsiu-to dur' ego*). Her ultimate aim is to fulfil Komsomol expectations and develop her body in the Sportintern (*Komsomolkoi zakhotela/Byt' primernoiu,/Razvivat' poidu ya telo/ V Sportinerniiu*). This final *chastushka* was even more representative of the woman who wished to use physical culture as a means of upward social mobility and self-betterment, and appealed especially to younger women (as evidenced by the disregard for the advice and harangues of older women and by Komsomol aspirations). These women were urged to abandon older, superfluous habits associated with the peasants or the bourgeoisie, whether it was prayer, smoking, drinking, or clothes styles. Being an active *fizkulturnitsa* meant embracing an entirely new existence. This *chastushka* also connotes female workers as muscular, an association which assumed increased importance in the latter half of the 1920s and which was linked to the labour campaigns for fitter, stronger women, where women were encouraged to change their physical appearance through exercise. The message of these latter two *chastushki* was reinforced through visual imagery, in particular through the works of Aleksandr Deinika and Aleksandr Samokhvalov.[38]

BODY MATTERS: THE PHYSICAL CULTURE IMAGE

This new emphasis on raising the physical capability of women meant that they had to assume additional roles and responsibilities. The earlier demands of increased hygienic awareness and improved health were no longer sufficient. Not only were women to be excellent homemakers; they were now also expected to join the industrialization drive.[39] Five Year Plan fever had truly gripped the nation by 1930 as posters and slogans encouraged workers to complete the plan in four years. These outstanding workers, wives, and mothers were to be tough and healthy, strengthened through physical culture and labour. At the beginning of the 1930s, women, though faced with these demands, were also presented with opportunities that had never before been available to many of them. Therefore some of these embraced the prospects of the new socialist life that were on offer, seizing the chance to work their way up in society. That many of these did make this choice cannot be denied—during this decade, of all those entering the work-force for the first time, 82 per cent were women.[40] Neither can it be denied that a great many capitalized on this new venture, leaving behind their roots in the peasantry and working class to become professionals, managers, and government bureaucrats.[41] With sport and physical preparedness still being strongly endorsed, Lynne Attwood attests that in the 1930s there was a new attitude to dress and appearance, largely owing to a desire to raise the level of *kulturnost'*. The many women climbing up the social ladder had to acquire suitably new "cultured" lifestyles. To fit in to the new Soviet life, they (both women and indeed men) were expected to dress accordingly. For women, this meant dressing in a more feminine, natural, and, above all, practical manner. As Attwood noted, "Socialist women should . . . only wear clothes which would not hinder the work process" and "[m]ake-up was unacceptable because putting it on wasted precious time".[42] The image women were encouraged to project was not sensual, playful, or frivolous. If they were to be considered serious workers, they had to look the part. While dressing smartly at work is not at all unusual (in any society), the Soviet approach differed in that this image was prescribed for the private lives of women also.[43] *Komsomol'tsy* and shock-workers were expected to be model citizens whether at work, at home, or in their leisure time in the club.

Image was an essential component of the physical culture discourse and the way women looked was considered very important by the state, society, and women themselves. For women this was not just an esteem or vanity issue—women were actually judged socially and politically by how they looked. Every detail of their appearance mattered. Some *chastushki* in the late 1920s underscored the characteristics appropriate to *fizkul'turniki* and women more generally: "If a boy breaks records,—it means he's a recordsman/If a girl wears powder,—she's a bourgeois"

(*Ezhli paren' b'et lekordy, eto znachit-lekordsmen./Ezhli devitsa pri pudre,-burzhuaznyi elemen* [sic]); "If a girl wears heels, it means she has no brains" (*Ezhli devka s kablukami, eto znachit-bez mozgei).*[44] In 1930 *Fizkul'tura i sport* reported that in one *kruzhok* a girl who turned up to classes wearing lipstick and a felt hat was reprimanded and warned of future expulsion by the *kruzhok* bureau.[45] The bureau had hoped that this action would deter other girls from doing likewise. Vladimir Brovkin has observed that during the 1920s women were mainly interested in "dating, dancing, looking attractive, and building a family" and their role model was not a "tough, leather-jacketed, masculine-looking commissar but a bourgeois lady in silk stockings and low-cut dress".[46] This may very well have been the case but it seemed to co-exist with a mix of other attitudes lingering into the mid-1930s. The type of image women chose to follow depended on whether they lived in the city or village, their age, and social background. Urban women were more likely to embrace fashionable styles irrespective of propaganda; younger rural women might have tried to imitate these urban styles. As Victoria Bonnell has shown, the type of images portrayed by propaganda posters in the 1920s and 1930s at any rate changed considerably (masculine/rotund/sporty/curvaceous) and as well as that the target audience varied from industrial worker to *kolkhoznitsa* and on the latest political campaign (collectivization/industrialization).[47] It would appear that clothes and style were ultimately an individual choice governed mainly by local and peer mores, especially outside of the major cities. If women learned anything from propaganda and politics, it was that their style of dress reflected who and what they were and so represented an important personal and social statement.

Physical culture imagery was further publicized through the media of film and art. Dziga Vertov's *Man with a Movie Camera* of 1929 depicted women participating in a variety of sports and exercises, as well as engaging in general physical culture activities such as bathing. In the 1936 film *Vratar'*, the leading actresses were portrayed as natural and feminine but at the same time were fit, active, and healthy. Women were given new idols and ideals, their heroines transmuted to that of "a working-woman, a sportswoman, a record-holder".[48] These images were closely followed by portraits of women as *fizkul'turnitsy*. As Mike O'Mahony has shown, portraits of women involved in labour, especially those by Samokhvalov, appeared at the end of the 1920s and beginning of the 1930s.[49] Aleksandr Deinika also produced pictures that "are usually understood as examples of [his] generic images of strong, physically fit Soviet women representing the official optimism of the early 1930s".[50] The new images of women, as well as the *chastushki* and other forms of propaganda, attempted, on the one hand, to breach social concepts of the traditional role of women (relating to clothes styles, sports participation) and, on the other, reinforce some of these traditional images (predominantly as mothers and caregivers). Here

Figure 4.3   On the skating rink. "Vykhod na katok" ("Exit to the Skating Rink"), *FiS*, no. 8 (1930): 10. Courtesy of the Russian State Library.

Robin's axiological and symbolic levels of acculturation combined to create a vision of the New Soviet Woman, a vision that essentially merged the traditional with the modern.

The physical image of the New Soviet Woman was not an image that was universally well-received, especially outside of the urban centres. The clothes worn by women in villages and the republics were often highly traditional and symbolic and at odds with sporting attire. Participants in sports events, competitions, and parades wore shorts and vests which put their bodies on display. Such exposure was uncommon and unpopular in villages and in Central Asia, and as Karen Petrone observes, "[t]he attitude toward dress and the body that was standard in an urban physical culture parade was alien to at least some younger inhabitants of rural Russia".[51] In the national republics wearing sports attire was controversial and socially frowned upon.[52] Local opposition did not discourage physical culture organizers and activists though, and if anything spurred them on to increase propaganda campaigns. It was still hoped that new images of women in sports, aviation, industry, and tractor driving would supplant the older iconography of the rural traditional woman as well as the revolutionary militaristic and masculine woman. The new, later iconography targeted those women who, like the characters from the above *chastushki*, no longer wanted to live "as before". These women were encouraged to embrace new, so-called more attractive images and to help play an essential role in socialist society.

In light of the preceding discussion it seems fair to argue that the preoccupation with the female form was not a curious product of NEP society or Proletkul't politics. The way women looked was actually important. Semashko, for instance, was concerned with female appearance and was dismayed at some women's militaristic interpretation of the revolution in their attempts to dress in a masculine fashion.[53] Nor could this be dismissed as the reaction of someone of Lenin's generation to current fashion trends. This attitude was expressed by younger generations and persisted into the 1930s when then chairman of the Physical Culture Committee, Ivan Kharchenko (aged thirty in 1936), complained that one female physical culture representative, Bol'shakova, looked like a boy. He wanted to see a woman before him, not in the sense, he explained, that she "should cook porridge", but that she should possess a feminine quality and at least try to look like a woman physically.[54] "Comrade Bol'shakova", he continued, "first and foremost tries to look like a man with her dishevelled cap and unfastened buttons".[55] The chastised Bol'shakova would know to dress more tidily when next meeting Kharchenko. Furthermore, he added, the time had passed for women to go about "smoking cigarettes, spitting on the footpath and wearing men's blazers and boots".[56] There was, he concluded, only space for highly cultured young ladies. Clearly the avant-garde fashion moment was over.

Apart from the industrialization drive and their roles as mothers, why did the Soviet authorities seek to place so much emphasis on the female body? Why was the female body important? One explanation is provided by Bryan Turner, who notes that, "[t]he unrestrained body is a statement or a language about unrestrained morality. To control women's bodies is to control their personalities, and represents an act of authority over the body in the interests of public order organized around male values of what is rational".[57] Once again emerging is the contradiction between the public illustration of female emancipation, strength, and empowerment and the ulterior motive of state/male interests in controlling them. This is not to say that the opportunities on offer were illusory; they were in fact very real. It was simply that the motivation served dual purposes, both female and male. Considered most important of all by the party in this regard was that women would have an image with which to identify—an image that defined socially acceptable goals and aspirations.

The dream of attaining socialist bliss was one that had to be shared by everybody if it was to be rendered truly effective. This was an idea heavily promoted by state propaganda and in some cases did meet with success. As Jochen Hellbeck showed in his analysis of the diaries of Zinaida Denisevskaya, Stepan Podlubnyi, and others, surrendering to the collectivist ideal was often the easiest way out. Likewise Christina Kiaer points out that "the ideological images of sport succeeded . . . because of the active participation of Soviet subjects".[58] Participation was intrinsic to both individual, personal success and collective, state success. The latter became even more dominant in the mid-1930s with the greater imposition of state values and erosion of female independence. The state attempted to tighten its grip on the female body with concerns over the declining birth rate leading to more urgent calls for women to combine work and motherhood (the 1936 illegalization of abortion was an example of this). Maternity leave, paternity leave, and other incentives were introduced in order to encourage women to have families. Yet, in spite of increases in the birth rate, state propaganda appeared not to have won women over as the birth rate soon began to decrease once more as women opted for illegal abortions rather than obeying state policies.[59] As David Hoffmann argues, the state emphasis on women as mothers reduced equality between the sexes.[60] Women came under increasing pressure as they were expected to perform the functions of mother and housewife as well as worker, Stakhanovite heroine, and *fizkul'turnitsa*.

SPORT AND MOTHERHOOD

A supposedly ordinary woman's personal triumph and tragedy, as demonstrated through her involvement in sport, is explored in Igor Savchenko's 1936 film *Sluchainaya Vstrecha* (*Chance Encounter*). As Emma Widdis has argued in relation to Savchenko's 1934 film *The Accordion*, such films are important historical documents because they present the "kinds of images that surrounded ordinary men and women during the 1930s, images that were part of their reality".[61] In *Sluchainaya Vstrecha*, Irina Mikhailovna (played by Galina Pashkova)—the best shock-worker in a provincial children's toy factory—develops a relationship with the newly arrived and charming physical culture instructor named Grisha Rybin. The factory features as a focal point of the lives of the town's inhabitants, for the workers, and more so for the children, who naturally have a keen interest in the latest toys produced by the factory (the factory director is even depicted as a kind of "pied piper", blowing his horn out of his office window to call the local children to the factory for "consultation" on the latest products). Popular and pretty, Irina has won the affection of the children and her fellow workers (especially Petr Ivanovich). Grisha thus enters a world of idyllic rural bliss, where a montage scene shows the factory workers swimming in the river, practicing gymnastics by the river's edge (all evidently combining physical culture and nature), as well as practicing athletics in the stadium. This montage unfolds against the musical backdrop of *fizkul'turniki* singing about a strong and healthy body, including a shot of Petr singing in the shower (portraying hygiene as an important facet of physical culture). We are informed that this happens everyday after work and that the physical culture collective is preparing for the autumn spartakiad. Then Irina takes centre stage as she runs the 400m, beating the record by 1.5 seconds. Those watching in the stadium are in awe of her speed and grace, while Grisha is clearly taken with his new "protégé". Irina is also attracted to the handsome Grisha, though training comes first for her. The best worker in the factory, "loved by all children of the USSR", Irina is set to participate in the spartakiad. In order to prepare for this, Grisha requests that Irina be granted three months leave from work, but this is denied by the factory director, an action which prompts Grisha to quit as *kruzhok* instructor and to decide to leave the factory entirely. However, once he tells Irina of his intentions and their feelings towards each other are revealed, he stays and when we next meet them they are married and decorating their apartment.

Soon we learn that Irina is pregnant. Disappointed and angry on hearing her news, Grisha asks her about what will now happen to all their dreams, her training, the records, and the spartakiad—with a child everything will be lost. Grisha declares that he does not want a child, not now, but maybe when he is forty years old. Irina walks away, and, looking on, Grisha utters the word "baba" to himself. Irina is convinced that she should keep the baby and, even though still in love with Grisha, does not return home to him. Petr Ivanovich then tells the factory director what has happened. The director, whom we see nursing a child (his wife left him and their children), is aghast to hear that someone working in the factory is "against children". As Petr leaves, the director reminds him that the "party teaches them to take care of the family". Later we see Irina at a party held by a truck driver in honour of the birth of his son. Grisha, seen outside lurking in the bushes, is invited inside to mark the occasion. Though reluctant, he is amicably forced into the house where an anxious Irina, keen to leave, is persuaded to stay. Irina raises a toast to the driver (she also remarks that she never drinks but asks Petr to drink the glass of wine in her place) and then continues, saying that many young girls shed tears for those who they loved who turned out to be different to what they had first expected. She says she was such a girl. Then she speaks about children, and how the first word uttered by a child is "mama", and the second word she does not say, but pauses. Grisha stands up and then leaves, with everyone in the room left seething with rage. Irina however, is now strong and, with Petr by her side, declares that she will cry no more.

Following this we next meet Irina three years later, three years which, we are informed, were filled with great joy. We are also told that she in fact did cry, quite often, as did many girls for their first love and their "first major insult". The action has by now moved to Moscow. As crowds of excited people flood into the city's stadiums and parks, we are shown posters informing us that this is the year of the All-Union Spartakiad of Physical Culture (presumably the 1936 Spartakiad). Grisha is there, holding a cigarette and asking his girlfriend for a match. The action then switches to Irina and Petr as Irina prepares for her race. Cheered on by the crowds, the five athletes take their places. Irina, supported by her daughter, Petr, and the factory director, wins the race. Afterwards Grisha comes to her, looking for forgiveness and asking to return to her. Irina kindly refuses, saying she has a child and that she in any case is happy as she is. She says goodbye, shakes his hand, and returns to her daughter and Petr. The champion, followed by her daughter and Petr, then does a victory lap to the applause of the crowd. When Grisha returns to his girlfriend to leave the stadium, she asks about Irina and is told that it was just a "chance encounter". We next see Grisha's abandoned, sobbing girlfriend sitting next to Irina, Petr, and the daughter, being comforted by Irina and the young girl. The film ends with the words of Irina's smiling, happy, young daughter telling Grisha's girlfriend not to cry, "never to cry".

Sluchainaya Vstrecha was a film with a message for young girls in particular. It sought to show them that juggling a career, sport, and family was indeed possible, and moreover, a means to overall happiness and fulfilment. Being spurned by a lover was not to mean devastation, but would actually make one stronger emotionally and psychologically. Likewise, the birth of a child and abandonment of a husband did not signify hopelessness. One could still attain happiness and success in work and leisure, as well as turn to the support and help of others. In Irina's case, the love and support in her time of need came from Petr Ivanovich and the factory director. These were Irina's family, with the factory and the stadium effectively functioning as a surrogate home and her co-workers as her family. In spite of her troubles, Irina is never portrayed as bitter or angry—when she meets Grisha in the stadium after her race, she is warm and friendly towards him. The only time when she expressed any signs of anger or bitterness was at the driver's party, but even here she barely raised her voice and managed to stay largely in control of her emotions. Again, we are reminded of how model citizens were expected to behave. This is also conveyed through the character of the factory director. In his position as factory director, he did not only oversee production but was also deeply involved in the welfare of his workers and the larger community. When Irina tells Petr of Grisha's reaction to her news, it is the factory director to whom Petr goes to seek advice. He is a figure of respect and authority, but is at the same time portrayed as a good friend and an attentive and loving father. His devotion to his children stands in stark contrast to Grisha's ambivalence and even disdain towards them. There is a clear message here for male viewers—as fathers they should accept responsibility in the care and upbringing of their children.

Irina is the best shock-worker in the factory as well as a *fizkul'turnitsa*, and she also desires a family. This is the other key theme dominating the film—children. From the director of the children's toy factory, to Irina's popularity among the children, to the birth of her own child, the health and happiness of children and family values vie with physical culture for audience attention. As the director of the factory leans out of his office window to "consult" with the children, a picture of Stalin hangs

Figure 4.4 Victory of a true champion: A scene from *Sluchainaya Vstrecha*. L–R: Irina, her daughter, Grisha, and factory worker Patek at the spartakiad.

in the background, watching over the children and the factory. The factory director almost acts as a symbol of the state and patriarchal values, himself raising his children alone and reminding Petr about the party line on the family. Typically, it is the image of a happy, smiling child that we are left with, telling the slighted girlfriend and the audience in general not to cry. In Stalin's Russia, no one was to be sad, and everyone could achieve their dream (as long as their dreams coincided with socialist ideals). While it has been argued that "Soviet visual materials did not link sporting women with children, show them in a family setting or explicitly link sport with physical beauty and attractiveness to the opposite sex", the story of Irina clearly indicates otherwise.[62] This argument is not "missing from the Soviet context" but is in fact quite visible.[63]

This type of visual representation of Soviet life was reinforced by press coverage of "real" female athletes and stars. After the Stalin Constitution and the ban on abortion, motherhood was heavily promoted in the Soviet media. The press, as *Sluchainaya Vstrecha* demonstrated, was keen to show that sport and motherhood were not mutually exclusive. Several mothers involved in sports wrote about the rewards of combining the two obligations. One such woman, Galina Tusova, had represented the USSR in France and Czechoslovakia in athletics and had five national records to her name.[64] When she had a daughter she was told she was "mad" to think about returning to the track. Yet return she did and, she stated, she brought her daughter along with her. She encouraged others to follow suit and have strong healthy children while at the same time continuing to participate in sports. Tusova had not only returned to sports but she had also broken her previous records. The same could be said of others, including Klavdia Aleshina and Maria Shamanova. Shamanova even warned that she had heard of record breakers who were no longer able to perform after they had had abortions.[65]

More articles in support of motherhood came from students from the State Institute of Physical Culture. Gymnast Zinaida Shumova, a student from the third course, wrote that she was "really pleased" to have become a mother and had returned to full form three and a half months after giving birth.[66] However, she was anxious because her former husband and father of her child (a physical culture instructor) lived in Astrakhan and had not paid any alimony for several months. Meanwhile, the child lived with Shumova's mother in Astrakhan, and she saw no possibility of her child, aged just nine and a half months, being able to live with her in Moscow. When she approached Infizkul't director S. M. Frumin (who was soon to be purged) she was told that she would not be provided with suitable accommodation to raise a child. Such circumstances prompted one young father to write to the newspaper in support of abortion.[67] He claimed that circumstances were so appalling for young mothers who wanted to study that they had little choice other than to opt for abortion. He said that he was able to help and look after his wife and child but that many mothers did not have this support. The reality would seem to be that abortion was in fact the more plausible option for women involved in sports, and that these press excerpts were designed to stem the tide of abortions among Soviet women. Even Luisa Vtorova, in spite of her star status and the presence of a boyfriend, had—according to her sister—three abortions in the 1930s.[68] Nonetheless, it was the image of the childless Luisa that Deinika used in *Mother* (1932), depicting the figure of a mother with a child in her arms.[69]

SHATTERING ILLUSIONS: WOMEN SPEAK OUT

How did women respond to the model of the new socialist woman? What did they themselves make of the various debates such as female emancipation or women in physical culture? In 1929 the female contributor Barkhasha, writing in *Smena*, had her say on women in physical culture.[70] She argued that women were just as capable as men and worked just as hard. Their day consisted of work both inside and outside the home, far exceeding their male counterparts and lasting fourteen to fifteen hours.[71] She also acknowledged the difficulties of peasant women, particularly peasant girls, and contended that they often aged more quickly. Strenuous work and multiple children meant that, by the time these women had reached the age of thirty, their appearance was closer to that of a fifty-year-old.[72] As soon as they had given birth, they were back working. After ten years of married life, the women already had a curved spine and other ailments and illnesses. In order to better prepare women for this work and improve their health, Barkhasha wrote that physical culture was essential. This was because, she surmised, physical culture was not solely concerned with exercise, but rather, with a correct regime of work, rest, diet, and lifestyle. Her article featured a picture of a forty-five-year-old female worker from the *Sverdlov* textile factory. Wearing a knee-length, loose-fitting, pleated skirt or shorts, and a white T-shirt with her hair pulled back, this woman appeared strong and healthy, was an active *fizkul'turnitsa*, and mother of twenty children. There were also photos of younger women wearing shorts and vests, walking side-by-side in a parade, laughing and smiling.[73] The images portrayed depicted happy, healthy, and strong women.

Yet Barkhasha argued that female participation in sport did not always assume a healthy nature, echoing concerns about women trying to match men in the factories. Although women now strove for equality, they were discouraged from believing that they were equal in other senses.[74] Certain contingencies had to be put in place to protect and assist women. Women were to be deterred from competing with men in a physical sense, as this had negative consequences for their health and safety. It was cautioned that women who tried to outperform men in physical culture frequently did more harm to their

Figure 4.5   Rodionova from the Sverdlov textile factory. The caption accompanying the photograph reads, "Comrade Rodionova, worker in the Sverdlov textile factory. She is 45 years of age, mother of 20 children, and active *fizkul'turnitsa*. The Leningrad provincial textile section awarded Rodionova a diploma", *Smena*, no. 5 (1929): 7. Courtesy of the Russian State Library.

bodies than good. In conclusion, Barkhasha observed that physical culture was very important for women, but that this was not as yet reflected in the numbers participating in physical culture, especially in rural areas. Her article demonstrated that the issues of health and lifestyle were important to women and thus warranted considerable attention and that physical culture was certainly seen as one means of enlightening peasant and even male attitudes towards the traditional role of women. It also raised important questions concerning the practical application of equality and how this needed to be more adequately addressed to prevent some women from harming themselves physically through attempts to outdo men in labour and sport.

By the start of the 1930s women began to feature more prominently in physical culture propaganda, and there was a growing interest in women's personal experiences of physical culture and sport.[75] While the veracity of the following accounts may be somewhat questionable, given that they were published, they nonetheless provide an indication of wider female concerns regarding physical culture. Based on her experience, one worker considered that the best way of attracting women to physical culture was to increase the number of female instructors, as male instructors never made an effort to involve women.[76] Furthermore, when male instructors raised issues such as sweating or other hygiene issues, women felt insulted and uncomfortable, often leaving as a result.[77] Problems with instructors were generally a major obstacle for women, with some classes for women being stopped altogether.[78] Another contributor urged older women to go to the physical culture *kruzhki*, though admitted that this was often difficult because many felt ashamed and embarrassed.[79] She argued that women needed to understand that they had to take care of their bodies and health. If they were strong and healthy, they would be better able to take care of their own children's health and well-being. A woman who worked in the Park of Culture and Rest as a physical culture instructor also acknowledged that many women were simply shy or embarrassed depending on where they practiced physical culture.[80] The park organized special women's sports' squares where female instructors supervised and helped the women, but she observed that older women were reluctant to mix with younger women when participating in sports and games. They felt ill-at-ease when confronted by fitter, stronger, and healthier women or girls. Therefore, she concluded, stricter differentiation amongst the groups was necessary if physical culture was to succeed in winning older women to its cause.[81] The women interviewed obviously had experience of physical culture participation, an experience that was far from satisfactory and which highlighted the range of personal and social challenges faced by women involved in physical culture and sport.

Figure 4.6 The swimmers. Fizkul'tura i sport, 40 (1928): 1. Courtesy of the Russian State Library.

In terms of responding to state calls for increased female participation in physical culture, it was initially at least urban working women who responded most positively. Some women even claimed that they had been empowered by physical culture and sport. One such woman, Kadnova from the *Kauchuk* factory, explained that she had been working in the factory for more than eight years and had been a part of the physical culture *kruzhok* there for about six years, on and off.[82] She claimed that active involvement in physical culture allowed her to exert more influence and control over her life. When she was not involved in physical culture, she admitted that she often felt sick, she caught colds, her overall state of health deteriorated, and when at work she felt poorly and listless. When she resumed her involvement in the physical culture *kruzhok* and classes, she immediately felt better, fresh and more cheerful. Slivina, a Soviet diving champion, echoed how sports improved her physical and mental well-being.[83] She noted that she followed a highly regimented regime and diet, and was active in swimming, athletics and gymnastics as well as diving. Diving and water sports, she admitted, were especially complicated and difficult, and consequently required enormous commitment. One needed to attain complete mastery of one's body and possess qualities such as decisiveness and will-power. While the state gained healthy, fit, motivated, and committed workers and athletes, these women in return received social promotion, confidence, and increased control over their lives. It should be borne in mind that these and other positive accounts were undoubtedly designed to please and, as Stephen Kotkin notes, served a "definite purpose", for such people were being "exhibited as the standard bearers of the 'new culture'".[84] All the same, and perhaps more likely in this case, successful athletes who were "standard-bearers" or producers of this culture could equally be understood to be genuinely appreciative of it as they directly benefited from it.[85]

While some women might very well have felt "empowered" by physical culture and enjoyed participating in sports, other evidence would suggest that these were in the minority. Press accounts and images of women in physical culture told the idealized Soviet story, but the reality was that few women were actively involved in physical culture, as Maria Glebova and others had argued in the mid 1920s. One worker commented that in her factory the physical culture uptake was very low. The reason for this, she explained, was that, until recently, there were no physical culture premises.[86] She noted that the managers of the club and factory committee of another factory, despite its workers all having the same days off, had failed to organize any sort of excursion or activities.[87] Tram conductors A. P. Vasil'eva and O. A. Ivanova complained about their working conditions in the *Artamonovskii* tram park.[88] They stated that, as conductors, they spent all day on their feet, wearing dirty clothes and breathing dirty air. Vasil'eva claimed that she would have liked to partake in athletics but did not have the opportunity. Ivanova

Figure 4.7 N. Slivina, *FiS*, no. 47(1928): 12.
Courtesy of the Russian State Library.

recounted how before travelling to Moscow, she had lived in the Crimea, where she had been involved in all types of sports. However, on finding work in Moscow, she had to abandon her interests in physical culture. They stated that a few workers had tried to agitate for physical culture, but that the *Artamonovskii* tram park had no physical culture *kruzhok* at present (though it had one in the past which had since disbanded). For women who wanted to become involved in physical culture the opportunity was not there as busy factory bosses had neither the time nor interest to invest in physical culture.

The textile production dominated city of Ivanovo, where the vast majority of factory workers were women, serves as a good indicator of how women responded to physical culture. In the city's main factory, the *Melanzh* plant, 10,000 of the 12,000 employees were women, and yet physical culture work was done among just 100 people. Only thirty-six workers received the GTO badge in 1935, and only two of the recipients were women.[89] In the Dzerzhinsky factory, one woman (out of a total of 6,000 working in the factory) was awarded the GTO badge. Similar statistics were reflected in numerous factories across the city. The provincial and city physical culture councils reported "with bewilderment" that women were "not interested in physical culture", while "slovenliness reigns in the physical culture *kruzhki* of Ivanovo".[90] Once again, instructors were a problem. In the *Melanzh* plant the instructor turned up drunk and insulted the girls there. In the Kineshemsk district an instructor weighed girls "in an exposed state" and asked that each girl be weighed separately in a storeroom so that an accurate weight could be ascertained. Some instructors, according to one *fikul'turnitsa*, "supported" or "stood by" those girls in whom they were "interested". Of course sometimes there were no instructors at all. The secretary of one factory committee wrote that he had been requesting an instructor for three months and in the end had to promote a couple of demobilized Red Army soldiers to work as instructors. Those in charge appeared indifferent to these problems, "accustomed to the shortcomings" and "too lazy" to do anything about them.[91] The fact that women who were interested or involved in physical culture were made to feel uncomfortable, and in some cases possibly taken advantage of by male instructors, no doubt hindered female participation in sports and physical culture.

The positive attitude towards women in physical culture often seemed limited to the press and utterly divorced from reality. Again the situation in Ivanovo provides a good example of attitudes towards women in physical culture and the difficulties encountered by women who chose to play sports or exercise, whether in work or at home. In parts of this city the negative attitude towards physical culture was not limited to the factory and actually extended to include home life as well. One landlady where some of the factory girls lived forbade them from practicing physical culture, as it was for "hussies" and "shameless people" (*"sramnitsa"* and *"besstydnitsa"*).[92] The danger of being labelled some sort of a "loose" woman was a stigma that no doubt put many girls off participating in physical culture, particularly in smaller towns and villages. Women could not be assured of finding solace or sympathy among other women working in the factory either. One young cotton worker and *fizkul'turnitsa*, twenty-two-year-old Liuba Naboishchikova, injured her leg but was told that she was "faking" her injury.[93] The other (all female) cotton workers said that she was a "worn out tart". By the end of the working day this "good cotton worker" was hardly able to stand, and despite repeatedly telling the instructor that she could not participate in competitions and needed medical expertise, was instead forced by the instructor to practice physical culture without receiving medical attention. As a result of being forced to participate in these competitions she fainted and was told "maliciously" that now without her there would "be no *fizkul'turniki*". All of the women in the factory shop apparently knew of this case and were consequently "convinced that practicing physical culture was useless and impossible".

For such women the famed sportswoman in shorts and vest, who was both popular and attractive, was non-existent. The daily grind of life in the factory saw to this. Work, motherhood, and social stigma sidelined any physical culture interests for the women of Ivanovo and other towns and cities across the Soviet Union. Women who dared to participate in physical culture were not popular or heroic but instead sometimes earned a reputation for being sexually loose. They were vulnerable, liable to being exploited by instructors, and ostracized by colleagues. The Soviet *fizkul'turnitsa* did of course exist, but she appeared to inhabit a different world to the one experienced by most ordinary working women. Those not fortunate enough to have the right body shape or sufficient talent were doomed to the role of spectator rather than participant. As Christina Kiaer notes in her study of the swimming Vtorova sisters, their elite status as athletes protected them and separated them from other, "ordinary" citizens.[94] For many "ordinary" women involvement in physical culture was not an enjoyable but rather an arduous and socially compromising experience.

A SOVIET KIND OF EMANCIPATION

Physical culture propaganda was disseminated to both educate and control women, reflecting wider state policies for the care and control of its citizens. Its message to women was largely positive and encouraging, but with underlying negative tones as their "emancipation" came with restrictions, especially in the 1930s. Women still had to conform to certain social identities such as mother, wife, and homemaker. Physical culture undoubtedly contributed to a change, albeit a slow change, in attitudes, both among men *and women*. While much of the criticism generated by women and sport has centred on male attitudes to women and especially to the *new physical image* presented by women in sporting attire, the actual attitude of women themselves has frequently been overlooked. Women, after all, were also slow to adjust to the new images of themselves as *fizkul'turniki*. They had to overcome feelings of embarrassment and discomfort, feelings which, although heightened by the largely negative reactions of men, were also produced by female scepticism and suspicions. As for the role of women in society, physical culture exemplified the multitude of roles incumbent upon women—women were expected to become important contributors to the socialist world, and not just as mothers. While female emancipation had been proclaimed, women were still considered and treated far from equally. As Dr. Korolev's theories attest, attitudes to women were mixed and contradictory. While the state declared women to be equal with men, this was not realized in reality because of both male and female recalcitrance to adjust to new ideals. Physical culture itself was of course also subject to much change and inconsistency, initially focusing on raising the poor standards of health and hygiene and later developing and moulding strong and fit workers. It was only in the 1930s that the notion of the sports star was officially acclaimed. If the party's promotion of women's participation in *fizkul'tura* did help women to become more "enlightened" citizens, it was only on a smaller, more sporadic, and ultimately much slower scale than had initially been anticipated in the heady years of the Soviet state. This was the case for both urban and rural women, the latter whom, as we shall soon see when looking at peasants and national minorities, seemed to have an even longer road to travel in reaching the status of "enlightened" citizen.

5 The Pursuit of a Rural Civilized Citizen

Rural physical culture seems like somewhat of an oxymoron. One is severely challenged to picture the "darkened masses" doing morning exercises before heading to the fields for a day's work, then coming home to clean their nails and brush their teeth. Rural societies did not have easy access to facilities such as toilets, washbasins, showers, or even soap. In the countryside and in parts of the national republics, as the *chastushki* from the previous chapter showed, resources were scarce, vast distances severed many families from cultural or social centres, and deeply imbedded rural or national customs and traditions neutralized the reception of Soviet ideology. In penetrating the firmly entrenched habits and values of the peasants, and indeed non-Russians, physical culture acculturation would have to stage a physical and psychological transformation. The Bolsheviks did not flinch at such an undertaking, and as Aaron Retish notes, "the village became a laboratory for . . . state agents to test their methods and ideologies".[1] This was not only the case in the villages but in the national republics too, where Douglas Northrop has argued that in Central Asia the Bolsheviks set out to bring "modern European cultural norms (such as gender equality)" and "European notions of social reform (which meant public health and hygiene as much as class revolution)".[2] While this chapter focuses predominantly on peasant physical culture, the national minorities—also considered benighted and ripe for reforming—are examined.[3] There are naturally problems in taking such an approach. One is reminded in particular of a local Transcaucasian organizer's complaint that all the "nationality eggs" were lumped together in "one basket". This organizer argued that they "cannot all be treated the same" and that each individual nationality could not be generally labelled "the nationalities".[4] That is of course true in the case of both nationalities and indeed peasants, but ethnic diversity and local norms or customs coupled with the vast geographical expanse of the Soviet Union makes it extremely difficult to examine here individual local cases on a comparative scale.

One of the main problems with the peasants, and perhaps more particularly with the national minorities, was the perceived lack of hygienic awareness and the continued presence of "anti-physical culture" habits and customs.[5] In an effort to improve hygiene standards physical culture activists and propaganda encouraged Soviet citizens to enjoy the sun, bathe in the water, and breathe in the fresh air. Greater attention was to be paid to sanitary and hygiene education in schools and in the Pioneers, as well as in institutes of higher education, Soviet party schools, and secondary schools. The physical culture *kruzhok* in the villages was instructed to examine social issues and help popularize sanitary and hygienic work among the peasants. It was also considered imperative that popular brochures were published in the national languages, that propaganda was introduced in magazines and newspapers, and that these were published in the centre and the localities in the national languages, as well as all being widely available in the Russian language. These campaigns were not entirely altruistic endeavours. Northrop argues that in Central Asia the public health campaign was "deeply political" and contributed to the "power relationship" within that society.[6] As with physical culture campaigns directed at young people and women, the health and well-being of the individual were indelibly bound up with the social and political advancement of the nation.

An examination of the physical culture campaigns shows how, in its attitude towards acculturation, the state did not intend to simply apply Soviet cultural methods or "bourgeois" standards of culture to the peasants or national minorities. Traditional physical culture in the 1920s, as this chapter will show, was recognized as having its own merits. The process of acculturation therefore sought to integrate the beneficial aspects of pre-existing rural culture with the new, Soviet culture. The objective was to instil socialist values into everyday life through the practice of traditional games and sports and to add to this a programme for general improvements in health, hygiene, and educational standards. This was to be achieved not only through encouraging so-called "backward" people (in this case peasants or national minorities) to adopt more stringent hygiene habits, but also through increased health awareness, exercise, sport, education, and social work. The extent of any level of acculturation and "sovietization" is, as Sheila Fitzpatrick argues, an "open question", for it is difficult to judge how any kind of accommodation with Soviet values denoted actual acceptance or not.[7] Irrespective of acceptance or non-acceptance, exploring various attempts at acculturation and sovietization is important in helping to understand the relationship between the state and its citizens, providing a means of ascertaining the various levels of state commitment to policies of acculturation.

In order to do this it is necessary first to explore the Bolshevik understanding of physical culture in relation to the peasants and national minorities and examine how the party and physical culture activists sought to promote the practice of physical culture in non-urban centres. The first of these centres was the village reading-room, which was one of the few places where the peasants were exposed to party propaganda, mainly through the work of Komsomol activists. Schools formed another important outlet for introducing rural children to physical culture practices. The final area analyzes the policy of *shefstvo* or patronage, a means of sending the Soviet message from the city to the countryside through agitation brigades from factories or universities. These were, more or less, the main cultural links tying the countryside to political events and social developments in the rest of the Soviet Union. There were of course other less officially organized links, such as demobilized soldiers who, because of their physical culture training, were often encouraged to help train and educate those in the villages. Also as an unofficial source of spreading agitprop, *otkhodniki*—seasonal workers who moved between the cities and the provinces—became another important link in relaying news of life in the cities back to those living in the villages. The unprecedented levels of population displacement in the early 1930s as villagers flooded into the cities following the immense devastation of collectivization in many ways increased correspondence between urban and rural populations.[8] Whether driven from their native villages and towns out of fear, famine, or a desire for a better future, great numbers of people were on the move. In the early 1920s this occurred in an urban—rural pattern but in the late 1920s and 1930s the pattern was reversed as people sought work in the cities.

SOVIET AND "NON-SOVIET" PHYSICAL CULTURE

It seems safe to assume that rural physical culture, as envisioned by the authorities, was virtually non-existent in the early years of the Soviet state. Even by the mid-1920s when there were supposed to have been at least some propaganda campaigns conducted, the situation appeared hopeless. The ever-active and vocal *Zhenotdel* representative Maria Glebova commented in 1925 that, having travelled around five provinces over the course of three months, she encountered not one peasant who practiced physical culture.[9] In the same discussions Genrikh Yagoda noted that there was no physical culture in the provinces, simply hooliganism and *samogon* (home brew). He was unable to understand what it was "physical culture was doing" in the villages and why hooliganism was "spreading like wildfire".[10] He accused those in charge of promoting physical culture of not understanding the village—how, he wanted to know, could peasants be told to go skating and skiing when people living in the cities could not obtain skates or skis.[11] Or if told to row, were peasants to do this in an old tub?[12] Organizers and agitators were often out of touch with the realities of life in the villages and the fact that rural inhabitants had different needs and conditions to those living in urban areas. While Yagoda and some others recognized this, instructions from the centre and the press continued to promote physical culture from a singular viewpoint without properly differentiating between rural and urban requirements.

Similar problems occurred in the national republics throughout the 1920s and even into the 1930s. According to the All-Union Council of Physical Culture in Transcaucasia there was "no organization of the masses, no physical culture *vospitanie*, [and] no correct physical culture".[13] Another Transcaucasian correspondent noted that there was "not one physical culture *kruzhok* in a single local village."[14] In the North Caucasus local physical culture correspondents communicated that there was no equipment; nobody educated in physical culture literature (and there was in any case an absence of literature in the native languages); there were no specialists, instructors, or teachers; and there was an "incorrect" understanding of physical culture.[15] Young people there were only interested in *dzhigitovka*, wrestling, and dance.[16] Correspondents in Central Asia reported negatively on the development of *fizkul'tura*, where it was said to be particularly weak in the *auls* or villages, and there was no competition whatsoever.[17] A representative of the Supreme Council of Physical Culture in the Tatar Republic claimed that the number of *kruzhki* in Kazan stood at forty but that growth was sluggish, physical culture and educational work was weak, and equipment was non-existent.[18] Such reports in conjunction with the harsh economic circumstances of the 1920s suggests that physical culture activists struggled to establish any sort of a physical culture base in the national republics. The likelihood is that, the farther away from Moscow one travelled, the less likely one was to encounter physical culture and sport, at least in its Soviet context.

Contrary to the impressions created by these reports, it was not the case that there was no physical culture, but rather an absence of Soviet physical culture. Russians and non-Russians had a rich physical culture heritage long before the arrival of the Bolsheviks. Popular among peasant children, for instance, were games such as "blind man's buff" and "hide and seek", while during Easter especially "egg and spoon" racing was popular with all age groups. Among the peasants traditional games such as *lapta* and *gorodki* were widely played.[19] For children, *lapta* and other games were considered a good means of strengthening their young bodies for the physical demands of peasant work that lay ahead of them.[20] After all, peasant life was tough, with outdated farming methods placing extreme physical demands on those working in the fields.[21] Physical strength, besides being a prerequisite for life on the farm, was a matter of pride and prestige among peasants, and stories of famous "strongmen" were passed down from generation to generation.[22] As the opening chapter suggested, the cult of the body was embedded in village culture since the nineteenth century. When it came to physical culture and sports activities, peasants preferred simple games with simple objectives or entertainment with elements of social interaction. In her study of peasants in Penza in the 1920s, Larissa Lebedeva notes that games were often a means of fraternizing with the opposite sex, especially for young people.[23] Male peasants liked to use games as a way of impressing girls with their strength, and on certain holidays village men gathered together to mark the festive occasion through fist-fighting matches ("*kulachnye boi*" or the "*stenka*").[24] These were of course not recognized as a form of Soviet physical culture. Fist-fighting or boxing in particular had no official place within the early spectrum of physical culture, even though it enjoyed some popularity. Fist-fighting, wrestling, or dance, as interpreted by peasants and national minorities, were simply unacceptable as part of the "new culture". The challenge for Soviet activists consequently lay not in convincing rural inhabitants to actually become *involved* in physical culture, but to change their habits and adopt a more "Soviet" style of physical culture.

To claim therefore that physical culture per se did not exist among peasants or national minorities overlooked the existence of this body symbolism and the fact that Russian and non-Russian culture already had this wide variety of traditional games and activities. The Georgian Supreme Council of Physical Culture, for example, was keen to incorporate Georgian games into Soviet physical culture. The traditional peasant Georgian games of horse racing, *tarchiya*, and *lelo-burti* were advanced as possibilities for inclusion into the Soviet pantheon of sports.[25] While the former demanded agility and speed on horseback, the latter ("field ball") was a game similar to rugby and had been in existence for over 300 years.[26] The problem was that these were not organized and *lelo-burti* in particular was a game that could easily turn violent. Some of these folk games, again such as *lelo-burti*, were associated with religious festivals, and often took place on May 1. While some of these contests and games often led to an escalation of

Figure 5.1   Young peasants playing *lapta* in the village of Ignat'esya, Kadamskii district, Ryazan, *FiS*, nos. 31–32 (1930): 8. Courtesy of the Russian State Library.

tensions between Georgians and Mingrelians and could also inflict serious injuries on participants and bystanders (*lelo-burti* especially), they were all advanced as being contenders because of their popularity. To prove the point, central authorities were informed that at the tenth anniversary of the October Revolution a programme for a sporting celebration had been agreed with all types of sports included and a total of some 15,000 locals turned up to the festival. The efforts of the Georgian Supreme Council and others did not seem to be in vain as some of these folk games were indeed standardized during the Soviet period, forming a hybrid between the traditional, folk, and modern Soviet forms of physical culture.

In its physical culture policy it seemed more plausible for the state to merge some of these long-standing traditions with new Soviet values, rather than completely destroy them. Semashko considered it important to cultivate the older games such as *gorodki* or *lapta,* although he suggested that they be re-invigorated by new socialist methods.[27] If this was done correctly, then they could be used as a modernization strategy, easing peasants into the Soviet mode of life on more familiar and agreeable terms. To make national dances and games more amenable to the Bolshevik vision, he advised propaganda workers and organizers to choose sports and games which emphasized collectivism, solidarity, discipline, and similar characteristics. Peasant and national dance were favoured over "bourgeois" dances, preferred so long as they were healthy and helped the biological, psychological, and emotional development of performers, especially in schools where national and traditional dance were less likely to lead to sexual deviancy.[28] One criticism however, was that sometimes these dances were slow paced, depriving rural dancers of the "motions and rhythms . . . for the new conditions of work".[29] Games had to be interesting and "emotive" in order to attract villagers.[30] Policymakers realized that making peasants into active *fizkul'turniki* meant educating and impressing them on terms that were agreeable to them. In physical culture, indigenous games thus represented an important element in the overall state policy of *korenizatsiya* or "nativization". Throughout the 1920s and into at least the beginning of the 1930s central authorities considered it necessary and advantageous to utilize native peasant games in an effort to establish the values of Soviet physical culture. As Mark Saroyan argued, this "process of national-cultural construction developed not simply from the amorphous activization of 'tradition' by the cultural intelligentsia but reflected the 'modern' institutional innovations of Soviet national-state formation".[31]

An example of state appropriation of traditional customs in order to promote Soviet ideals and concepts of physical culture was the national holiday of *Sabantui,* a Tatar labour festival celebrating the end of one season and beginning of the next.[32] *Sabantui* was a prime example of how traditional and "new" cultures fused together to create a special blend of Soviet culture.[33] In 1922 "the question of its organization was considered by the Presidium of the Central Electoral Committee of the TASSR" and it thereafter became the "national sports holiday" and the holiday of spring.[34] The revised holiday included military speeches, national games, competitions, and entertainment. The beginning of *Sabantui* was now heralded by the rising of a red flag accompanied by the sounds of the Soviet national anthem. The ceremony was even broadcast on radio. Eventually the programme came to include "national kinds of wrestling competitions and games with the compulsory attributes of physical culture and sports of that time: a parade of athletes, free-style exercises, boxing, weight-lifting, track and field athletics, parachute-jumping, performances of cavalrymen, artillerymen, mass games", and hundreds of people from amateur choirs, circus performers, and actors participated in the event. Deemed permissible in the overall context of rural sports and games were sports competitions in the various types of national sport. In his work on festivals Malte Rolf has observed that they "helped the regional power cliques to display a local *korenizatsiya* of Soviet rule", although officials "strove everywhere to copy Moscow's role model".[35] Once again it was evident that central authorities seemed quite willing to yield on certain matters in an effort to advance the basic principles of Soviet physical culture among the peasants and national minorities. The objective was to familiarize the Tatar population with the basic precepts of Soviet culture. The addition of military speeches and a red flag to the *Sabantui* festival was the Bolshevik attempt at placing Tatar culture within the broader framework of communist culture and politics.

The *Sabantui* festival provides a good example of how folk or religious traditions were preserved or "hijacked" by Soviet authorities. Not all festivals or games made the cut though, and figuring out which types of native games were suitable for "sovietization" sometimes posed a serious problem for central and local organizers. Different regions had their own types of sports and games, such as horseracing and wrestling, which had been in existence "since time immemorial".[36] Official policy in regard to native games in the 1920s was that elements of these sports and games (as evidenced by *lelo-burti*) were harmful and had to be "discarded", but that essentially they were in agreement with Soviet principles. The same reasoning had applied to events such as *Sabantui*. In the view of physical culture leaders, these events were in fact undervalued and underused by local organizers, with little or no participation by the local organs of physical culture. According to a report by the physical culture presidium, the "general tendency" of the physical culture councils in the localities was to simply "transfer European types of sport without any consideration of local peculiarities".[37] The situation was not helped by the fact there were no physical culture instructors among the indigenous population of the national republics, at least not by 1929. The difficulty for organizers in determining the principles of Soviet physical culture makes clear that there was deep uncertainty, confusion, and misunderstandings between centre and periphery, with the message of how to handle local customs and culture often not understood or implemented by organizers in these regions. There is some evidence to suggest that this was beginning to change somewhat by the 1930s. By this time there seemed to be a more concerted effort to attract indigenous populations to physical culture leadership positions and popularize physical culture and sport, with additional numbers now becoming involved in physical culture.[38] There was even an effort to showcase national minority participation in physical culture by using "rich material" for a film showing "the variety and beauty of national and other forms of physical culture", filmed in the Russian Republic, Buryatiya-Mongolia, the Altai, Central Asia, and Dagestan.[39] This would again, it was supposed, help raise standards of physical culture in "the backward national republics" and draw attention to the relationship between folk culture and Soviet culture.[40]

Soviet authorities were certainly faced with different challenges when it came to introducing Soviet concepts of physical culture to peasants and different national minorities. Local organizers did not seem to take a nuanced approach, as instructed by the central physical culture leadership, and so the reception of Soviet physical culture varied considerably on a case by case basis. The approach appeared to vary too as the 1920s progressed with collectivization and the rise of Stalinism impacting upon how policy was carried through in the regions and provinces. By the mid-1930s it was evident that physical culture in relation to the national minorities had progressed from simply establishing a Soviet type of physical culture among local communities to articulating a more defined approach to nation-building and establishing a Soviet identity amongst national minorities.

THE VILLAGE READING-ROOM, THE KOMSOMOL, AND RURAL PHYSICAL CULTURE

In his study of propaganda and political education Peter Kenez notes that the "reading-rooms played a central role in the many campaigns initiated by the Party".[41] The reading-room was to be a beacon of Soviet progress within village society where illiteracy would be eradicated and peasants acculturated.[42] Not only did it function as the focus of political campaigns but also as centres of leisure and entertainment. In many cases the reading-rooms hosted the physical culture *kruzhki* and so had responsibility for physical culture propaganda. The village *kruzhok* attached to the reading-rooms were tasked with introducing peasants to literature regarding cleanliness, sanitation, hygiene, and health, and took the form of speeches, talks, lectures, brochures, posters, leaflets, and so forth. There were several obstacles which the village *kruzhok* had to first overcome. One of these was that there were not enough reading-rooms: in 1923–1924 there were 11,357 reading-rooms which grew to an NEP peak of 24,934 in 1925–1926 and then fell slightly to 22,125 in 1926–1927.[43] Moreover, those that did exist were basic huts and the funding available to them did not improve drastically over the course of the 1920s.[44] Another problem was that the provincial *kolkhozy* faced a shortage of physical culture literature because it was either too expensive or never even made it as far as the villages, having been lost or delayed in the cities.[45] This proved a huge problem for those in the provinces, where the instructors were "semi-literate" and knew nothing about any of these books and so worked according to "old materials".[46] In the national republics similar problems regarding access to literature existed, with apparently no physical culture literature available in the native languages of Azerbaijan and only four books available in Armenian.[47]

As a response to basic deprivations Komsomol activists were to step up propaganda campaigns in order to attract more peasants towards physical culture. During the NEP the Komsomol, as Isabel Tirado notes, was "asked to recast its public image" to that of "peacetime builders of the socialist village".[48] Young people were to be instructed on how to behave. The extent to which village youth were entrusted with embodying socialist life was evident in a 1928 illustration of a young Pioneer shown brushing his teeth in a peasant hut while several older peasants, presumably family members, watch from a "safe" distance, their expressions a mixture of both fear and curiosity.[49] The simple action of the young child brushing his teeth represents the clean, healthy Soviet lifestyle. As a Pioneer, he is an exemplary figure within society and a living symbol of Soviet values. Reminiscent of the women from the Komsomol *chastushki*, this leading light should not be frowned upon but heralded as an example for all to follow. However, while some Komsomol and Pioneer members relished the role given to them by the party, others were less enthusiastic and as Tirado also observes, "Komsomol members could be found on both sides of the hooligan divide".[50] Consequently, attempts to educate peasants in the ways of physical culture were often a futile exercise as its basic ideals were often misunderstood or ignored. One report highlighted the failure of organizers and propaganda when it noted that "*fizkul'turniki*" often smoked during lessons—hardly a feature of the new, healthy Soviet citizen.[51] The offenders apparently did not know any better because nobody had told them that this was not the correct practice for *fizkul'turniki*.[52] Problems with instructors, as the chapter on young people demonstrated, were commonplace with real, everyday examples of healthy physical culture hard to come by. These problems with instructors, combined with institutional problems within the Komsomol, meant that young people in the countryside were more or less left to their own devices.[53]

Figure 5.2   Pioneer brushing his teeth. "Pioner v glukhoi derevne". ("Pioneer in the depths of the countryside"), Griffel', *Zhurnal krest'yanskoi molodezhi*, no. 18 (1928): 1. Courtesy of the Russian State Library.

In attracting peasants towards active physical culture and sport, dance and traditional folk entertainment were to be introduced to the reading-room or *kruzhok*. This once again reflected the "nativization" policy and the decision not to exclude all forms of existing traditional culture, with the authorities reasonably content to integrate national games into the new *fizkul'tura* regimen. Using dance and folk games seemed a logical means of promoting physical culture—these were familiar and entertaining and represented a possible stepping stone onto sports as well as a way of drawing young people to the reading-rooms. As physical culture in the republics displayed few or no signs of "bourgeois tendencies", it was thus not considered a major threat and so national games and dances remained. At a time when much of traditional peasant culture was being eroded and destroyed, it was important that at least some of their customs received official sanction and support.[54] This policy did not always translate well into practice, however, as one Transcaucasus representative had learned from his experience in applying traditions such as *dzhigitovka* or national dance: "You tell us to use local peculiarities but how are we supposed to use them? It is not easy to maintain control . . . not every dance is healthy".[55]

The use of indigenous games was a real cause for concern among local organizers, who struggled to find the right balance of a healthy and controlled physical culture that was both traditional and modern. Attempts to educate peasants and use methods such as dance to attract peasants towards physical culture often backfired. In one case several *izbachi* (those responsible for the reading-rooms) reported that dances in fact had a negative influence and only interested younger peasants.[56] One observer wrote that when dances started in the room, older people who had gone there to read walked out.[57] When the dancing ended the floor was covered with cigarette ends, phlegm, and *semechki* (sunflower seeds) shells.[58] Not only had the introduction of dances created an unsightly mess and led to "anti-physical culture behaviour" among youth, but it had also alienated older peasants. The latter was something that those frequenting the reading-room often seemed wont to do. Such behaviour undoubtedly gave a certain reputation to reading-rooms and depicted them as being far removed from "cultural" centres. Kenez draws the conclusion that the high proportion of young people "who found no other amusement . . . lowered the prestige of this institution in the eyes of the older, more conservative peasants".[59] This is echoed by Tirado, who comments that "[e]ven village reading-rooms, the symbol of Komsomol *kul'turnost'*, were tainted with hooliganism in the eyes of peasant adults".[60] The disparity between the illustration of the boy brushing his teeth and the problems experienced by the reading-rooms highlights the serious problems facing Soviet authorities. Propaganda designed to instruct and inspire peasants of all ages seemed to have little or no effect, its power diminishing in the face of reality where it more often than not transpired that peasant youth behaviour tarnished the image of physical culture.

SCHOOLS AS HARBINGERS OF CULTURE

Along with the village reading-rooms, schools were also to function as important nerve-centres of physical culture discourse and centres for instilling Soviet values.[61] During and immediately after the civil war schools were in ruins and the state simply did not have sufficient resources to construct or rebuild schools throughout the country. Chapter 3 highlighted the serious problems in physical culture education and showed how rural and national republic-based schools struggled to procure equipment, instructors, and facilities. Many rural schools had no physical culture teachers and some had only activists with a few months training.[62] The challenges faced by educators varied from one province, region, or republic to the next.[63] One of the main problems for rural youth was that they were often used as cheap labour and denied a full or complete education. If forced to work in the fields and denied access to education or to the reading-rooms, children consequently received minimum exposure to physical culture propaganda. Coupled with this frequent problem was that those rural youth who received some formal education may not have benefited significantly from physical culture propaganda when the schools were so woefully under-funded and under-equipped. Some of this was down to a basic lack of interest or logic, as evidenced in Adzharistan when organizers trying to attract sixty children to the school only succeeded in attracting three. The next day, when the organizers brought an actual football to the school, thirty children turned up.[64] Having material provisions to entice young rural inhabitants towards education was also proven to be successful in attracting children of the north.[65] It was shown that having something as simple and basic as a ball could make a difference in drawing people towards active physical culture.

In a 1930 physical culture press review of village *kruzhki* and schools it was found that those *kruzhki* attached to the *kolkhoz* youth school most needed to be taught about personal and social hygiene. The review concluded that students should partake in competitions and festivals, should be taught exercises and theory, and should be given seminars and lectures.[66] Included in the educational review were dress-making schools. These were composed primarily of female farm-hands, day labourers, and peasants. For these girls living in the countryside questions of hygiene, sanitation, biology, children, and the "struggle against ignorance" had to assume high importance. The best forms of propaganda suggested for this group were talks, exercises designed for women, lessons, games, and dances (no lectures, theory, or seminars were on the agenda).[67] From this survey alone the propaganda used to mobilize the peasant population around physical culture differed considerably. A degree of social stratification was also present—those in the countryside were assigned a class and segregated accordingly. Although the peasant classes of *bedniaki*, *sredniaki*, and *batraki* applied, this was here accompanied by further gender divisions.[68] The combination of class and gender differentiation was a prevalent feature of physical culture propaganda directed towards women as it sought to engage the two audiences of rural and urban women.

In the survey examined here the dress-making schools were encouraged to use a different type of propaganda that appealed to the "poorer" classes and a female audience. There was an explicit assumption that the girls in the dress-making schools need only to be required to absorb physical culture through more simplistic and demonstrative means such as dance.

They were not required to participate so much in competitions or become involved in theories of physical culture but instead expected to focus on children and biology. These girls were required to stay in the home and so physical culture was necessary in that it could be applied domestically. The *kolkhoz* school for youth, on the other hand, consisted of both boys and girls who were considered to have higher education and literacy levels, thus elevating them above the lowly dress-making girls. Some of these students were expected to become active Komsomol members and later progress to become party members. Consequently the propaganda directed at these students was slightly more sophisticated and ambitious.[69] This ambiguity in state attitudes towards the young female peasants reflected the wider gender divisions that prevailed. In spite of party rhetoric and propaganda, women—especially those living in rural areas—often found it difficult to lead a life apart from domestic duties and household chores. This situation was worsened by parental and social attitudes to how a rural girl should be raised, which reflected those of the older peasant women in the *chastushki* from Chapter 4.

Rural children, both boys and girls, were often considered in an unfavourable light when compared to urban children. The instructions for the conduct and implementation of the third city and first rural festival of physical culture in Tambov region for the academic year 1929–1930 revealed how rural children were treated as less capable than their urban counterparts.[70] Although ostensibly framed as a friendly cultural exchange, with the Tambov city children charged with familiarizing their rural acquaintances with everyday life in the city and rural children in turn expected to teach city children about the new way of life (*zhizn'* and *novyi byt*) in the village, there were underlying notes which portrayed the rural children as inferior. Sports attire, for example, marked exceptions between the two groups of schoolchildren, with the rural visitors not expected to conform to the sartorial standards of the time. Preferably most children would wear special physical culture costumes, but if this was not possible boys had to wear light shirts and dark pants while girls had to wear light dresses or a blouse (*koftochka*) and dark skirt. City children were also obliged to wear badges, but it was not obligatory for rural children to wear badges or sports costumes.

There was further differentiation in the performances that both groups of children had to learn. For example, all schools had a set number of assigned performances, but city schools had five combinations of free exercises to prepare, whereas the rural children only had to perform the first three. Even if the children had wanted to learn more, the option was not available to them. Consequently, by their lack of sports costumes, badges, and restricted performances, the rural children visiting Tambov, whether they were aware of it or not, appeared inferior and less able than their urban counterparts. This was not a direct result of their own but of the restrictions imposed upon them by local organizers. If, as Régine Robin argues, schools as centres of learning and knowledge were critical for social integration, then in this case of school participation in the Tambov physical culture festival it is evident that schools were clearly divided along social lines, with urban schools having greater access to knowledge and learning. Instead of bridging the social divide, schools in fact further separated urban schoolchildren from rural schoolchildren.

Some of the issues raised by this festival in Tambov were common and experienced elsewhere. One of these—sports attire—was again a divisive matter. As the photograph in Figure 5.3 shows, shorts and vests were generally not worn by those living in rural or republican areas. In some instances it was the case that these were simply not available in schools with limited resources, but in other cases, where such items were available, problems sometimes arose. In Transcaucasia the Adzhar population, for example, tended to practice physical culture in the type of trousers traditionally worn by Adzhar locals. There is an account of one Adzhar instructor who wore shorts and was consequently ridiculed.[71] As the last chapter highlighted, clothing was highly symbolic, and this was not just in relation to women. In the Caucasus region it was noted that "a cultured boy ought to wear a local *papakha* (a tall Astrakhan hat) and that only in these conditions could there be work".[72] The recent work of Douglas Northrop shows

Figure 5.3   School sportswear. The caption accompanying this photograph of physical culture among national minority children reads, "Pay attention to the 'ungymnastic costumes' of the instructor and the schoolchildren", *Fizkul'tura v shkole*, no. 7 (1931): 31. Courtesy of the Russian State Library.

the significance of dress, clothes, and image, with the party's longstanding struggle concerning the veiling of Uzbek women highlighting the failings of Soviet policy in the outlaying territories of its vast borders. Physical culture and sport, touching upon these important issues of dress, meant that it conformed to one of those broader cultural policies not often welcomed by local populations.

By the 1930s conditions, on paper at least, seemed to be improving for schools in the countryside. Physical culture classes for two and a half hours a week and classes to be conducted by a specialist instructor were introduced in 1936.[73] Another significant boon for physical culture was that *sovkhoz* and *kolkhoz* schools were to function as physical culture centres all year round and were to extend their influence beyond schoolchildren to include all village youth and adults.[74] However, on the whole such positive developments did not necessarily entail support or success. In the 1930s physical culture in the villages was still struggling and propaganda largely ineffective. Books sent to the villages were unappealing and illiterate or semi-literate peasants struggled with scientific or technical manuals on physical culture.[75] In the absence of trained agitators and instructors there were calls for demobilized Red Army soldiers, Komsomol activists and even just "Bolsheviks" to become more involved.[76] To further help matters along, the young and active members of rural *kruzhki* were encouraged to conduct talks, lectures, and readings. Shock brigades were urged to go to the provinces to help educate the rural population in physical culture matters, but especially in hygiene and sanitation, whether personal, in the home, or at work. In spite of these efforts the authorities were still struggling to turn all citizens into *fizkul'turniki*. Moreover, this was soon taking place against the backdrop of collectivization; consequently any achievements in physical culture were overshadowed and rendered futile in the face of the hardship and upheaval experienced by those living in the countryside.

SHEFSTVO

Given the difficulties experienced in trying to transmit the importance of physical culture to rural and non-Russian societies, a more practical and direct way of reaching peasants was developed. This was the practice of patronage or *shefstvo* of physical culture. *Shefstvo* emerged in the 1920s as a solution to the divide between urban and rural societies and was an attempt to strengthen the worker-peasant alliance (*smychka*). The urban working proletariat was offered the "opportunity" to set an example to backward peasants through factory sponsorship of a village. *Shefstvo* applied not just to factories but also to universities, party schools, or military units—any group willing to assist and teach the "benighted". As Lynne Viola notes, the primary orientation of the movement was cultural, "limited to the organization of village libraries and literacy classes and the sending of literature and newspapers to the villages".[77] The *shefstvo* movement grew considerably throughout the 1920s, and by 1927, 1.5 million people were estimated to be involved in *shefstvo* work, with 59 per cent of these industrial workers and the rest soldiers or students.[78] *Shefstvo* was closely associated with shock-work, which had begun to exert a dominant influence over the nature of agitprop and could also be likened to *Kulturträger*, by virtue of its transmitting modernization ideals from city to village. Following the election campaign and during the initial years of the first Plan, *shefstvo* extended and assumed a somewhat different character, "when over one hundred thousand factory workers participated in one aspect or another of the implementation of state policy in the countryside".[79] These differed from the campaigns of the 25,000ers in that the latter aimed to recruit workers to "serve in permanent positions on the collective farms to ensure the reliability of the collective farm movement".[80] The campaigns and *shefstvo* that follow here were more relaxed, ad hoc affairs with less stringent criteria than those required to become a 25,000er.

In physical culture, *shefstvo* was most often carried out in the form of a factory or university agreeing to send instructors and agitation teams of *fizkul'turniki* to the villages. These would then propagate and help organize physical culture. Having already been firmly established in industry, many physical culture commentators believed that *shefstvo* could genuinely contribute to raising physical culture awareness and standards as well as help in the modernization of Soviet society. It was especially important for older or illiterate peasants who were excluded by other forms of physical culture agitprop carried out in the reading-rooms, in schools, or by the Komsomol. Physical culture *shefstvo* assumed various forms. Some argued that *shefstvo* did not have to be organized around one-day trips to the villages or restricted to demonstrations by the urban *kruzhki*.[81] Longer stays made more sense and should have proved more beneficial to the rural *kruzhki*. This approach would mean that propaganda workers would have more time to educate peasants and teach them some games and exercises as well as perhaps establish a relationship with them. Spending a few hours with the peasants was hardly going to turn them into instant *fizkul'turniki*. Limited resources more than likely meant that longer stays were not possible however. In any case the policy of *shefstvo* rarely met with much success and as Kenez comments the "visitors came, brought some gifts, provided diversions, and then returned home without changing very much in country life".[82] Lynn Mally makes similar observations relating to agitprop theatre, commenting that "agitators maintained that they could discover and isolate problems within a village after a few hours of hasty research and then eradicate them in the course of a performance".[83] The *shefstvo* scheme in many ways resembled little more than a public relations exercise to improve the image of urban/rural relations rather than assert any meaningful changes through agitprop.

An example of physical culture *shefstvo* in action was illustrated by the work of one brigade in northern Kazakhstan.[84] At the end of January 1930 Narkompros and the SKhLR (Union of Agricultural and Forestry Workers) Central Committee sent fifteen shock-worker brigades comprising eight people each to the main *sovkhozy* in the Soviet Union.[85] Each brigade had a doctor, schoolteacher, pre-schoolteacher, *fizkul'turnik*, political education speaker, a group speaker, and a librarian. The *sovkhoz* in northern Kazakhstan, the brigade noted, appeared to have "basic and backward Kazakh forms of physical culture" and it was in fact claimed that physical culture was non-existent until the arrival of the brigade.[86] The brigade's appearance and setting up of a *kruzhok* was reportedly greeted with much delight, as was the brigade's presence in general.[87] This "delight" must naturally be read with care. The brigade might have been reporting what they assumed their audience wanted to hear or the Kazakhs might have feigned this delight in order to temporarily satisfy Soviet demands and then return to their usual lifestyle. In any case, the *shefstvo* team claimed to have become heavily involved in its work and organized three groups—men, women, and children. However, this work was inhibited by some unforeseen problems. For instance, in spite of the enthusiasm reported, there were still only ten people in the *kruzhok*, and it proved difficult to involve adult workers in group activities.[88] There was also the problem of an absence of sports attire and inadequate accommodation. On a positive note it was discovered that almost all the workers had access to skis.[89] The brigade stayed for two weeks (after a journey lasting twelve days covering 240km by horse to get there!) and then returned to the city, dispatching a physical culture worker to oversee progress.

Having gone to so much effort (and cost no doubt) the *shefstvo* mission met with limited success. Only ten people attended the seminars organized by the brigade. Yet this was apparently not sufficient reason to be too despondent—as a result of the brigade's efforts these ten people "very consciously" related to physical culture and had received some political education, even if just a short anatomical and biological course on the basics of physical culture and materials pertaining to work habits, exercise, and games.[90] Still, this was hardly the "masses" that physical culture agitprop was supposed to be reaching. Even if the other fourteen brigades sent to the *sovkhozy* by Narkompros and the SKhLR managed to "convert" similar numbers of peasants to the practice of physical culture it was nevertheless a piecemeal effort. This was made all the more difficult because the *shefstvo* mission included just one *fizkul'turnik*. That Narkompros and the SKhLR saw it necessary to include a *fizkul'turnik* in the brigade is all the same significant. Along with teachers, a doctor, librarian, and political-educational agitator, a *fizkul'turnik* was deemed a necessary emissary of the new Soviet system. Nonetheless, this one *fizkul'turnik* was heavily burdened with organizing and disseminating the principle of physical culture. Such difficult experiences were not confined to physical culture.

Paula Michaels, in her work on biomedicine in Kazakhstan, has shown that the "red yurt" campaigns (more sustained and organized versions of *shefstvo* directed at advancing Soviet biomedicine) received mixed local reactions also, with activists struggling to convince nomads of the apparent benefits of Soviet power.[91]

Shefstvo campaigns in Russian villages noted similar problems to those encountered in Kazakhstan, with hostile locals posing a threat to campaigns. The successful construction of gym halls, clubs, sports squares, and football fields tended to win activists support in some instances, with old, "grey bearded men" who had previously run scared of physical culture now happy to wear shorts and vests.[92] *Shefstvo* agitprop seemed to increase considerably during the course of the Five Year Plan when workplaces and individuals were even more fervently encouraged to increase the tempo of social as well as industrial work. As a response to such calls one *kruzhok* stated that physical culture *kruzhki* were "growing every day, strengthening working youth and its immediate leadership, fighting with apoliticism, and seeking to realize the Five Year Plan in four years".[93] As a part of physical culture campaigns carried out by the party in the villages during 1929 and 1930, this *kruzhok* had sent twenty-five physical culture members to help in the practical work of the village councils and *kolkhozy*. In addressing collectivization, physical culture had been used for the harvest (*urozhaya*), where five brigades numbering eighty-seven in total had been sent to work in collectivization and the harvest.[94] There had been five meetings with peasants (who numbered about 1,031) on questions of collectivization and the harvest, about meeting the plan in the fields, about contracting, and concerning physical culture matters. It was proposed that they should conduct two physical culture performances and have ten physical culture "repair" brigades to help in repairing a sowing machine, a harrow, a winnowing machine, to help build a pigpen, and to plant fifty apple trees.

There were two different, though not mutually exclusive, types of physical culture *shefstvo* in action from the late 1920s and early 1930s. The first (the example in Kazakhstan) was where physical culture workers actually went to the provinces to teach the peasants about physical culture issues such as health, hygiene, and sports. It is reflective of the red yurt campaigns as discussed by Paula Michaels, where there were efforts to go to the people and educate them in the Soviet way of life. The second type of *shefstvo* (as in Leningrad example) had less to do with popularizing concepts of physical culture or culture per se and more to do with helping to reinforce the collectivization campaigns and assist peasants in their work on the *kolkhoz*. This kind of physical culture work was a major feature of the physical culture ideology during the Five Year Plan, where letters and reports to "our great leader, Stalin" recounted the lengths to which local factories and collectives had gone in spreading physical culture and relating it to their social and political work.[95]

A "POTEMKIN" PHYSICAL CULTURE

Under Stalinism more direct state control was sought and previous efforts to gently introduce the "new way of life" to the peasants were replaced by forcibly imposing socialist policies. In the countryside devastation was wrought through collectivization policies, famine, and demographic change. The relationship between the state and the peasants becomes further blurred in the 1930s, owing to what Sheila Fitzpatrick has described in Stalinist discourse as a form of "Potemkinism" in the villages, the depiction of a type of rural idyll where the "sun always shone".[96] Physical culture was a perfect medium for the Potemkinist spirit. In 1937 a rather typical piece of propaganda featured in the weekly newspaper *Krasnyi sport (Red Sport)*— lauding parachutists, snipers, and pilots—and which was dedicated to the "happy life" in the Soviet Union. The song proclaimed the joys and merits of physical culture and was reportedly the latest type of song popular among *kolkhoz* youth. The supposedly popular ditty came from Saratov where, according to its verse, all the rifle-shooting girls were very agile, grandsons taught their grandfathers how to wear an anti-gas mask, and girls no longer liked boys who could not shoot straight.[97] Girls were here portrayed as being successful physical culture participants, and young people were depicted as leading the way. In this *kolkhoz* song ordinary peasant boys were no comparison to pilots, parachutists, or snipers. Improving their fitness and honing their military preparedness was apparently the best way to a woman's heart in the new Soviet Russia of the 1930s. Soviet culture was being increasingly painted as an attractive, desirable, and attainable form of culture for all, whether male or female, worker or peasant.

Potemkinshchina seemed to gather force towards the latter half of the 1930s as physical culture campaigns and propaganda increased.[98] *Chastushki* such as the following were printed to attract villagers and show them that physical culture was healthy and fun:

If
You have been sitting for a very long time
You want to loosen up those legs
Go for a kick with a football and become good and happy

March on, rural physical culture![99]

While the sentiments expressed here initially seem quite curious—asking peasants who more than likely spent the day doing very physical farm chores to "limber up" their legs—this *chastushka* more than likely had another target in mind. It seems reasonable to assume that it was directed at the young men, usually aged seventeen to thirty years, who worked in the MTS tractor depots. Tractor and combine drivers, of whom there were more and more throughout the 1930s, often had to sit for long periods of time in conditions that were dirty, dusty, hot, and uncomfortable.[100] Exercise and sport such as football were precisely the kind of physical culture required by these drivers, according to physical culture and sports writers. Other propaganda included non-official, folk *chastushki* which some of the youth in Moscow Oblast' were apparently singing. They sung that they had long since passed the GTO norm and they now had their sights set on rifle-shooting and parachuting.[101] Such *chastushki*, which boasted of sporting achievement among the villagers, were supposed to "raise their mood" and, most implausibly, to "register the modern village's love for physical culture".[102]

Campaigns were then bolstered by "raids" on the *kolkhoz*. These raids were yet another form of agitprop specifically designed to target sleepy provincial villages and awaken in them a new-found love for physical culture. In a raid reported in *Krasnyi sport*, 162 new physical culture collectives were recruited in the *kolkhozy*.[103] In Alaverdy, Armenia, work was conducted among the local nationalities by organizing a competition. Before the competition there were only four Persians in the collective, but during the course of the competition more Persians had been attracted to the collective so that there were now twenty-seven in total.[104] In 1936 an article and photograph featured in *Krasnyi sport* drew attention to Shari Dzhumbaeva, the first woman from one of the national republics to become a physical culture organizer.[105] Although this was reported in the press as a success story, in reality it shows that it took many years for physical culture agitprop to reach and influence those in the provinces and republics. Ceaseless agitprop campaigns and raids were overt attempts by the authorities to force indifferent or even hostile peasants and national minorities into physical culture and sport. The problem with these campaigns was that, once they finished, the wave of enthusiasm associated with them also dissipated and so they often became short-term solutions to long-term problems. Raids, campaigns and competitions were deployed to round up locals and get them involved in some form of physical culture. Although some statistics suggested that regional, republican, and provincial physical culture were improving, these should be treated with a degree of caution.[106] The likelihood is that improvements were temporary, serving to satisfy the media desire for capturing the "potemkinist" mood.

The development of a rural form of Soviet physical culture did seem to have some genuine success stories. One positive step for physical culture would appear to have been the establishment in 1936 of the first rural voluntary society, *Kolos*. The society "produced good sportspeople" and had set up various sports teams including six football teams and seventeen volleyball teams, of which four were female.[107] There were positive accounts of some initiatives by local *kruzhki* towards improving *kolkhoz* physical culture and of village inhabitants who worked towards improving conditions in physical culture, especially for children, by working with the Komsomol *yacheika* to "help re-build roads and bridges".[108] More encouraging for organizers (and more closely related to actual physical culture) were the initiatives of the *Krasnyi Partizan sovkhoz* in Dnepropetrovskii oblast'.[109] The *sovkhoz* had 300 *fizkul'turniki* who regularly practiced physical culture and the *sovkhoz*, without any outside help, built physical culture squares and volleyball courts, and managed to construct a horizontal bar and trapezes. The volleyball team could then "prepare for the summer spartakiad". Another rural *kruzhok*" decided to build a *kolkhoz* stadium in the centre of the village. In the square where it was intended to construct the stadium, five peasant huts were destroyed, and within thirty-one days 150 *kolkhoz* workers were said to have completed construction of this stadium.[110] Assuming that any peasants living in the "destroyed huts" were rehoused, and the hastily constructed stadium was of sound structure, this was a positive development for locals with an interest in sport.

While local success stories show that some communities were indeed interested in physical culture, they also show that it was solely the collective will of these communities which determined the fate of physical culture. Local authorities and physical culture officials seemed to have other concerns. Whatever happy images of physical culture the state projected, whether through rural representations of *fizkul'turniki* on the farm or in the physical culture parades, in rural life it was clear that collectivization was the priority and any individual interests of the peasants were subordinate to this.[111] One *sovkhoz* director refused to organize some sort of sports square for the *sovkhoz* saying that "we never practice physical culture; we need to conduct the harvest campaign".[112] This happened in spite of the fact that the workers there had shown an interest in physical culture. A similar case occurred in another *sovkhoz* where the workers' committee "paid absolutely no attention" to the work of the eighty-five strong physical culture collective.[113] It was even stated that, if one out of ten *sovkhozy* was doing some sort of physical culture work, this was a very good result.[114] There were also the usual complaints of instructors who did no work. One instructor who was considered to be a very good sportsman did no work whatsoever. When only seven people attended the oblast' conference which he was supposed to have organized, he flippantly remarked that he would organize it another time.[115] There were other reports of no work being done. One representative from Georgia who had worked in the union for two and a half months reported that the cultural sector there was dealing with physical culture matters. It had a physical culture section, a wall-newspaper, and a radio, and was supposed to ensure that physical culture was included in its work. However, there was in fact no physical culture representative there and "the whole business existed on paper only".[116] In 1931 there was some official scepticism surrounding physical culture collective figures in Ukraine and as an acknowledgment of the problem there were calls for attention to be paid to reports citing a "growth in the collective" as a "large number" of collectives were really just "dead souls"—people signing up for physical culture to receive free equipment.[117]

Those in charge of organizing physical culture in rural areas were left on their own, with minimal support and seemingly no interest from Moscow. In a letter to Kharchenko one organizer in 1937 claimed that he had to work alone as two other workers had been transferred (while he had been absent on army service and other duties).[118] The basic message of his report suggested that, in spite of communication and local organizers conveying their concern to those at the top, they were left to deal with matters by themselves. There seemed to be either a lack of interest on behalf of the central authorities or there was a chronic personnel shortage. General reports and documentation confirm elements of both. The written evidence, as opposed to the visual, indicates that even by the late 1930s physical culture was not in a strong position. The existence (or non-existence) of "dead souls" floating around the countryside makes it difficult to assess the true success of physical culture and the impact that it might have had on the cultural development of peasants or national minorities. It also calls into question the actual commitment of the state to its ostensible task of acculturating its citizens, where promises of help and support increasingly resembled hollow rhetoric.

Figure 5.4 Some of the many problems with physical culture instructors. The caption accompanying this illustration reads, "In their personal lives instructors and leaders of physical culture often provide bad examples of *fizkul'turniki*. Only look at the meetings and conferences of instructors", *FiS*, no. 50 (1928): 11. Courtesy of the Russian State Library.

Agitprop efforts could not disguise that the dominant peasant attitude towards physical culture still appeared to be ambivalence. In the face of collectivization, famine, and a generally hard life in the provinces or republics, rural inhabitants seemed to have no particular appetite for physical culture (at least in its Soviet guise), and propaganda campaigns appeared to do little to change this. Rural priorities were aptly encapsulated by a letter from a physical culture organizer from an MTS station. Relaying the results of the MTS spartakiad to the *Kolos* voluntary sports' society's provincial bureau, he commented that all was satisfactory and 250 people turned up.[119] More tractor and combine drivers would have turned up, but some had work commitments and so either turned up late or not at all. The overwhelming impression is that the Soviet Union appeared to be haunted by a kind of "phantom" physical culture. Nor was the spurious state of physical culture one-sided; it was the result of both local and state attitudes. Irrespective of rural attitudes towards organized Soviet physical culture and sports, state support seemed to be lacking in providing even the most basic elements of physical culture to peasants and national minorities. As late as 1933 some rural communities complained of difficulties in obtaining soap, especially good quality soap, the absence of which deprived them of living "clean and cultured" lives.[120]

If obtaining soap was a problem, then obtaining sports equipment was an even greater one. When it came to sports inventory, rural areas lost out to the cities. Whereas the cities could count on receiving a massive 86 per cent of sports inventory, villages had to cope with just 14 per cent.[121] If voluntary societies such as Spartak or Lokomotiv could open their shops in the main provincial cities, it was considered that this would make a huge difference.[122] As it was though, these were concentrated in the major centres such as Moscow and Leningrad.[123] If the authorities really wanted to help physical culture in the provinces and national republics, why did they not focus efforts on providing more equipment and material resources? Even if funding was scarce, surely a more equal distribution between urban and rural funding was necessary, especially when the villages were so under-equipped and under-served by physical culture instructors. Either central authorities were unaware of the extent of the difficulties experienced in implementing physical culture in the provinces (unlikely), or they simply concentrated efforts in showcasing urban efforts and achievements, hoping that such successes would, somehow, eventually filter down to the "uncultured masses" elsewhere. Rural communities, in spite of the various plans for acculturation, continued to be marginalized by distance, under-funding, and general inaction on the part of local officials and those in authority.

THE RURAL WAY

In a biography written by one physical culture leader, physical culture was not a "career" he had worked towards or had been inspired to engage in owing to propaganda. It was simply the job in which he found himself working. Pavel Alekseevich Tishchenko was born in the village of Otradovka, Militopol'skogo Okrug in 1914 to a peasant family.[124] Between the ages of eight and eleven years Pavel completed four years of education and then worked with his father in the *kolkhoz*. In 1929, at age fifteen, he was sent by the *kolkhoz* to work in the town of Kherson on a construction project. When this finished two years later Pavel went to Kharkhov to work in a factory. There he moved up the ranks quickly. Having started out as an unskilled labourer he within a few months became a storekeeper, then a trainee lathe operator and after over a year he was working as a mechanical fitter. He was by this stage a shock-worker, Stakhanovite, and Komsomol member. In 1932 he joined the factory trade union and remained working in the factory for another four years. In 1936, at age twenty-two, Pavel was called to serve in the Red Army for one year until he was demobilized in 1937. The Komsomol then instructed him to work in a Moscow Oblast' *sovkhoz* school as a physical culture instructor. In 1938 he was awarded for his work by the MTS and received a tourist pass and 400 roubles. He was then transferred from the Moscow MTS to Kuntsevskii MTS where he continued to work as a physical culture leader. In November 1938 he was sent by the MTS to work in the Khot'kovskii *kolkhoz* rural mechanization school as a physical culture instructor. This was where his biography ended.

Tishchenko's story illuminates the incidental nature of physical culture for rural natives, and his biography is hardly exceptional in the overall context of the Soviet collectivization process. Having left the countryside for the city at the start of the first Plan he formed part of the broader population pattern moving from working in agriculture to working in industry. Also like many others, his time spent in the Red Army had brought him into contact with practices of training, discipline, and physical culture. Consequently he was considered a good candidate for physical culture instructor upon demobilization, as the Komsomol had quickly realized. There is no real way of knowing how Tishchenko weathered the Terror or what became of him following his appointment to the Khot'kovskii *kolkhoz* rural mechanization school. Whatever his fate, there were no doubt myriad other Pavel Tishchenkos produced by the Soviet system, who, lacking the drive and desire of some of those featured in Jochen Hellbeck's study of Soviet diarists, found themselves washed along by the political and economic tide and ended up in whatever occupation destiny or the Soviet system dealt them—in Tishchenko's case, as physical culture instructor.[125]

Rural physical culture was never in a particularly strong position. As Vladimir Brovkin has commented, peasants were the "people least affected by Communist propaganda" and "lived in their own cultural world quite apart from Communist visionary projections".[126] Life on the farm was a lifestyle and one that was not particularly accommodating to Soviet concepts of physical culture. Even if peasants and national minorities were receptive and eager adherents of organized physical culture, the resources for wide-spread uptake were anyhow not in place. Isolated rural communities were the last to benefit from sports equipment, facilities, or even just good quality soap. For the most part physical culture, in its organized, Soviet form, did not penetrate the villages until well into the 1930s, aided in particular by the schools and the curiosity and enthusiasm of rural youth. Those who were most affected by physical culture agitprop were thus the young who were exposed to it in the reading-rooms and schools, through the Komsomol and *shefstvo* campaigns, and perhaps by *otkhodniki*. These were also the type of rural inhabitants who were curious about urban life and the life lived by their urban counterparts. Or like Pavel Tishchenko they were sent to the city to work in the massive construction campaigns during the Five Year Plan and were drawn towards physical culture through the Komsomol, trade unions, or army service. The cause of any peasant, or indeed national minority, initiation into organized physical culture and sport was in many instances not a love of physical culture and socialist ways but rather a utilitarian response to circumstance.

6   Visualizing the New Soviet Citizenry

Hold up high the banner of Soviet sports!
Take broad strides from record to record!
Glory to the strong, the daring and the proud,
Patriots of the land of labour!

We have come from the factories and fields,
And our muscles hold the power of the people.
Our banner proclaims freedom and peace
For all the peoples of the world!

You represent a progressive land
And you must always come out in first place.
You go forth in the battle line
Of defenders of her sporting honour.[1]

In spite of the individual and collective hardships endured by the young, peasants, women, or national minorities, all were expected to participate in socialist life, and this included celebrations. New songs and heroes introduced in both everyday life and the ceremonial—what Robin refers to as the symbolic level of acculturation—were becoming more prominent features of Soviet life and physical culture as the 1920s progressed. Physical culture symbolism appeared to have become ever more pronounced with parades and festivals celebrating "the strong, daring and proud". Spartakiads and parades, by virtue of their mass nature and the element of spectacle, presented the state with a powerful visual "programme of identity". Physical culture and sports themes became popular among artists, sculptors, and photographers. Certain artists in particular came to be associated with this theme, for example, Aleksandr Deineka, Aleksandr Samokhvalov, Aleksandr Rodchenko, Gustav Klutsis, Ivan Shagin, Iosif Chaikov, and others. Paintings, sculpture, and other artistic forms became integrated into the everyday existence of *fizkul'tura* as stadiums, parks, and metro stations represented ideal canvases for *fizkul'tura* expression. Deinika's *Fizkul'turnitsa* and *Goalkeeper*, Samokhvalov's *Girl Wearing a Football Jersey* and *Girl with a Shot Put*, Chaikov's *The Football Players*, as well Mayakovskaya, Ploshchad Revolutsii, and Dinamo metro stations were all reminders of the relevance of physical culture in Soviet culture and society.[2] Meanwhile, the photographs of parades and festivals taken by Rodchenko and Klutsis captured not only the organization involved in such events but also their symbolic significance. The images they produced served to validate and reinforce the importance of physical culture and sport. Besides these, there were other visual modes of popularizing and indeed glamorizing physical culture. Films such as Dziga Vertov's 1929 *Chelovek s kinoapparatom* (*Man with a Movie Camera*) and Semyon Timoshenko's 1936 *Vratar'* (*The Goalkeeper*) served to bring *fizkul'tura* to an even wider audience, portraying *fizkul'turniki* as desirable, transformative, and inspirational.

While parades and festivals had been taking place since the revolution, their potential impact had not really been recognized. It was only with the momentum created by the Five Year Plan that the spartakiad and parade truly developed. The images produced by parades and spartakiads were in keeping with those of the New Soviet Person. They portrayed happy and healthy Soviet citizens who apparently derived immense pleasure from participating in Soviet life. With Red Square as the setting, the well-rehearsed participants starred in their very own Soviet fairytale. This chapter shows that parades were highly contrived and organized events, and if there was a "fairytale" quality then this was part of the constructed ideal. In many cases ordinary people cared little for such celebrations. Behind the scenes, parades were often the source of discord, petty competition, and stress. As the years went by, an increasing amount of planning and resources went into the production of these parades. The same could be said of the spartakiads. These grew in importance and prestige, diversifying from the major international spartakiads that were held every four years to the smaller scale factory and local spartakiads. Parades and spartakiads were to demonstrate a sense of community and show a united front, a feature also noted and exploited in other European countries. In Weimar Germany it was acknowledged that the "highest form of body culture is its representation of community".[3] In the Soviet Union the spartakiads and parades were also to cultivate an image of a harmonious national body and sense of community spirit.

Physical culture parades and spartakiads were important because bodily expression, as Mary Douglas notes, acts as a vital mirror of state concerns and attitudes. Douglas considers the importance of the body as a reflection of society, maintaining that "the social body constrains the way the physical body is perceived"[4] and that "the human body is always treated as an image of society".[5] Whether in public mass gymnastic displays, physical culture parades, or even personal exercises, how the individual body is perceived is important. The value of physical culture parades and body matters are also acknowledged in the work of Christel Lane.[6] In *The Rites of Rulers*, Lane notes that ritual is a "very important propaganda function"[7] and could be used "as a tool of cultural management and political socialization".[8] She convincingly argues that Soviet society was a highly ritualized society. Lane's stimulating discussion on body matters and the role of symbolism points to the significance of the symbolism of body movement in massed choirs, gymnastics displays, and military modes of action, showing how these events became much more regimented and organized in the 1930s.[9] As discussion of the physical culture parades will attest, Lane's argument is certainly true when it came to the organization of such mass, public events.

Parades, festivals, and celebrations assumed a variety of meanings under Stalinism. Some regarded celebration as a release, others considered it the ideal avatar of collectivist spirit and unity, while for a few celebrations and holidays often came to signify resentment in their Soviet incarnation.[10] One diarist from Tiumen wrote that the 1936 anniversary of the October Revolution with its display of posters, decorations, music, and shows was all "false and strained", and was a huge waste of resources when for the rest of the year they were subject to food shortages.[11] The express purpose of parades and festivals under Soviet power was not, despite some appearances, for participants and spectators to have a good time. Parades and festivals assumed a different conceptual dimension under socialism. Rosalinde Sartorti, in her article "Stalinism and Carnival", acknowledged that holidays were a means of educating the "illiterate masses who still lacked the necessary political consciousness through colours, images, slogans, sounds, in short, by acting on the senses, the visual and the auditive, what this new society was to be all about".[12] If anyone had been untouched by official propaganda campaigns, then surely they would take note of the parades and festivals. Malte Rolf convincingly argues that "[m]ass celebrations turned into a central reference point of the Soviet cultural cosmos and served as a metaphor of the better world that was being realized in the Stalinist Soviet Union".[13] Soviet festivals were above all else to serve as signifiers of the socialist good life, and no matter what the exact content (sporting or otherwise), this was the meaning they were to convey. Under Stalin, as Robert Edelman has observed, sports festivals were "not necessarily sports events [but] . . . political events that used sports as their subject".[14] In their official form, festivals and parades were designed to portray and reassert the might, glory, and unity of the Soviet Union. They were, in fact, designed to be the biggest propaganda coup of all.

SPORT IN ACTION: THE INTERNATIONAL SPARTAKIAD

Spartakiads almost rivalled parades as mass demonstrations of physical supremacy and bodily perfection. The difference was that these were a more serious sporting affair. Beginning in 1928, the International Spartakiad took place every four years, while in the interim there were national, republic, regional, provincial, and trade union spartakiads.[15] Although some of these provincial spartakiads, as Edelman comments, were only "glorified field-days", others yielded "impressive results".[16] The International Workers' Spartakiad[17] was to mark achievements in Soviet sport on an international level; the other spartakiads were to inspire and maintain the drive and motivation for sports success on an annual basis. All were to register the importance of Soviet forms of culture on the national psyche.[18] The official task of the spartakiads was to maximize the scope of membership in the trade unions, in the GTO, and among those involved in general shock-work, while the form and content of the spartakiads fused different elements of traditional western sports events such as the Olympics with Soviet idiosyncrasies, such as the inclusion of national dance.[19] The Spartakiad, like the Olympic Games, was a multi-sport event, so in essence the sporting content of the two events was more or less identical. Although Edelman contends that the "inclusion of military events, folk dances, and non-competitive pageants" distinguished socialist from proletarian sport, this feature was arguably another commonality between the two.[20] Just like the Spartakiad, the Olympic opening and closing ceremonies embraced the idea of mass participation with its parades of participants and it also devoted considerable time to mass artistic displays and dances. However, the Spartakiad did differ in that it included some particularly Soviet features such as the celebration of production and agricultural achievements, but essentially the concepts of mass demonstration and competition were generally the same as the Olympic Games.

In 1928 both the "bourgeois" Olympics and the proletarian Spartakiad were held with the latter including some 7,000 participants from the union republics as well as fourteen delegations of foreign worker sportsmen.[21] That the Olympics and Spartakiad were held in the same year was no coincidence, for the Spartakiad was to symbolize the supposed contrasts between western and socialist sport and, as Edelman argues, was a conscious challenge to the western Olympics.[22] For the Soviets, the spartakiads were to become the visual embodiment of physical culture and sports success. They demonstrated the alleged natural affinity of its citizens with socialist sport and represented the desire of the people to become involved in such events. Western, bourgeois sport, as epitomized by the Olympics, was looked upon unfavourably. Unsympathetic accounts of western sports events were provided, portraying a suitable contrast between "honourable and clean" socialist sports and "disreputable and dirty" bourgeois sports. This was evidenced further by a letter from an observer at the Amsterdam Olympics, who described the chaos involved in buying tickets to the Holland and Uruguay football match.[23] He bemoaned the enormous queues, the disregard for order, and the shameless speculation in the selling of tickets. It was noted too that the Olympics received substantial funding from the capitalists and that athletes had already been training for fifteen months.[24] The Soviet sports authorities, on the other hand, received "moral encouragement" and "organizational instruction".[25]

In a demonstration to highlight the importance of the 1928 Soviet Spartakiad, as well as to mobilize support and raise awareness, a magazine was established in its honour. Three months before the event was to take place, this magazine, *Spartakiada*, informed readers on preparations, locations of events, and the importance of physical culture and sport in general. It featured letters from the regions and accounts of physical culture festivals in the various republics.[26] In the run up to the Spartakiad short films were also to be used by local organizers in order to help train and inform others as well as to "show the achievements of socialist industry and culture".[27] Lasting just seven to ten minutes, these films would show how physical culture work was to operate in the factory, how to conduct internal factory spartakiads, or link physical culture work to *zaryadki* in the factory, *sovkhozy* or *kolkhozy*.[28] They were to address the different geographical and climactic conditions of the national republics and incorporate different national games and work processes (whether depicting the taiga, deer-hunting, cotton work, etc.). The films were to attract both Soviet and international attention as well as highlight Soviet achievements and capture the final months leading up to the Spartakiad.[29] Films such as these fitted in with the general trend of Soviet cinema which at this time, as Lynne Attwood and Catriona Kelly note, "mediated between transforming personal identity and official conceptions of national character, which were to become increasingly important as the internationalist ideals of the 1920s were eroded by the rise of a new Russian imperial spirit in the 1930s".[30] The combination of film and festival provided the perfect conduit for disseminating official ideals and concepts of Soviet identity to the wider public.

On the opening day of the Spartakiad mass events were to be organized, with a funfair, games, and activities for those gathering in the Lenin Hills. Dances from various national republics were to be an important part of the festival, with Ukraine, Uzbekistan, and other republics applying to participate in the festival.[31] This emphasis on national culture and folklore, so strongly projected in the 1930s, was already a strong presence in 1928. Spectacle was another important characteristic. There were 30,000 spectators and 10,000 participants expected to attend the event. On the Moscow River, a "grandiose" carnival was to take place with all the water-sports facilities illuminated.[32] From there all along the river as far as the Park of Culture and Leisure there would be an "arc of lights". Boats and other crafts would also be illuminated. Even more spectacular was the fireworks salute taking place every thirty minutes during the carnival. Prizes would be awarded to the most impressively turned out craft.[33] Competitions were to be run for the best sculptures, poetry, and art relating to the Spartakiad theme.[34] There could be no doubting that this event was to signify both the power and splendour of Soviet life, with a display of young and old, male and female, urban and rural united together in Moscow in a spectacular show.

Both the Spartakiad and the festival on Lenin Hills were accompanied by another celebration of physical culture, an exhibition at the Central State Institute of Physical Culture entitled "The Achievement of Physical Culture in Ten Years" that was open to the public from 10–25 August. The exhibition was to showcase physical culture over the last ten years and offer a picture of the "cultural construction" of physical culture from the October Revolution, demonstrating the "link between theory and practice in the areas of physical health, *vospitanie*, education, and strengthening of labour and fighting strength of the people of the USSR", and also to show the achievements in physical culture by the various republican Supreme Councils as well as in the departments and organizations.[35] Besides the exhibition there were also to be demonstrations of different types of physical culture (individual, corrective, and artistic gymnastics) and methods of scientific research, scientific speeches, and mass work. Competitions were to be conducted in the different aspects of physical culture, such as in the arts (sculpture, posters, etc.) and in the press. Apparently, there had been a lot of interest in the exhibition by those wanting to take part and any remaining republics or departments not involved were urged to hurry if they were to participate. All of these events, from the press reports, establishment of a magazine, films, carnivals, exhibitions, and other related cultural events conveyed a definite sense of anticipation and achievement, as local collectives and communities prepared to celebrate the first major International Spartakiad.

The Spartakiad functioned as an important means of drawing centre and periphery closer together and also of highlighting the superiority of the city. As James Van Geldern comments, "[s]ocial legitimacy was concentrated in the centre not as a monopoly, but as a point of distribution".[36] This was particularly so in physical culture and in the structure of the Spartakiad. It was assumed that everyone involved in sports and physical culture, whether in Moscow, Minsk, or Mongolia, had the ultimate ambition of participating in the national and international spartakiads to be held in the major Soviet cities and it was intended that their local, regional and republican spartakiads were a means of preparing for this occasion.[37] Almost all the provincial press reportedly carried a "Spartakiad Section" which addressed issues concerning the preparation and conduct of the Spartakiad. It was reported that workers from the localities requested holidays during the time of the Spartakiad so that they could travel to Moscow and see it for themselves. Narkompros had even organized excursion guides to help these visitors, arranged through an "excursion bureau".[38] These guides could help provide accommodation and meals for the visitors. Transport for all participants would be free courtesy of the provision of a transport pass.[39] The Spartakiad confirmed the pre-eminence of city over periphery and was in many ways just as much a celebration of Moscow city than Soviet sports. Excursions had even been organized where "specialist supervisors" would help not only in showing the "out-of-towners" the Spartakiad during their stay, but also acquaint them with Moscow itself, more particularly with its "economic and cultural achievements".[40] It was also a huge propaganda opportunity for sponsors. In the hostels and competition venues participants and visitors could procure literature, badges, and postcards from kiosks that had been organized by the publishers *Molodaya gvardiya* and *Fizkul'tura i sport*.[41] On the closing day of the Spartakiad the agitprop committee (of the Spartakiad organizing committee) had planned a concert for all the referees and participants which was to take place in the grounds of the Bol'shoi theatre.[42] The Spartakiad was not just a sporting but a social, cultural, and political affair that appealed to a much wider audience than just those interested in sports. Whether partaking or not, the Spartakiad in Moscow was the place to be in August 1928.

The International Spartakiad was also to function as a catalyst for other spartakiads and competitions throughout the Soviet Union. In 1931 the city committee secretariat requested that part of the MOSPS and regional committees include no less than 7 million people in mass physical culture events (in spartakiads, physical culture groups, out of town excursions, stadium events).[43] It also charged the MOSFK and physical culture bureau of the MOSPS with organizing gymnastics before work and during breaks in 100 of the city's main enterprises. It was hoped that factory and work-place spartakiads organized by the physical culture bureaus would revive worker interest in the physical culture movement.[44] These could just be oriented around general sports, based on previous spartakiad programmes, and could take place over the month of August. The spartakiads and propaganda accompanying them seemed to help in motivating at least some workers, schoolchildren, and the populace as a whole around questions of physical culture. According to one representative present at an All-Union Council meeting, the Spartakiad experience had "forced some people to stir".[45] He noted that during an evening organized to discuss the city spartakiad "the guys came forward and asked questions about the conduct of the [next] 1932 spartakiad—regional, provincial and all-union".[46] The trade union factory spartakiads were not just receiving additional attention among workers, they were also valued by the trade unions themselves. The VTsSPS considered industrial trade union spartakiads a "mass social, political and physical cultural event" in trade union preparations for the International Spartakiad. [47]

The International Spartakiad itself was considered an excellent means of measuring the standard of Soviet sport against that of other socialist countries and hence a good deal of prestige and significance was attached to it. If the Soviet Union wanted to lead the way in international sport, then success in the spartakiads was a crucial means of showing its supremacy as well as asserting a strong sense of national identity. It was widely acknowledged that physical culture was an important facet of general culture and therefore sporting dominance could become a metaphor for political and cultural dominance on an international stage. The Sportintern was another means of achieving this objective, although as Barbara Keys asserts, it "remained a marginal organization" that was "often ignored by the Comintern".[48] Energies were focused on the domestic sphere, with emphasis placed on spartakiads and parades. It was hoped that the Spartakiad would show that the trade unions and Soviet physical culture movement represented the "continued development of the world revolution of the workers' movement and that achieving the Five Year Plan in four years was of international significance".[49] Through physical culture and sports the links between culture and politics could be vividly expressed and used to demonstrate different aspects of the practice of socialism within the Soviet Union to a western audience. For Soviet citizens, meanwhile, domestic achievement and international success were to foster a greater sense of patriotism and national pride.

FACTORY SPARTAKIADS

Although the International Spartakiad took place only once every four years, there were other national events and celebrations of physical culture and sport. The major factory competitions and spartakiads, for instance, received much attention and press coverage. The programme for the trade union spartakiad, to be held in Moscow, was divided into three parts: mass, demonstration, and sports competition. The "mass" section included the inauguration of the spartakiad in the Central Park of Culture and Rest, the "avio-avto-moto-velo" (aviation-auto-motor-cycling) relay, and mass physical culture festivals in all the Moscow stadiums. It also included mass gymnastics and exercise routines by all involved, a mass pyramid titled "Forward to Socialism", cross-country races, as well as mass outings and excursions.[50] The "demonstration" element entailed holding exhibitions, shows highlighting the achievements of various industrial and agricultural sectors, the growth of the working class, and the success of physical culture organizations and other achievements. The spartakiad was, after all, not just a celebration of physical culture, but also of the trade unions and industry in general. It was to portray to spectators the vital organizational branches and "depict the everyday struggle of the working class for the construction of a socialist society".[51] As with mass events and demonstrations in other countries, celebrations were to provide a sense of achievement, unity, and community. This was the case in Weimar Germany also, where the "active participation of its citizens" embedded the "republic into a national tradition of German history and culture".[52] By encouraging active participation in such events, these newly established regimes attempted to construct and reinforce their own cultures.

When it came to organizing events on a local level, bureaucracy and local rivalries sometimes undermined central objectives. Rather than showcasing unity or the achievements of Soviet culture, the spartakiads often highlighted tensions. This was sometimes the case with local parades where in spite of "strict orders from Moscow . . . instructions often got ignored".[53] In one case in Kemerovo the regional council of physical culture experienced difficulties in dealing with the trade union bureaus of physical culture, which had a tendency to organize events independently of the regional council, under whose authority it ultimately belonged.[54] Matters came to a head when the regional council of physical culture wanted to organize a regional (krai) spartakiad in the town (now city) of Prokopyevsk for the central committee of coalminers for 12–18 July 1935. The council requested a programme for competitions and other related matters but in spite of this the central committee of coalminers refused to conduct any work, claiming that the central committee would carry out this work itself without the agreement or support of the regional council. As a result the spartakiad was "ruined" because the central committee did not organize the event properly. When teams arrived from Central Asia and elsewhere, they were not met by any officials and so, after wandering around for a few hours, returned home. In this case the disharmony between the trade unions and the regional council of physical culture hampered the implementation of central objectives. While this debacle cast doubt over harmony within local physical culture authorities, the keen interest of both parties in the spartakiad, however, suggests that such events were worth fighting over.

For the factories spartakiads raised a number of opportunities. One magazine article commented that, among the party committee and Komsomol, the spartakiad raised considerable interest, "especially when the physical culture bureau began to speak about including serious production performances in the spartakiad programme".[55] The party committee and Komsomol bureau were particularly interested in physical culture's use in fulfilling the *promfinplan* (industrial financial plan), in reducing absenteeism, and in the adoption of production techniques and technical studies. A love of sport and a burning desire to compete in the spartakiad were not enough for workers and so incentives were provided. The MGSPS physical culture bureau decided to hold a "general Moscow competition with bonuses for the best collective, city committee union, district council of trade unions", as well as providing bonuses to "individual workers in physical culture and *fizkul'turniki* for the best preparation and conduct in the factory spartakiad". The factory trade union committee (*zavkom*) would then "consider this decision and decide to allocate the prizes for the best shop and factory *fizkul'turnik*". The incentives appeared to work—it was noted that, since 1 June, the physical culture factory collectives had been hard at work in their efforts to organize the spartakiad and had managed to obtain material on how to organize the spartakiad programme.[56] Spartakiad participation certainly seemed to have been greeted with enthusiasm by the factories, which almost immediately noticed an opportunity to secure factory and shop pride in the event. This was frequently matched by the enthusiasm of factory workers who were presented with the possibility of rewards.

One of the most successful factories in physical culture and in the spartakiads was *Serp i Molot*. The *Serp i Molot* factory "recognized the importance of the general factory and plant spartakiads" and hoped to have four thousand participants in the 1933 spartakiad.[57] The *Serp i Molot* spartakiad was set to take place during July, and so all of June was to be spent conducting propaganda campaigns and organizing the shops and sections for the spartakiad. Other major factories, such as *Krasnaya Znamya*, were also able to boast of successes in physical culture, but beyond the biggest city factories physical culture struggled. Increased propaganda was, as usual, suggested as a means of raising its popularity. For example, the city committee union of RATAP[58] had organized a mass seminar for training referees for the factory spartakiad in athletics, military applied sports, volleyball, basketball, *gorodki*, swimming, and rowing to which *Serp i Molot* and other factories had sent their activists. Plans were also put in place for an All-Union children's spartakiad to be conducted among all children aged between twelve and sixteen years in factories where *shefstvo* work was conducted.[59] It appeared that all kinds of initiatives would be explored to popularize physical culture.

While the ostensible reason for factories and clubs to participate in physical culture was for self-improvement and for the good of the collective, the real reason for any participation was evidently often much more mercenary. In mobilizing busy workers incentives more often than not had to be used. While it was claimed that *Serp i Molot* workers would "fight for the red badge of RATAP" awarded to the best factory performance in the spartakiad, worker commitment did not derive from a love for physical culture. No doubt inspiring this "fight" was the news that RATAP "unlike some other city committees . . . would award a four thousand roubles prize to the best physical culture collective" and to the winners of the MGSPS competition for holding the best factory spartakiad. There were distinct parallels emerging between the conduct of the factory spartakiads and the wider problems afflicting sports. Shades of the Starostin affair and a desire to receive material rewards often surfaced as a motivating factor in factory spartakiad participation. The spartakiad, it seemed, drew attention to certain problems within factory life and socialism in general. Every shop *fizkul'turnik* and every shop worker, it was noted, had to participate in the spartakiad under their "own" shop.[60] If in subsequent or future spartakiads a worker transferred from one shop to another, then this worker must represent the older or "original" shop in the spartakiad. There were two possible explanations behind this request. First, it may simply have been the result of workers being promoted or transferring from one position to another—as Pavel Tishchenko's employment history showed, workers tended not to remain in the same job or position for very long in the 1930s. A second explanation behind the stipulation was that it was put in place to prevent workers from moving from shop to shop in pursuit of more favourable conditions or better rewards for sporting success.

The factory spartakiad system embodied both the good and the bad within Soviet society. The *fizkul'turnitsa* T. Khorosheva was the head of a collective from a Moscow bicycle factory where more than 30 per cent of workers at the factory were women.[61] She claimed that, because the head of the collective was a woman, more female workers were attracted to the physical culture collective (although this could have been simply a case of "quota filling").[62] As Chapter 4 showed, women were called on by the state to play an increasingly important role in society, with sport a vital part of this. Yet participation was not so straightforward, and the spartakiads proved this. Khorosheva would have had no problem participating in the spartakiad as the factory where she worked had a male majority. However, factories employing predominantly women found that their participation in spartakiads was extremely limited. This occurred because factories had to enter a certain number of male and female teams—if factories could not fill these quotas then they were denied participation.[63] For certain types of industries this was a major obstacle—for example, textile factories in particular, with a vast majority of female employees, would have been denied entry. Of course the same problem would have applied to factories with a male majority, but this was less of a problem because the rule allowed for more male than female teams. The spartakiads thus served as further evidence of how sport and physical culture were used—inadvertently or not—to help cement the hierarchy that had begun to permeate Soviet society since the Five Year Plan. The stratification of society was abundantly clear in physical culture, where opportunities and obstacles were placed before Soviet citizens who had little chance of determining which obstacles lay before them and when.

Spartakiads, it turns out, were a hybrid of festival and competition. In order to be a truly socialist event, they had to be differentiated from the capitalist Olympics. This led to a high dose of demonstration and celebration being injected into the Spartakiad, which still did not succeed entirely in distinguishing itself from the Olympics. In spite of this, the significance of the International Spartakiad should not be underestimated for it offered a valuable opportunity to test socialist sport (although Soviet athletes were not really tested against many successful international teams). Even more importantly than results however, they portrayed the right kind of image of the Soviet Union in the 1930s, the type of image that authorities wanted the world to see, as exemplified by the film *Sluchainaya Vstrecha*. They portrayed a strong sense of community and active participation in socialist life. As for the factory spartakiads, these had close ties to sports stars, privileges and rewards. Participants, regardless of the ideology, were not uniformly on a level playing field and certain factories and institutes, owing to better material conditions, held an advantage over less well off clubs and societies. It was also still evident that there were problems attracting women and that, when women did want to participate, they were hampered by the very system encouraging them to become more active.

PARADES AND FESTIVALS

Hey you, sunshine, shimmer brighter,
Make us glow with your golden rays!
Hey you, comrade! Liven up there!
Keep up, step up, don't hold us back!

To make our hearts and bodies younger,
Become younger, become younger,
Do not fear the coldness or the heat.
Harden yourself, like steel.
Physicult-hurrah-hurrah-hurrah!
Be ready!
When the time comes to beat the enemy,
Beat them back from every border!
Left flank! Right flank! Look sharp![64]

According to one observer, Evgenii Riumin, mass proletarian festivals embodied the artistic and organizational visions of the revolution.[65] He considered that the immense organization and rhythms of proletarian festivals set them apart from bourgeois carnivals. The inclusion of physical culture elements was intrinsic to the success of a parade or festival and with this, he added, would come "increased organization and rhythm". The spectacle of seeing masses looking "sharp" and steel-like, as the *Sportsman's March* called for, as well the demonstration of such "intense discipline, exactitude, and dynamism" as described by Riumin, could be channelled through physical culture. All of this, Riumin argued, was reinforced by the powerful music, songs, words and movement. What was essentially created, Riumin averred, was a "living picture".[66] The depicted stars, pyramids, and other formations were images that reflected the "strength and agility of the collective". These festivals offered organizers the opportunity to promote military movements and skills, as well as exhibit national dances and the customs and costumes of the various nationalities participating.[67] He pressed for increased attention to be paid to parades, as they were such a valuable form of "organizing mass energy and impressing meaning and significance upon spectators". Yet as Riumin noted, the key ingredient was organization—these parading masses had to be strictly organized and controlled so as to avoid creating a scene of chaos and disorder. Images and iconography were an essential part of the "socialist myth". The images of those celebrating on Red Square and on the streets of the capital thus had to correspond to the political images of the state—structure, order, control, strength, and collective unity were to be portrayed through the parades.

It was only in 1927 that any significant attention was paid to physical culture parades and festivals as a major mobilizing force.[68] Until then, the primary concern of those in charge of physical culture had been organizational, health, and hygiene matters. When the Five Year Plan was introduced, parades were used to relate physical culture to industry and labour. By the early 1930s, parades and spartakiads were receiving increasing coverage, designed to reflect both the apparent general progression and expansion of physical culture and sport as well as the image of a modern, developed nation. Celebrations were viewed as the physical embodiment and expression of socialist achievement and were considered the ideal means of celebrating the Five Year Plan as well as the Spartakiad.[69] This thematic link to industry and achievement continued into the 1930s. In preparation for the 1933 parade, the Moscow Party City Committee stated that the parade should "reflect and be a powerful demonstration of the spirit of production and the Bolshevik struggle for a higher quality of work".[70] Factories, plants, and VUZy sent 70,201 of the best "shock-*fizkul'turniki*" to the parade.[71] On the façade of the executive committee's building there hung banners on which were written several slogans, including "Towards 10 million Soviet *fizkul'turniki* in the International Spartakiad!" and "Towards 2 million passing the GTO norm!"[72] Shock-work and record-breaking had come to infiltrate every aspect of Soviet life, including sport and physical culture. The parades and spartakiads served to further the worker's conscious engagement with the regime.

As the scope and scale of celebrations seemed to increase year by year, so too did the organizational input involved. City committees had to achieve certain targets and delegate responsibilities to the appropriate organizations such as the trade unions or Komsomol. They had to nominate and liaise with a special committee to oversee the implementation of the proposals and the general organization of the parade. The party district committees were to "observe the course of the parade in the districts".[73] With Moscow as the centrepiece and focal point of physical culture celebrations, the Moscow Party City Committee was under more pressure than most. Immense targets had to be met. For example, 75,000 *fizkul'turniki* were to participate in the 1932 parade, with 50,000 from the trade unions, 14,000 from the VUZy, 5,000 from Dinamo, 3,000 from TsDKA and 3,000 from the industrial cooperatives.[74] These figures were to include shock-workers, the "best physical culture workers", and recipients of the GTO norm.[75] By the time all of these groups congregated in Moscow to salute Stalin and the party, countless hours had been spent on organization by those in the various councils and committees as well as by the workers involved.

Just a few days before the 1932 parade the Moscow City Committee secretariat stipulated that "sections of the physical culture council, Moscow City Committee, Komsomol and MGSPS conduct before May 13 [the date of the physical culture parade] a meeting of *fizkul'turniki* and *komsomol'tsy*" as well as conduct short talks with the workers during their dinner-breaks on the significance of physical culture.[76] In the immediate run-up to the parade intense preparations were underway. Besides meeting targets and overseeing the conduct of the parades, those involved in the organization of the parade still had to hold agitprop sessions to motivate the workers. That the workers' dinner-breaks were to be the scene of physical culture talks indicated the significance of the parade and the time required to organize it. Not only were workers targets of *fizkul'tura* in their morning exercise classes and possible evening meetings in the club, but in the build-up to parades they were also subjected to increased physical culture agitation. Parade season meant more than just rehearsals and participation for workers—it also meant sacrificing their dinner-breaks. Even if sports were genuinely popular amongst the workers, it is likely that not all welcomed the increased agitation accompanying parades. Whereas Thomas Alkemeyer has argued in the national socialist context that through physical culture and sport the state's agenda was not forced upon an individual but rather became embodied so that it was not experienced as external compulsion but as inner nature, this was not quite the same in the Soviet case.[77] People were firmly pushed and persuaded to participate in physical culture activities, irrespective of consent. Following propaganda lectures held in April in preparation for the 1 May 1935 demonstration, some workers admitted that they could not remember the content of some of the speeches nor did they understand what they were about.[78] Yet such meetings and talks were considered necessary and after all, each level of organization involved in the parade, from the Moscow city committee to the ordinary worker, had specific jobs to do and roles to play if the "fairytale" was to be realized in practice.

Some workers could not hide their dissatisfaction with the regime. Party cadres working in the Moscow city committee in April 1935 reported ongoing difficulties with mobilizing workers for the 1 May parade. There were various reasons for worker discontent including no pay, not enough bread, exhaustion due to continuous work (some reported working fifteen days with no break) and having to work with poor equipment.[79] All of this had lowered morale and had even led to the perception that the party did not care about them. One woman commented that life was "better under Tsarism"—if in need one could "go to the palace and ask for charity whereas now this was impossible".[80] Similar sentiments were echoed by workers in Tula, who claimed that "the devil doesn't need this festival when there's nothing to eat. Before in the prisons they ate better—now we're being starved to death".[81] Even Nikita Khrushchev recalled the hunger of the early 1930s, remarking, "[i]t was a hungry time back then, even for people like me who held fairly high positions . . . even in your own home you couldn't always eat your fill".[82] Hunger was a primary reason for disenchantment with parade participation and some factories had a significant number of workers who did not turn up to the parades. One absentee worker commented "give me a can and I'll go".[83] Another despondently remarked that "under Communist power not even black bread was to be found on May 1", while another commented that they did not know whether their weary legs could carry them home, let alone to the demonstration.[84] A worker who had previously attended a parade remained unimpressed: "I went once . . . what did I get out of it? I just wanted to eat".[85] While some cited other reasons for not wanting to attend demonstrations, with one saying, "I don't have a good dress. I'm ashamed to go like this"—it was generally the lack of food that was the most frequently cited and biggest obstacle in mobilizing the workers to attend parades and festivals. The concerns of the party and organizational committees were far removed from the real concerns of ordinary citizens, who cared more about food and clothes than parades.

Officially parades were to be positive, happy occasions but with very serious political and social overtones. There was no mention in the press of hungry spectators—the focus was securely fixed on healthy and happy looking participants. Parades brought together all of the various elements within the physical culture family—the party, organizers, participants, and spectators. The sole objective of the parade, for organizers at least, was to impress the party, but all of the family members had different agendas. In public, sport, labour, and defence remained the ostensible goals. As one keen participant from the 1932 parade commented, physical culture was not just "about looking good for a day on Red Square—it was about devoting serious attention to sport".[86] Parades affirmed the might and solidarity of the Union, leaving no doubt that its citizens would be prepared to defend the country "at any moment".[87] It was observed that these parades were the "future social form demonstrating military preparation of *fizkul'turniki*" and showed that the Soviet physical culture system and the GTO complex engendered considerable physical culture successes. Parades, it was claimed, represented the "supreme form of demonstration and review of physical culture mobilization and organization". Their value was recognized by the presidium of the All-Union Council of Physical Culture, which considered:

> The enthusiasm and great activity of the Moscow and Leningrad *fizkul'turniki* in their preparation for the parades, the widespread involvement and help of the Soviet social organizations in organizing the parades (especially the Komsomol), in every way underlined the new importance assigned to modern physical culture parades, which embodied the ideals of preparation for labour and defence of the workers as its basis. The parades exemplified the system of physical culture as a mass form showcasing their achievements and in the militarization of physical culture; the parades represented the strengthening of organization and discipline.[88]

It was further noted that, in the 1933 parade the Moscow and Leningrad Institutes of Physical Culture, had, "as ever", performed supremely and had demonstrated the "highest forms of exercise techniques . . . showing the extremely high standard of the students".[89] The All-Union Council acknowledged the high quality of physical culture work and organization bestowed by the GTO system. The All-Union Council's statements were rather sombre ones, focusing on labour, discipline, and defence achievements and lacking any sense of celebration or frivolity, as one might normally expect from a "festive" occasion.

In spite of the outwardly celebratory nature of the parades, they continued to be the subject of extremely serious objectives. As if to signify their increasing importance, this solemnity was accompanied by rising participation figures. For the 30 June 1935 parade on Red Square, there were to be 100,000 participants.[90] The primary goal of the 1935 parade was:

> [t]o showcase the high quality of physical *vospitanie* of the workers, reflecting the full preparation of *fizkul'turniki* towards the defence of the socialist motherland, demonstrating the devotion of *fizkul'turniki* to the Bolshevik party and to its leader and teacher of the people, Stalin.[91]

Discipline and organization were reflected in the formation of the parade. This was to consist of the trade union physical culture organizations and enterprises according to district, different types of sports, and voluntary societies. According to this model, the parade would be formed of columns from Dinamo, Spartak, TsDKA, the columns of trade unions (according to sports), and columns of cyclists.[92] Once again, it was stated that these had to be the "most devoted, cultured and physically developed" *fizkul'turniki*, as well as medallists.[93] The Moscow City Committee also entered a team of some two thousand factory workers to perform free exercises in the 1935 parade, although in order for the team to represent "culturally and physically developed" *fizkul'turniki*, all participants had to take a full three days off work to rehearse in the run-up to the parade.[94] The workers must not have been particularly "devoted" to the cause either, as they had to be offered a 50 per cent discount on sports costumes and would be provided with free food during rehearsals.

The structure of parades imposed a hierarchy on its participants. All marched according to their importance. The leading column was the State Institute of Physical Culture, followed by the Moscow technical secondary school of physical culture, the Pioneer column, the column of participants for the gymnastics performances, the columns from the Leninskii and Stalinskii districts, the trade union columns, the columns from the Fruzenskii and Proletarskii (home to *Serp i Molot*, Dinamo motor plant and AMO automobile works) districts, the railway workers, the Dzerzhinskii and Sokol'niki districts, Osoaviakhim, the Krasno-Proletarskii and Oktyabr'skii districts, Spartak, the Red Army, Dinamo, and finally, the cyclists.[95] The performance of *fizkul'turniki* from the main enterprises with the gymnastics section and those in the pyramid were to consist of 500 participants. The trade unions and other "corresponding physical culture departments" were to finance the parade.[96] Evident from the order of the parade were a number of hierarchies within both physical culture and Soviet society in general. For instance, the educational institutes unsurprisingly claimed prime position, as these were responsible for the instruction of physical culture and consisted of the best conditioned and most devoted *fizkul'turniki*. With these then followed by the

Pioneers and a gymnastics display, the image of a young, healthy, and vibrant nation was reinforced. The eight districts of Moscow, divided into couplets of four and wearing their individual district colours, were next and led by the Leninskii and Stalinskii districts. Regardless of numbers or geography, these districts no doubt led the way owing to their names alone. Next on the list were the trade unions, their prominent position highlighting their importance within the physical culture organization. The railway workers—one of the most dominant unions within physical culture—came next and were then followed by Osoaviakhim. That some of the more defensive groupings within physical culture were placed towards the rear of the parade was somewhat unusual but may have been explained by the desire to have those groups specifically associated with youth at the helm or also in a more practical sense because defence and military groups were often accompanied by tanks and equipment. Very last in the parade were the cyclists, with the fear of accidents and time-delays no doubt having influenced this decision.

Figure 6.1 A sports parade in Red Square, Moscow, from Bertha Malnick, *Everyday Life in Russia*.

Parades revealed other hierarchies too. This was particularly so with the national republics, and as Karen Petrone has argued, "[t]he symbolic construction of the Soviet nation clearly revealed the contradictions inherent in Soviet nationality policy", as "the nationalities section of the parade affirmed Russia's geographic and ethnic hierarchy", with the Russian republic marching first.[97] The 1939 Physical Culture Parade, with the general theme "Friendship of the Peoples", placed particular emphasis on the contribution of the national republics to the Soviet Union. Parade directors and organizers were given creative licence to construct what Robin calls the "social imaginary" and illustrate the new Soviet culture. The performance of each national republic was clearly defined and rehearsed, and only approved when all the necessary arrangements were in place. Artistic and design standards were to be met, with a certain degree of thematic consistency to be attained by all eleven republics. No republic was to have more than 200 participants, and no performance was to last more than eight minutes.[98] All republics were to portray, through physical culture, the successful and happy life of national republican citizens. More or less the same image was to be portrayed internationally at the Soviet Pavilion at the 1939–1940 New York World Fair, where a quickly paced physical performance with fast changing scenes was to show "colourful pictures of Soviet national culture", with "happy young people . . . in national costumes", moving to national music.[99] These young people, the best *fizkul'turniki* from the republics, were to perform different types of national sports which showed their "strength and dexterity" as well as "a willingness to defend". The physical culture performance was acknowledged as being "unusually broad" so as to convey to the world a sense of the uniqueness of the Soviet character.[100] This uniqueness was, ironically, not always appreciated by Soviet authorities. Even for the 1939 parade Tadjik men were prevented from wearing traditional wide trousers (*sharovary*) and were forced to wear shorts.[101] While wearing wide trousers might have been permitted in their native clubs, for a national performance participants had to conform to accepted standards of Soviet physical culture.

SPORTS PARADE OR BEAUTY PAGEANT

The structural hierarchy of the parades was accompanied by a physical hierarchy. Parade participants had to be "thoroughly selected" and only "leading shock-workers and the best *fizkul'turniki* who had passed the GTO norm and been awarded the badge" could participate in the parade.[102] In the press coverage of the May 14 parade in 1933 it was reported that, to the "sound of drums, the creative march of the Moscow *fizkul'turniki* began".[103] Among their ranks almost every fifth person bore the GTO badge on their chest. According to one account, "with a firm, measured pace and lively bronze bodies, wearing their white sports attire and a twinkle in their eyes, [the participants] marched forward on to Red Square".[104] They were followed by detachments of "joyous" Pioneers, gymnasts, footballers, boxers, and other athletes. With image becoming increasingly important the physical culture parades sometimes blurred the lines between talented sportspersons and those who simply looked good. Svelte, muscular, and tanned bodies streamed by the streets onto Red Square as successful young men and women in colourful shorts and vests were watched by thousands of spectators. This was adjudged to be the best way of showcasing the health, pride, and happiness of the Soviet Union. As Petrone notes, the preoccupation with appearance was what distinguished the physical culture parades from others, with officials specifically instructed to "pay attention to the people on the right-flank . . . [where] there should stand a strapping, healthy, suntanned Communist or Komsomol".[105] Petrone notes too that the quest to find such rare commodities led to competition amongst the various institutions, shaping "regional and institutional identities" as healthy athletes denoted status.[106]

In its discussions of the 1934 parade, to take place 24 June, the Moscow City Committee stipulated that it show the "real strength of physical culture in the city of Moscow".[107] In doing this, they were to "organize the selection" of physical culture strength according to enterprise, choosing only "the best, most physically developed *fizkul'turniki* for participation in the parade".[108] Appearance was now deemed even more important than ability, as it was noted that these "well-developed" *fizkul'turniki* should be selected regardless of whether or not they were GTO medallists. This favouring of appearance over ability is confirmed by Petrone's research, where she notes the warning given to local cadres by trade union officials in Moscow region: "When you are forming up your ranks, do not include people who are particularly small, even if they are people with merit, because we need to show a healthy, tanned person, a Stalinist athlete".[109] Stalin seemed to appreciate the effort. When congratulating Shura Kirichenko of the Ukrainian Physical Culture Institute (who had been nominated to present Stalin with flowers), a delighted Kirichenko claimed that Stalin "approvingly commented on the beautiful tans of the *fizkul'turniki*' and on the "successful formation of the columns".[110] The excitement experienced by Kirichenko on meeting Stalin was not shared by all. The selection process involved in the parades must have alienated those who were not selected. When only 600 out of the 700 who attended rehearsals in *Serp i Molot* were selected for the parade, how were the excluded 100 who had spent hours rehearsing to feel? How could the Soviet state proclaim to stand for unity and collectivism when it disregarded its prized workers for not looking good enough for the *vozhd*? Some did not seem entirely pleased. Even as early as 1931 one *Serp i Molot* footballer remarked that, of the 250 *fizkul'turniki* chosen to represent the factory in the parade, only 100 were genuine sportspersons. *Fizkul'turniki* who excelled at sport but who were not chosen because of their physical appearance had to work side by side with those who may not have been as good or committed as them, but who looked more like a "Stalinist athlete".

Such attitudes also manifested themselves in the middle and lower level bureaucracies involved as institutions and committees responsible for parade organization became ever more preoccupied with image and appearance. Selecting the right athlete was only half the battle. Having gone to so much effort in choosing the most impressive bodies, it was important that they be draped in the appropriate clothing. There was much discussion surrounding the vests and shorts participants would wear, including sourcing the necessary dyes from abroad and improving the quality and distribution of sporting attire.[111] Curiously, there was a concern with what exactly should be done with these vests and shorts afterwards.[112] Should participants keep them? Should they be returned to the clubs? There was a strong argument for returning them to the clubs so that they could be recycled for the following year's parade.[113] In the army the matter of returning these was standard practice, but this had to be done immediately after the parade or else they would be "leaked".[114] Implementing such a policy for the voluntary societies would have been considerably more difficult. One frugal society representative asked, "Are we so wealthy that we can afford to produce clothing for just one day?"[115] Adding insult to injury was that the sports costumes were viscose, a fabric completely impractical for sports.[116] Yet, in spite of the concerns of some cost conscious organizers, the notion of recycling ran contrary to the general Soviet predilection to outdo past achievements— nicer and more impressive costumes would have to be worn in the next parade. Each year saw the parade introduce something new and original, and costumes were presumably to be no different.[117]

While some of these matters may seem trivial, they were real and serious issues for parade organizing committees. In organizing the 1936 parade, a Zenit committee was critical of some of the parade features from the previous year. The committee was unanimous in its criticism of a car being used in the parade—this was not "physical culture". If a car had to be used again, then there should be a *"fizkul'turnik* or *fizkul'turnitsa* sitting in it".[118] Questions over portraits of the party leadership and Stalin in particular were dwelled over for quite some time, as were any formations or slogans situated near these. Those watching the 1936 parade more than likely did not realize the deliberations involved in how best to display and arrange the words, "life has become better, life has become merrier".[119] Choosing a good artist for the *"oformlenie"* or design was very important and great lengths were gone to in getting the best.[120] Also at the Moscow city committee meeting it was noted that all district committees of the party be made aware of the "appropriate political preparation for the parade in the districts" and to check the "quality of physical culture organizations, taking the necessary measures to provide a timely and organized presence of *fizkul'turniki* in the parade".[121] Not only were these participants acting as a reflection of the state, but they were also representing their factories, clubs, institutions, and organizations. Therefore there was not just enormous pressure on the relevant organizations to select the "correct" participants—there was also a degree of pressure on the participants to perform well and not let their fellow workmates, classmates, or organizations down. There was of course the added pressure of the "omnipresent conspiracy" that, as Malte Rolf explains, "left its imprint on Soviet festival style, turning any variance from the norm into a political statement of potentially 'anti-Soviet' subversion".[122] The smiles and celebrations on the big occasion no doubt masked a great deal of tension felt by organizers and organized.

Tensions seemed partly justified, as Stalin did take an interest in the parades and their *oformlenie*. Having watched recordings of parades filmed by head of *Soiuzkino*, Boris Shumatsky, Stalin commented on the Leningrad athletic parade and 1 May parade, observing that the "music has to be synchronized" and that the full scale of the parade be filmed so as to show it as "mass and imposing".[123] He requested that these films of parades be shown in two to three parts, insisting that "such chronicles are politically important historical documents" and that such documents should "be seen by millions".[124] He also made suggestions as to film content, such as including the military salute and three to four fast moving tanks but excluding segments of film showing the *kolkhozy* from Uzbekistan, Baku, and Ukraine.[125] Stalin had evidently noted the propaganda value of the parades. To further emphasize the importance of image and physical culture, a special documentary appeared in 1938, titled *The Song of Youth*, which told the story of the 1938 physical culture parade and Soviet physical culture in general. When this film opened less than a month after the parade, it was shown daily in fifteen Moscow cinemas.[126] Through their involvement in the parades ordinary Soviet citizens—the participants and spectators—had now inadvertently come to serve the functions of target, subject, and producer of state propaganda.

Parades and spartakiads exemplified the pre-eminence of the body in Soviet society. The body and body image were fundamental to the physical culture ideology, and attaining bodily perfection was an obligation that every citizen was to fulfil. The ideology of the socialist world strove to create the ideal form, the New Soviet Person. This person was above the mundane, base level of the older, ordinary person. The Soviet person was aesthetically pleasing—in the sense that he or she was physically strong, agile, and well-formed. As Karen Petrone commented on body symbolism, "[t]he naked, tanned flesh and well-developed muscles stood for the might of the Soviet nation".[127] Body imagery played a significant role in this society, where not being able to join in with the masses and embrace the collective spirit often meant social isolation. This is attested in the diary of Zinaida Denisevskaya, as examined by Jochen Hellbeck, where she acknowledged that the "chief agent preventing her absorption into the collective organism of Soviet activists was her failing body".[128] She admitted that she "didn't have enough strength to join their ranks" and was thus "doomed to loneliness" until her death.[129] When Denisevskaya eventually did summons the strength to march in a demonstration, she enjoyed the sense of "merging with everybody", becoming in essence a "one million headed body".[130] For that brief moment, Denisevskaya felt complete, a true member of society. She wanted to belong to the "social imaginary".

State control was wielded through a combination of repressive measures but also through the stimulation of desire. The latter form of control is what is really relevant to sport and physical culture in the Soviet Union. The projection of desirable images—those of tanned, toned, attractive athletes—was a direct effort by the state to influence society's perception of the ideal Soviet body. As Hellbeck observed, "the Soviet regime prodded individuals to consciously identify with the revolution . . . and thereby to comprehend themselves as active participants in the drama of history".[131] People were encouraged to embrace and emulate these images of Soviet life, images which seemed attractive. French sociologist Pierre Bourdieu stated:

> If most organizations—the Church, the army, political parties, industrial firms, etc.—put such a great emphasis on bodily disciplines, it is because *obedience exists in large part in belief,* and belief is what the body . . . conceives even when the mind . . . says no . . . It is perhaps by considering what is most specific in sport, that is, the methodological manipulation of the body, and the fact that sport, as all disciplines in all total or totalitarian institutions, such as convents, prisons, asylums, political parties, etc.—is a way of *obtaining from the body a form of consent that the mind could refuse,* that one will best manage to understand the use that most authoritarian regimes make of sports.[132] (emphasis my own)

From Bourdieu's perspective, if the mind was initially unwilling, then the body could be used to establish control, hence the importance of body images and body symbolism. Bourdieu's ideas on "totalitarian institutions" are somewhat simplistic, however, as the totalitarianism model has in many ways been deemed unsuitable for examining the Soviet system, considered a relic of Cold War ideologies and politics.[133] Nonetheless, his statement does highlight two points in particular. First, it draws attention to the importance of the body as distinct from the mind. States, whether "totalitarian" or not, recognized to varying degrees the important role of the body as a form of manipulation, persuasion, or inspiration. This was made clear by the Soviet use of physical culture parades and festivals. Following on from this is the second point, the use of sports by different regimes. In spite of population management, Soviet state use of sports and the body did not always equate with control. Many of those marching on Red Square in sports formations might have been demonstrating their support for the regime, but others might have been simply showing support "in body" but not "in mind". Similarly in the factories workers might have gone to meetings and attended parade rehearsals, but attendance at such events was expected, if not compulsory, and even so not all workers paid attention to political education. Again, there were perhaps cases of "speaking Bolshevik" (Kotkin), with physical culture discourse showing that control and desire worked in a variety of ways.

THE SOCIAL IMAGINARY

Visual culture was very much a part of physical culture, and the parades and spartakiads provided abundant evidence of this. Parades and spartakiads reinforced more than just the significance of physical culture and sport—they reinforced state objectives. Discipline, order, organization, success—these were all objectives of the parades and also the spartakiads. Yet in the quest to achieve these something important was lost—fun and spontaneity. For some the parades and spartakiads came as odious obligations; for others, a means of integrating into the new society and a possible opportunity to further their lot in it. It might have seemed that those who derived most enjoyment from the parades and spartakiads were the spectators who did not have to suffer the rehearsals and pressures associated with performing. As it transpired, however, many of the spectators, hungry and tired, did not want to be there at all. So although the parades and spartakiads were used to demonstrate popular enthusiasm and participation in sports, this was not always the case. In many instances selection was not even based on merit—perfectly capable *fizkul'turniki* were excluded because they did not look the part. Those in the parade had been selected on appearance just as much as for ability. As previous chapters showed, basic equipment and facilities were still lacking, and much of the population were ambivalent or indifferent when it came to matters of hygiene and sport. More than anything else spartakiads and parades represented the state's concerns with discipline, image, and order, and bureaucratic interpretations of how these concerns should be carried through in practice. Parades and spartakiads projected an image of Soviet sport that was designed to inspire a sense of pride and community as well as patriotism. For short periods of time, physical culture, through parades and spartakiads, enabled the state to portray a united, happy front, an image that will shall soon see was in fact a world away from what was actually happening in the everyday practice of Soviet physical culture and sport.

7   The New Soviet Citizen in Reality

When at the end of 1935 Stalin stated that "life has become better, life has become merrier" and the Stalin Constitution of 1936 declared socialism to have been achieved, it was of no surprise that changes in physical culture would soon be afoot. As a reward for their contribution to the Plan and socialism, workers could now take the opportunity to enjoy their leisure time. The best way of capturing this "happy" new citizen was in a moment of leisure. Involvement in physical culture and sports came to be viewed as the perfect snapshot of the New Person and the perfect complement to images of parades and festivals. Whether sportspersons training in the stadium or a family day-out in the park—these were healthy and wholesome images fit for mass production. They simultaneously depicted a happy nation and instructed their citizens on how to behave in their leisure time.[1] The possibility of the average worker accessing leisure became more achievable in the latter stages of the 1930s as infrastructure and amenities were being constructed. One of the most dominant advertisements of this was the Park of Culture and Rest, or Gorky Park. This was described as the "factory of the new man" and a "school of happiness, of sensible rest, cultural recreation, healthy cheerful laughter, vigorous sport . . . [and] the new life".[2] It was also a place where it was stated that everyone could enjoy the pleasures of physical culture and sport including mothers, children, and older people. As the status of the family assumed mounting importance after the introduction of the Constitution, family leisure time and the welfare of the child received increased attention. Films such as *Tsirk*, *Sluchainaya Vstrecha*, and others demonstrated that the Soviet Union "loved" all of its citizens, especially children. The image of Soviet sport came to be defined by young people, an image that was reinforced by the parades and physical culture festivals, which promoted an ideal of young, healthy, and attractive athletes.

Sport, leisure, and relaxation were to form an important part of the cultured New Soviet Person's image and identity. City parks across the Soviet Union were to be filled with Stalin's workers. With leisure across Europe undergoing a revival, Soviet Russia was to be no exception. At the same time that this interest in catering to the masses was happening, the rise of elite sports meant that issues of collectivism and individuality came into conflict. With competitive sport becoming more popular this conflict would have to be somehow reconciled. Individuals enjoying sports successes were encouraged to do so not for themselves, but for the collective. In this way champions, athletes, and sports stars supposedly raised the morale of their respective factory, university, and other collectives. While talented individuals were encouraged to pursue sports, mass participation continued to be the ultimate objective. Not everyone could be a champion, but everyone could go to the park, exercise, or participate in the GTO complex. This was the minimum commitment to socialist life and society expected of the new Soviet citizen. Soviet champions were usually shock-workers, and later Stakhanovites as well as active participants in society and the GTO system. The GTO system itself embraced all-round, collective sport, avoiding any tendencies to develop championism or individualism. Talented and successful athletes were to be distinguished from ordinary *fizkul'turniki*, meriting titles such as medallists and masters. Those displaying a positive disposition towards military activities were also recognized and rewarded. The sports authorities realized that popularizing sporting achievement was one of the key elements in achieving success on a mass basis. This was capitalized on later when physical culture and sport followed other aspects of Soviet life with the adulation of heroes and stars.

In the mid to late 1930s, shock-workers, Stakhanovites, the GTO masters (or, full title—"master-engineers of sport"), and other high achievers earned status in the new society. In an effort to further improve skills and techniques, champions were called upon. With these no longer as demonized as in the past, the Soviet inclination towards smashing old norms had begun to find expression in physical culture. Champions (socialist masters as opposed to bourgeois champions) were now welcomed as valuable instructors, with their knowledge and experience in swimming, athletics, and other sports necessary if higher standards were to be achieved in physical culture. Old masters were encouraged to impart their wisdom and training secrets on to the young. Mass and individual achievements were both publicly lauded and valued. Four hundred thousand workers were involved in the GTO norm, 72,000 thousand of whom had already completed the norm and had set their sights on achieving the even more complicated GTO Level II complex.[3] As previous chapters showed, many of these successes in physical culture and sport were accompanied by shadier developments which the authorities were keen to eliminate but vacillated on how best to do this. These issues beg important questions over the nature of physical culture and the kind of sports system that was developing in the 1930s as well as how this reflected on society. With whom were ordinary people to identify when the ideal figure of the honest, hard-working sportsperson was becoming increasingly besmirched by unscrupulous stars?

If sports parades and festivals projected the ideal image of Soviet life and symbolized unity within the Soviet Union, then the rise of elite, professional sports tainted this image. Money-hungry, success-driven athletes interfered with the pure and innocent image of physical culture as cultivated by the authorities through the display of happy young people in parades and festivals. Power-thirsty individuals often sidelined the needs of the collective. Ordinary people, those who most likely did not make the cut for the physical culture parades, did not always have access to physical culture and sport. They did not enjoy the sense of community that participation in sport and physical culture was supposed to provide. This chapter identifies some of those groups that were marginalized and denied an opportunity to participate in physical culture and sport, as well as those who suffered as a result of fulfilling the state's call to participate in sports and physical culture. The chapter also deals with those who used participation in sports and physical culture to further their own ends at any expense. These sports stars are related to the rise of the hero in Soviet society, those individuals glorified by the regime for their achievements and contribution to socialist life. The existence of such heroes and stars jeopardized the Soviet claim to mass, collective sport, which in the 1930s appeared to be overrun by elitist sport. Before examining these, the basic infrastructural base merits further analysis, for no claims to attaining mass participation in sport could be made without providing the necessary resources.

CONSTRUCTING SPACE

> It is necessary to understand that the conditions for our workers have changed entirely. Workers today are not the same as before. Today's workers, our Soviet workers, want to live with access to all kinds of material and cultural necessities, food supplies, and living quarters. They have this right and we must provide such conditions.—Joseph Stalin.[4]

If the achievements of the GTO and the growth of physical culture were to continue, then certain issues still needed to be addressed. In the spectrum of "cultural necessities", physical culture was certainly important. Yet how accessible was physical culture to the average worker or indeed any Soviet citizen in the 1930s? Where could they go to practice sports and physical culture? In 1929 the urban population in the RFSFR was 18 million, with one club serving on average 8,180 people.[5] If quality leisure was to be achieved then more leisure outlets needed to be constructed. The absence of facilities such as clubs and premises proved a constant hindrance to widespread participation. Until such issues were resolved, the numbers involved would be severely limited. The most basic space available for anyone wishing to practice physical culture was in their homes, but this was often restricted due to cramped conditions. Sometimes communal living may have offered a recreational area, but this again was not ideal. In the cities there were also courtyards, squares, and even boulevards where some physical culture activities could have taken place. However, these more than likely would have only accommodated games such as chess, *gorodki*, or at a stretch *lapta*. For those wanting to partake of more active sports and exercises, clubs attached to schools, factories, and elsewhere were the main loci of *fizkul'tura*.

The other possibility was of course the parks and stadiums. Yet these were not sufficiently widespread and also had their shortcomings. According to the findings of Katharina Kucher, there were 202 parks of culture in the Soviet Union by 1933, increasing to 348 by 1938.[6] The vast majority of these were in the Russian and then European republics. Between January 1937 and December 1938 the total number of visitors to parks in the Soviet Union was 87 million (including Moscow's Gorky Park, located just south of the Moscow River and opened in 1928), with 5 million having visited Leningrad's park of culture.[7] In the case of Moscow, as Kucher notes, the fact that the metro line was extended to the park in 1935 no doubt improved accessibility, increasing park popularity for city dwellers on the Moscow outskirts. Prior to the opening of this route, the vast majority of visitors to Gorky Park came from the neighbouring areas— the Zamoskvorech'e (11,175/ 33.5 per cent), Khamovniki (6,890/ 20.7 per cent), and Krasnopresnenskii districts (5,358/ 16.1 per cent).[8] Northern Moscow was home to Dinamo stadium, originally built for the 1928 International Spartakiad and later extended in 1935.[9] Dinamo, with a capacity of some 30,000–40,000 spectators, was primarily used for the practice of *fizkul'tura* and had a number of physical culture facilities in its vicinity.[10] Like Gorky Park, Dinamo enjoyed the benefits of the metro line in 1938. Discussions were initiated in 1936 to plan the construction of a central stadium of the SSSR at the northeastern edge of Moscow city, in Izmailogo (although discussions were ongoing until the 1940s and the stadium was never built).[11] The park (*Izmailovskii Park imena Stalina*) was to be used to develop mass physical culture and to train 50,000 workers to achieve the GTO norm.[12] The objective was that these huge parks and stadiums would help serve the leisure and sports needs of the workers. However, in spite of stadiums such as Dinamo there were claims that there were still not enough stadiums and that those that had been built were geared towards spectators and not participants.[13]

The Five Year Plan played an important role in facilitating the construction of parks and stadiums, and by 1931 an estimated 21 million roubles had been allocated to physical culture. In the same year a decree announced that parks of culture and leisure were to be constructed across the Soviet Union taking Moscow's Gorky Park as the template.[14] In the provinces funding made available for stadium construction was to be distributed fairly so that they "would not be overlooked or squeezed out of their share".[15] Yet with the trade unions leading the way (with 12 million roubles) it was more likely that urban areas would be first to benefit from financial support. Those living in the provinces and far-flung republics were once again at a disadvantage in terms of resources. This shortcoming was reflected in the construction of sports and leisure facilities in the republics, where some republics fared better than others; for example, the Armenian republic had only three parks of culture, while the Kirghiz republic had just one park.[16] In terms of stadiums, in 1936 there were 24,124 stadiums in the *kolkhozy* and construction seemed to be on the increase. In Belarus there were 2,820 stadiums in 1935, but in 1936 there were 3,000. In Bashkiria in 1935 there were 939 *kolkhoz* stadiums, but a year later this had increased to 973.[17] For the improvement of physical culture and sport in Kazakhstan, it was planned in 1935 to build 11 stadiums, 355 sports squares, 9,310 skiing bases with 13,000 pairs of skis, 6 aquatic centres, and 7 gymnastics halls.[18] It remains unclear whether or not "allocated" funds were indeed allocated accordingly. In Armenia there were reports of unfinished stadiums in several districts, where corrupt officials had found other uses for the money designated for stadium construction.[19] In cases where funding did make it into the right hands, then there were still massive disparities in centre–periphery distribution or, as the case of Izmailovksii Stadium showed, plans simply never got off the ground.

Using VTsSPS statistics one writer attempted to prove that resources and materials were improving, by showing that in 1931 there were more sports shoes, skates, skis, and football boots available than in the previous year.[20] Similar reports featured elsewhere—the manufacture of skis in the Soviet Union was reported to have increased from 560,000 pairs in 1930 to 670,000 in 1931 and to 1 million in 1932.[21] In various correspondences between Vyacheslav Molotov, Ivan Kharchenko, Nikolai Antipov, and Grigory Grin'ko,[22] the release of funds for use in physical culture was outlined—the party and All-Union Council of Physical Culture finally seemed to be coordinating their efforts to improve the situation.[23] Political intentions still took a while to filter down into practical, everyday life however, as could be observed from the futile search of one *Krasnyi sport* correspondent who struggled to find a standard size javelin and running shoes in all of Moscow.[24] In spite of this, it did appear to be the case that more attention was being devoted to creating spaces for the practice of physical culture and that some results were beginning to appear. Naturally, the construction of physical culture facilities varied from city to city and region to region, depending largely on the financial situation.

Another example of the sources of finance available for physical culture is provided by a survey of the situation in Baku during the first Five Year Plan. A republican capital, Baku was an important centre. From 1928 to 1932, physical culture there was financed by five major sources: the trade unions, schools (Board of Public Education), the Supreme Council of Physical Culture, the Baku Council of Physical Culture, and the Regional Council of Physical Culture of Azerbaijan.[25] Each year funding increased substantially, with the exception of 1932, which saw only a slight increase (from 650,949 roubles in 1931 to 658,693 in 1932). The primary source of financial support was the trade unions, with a total of 1,233,576 roubles, followed by the BSFK with 238,440 roubles and then the VSFK with 188,173 roubles.[26] What this shows is that, by the end of the Five Year Plan, physical culture in Baku was certainly (in theory at least) in a better financial position. However, how adequate was this financial support in terms of funding various construction projects? Stadium construction was expensive and in spite of the state emphasis on improving access to sports, finding funding was difficult when so many other projects demanded time and money. In some instances it was even up to workers themselves to raise the money.

There was no doubting that an intense interest in constructing and equipping sports facilities existed, especially in the mid-1930s, a period which Robert Edelman notes witnessed "the first great wave of stadium building".[27] The building of parks and sports centres was just as important from a social as well as a physical culture point of view. Children and young adults with idle time on their hands needed some place to go. Summertime and weekends were most suited to organized events for children and families who were encouraged to visit the parks. Moscow devoted particular attention to addressing the recreational needs of children. The Moscow city committee requested that the city branch of the ONO (the local education department) conduct mass health and cultural work in the summer, encompassing about 50,000 children of school age and 32,000 of pre-school age.[28] A square for 23,000 persons, a sanitary area for 7,000 and other facilities were to cater for the needs of school-age children.[29] The parks were to have special playgrounds or "children's parks". The city committee stipulated that the Central Park of Culture and Leisure (Gorky Park) was to attract 1,400 to the children's park (situated on its grounds) and was to have 3,000 children on its territory in total, Sokol'niki park was to have 1,000 in its children's park and 2,000 in the park in general, while finally in the Stalin and Krasno-Presnenskii park there were to be 500 children in the children's park area, with 1,000 catered for in the park as a whole.[30] It was also noted that the city branch of the ONO, together with the park directors, were to organize mass children's festivals in every park throughout the summer period.[31] These facilities for children were, as Claire Shaw notes, in accordance with Bukharin and Preobrazhenskii's *ABC of Communism* on how to raise children and more generally reflected acculturation policies.[32] Given the importance placed on youth, this attempt to place children in a healthy environment was a logical step in achieving a strong and loyal cohort of young communists.

It was not just the parks which were to become sport hotspots in summertime. The Moscow city committee requested that the Moscow city trade union council and Moscow city physical culture council organize daily work to take place in all stadiums, aquatic centres, as well as on beaches (in Moscow's case beaches meant riverbanks).[33] In undertaking this work they were to allocate specialist instructors and equipment. As well as that the Moscow City Council of Physical Culture was to "assign 300 physical culture games directors for work in the squares and in points of mass work". Narkompit (Commissariat for Food) and other agencies were to oversee the feeding of the hungry *fizkul'turniki*, with 50,000 to be catered for in the various parks.[34] The Gorky Central Park of Culture and Leisure had its own canteen which could meet some of these needs. Buses and trams were also organized to transport the children to and from the parks. Thus by 1933 definite plans were in place, in Moscow at least, to see that inhabitants had access to physical culture. Children, rather than spending their free time at home or on the streets, were encouraged to visit the parks instead. There they could become involved in planned, monitored events and activities. This organized system benefited both the children and the state, allowing the latter to exact a degree of both care and control.

When it came to stadiums, not all stadiums were necessarily in good condition or catered to everyone. Boasting about a certain number of stadiums might have looked good on paper, but in reality there was no real way of telling how a stadium functioned or if it really served the needs of the local population. The Gorky Park of Culture and Leisure's purportedly positive policy towards children was not replicated elsewhere. Moscow's Iskra stadium, for instance, did not admit children past its gates because the workers did not want to "work with hooligans".[35] The workers in Dinamo stadium only admitted "their children", which included just 80–100 of the youngest, pre-school age children. Moreover, these facilities were not always the safe haven that one was led to imagine. At many stadiums and aquatic centres there was no interest in developing work programmes for children, and nobody considered themselves responsible for the children. The thousands of children who walked past the gates of stadiums and parks were often not organized or supervised. The lack of responsibility extended to children who were not prevented from swimming in forbidden areas or climbing over fences, with many accidents occurring as a result.[36] According to the Moscow Council the situation was no better in Leningrad, Stalingrad, Saratov, Kharkov, and other major cities. A Komsomol representative even requested that measures be taken against those guilty of inactivity in the stadiums and aquatic centres.[37] This was a particularly timely demand as within the next few days 50,000 children were expected to arrive from Pioneer camps. There were also complaints about the quality of summer work being carried out in Moscow. The majority of organizations had not carried out the proposals of the party regarding children and did not seem to "understand the significance of this".[38] According to one source from the Iskra stadium in Moscow the reason for this was that "children vandalize ["hooliganize"] the squares, break glass, and generally harm work". The Dinamo aquatic centre stated that the "children are absolutely not allowed into the stadium" as it was too dangerous for them and officials working there were "overwhelmed with having to answer for them". Soviet children, socialist progeny, were evidently slow to take on board the values of the young Pioneer.

Although constructing physical space was admittedly a costly and time-consuming enterprise, it was still one that was nonetheless undertaken in the 1930s. Inspections of the aquatic centre *Mukomol Vostoka*, however, revealed serious problems which cast into doubt any claims about quality stadium construction. The centre catered for around 5,000 *fizkul'turniki*, merging together (a rather vast) seven oblasts, four krais, and five republics. The centre, just built in June 1940, had myriad problems including no tower, no swimming pool, a viewing platform that was not in good condition, and a dirty, stony beach.[39] This new aquatic centre had only a small stadium in very bad condition with a 100m running track beside the centre. The track was dusty and there had even been two accidents where athletes suffered ankle and knee injuries.[40] In terms of social amenities it had a dance square and billiards as well as a restaurant which had a constant supply of vodka.[41] The upshot of this was that there were masses of drunken people wandering about the centre. These latter measures had, ironically, been put in place to keep the aquatic centre financially afloat. The example of this new but clearly inadequate sports centre again undermines any official claims to achieving progress in the field of physical culture and sport, with ordinary people still being denied access to proper facilities, even in 1940. The completion of construction projects did not necessarily entail success and problems with poor facilities, lack of maintenance and equipment, and personnel shortages were just some of the issues that continued to impede any endeavours to establish a form of "mass" participation in physical culture and sport. Soviet citizens who were being continuously asked to commit to the socialist lifestyle found that they were not always able to do so. The "modal schizophrenia" of socialist realism was vividly clear in the world of physical culture, where the juxtaposition of the real and ideal or the "mythic or utopian" exposed the striking contradictions within Soviet life.[42] Soviet citizens, if denied the opportunity to actually participate in sports themselves, could perhaps be consoled by reading about ambitious construction plans, the feats of sports stars or seeing images of impressive physical culture parades.

INCLUSIVE PHYSICAL CULTURE

Although the image projected by physical culture and sport was above all a positive one, promoting health and instilling "wholesome" socialist values, many continued to view active physical culture and sport as a reserve of the young and talented. Even in the 1920s when "stars" and "heroes" were not publicly lauded, those who excelled at sport tended to receive more attention with some instructors "only paying attention to good sportspeople".[43] Meanwhile, physical culture for older participants was by and large neglected. As the experience of women and physical culture testified, older participants undoubtedly felt uncomfortable when mixing with younger sports enthusiasts, but no serious efforts had really been made to accommodate their needs. Aside from sedate exercises and games, activities for older sports enthusiasts—male and female—were not given much consideration. In 1927 the physical culture *kruzhok* of the Lenin railway club had given some thought to this issue. It was keen to attract older workers to sport, as some of them had been complaining that "young people can run and jump but for us—old people—there is nothing".[44] In response to this it was decided to arrange a summer excursion to the forest where the club would organize a contest for the best mushroom gatherer. Although a pleasant exercise, this was probably not the type of active physical culture envisioned by the older workers. Nonetheless, mushroom gathering—incorporating enjoyment of the fresh air and sun—qualified as a form of "cultured leisure" even though it was not "sport" in the traditional sense. Whether intentional or not, older workers were overlooked and the issue of older workers' health still needed to be improved with more active and attractive forms of exercise required to achieve this. In the culture of youth that dominated it was easy for older men and women to feel excluded, seemingly forgotten, and abandoned by the new society hurriedly being built around them.[45]

The issue of older people's participation in physical culture came to the attention of Narkomzdrav in 1935. Professor Valentin Vladimirovich Gorinevsky, member of the Scientific Medical Council in Narkomzdrav as well as a physical culture theoretician, acknowledged that something had to be done to address this issue. He noted that, as one of the oldest scientific workers in physical culture (he was seventy-eight years old) he empathized with older people and would welcome the introduction of specialist exercises for middle-aged and older people.[46] Such efforts had in fact been undertaken by the "pioneering" study of Vladimir Petrovich Il'in, a sportsman since 1910, experienced in swimming, rowing, figure skating, skiing, and golf. Il'in had an impressive resumé. He had been involved in training and instruction and in 1926 had begun working with "elderly" people, which he continued to do until the present day (1935). On top of this he was a representative and consultant on American sports issues for the physical culture *kruzhok* in the All-Union Council for the National Economy (VSNKh). His research had led him to conduct a study of middle aged and elderly participation in physical culture. Middle aged and elderly were here considered to be those aged between thirty-years and sixty-two (the ages of the youngest and oldest participants; the average age was forty-three). Troubling as this may be, it was a fair reflection of wider attitudes in Soviet sports, where the age for competitive athletes and women in sport was even more restrictive. Take, for example, the complaint of one woman, who lamented that at age twenty-two women were considered to be too old for sports.[47] Another, a Stakhanovite worker, complained that she had to switch from gymnastics to hockey because "at twenty-six years she was an old woman".[48] Age was evidently another divisive issue and one that denied many access to full participation in Soviet physical culture and socialist life more generally.

At least Il'in was attempting to help the more "mature" members of society. His study consisted of thirty-two women and twenty-two men who participated in dances, exercises, games, and other activities over an eight-month period (1 October 1934–1 June 1935), divided into two groups. The frequency was two times over six days for two hours in the evenings.[49] One of the initial hurdles to be overcome was that of attire. When dressed in what younger people would wear participants were "shy" and reticent. Instead of wearing shorts and vests, Il'in provided them with blouses and long, wide, loose-fitting trousers. This disguised the "less attractive exterior form of the older *fizkul'turniki*" (with comments like this it was no wonder they were "shy"). Upon donning their new, less figure-hugging outfits, participants felt more comfortable, with Il'in noting a marked improvement in their mood.[50] Those involved in the research were mainly scientific workers (90 per cent) and families of scientific workers (10 per cent). The consensus amongst those interviewed afterwards was that the experience had been a positive one. A thirty-seven-year-old doctor (a nervous psychiatrist) commented that the exercises had "lessened both his physical and mental fatigue" and that his mood, appetite, and sleep had improved.[51] A sixty-two-year-old law professor remarked that after the gymnastics he felt cheerful, fresh, and "young". For the four months that he had been involved in the study he claimed that his health had improved. Another professor (aged fifty-eight) noted that he arrived at gymnastics feeling tired and left feeling refreshed and upbeat. The potential health benefits for all were clear but extending such trials on a mass basis would be considerably more difficult. Owing to financial and other constraints the setting up of separate *kruzhki* for older physical culture participants was not an entirely realistic objective and so older sports enthusiasts marginalized by mainstream clubs and *kruzhki* were left to entertain themselves by playing *gorodki* or mushroom picking.

While the "age" question was important there were also other groups within Soviet society on the sidelines of physical culture but who were nonetheless bundled into the catch-all concept of the "masses". This had begun to change somewhat by the late 1930s when the desire for a more inclusive type of physical culture was beginning to extend to other traditionally neglected segments of the population. In 1937, for example, plans were proposed for establishing sports clubs for the deaf. This was not an initiative on the part of the Physical Culture Committee but rather, once again, a response to calls to address an overlooked issue. Organizing deaf *fizkul'turniki* had previously come under discussion in 1935, when the trade unions toyed with the idea of setting up a committee for work among the deaf, with specialist physical culture workers working with members.[52] The problem, according to the trade unions, was that deaf workers did not participate in general physical culture activities, but only in those activities conducted under the aegis of the Society for the Deaf. In any case, nothing came of discussions with physical culture work having "collapsed" and been "liquidated".

The request for the sports club in 1937 had come from a group of deaf physical culture activists who sought to improve conditions for physical culture among the deaf community.[53] Kharchenko responded by granting permission to create a sports club for the deaf in Moscow and Leningrad under the direction of MOOVOG and LOOVOG (the Moscow and Leningrad sections of the All-Russian Society for the Deaf). These sports clubs were then to be approved by the Moscow and Leningrad councils of physical culture. Although the deaf community had been provided for in other ways, for example, through the setting up of drama circles, and although they had participated in GTO and Osoaviakhim activities, it was not until the rather late date of 1937 that they were finally rewarded with a sports club.[54] In spite of this group's success, there were undoubtedly other marginalized groups in society who were unable to avail of physical culture and sport. Providing physical culture for the elites had eclipsed providing physical culture for the genuine "masses". Soviet authorities, intent on identity building, had concentrated on forging links with young people, women, peasants, and the nationalities, but in so doing had neglected to serve the interests of older people, the deaf, and others who wanted to join the wider physical culture community.

ORDINARY PEOPLE

Ordinary people—those not classified as stars or heroes—encompassed a broad cross-section of society and did not exclusively denote those with limited access to sport and physical culture. While "stars" made the headlines and conferred prestige upon clubs and factories, the less sports inclined masses, or ordinary people, were still expected to achieve the GTO norms, join clubs, and participate in the factory exercises. Fulfilling GTO norms posed significant problems, however, and many factories were unable to achieve set targets. Club membership figures were frequently described as existing only on paper. This was even the case among the young, supposedly the most receptive audience to physical culture. In one institute, students were reported to have a "disparaging attitude towards the obligatory physical culture classes", while poor attendance of morning exercises in the dormitories was reported amongst other students.[55] The social organizations were blamed for this lack of enthusiasm as well as for the departure of those who were really interested in physical culture and sport and who sought a "better physical culture collective". The result would appear to have been that good sports clubs and physical culture collectives continued to improve due to their ability to attract the best, while the lesser clubs and collectives struggled to improve owing to the desertion of their best sportspersons, lack of interest by social organizations, and a consequent deficit in financial and material support. As a result the divide between elite and mass sport continued to widen.

The situation for ordinary workers was far from ideal. In Ukraine, for instance, a worker by the name of Voitkovskaya wrote to the sports-technical committee of the All-Union Council for Physical Culture in a desperate bid to be reinstated to her old job.[56] She had recently been fired for "truancy" when she had travelled from Odessa to Kiev to attend the All-Ukrainian volleyball championships. Although she stated that all her documents regarding the trip were in order and she had been permitted to travel, she nonetheless lost her job. She had approached the factory's physical culture council about the matter, but this was to no avail. As she was no longer a worker, her case was not considered. It had been a week since the incident occurred and she was now hoping for assistance from higher authorities, hence the letter. In the case of Voitkovskaya, the physical culture council was of no use and offered absolutely no protection to the workers, leaving Voitkovskaya to fend for herself. If her case was genuine (and the All-Union Council was investigating the verity of her complaint) then such incidents were hardly encouraging for other workers wanting to become involved in sports. Naturally such stories did not feature prominently in the press of the mid to late 1930s, which primarily focused on covering the success of star teams and athletes, rather than covering the problems of ordinary people interested in participating in sport and physical culture. The case of Voitkovskaya accurately depicts the random nature of Soviet life where bureaucracy, corruption, politics, or personal grievances meant that apparent victims such as Voitkovskaya were easy prey with nobody to support them or defend their rights.

There were other victims and types of victim too, including the other type of Soviet hero who should not be overlooked—the martyr who had died in the service of socialism. Under Stalinism these were typically young *komsomol'tsy*, eager to show their commitment to the new system. In physical culture and sport, Liuba Berlin and Tamara Ivanova were two such examples.[57] Both girls, despite their experience, had died in parachuting accidents in March 1935. In June 1936 another parachutist died. The twenty-one-year-old *komsomol'ka* Nata Babushkina had been a student of the Institute for Physical Culture since 1931 and had been awarded the Red Star in 1935.[58] Despite her experience and expertise, she too perished during a jump. Her funeral in Moscow witnessed "thousands of workers including parachutists and pilots" lining the streets as her remains were brought from the *Dom Pechatnyi* (Publishing House) to the Novodevichy Convent. The urn with her ashes, surrounded by flowers, was carried by Kosarev, Kharchenko, Luk'yanov, and others. A salute was even organized. These kinds of tragedies were highly publicized, underlining that sport was not just for leisure, but was a highly important social obligation serving to restore Soviet defence needs. Those involved in such military and defence sports such as parachuting were highly valued and respected members of society, considered patriots by the state. While the successes enjoyed by heroes such as Valery Chkalov or Aleksei Stakhanov made them instant sensations, the heroic efforts of the young, including the deceased, also played a significant role in Soviet (and Russian) popular memory and history.[59] These deceased martyrs became popular heroes.

Death came to many while participating in sports, but not all of these were eulogized. Sport was often poorly organized and lacking in proper medical control. Technical and physical sports such as skiing, boxing, and parachuting demanded medical supervision but often took place without any at all. Medical control was considered important but often overlooked and, although the authorities and doctors were usually blamed when problems arose, sometimes sports participants themselves were to blame. One such instance occurred in Penza, where one official there claimed that ten footballers with heart-related illnesses, who had been banned from playing sport by a doctor, ignored the advice and played regardless.[60] The more frequent occurrence, however, was that medical control had simply been overlooked. This was sadly shown to be the case when a schoolchild was injured while on a skiing excursion. The injured child had to be carried by the instructor to the nearest village for medical attention, as there was no medical support present on the excursion. By the time the child had finally been transferred to a city hospital, he had died from his injuries.[61] Doctors in the regions and provinces were few and overworked. In some cases a doctor might have been present only at the start of a competition, and in other cases recently qualified medical assistants or feldshers were present.[62] In an April 1937 boxing match between a Zenit Stalingrad and Kryl'ya Sovetov Moscow, one of the boxers died.[63] This was blamed on the judges, referee, organizers, and the sports societies. The Zenit boxer had been allowed to get away with a number of illegalities, the rounds had continued for too long, and there was no medical supervision. Moreover, the boxer involved had only been seventeen years of age. The secretary of the society, head judge, referee, and trainer was all considered responsible for the death, and it was left to the main sports inspectorate to investigate further. After these incidents medical supervision was to be increased, and in the case of the latter incident Kharchenko warned that all sports clubs and societies were to be made aware of the rules and that they were to have received permission from the relevant authorities before any regional competitions were held. The quest for success and records was apparently often conducted at any cost, including lives. Whether through carelessness or greed many ordinary people, and indeed some stars, had to pay a high price for their involvement in sport.

TROUBLE IN PARADISE: SPORTS TOURISM

Earlier discussion of the Starostin affair and the organizational development of sport in the 1930s showed that sport by this time had assumed a semi-professional character. While successful sportspersons had been rewarded under NEP, this increased in the mid-1930s following the introduction of a structured football league and the establishment of sports societies. As Robert Edelman observes, the "modern era of Soviet spectator sports began in May 1936" when a "more serious, systematic, and professional approach" to sports emerged following the league's establishment.[64] The league was structured on a similar basis to the western model, albeit with matches played in the summer rather than winter months. Football was the most popular sport and came to be dominated by two teams in particular—Spartak and Dinamo. The former had been organized into a voluntary society in 1935 (having originally started out as the Moscow Sport's Circle 1921 and later known as *Krasnaya Presnya*), while the latter had been formed by Felix Dzerzhinsky in 1923. Other societies such as Lokomotiv (railway workers) and Torpedo (automobile workers) and more soon formed and enjoyed some successes in a variety of sports, not just in football. Other sports—particularly track and field athletics and hockey—enjoyed popularity and success, but football claimed the largest following. Contrary to the socialist concern for the collective interest, the hunt for sports stars was a salient feature of the top sports societies. As Edelman notes, "[s]ports 'businessmen' roamed the country in search of good soccer players" which proved to be to the detriment of developing young local talent.[65] This was hindered further by inherent problems in the structure of the football league. In a letter to Stalin in 1938, Lavrenti Beria acknowledged, that, in spite of large crowd attendances throughout the union, "the football championship does not promote the development of football".[66] This was because, he explained, out of the twenty-six teams in the Soviet league, seventeen were from the Russian republic, with ten of these teams from Moscow. Seven union republics were entirely unrepresented.

The separation between mass and elite sports increased as the 1930s progressed and was prevalent on various levels—individual, factory, provincial, and even republican. This divide was the result of the sports structure, societies, and the sports stars who commanded large sums of money for their skills. Here we will call the latter "sports tourists"—a term encompassing the very talented "stars" but also including the lesser talented sportspersons who tried their luck at obtaining higher salaries and rewards. The popular term for this practice at the time was "chempionstvo". Sportspersons moving from one physical culture organization to another was a significant problem and it was an indisputable concern of those charged with overseeing sports. Edelman has already convincingly showed that this trend can be traced to the 1920s, noting that in 1926 *Krasnyi sport* reported that "players move about according to their own taste" and that "with the approach of the close of the transfer period, a small but substantial number of players appears, ready to sell themselves to whomever they want to, whenever they want".[67] This was recognized in 1925 by the Supreme Council and Komsomol, which acknowledged that "specialists and sportsmen 'sew up' money".[68] In spite of the problem, it was not until 1934 that serious action was taken against the trend. Then Ivan Kharchenko considered it necessary to introduce measures to look after the interests of clubs and monitor more carefully the transfer of players who seemed to be able to go where they pleased regardless of the consequences for club or factory.[69] The resolution passed sought to eliminate the "corrupt, careerist and disruptive ambitions" of certain *fizkul'turniki* and to regulate transfers from either one department to another, such as between the trade unions, Dinamo, the RKKA, and industrial cooperatives or transfers from one city to another.[70] Any transfers should be authorized by the appropriate organs (normally the responsible council for physical culture or internal department). The transfer of masters of sport received greater attention and decisions concerning their movements had to be made by the presidium of the All-Union Council of Physical Culture and Sport. The leadership of the physical culture organs had the power to exclude from the physical culture organization and work any *fizkul'turnik* caught violating the new rules.[71] The legislation was not entirely effective, however. In some cases the councils could exercise their authority, but in others *fizkul'turniki* seemed to be able to get around it.

One such example occurred in March 1936, revealed in a letter sent to Mantsev (chairman of the All-Union Council of Physical Culture) and Lukyanov (the Komsomol representative) from F. Rodionov, one of the heads of the TsDKA.[72] Rodionov explained that he had read an article in *Krasnyi Sport* referring to a football player from Dinamo who had gone to Kislovodsk for training. At first Rodionov supposed that this was a misprint, for the player referred to—Semichastnyi—was in fact in the TsDKA team and had never mentioned anything about transferring to another organization. Furthermore, he maintained that no decisions had ever been made about such a transfer by the All-Union Council of Physical Culture presidium or the Moscow Council of Physical Culture. Upon running some checks, Rodionov discovered that he had not been mistaken, and Semichastnyi really was included in the Dinamo team which had gone to Kislovodsk for training. He went on to state that in the Red Army "they were used to greater respect in relation to Dinamo", since it was one of the leading physical culture organizations in the country. It seemed to him that this was the fault of some "irresponsible person" who had enticed TsDKA's best player and had occurred without the consent of the Dinamo leadership. He added that Semichastnyi had "grown up" with TsDKA and had become a master of football as a part of its sport's collective. Rodionov continued that TsDKA could not become accustomed to the poaching of sportspersons and that now, just before the start of the football season, it could not bear the loss of its best player. He expressed "extreme protest" at this transfer and astonishment at how it could have occurred without consent from TsDKA. Finally, he stated that a Komsomol Central Committee and All-Union Council of Physical Culture resolution had to discuss in a "most decisive manner" the luring of sportspersons from one club to another and examine especially the case of Semichastnyi. The 1934 legislation introduced by Kharchenko had clearly not been "decisive" enough.[73]

Another strange case of early sports tourism was that of the footballer Zhukov. Zhukov was not a "star" such as Semichastnyi and represented that other type of sports tourist—the not-so-talented sportsperson who tried his luck at various clubs to get the best deal. His case was brought to the attention of the Moscow Council of Physical Culture in 1933 by Trekin, a representative of the Stalin Avtozavod factory.[74] The factory bureau wanted to rein in the "anti-physical culture actions" of their football player Zhukov, who had become "corrupted by self-seeking champion moods".[75] Trekin wrote that Zhukov had been accepted into its physical culture organization as a *fizkul'turnik* but had decided "not to follow the physical culture way".[76] He claimed that Zhukov considered playing for the football team "work", for which he should receive money. The factory, according to Trekin, "took all measures to educate and correct Zhukov's character" and he was shown help and support. Yet he reportedly avoided work and did not fulfil his given work quotas. At the most recent factory meeting he had declared, "Either I work, or I play". The physical culture bureau, Trekin wrote, considered that there was no longer a place for Zhukov in its organization. He was excluded from the football section and Trekin now looked to the Moscow Council of Physical Culture to ratify this decision and "deliver a strong blow to this infected champion".[77]

That was not the only time this apparent "prima donna" footballer came to the attention of the authorities. Some years later, in 1936, the Stalin Avtozavod factory's sports club once again felt compelled to highlight the case and described the actions of Zhukov during the intervening three years.[78] A letter was written stating that the Stalin Avtozavod factory wanted to disallow the transfer of Zhukov from their collective to Lokomotiv. Meanwhile Zhukov had also been a part of the district club Proletarskaya Kuznitsa and a part of the Dinamo collective. According to factory director Likhachev, this was the last collective to which Zhukov belonged as an "honest, Soviet *fizkul'turnik*". Then, "in the pursuit of the 'long rouble' he began his journeying".[79] Having "toured" up to five different organizations Zhukov then "yearned for his roots" and returned to Avtozavod. After a trip to the Donbass in 1933, Zhukov "returned to his old ways and eventually ended up with TsDKA". This last move, Likhachev noted, could be explained in part by his conscription to the Red Army. He was soon demobilized however, having lost three of his fingers after falling under a tram. Likhachev recalled that Zhukov's time in the army had not changed him and (once again) having been offered every opportunity to change his ways through work or study Zhukov continued to want to "work" in football. The Stalin factory's Orgburo suggested more "practical" work which would "solidify the educational (*vospitatel'noe*) influence" on Zhukov, but this did not work and he moved to Lokomotiv. This latest move to Lokomotiv was, Likhachev wrote, "conditional exclusively on the self-seeking moods which Lokomotiv encouraged".[80] In conclusion Likhachev reiterated that this kind of behaviour was unacceptable and that the factory collective, with the help of the various physical culture councils and trade unions, would attempt to re-educate Zhukov and make him "not only a good sportsman but a Soviet citizen, able to work and participate in the construction of a socialist society".[81]

Zhukov may have represented an extreme form of sports tourism but he was by no means the only adventurer in search of "the long rouble". As Robert Edelman has also shown, switching sports organizations was a regular occurrence, particularly at the start of the football season.[82] The Zhukov saga highlights that this was not an issue restricted to masters of sport. Players went in search of better conditions but did not always find them. Some having moved, like Zhukov, suffered from homesickness and wanted to return to their native clubs. Others saw the error of their ways and recognized that moving from club to club was harmful. One such repentant adventurer was the young master of sport in football and hockey, S. Artem'ov, who admitted that his transfer decisions of the last

Figure 7.1 Sports tourism. "Chempion po begu . . . iz odnogo obshchestva v drugoe" ("Champion at running . . . from one society to another"), by Iu. Uzbyakov, *Krasnyi sport*, no. 63 (1937): 3. Courtesy of the Russian State Library.

two years had been "harmful to labour and social life" and he now wished to return to his native Spartak where "he was raised" for which he felt a "connection".[83] Remorse and a sense of moral propriety was generally not a characteristic shared by these sportspersons however. The real reason why this player returned to Spartak was likely connected to more mercenary motivations, not a concern with labour or socialist life. The fear of being excluded from the organization for which these "tourists" worked did not seem to have any effect and the All-Union Council appeared to have no power to stop such behaviour. Achieving the ideal of the new Soviet citizen, as the case of Zhukov and others demonstrated, continued to remain out of reach. With the public largely aware of the prizes received by stars and their behaviour reported (and condemned) in the press, the New Person myth and positive image of the sports star became harder to sustain.

In spite of the failure of political and organizational interventions there was some hope that a cultural and social shift might take place that would discourage such behaviour. Part of the shift was to be pioneered by agit-prop, especially film propaganda. For instance, in the film *Sluchainaya Vstrecha*, released in 1936, the character of Grisha epitomizes the "self-seeking tendencies" that were pervasive throughout sports, representing the kind of superficial self-interest that the state condemned. His character serves to remind the audience that, while a fit and healthy body were desirable, so too was good moral behaviour and a commitment to the party and the family. By focusing all of his energy on his protégé Irina, Grisha neglects the interests of the collective. When Grisha quits the *kruzhok*, and accuses the director of undervaluing the importance of physical culture the director responds by reminding Grisha that it was he and the factory who built the stadium in the first place. Although a physical culture instructor, Grisha does not appear to have the same passion or commitment as Irina. His "love" of physical culture is depicted as more transient, and he is attracted only towards fame and success rather than by a healthy lifestyle and the true principles of physical culture.

In the end, Grisha's desire for fame and recognition leads to him being left alone and unsuccessful while Irina, the true *fizkul'turnitsa*, is triumphant. The right attitude to physical culture and sport are depicted as offering women and men a means of achieving their goals. Irina, a young and hard-working girl from the provinces, is able to become Soviet champion. Yet, unlike Grisha, sporting achievement and fame are not her "dream". For her, athletics is portrayed as a passion, but not as "an end in itself'. Of course she wants to realize her talents, but she does not pursue athletics solely for the sake of breaking records. She has other hopes and aspirations, as well as other important roles to fulfil. Aside from the propaganda efforts of the silver screen this official image was far removed from what was actually taking place in the clubs and factories which had innumerable Grishas and other success-hungry characters trying their patience. Notwithstanding these growing contradictions within Soviet society, programmes for identity—as

Sluchainaya Vstrecha demonstrates—were relied upon as important counterpoints to reality. The idealized principles of Irina combined with the real achievements of Soviet stars formed a seductive and powerful narrative. The juxtaposition of the everyday and heroism, as Catriona Kelly argues, meant that "[m]any who did not have it in them to become Stakhanovites [or, for that matter, sports stars] could still feel a disinterested sense of pride in living in a land of supermen and superwomen".[84]

Apart from appealing to higher authorities there was not that much which organizations could do to retain their star players or "supermen" and "superwomen". They could try to improve material conditions, but this was often beyond the means of many. At the first regional Zenit conference in 1936 in Tula a representative from the Kalinin factory claimed that enough was not being done to improve the conditions of physical culture, whether for participants or instructors.[85] It was this lack of attention which, he maintained, led to the decision of rising star athlete Maria Shamanova to leave Zenit and move to Lokomotiv. At the time she had been close to breaking the all-union record in the shot-put. Though another representative at the conference remarked that she left to go somewhere better, it was countered that she—and others—left to go where they could "work better and have better conditions for work".[86] If better conditions could not be created, then Zenit and its members would never achieve the same results as Lokomotiv. A situation had now arisen where "champions could be bought, people could be bought" who would break records and move from one society to another.[87] This was also the case with instructors and trainers. One factory worker commented that there had been a "wonderful" master trainer who had left for Lokomotiv.[88] The reason for the departure was explained by the better pay, better material conditions, and the provision of better training facilities. Smaller factories and unions, such as Zenit, could not compete with the larger factories and unions. Even one of the bigger Tula-based factories such as the Kalinin factory struggled to maintain their sports masters.[89] Those in charge of physical culture in various organizations seemed outraged at the actions of certain organizations and individuals yet powerless to take any real action.

In light of negative developments within the world of Soviet sport and physical culture, it would seem more probable that the June 1936 restructuring of the sports movement may have had more to do with the "corrupt" tendencies developing in physical culture and sports than with just marking the Stalin Constitution. As reports of "anti-socialist" behaviour from sportspersons mounted and as political tensions in the country deepened, it was no surprise that sports was subjected to further organizational and structural change. Centralization and control took precedence over workers' rights to leisure and the demands of sports stars. All the same it must be asked why the authorities left it so late to deal with charges of sports tourism. Both Riordan and Edelman's research demonstrate that this was ongoing since the 1920s but legislation (that introduced by Kharchenko) dealing with the matter was not introduced until 1934, and this was in spite of the fact that the authorities were clearly not happy with the situation. There are a number of possible explanations for this. For one, club directors were seething with rage over the loss of important players and, since the setting up of a proper football league in 1935, the stakes were higher as club prestige was on the line. Moreover, this in turn meant that higher financial rewards were there to be won, and trainers and directors were no longer willing to tolerate the disappearance of their best players. Sports stars had become valuable investments and since the 1936 organizational re-structuring, champions were acceptable so long as they were motivated by collectivist rather than individualist desires.

Another possible explanation is the political atmosphere of the 1930s. During the NEP certain "un-socialist" elements had flourished but with the advent of Stalinism society became much more regulated. All actions from below had to go through to the centralized system at the top. Therefore the Physical Culture Committee was to have increased legal control over sports affairs. This had an important political dimension and, as previous chapters showed, allowed the hunt for enemies to be conducted with greater ease. Those involved in sport who were accused of being a "bad champion", that is, of harbouring bourgeois tendencies or displaying "un-socialist" behaviour, could in the late 1930s have been swept along in the tide of arrests and executions. The legislation of the 1930s might thus be viewed as part of the Stalinist trend for regulation and higher forms of control.

WE COULD BE HEROES: PAYMENTS AND PRIVILEGES

The cases of Shamanova, Semichastnyi, and even an apparent journeyman such as Zhukov illuminate much about the developing world of "professional" Soviet sport. They show that, in spite of socialist ideals and Stalinist proclamations of equality, conditions were variable for everyone involved in physical culture, no matter what the level. It was seemingly worth moving from one organization to another in search of better offers. Regulation in this regard was only catching up on what was happening at ground level. It was the frustrated physical culture workers in the clubs and factories who were left to deal with messy transfers and disgruntled sportspersons. Likewise sportspersons, even successful ones, did not always receive considerable material advantages. Depending on the status of union and factory, the circumstances and rewards for each sportsperson varied considerably.

One worker, a champion skater from the Kalinin factory, did not apparently enjoy any improvement in living standards and was reportedly living in "very bad conditions".[90] She was one of eight living in a room measuring 18m squared. Her brother, a promising *fizkul'turnik*, had to endure the same conditions. The representative from the factory argued that the "best *fizkul'turnitsy* should have been provided with better accommodation and shown some material support".[91] The case of Shamanova appeared to have rankled those in the Kalinin factory, and they vacillated between the two opposing ideals of creating better conditions for successful sportspersons while at the same time not encouraging avaricious "stars". A comment from one worker seemed to sum up the general dilemma faced by factories when he acknowledged that Shamanova should have been entitled to better living conditions, but was concerned that if "today she or any sportsperson wanted an apartment then when we would search for one for them, they would refuse point-blank".[92] When could a club ever be sure that their workers would be satisfied and not want to leave or be enticed elsewhere?

Sports stars quickly learned that they were valuable commodities, and there were attempts by several stars to capitalize on their special position within Soviet society. The major voluntary societies such as Spartak, with its host of stars, were particularly associated with privileges and favours (as the Starostin affair showed).[93] Clubs were not always willing to succumb to a sportsperson's demands, however. This was exemplified by a Spartak presidium representative who did not grant permission to send a ski team to the south. The ski team had requested the trip in order to train for the upcoming season, and while it was agreed that preparation was indeed necessary, the presidium representative considered that it would be more in the ski team's interests to go to the north, where there would be snow.[94] The representative stated that he had been in touch with Nikolai Starostin who had said that the skiers had given him an ultimatum: either they went to the south or they would leave altogether. The representative supported the right of sportspersons to have the best conditions for their work and to spend time at resorts and in sanatoriums, but that clubs should not be held to ransom by these sportspersons. It was decided that this type of behaviour was unacceptable and would not be tolerated. People with such attitudes did not belong in the organization and should be removed.[95] This problem was not exclusive to Spartak, and it seemed to be a frequent occurrence that those involved in physical culture made demands that frustrated and angered factory and union bosses. Some factories suffered from extreme absenteeism from workers who were on sports teams, with some spending up to six months away at training camps or competitions.[96] While this was obviously bad for work at the factory, it was also bad for physical culture as there was nobody there to organize it in the absence of missing players and instructors. Robert Edelman has noted the significance of this problem, with the actions of many societies leading to the neglect of mass sport.[97]

The Moscow City Council of Physical Culture also took a stand against "corrupt" behaviour in sport and issued a decree against "perversions in the practice of sport's work by those in Moscow physical culture" which had been ongoing up until that time (1935).[98] It was stated that, after an investigation into the voluntary sports societies of Spartak, Burevestnik, the Union of Economic Workers, and others, many "perversions in the creation of normal work conditions for masters of sport had come to light".[99] There was widespread practice of distributing stipends among *fizkul'turniki* and instructors, some of which had frequently been given in addition to basic pay. The example of Burevestnik was cited where there the entire male and female hockey team were in receipt of stipends. In Spartak the practice was even more endemic. It was known that every team in every sport including instructors and social workers attached to Spartak received stipends. In the Union of Economic Workers seventeen stipends had been distributed amongst those in the ski school, and fifteen of these had been distributed to members of other societies. Furthermore, it was disclosed that in these organizations up to 80 per cent of their instructors had been hired without producing any instructor's identity card (from the latest round of testing) and did not have any special training. While sport was supposed be "for the interest of working youth", it had changed into becoming a supplementary trade and income for certain *fizkul'turniki*. It was considered that these stipends corrupted sport and led to antagonisms, essentially "poisoning" or polluting the entire sporting environment.

In response to this, the Moscow City Physical Culture Council in 1935 outlined five steps to take in order to combat the growing corruption problem. Firstly, it banned all physical culture organizations in Moscow city from distributing stipends to *fizkul'turniki*, forbade organizations for "taking them [*fizkul'turniki*] out of work for some course", as well as for providing them with additional financial benefits such as food allowances.[100] Secondly, it banned students and postgraduate students from the Stalin GTsOLIFK (the renamed State Institute of Physical Culture) and the Antipov Regional Technical Institute of Physical Culture from competing for other societies and receiving payment for this. Thirdly, it warned all physical culture organizations in Moscow that in the future, the "presidium would be taking the most severe measures in regard to those persons who would be revealed in further resolutions".[101] Fourthly, in relation to instructors, it stipulated that instructors with two occupations were only allowed to work with the permission of the organization in which they were primarily employed. Finally, the MGSPS resolved to remove from work any physical culture instructors who did not pass the most recent round of checks. Decisions regarding their work would in the future only be made after they successfully passed through the central examinations commission of the MGSPS.[102] The Moscow City Council of Physical Culture's decision to act on corruption at the end of 1935—closely following the establishment of the league and voluntary societies—was further proof that problems within the sports structure had been rife before the "professionalization" of Soviet sports in the mid-1930s.

For those working side by side with better paid absentee sports stars in factories, the atmosphere must have been tense. At least now the authorities were seen to be taking affirmative action. As a response to masters of sport continuing to request better living conditions, a commission was charged in 1936 with drawing up an appropriate hierarchical payment scheme.

The commission recommended that sportspersons training for competition should have access to medical support, massage, and a canteen with a "good quality chef" at their training base.[103] Payment was to be graded on four levels which saw masters and record-breakers of international standing receive the top wage of 600 roubles per month. Champions of international standing with some records to their name were to receive 400 roubles, while first-grade holders were to receive 250 roubles. The final rung on the scale was, unsurprisingly, occupied by students and young sportspersons who were entitled to a meagre one hundred roubles per month. This scale still did not reflect the growing stratification in Soviet society and was in many cases ignored anyhow. Just over a year later certain physical culture organizations were suspected of going to extraordinary lengths to ensure sports success. One trade union bureau reportedly spent 40,000 roubles on training and preparation for a swimming event.[104] To make matters worse, the two swimmers involved were relieved from work for a period of four months in order to train, while 3,600 roubles had been expended on providing them with a "specialist swimmers' diet" and 200 roubles a month spent on trainers, personal doctors, and massage.[105] The specially appointed commission evidently needed to clarify the minutiae of "medical support" and afford closer consideration to its definition of a "good quality" chef.

It was in the same month as this had come to light, May 1937, when it was decided that enough was enough. The Starostin affair of 1937, discussed in Chapter 2, highlighted the infiltration of the new political mood into the world of sport and physical culture. This political mood permeated further into physical culture and sport when the Physical Culture Committee made a declaration on the transfer of players from one organization to another, and on the awarding of prizes to sportspersons. It decreed that *fizkul'turniki* had to remain within their respective work collectives regardless of their sports status.[106] In one calendar year *fizkul'turniki* could only represent one organization. The transfer of masters was subject to stricter criteria and had to be authorized by the All-Union Committee. These were similar to the 1934 rules passed by Kharchenko, rules which carried little meaning in practice. The Committee acknowledged that there had been a growing trend in recent years for physical culture organizations to lure sportspersons through the awarding of prizes. These included money, apartments, furniture, sports attire, resort passes, and more, all of which had created a "mood of corruption".[107] The Committee therefore resolved to forbid the awarding of monetary sums or prizes which were only "materially valuable" by the physical culture organizations. Instead, prizes received in sports competitions had to be diplomas or badges, statuettes, cups, vases, pictures with physical culture themes of artistic value, or "cultural" items such as library cards, watches, binoculars, bicycles, musical instruments, radios, cameras, and other items. These prizes had to correspond to the standard of competition. In cases where regional prizes were concerned, these had to go through the Central Committee for authorization.[108] It remained to be seen whether or not stars could successfully make the transition from receiving hundreds or thousands of roubles to receiving a "cultural" reward of a library card or bicycle.

PHYSICAL CULTURE UNRESOLVED

Just as in other areas of Soviet life, physical culture was also subject to increased stratification, where the young, ambitious, wily, and just plain lucky got ahead. Commitment and ability did not necessarily entail sporting success as political games had to be played and bureaucratic structures adhered to. As sports tourism showed, some were able to master (or evade) this system with considerable aplomb, while others were for various reasons unable to do so. The experiences of those participating in sports shows that honesty and morality—two key tenets of Soviet socialism and characteristics of the New Person—were repeatedly trodden over by officials and self-interested stars whose dishonesty and corruption often found reward. Under the skewed morality of Stalinism it transpired that the enemy was oftentimes the innocent party, while the system of justice frequently favoured those guilty of committing "crimes". The so-called happy Soviet citizens who wanted to enjoy life in the "utopia" were still largely unable to do so for several reasons. Sports infrastructure, though improving, was far from satisfactory. Regulation and organization were still weak. Large segments of the population such as older people, social minorities, and rural inhabitants remained marginalized and cut-off from physical culture and sport. It was ultimately proven that mass participation in physical culture, and by extension the wider socialist community, was impracticable, and, what was more, socialist principles were shown to be elastic, inconsistent, and easily flouted.

Conclusion

After the revolution and civil war Soviet citizens were continually encouraged to remodel and refashion themselves, both in body and in mind. Physical culture was an integral part of this project, with the incorporation of style and image, strength, and well-being, as well as determination and enlightenment. This project was initially undertaken under the NEP with a fear of what Igal Halfin has called "degeneration"—"the propensity of the proletariat to contract diseases that could not be described as either physical or moral, but had to be characterized as a hybrid of both".[1] These diseases threatened the "health of the entire body politic". The constant fear of degeneration or loss of consciousness was combated in numerous ways, but particularly through programmes for identity such as physical culture. The unfettering stream of physical culture propaganda from the centre to all parts of the Soviet Union aimed to fortify and maintain the health of the social body. This vast campaign of transformation and self-betterment continued after NEP and in many ways gained momentum during the Five Year Plan, when attention had turned to the labour and collectivization drives. Physically capable and socially aware workers and peasants were to be forged through their identification with Soviet ideals and shared objectives of constructing a socialist paradise. The mid to late 1930s witnessed the introduction of Stalin's Constitution and an intense juxtaposition of the opposing forces of good (heroes, happiness, leisure) and evil (enemies, purges, fear).

While physical culture was part of a wider modernizing and civilizing project, it was also intrinsically bound up in party politics. The conflicts among leading political figures involved in physical culture organization, aside from hindering progress, showed that physical culture was an important battleground over which senior figures, such as Semashko, were willing to argue. Turf battles were a salient feature of the young Soviet state and, as it sought to establish itself, so too did individuals seeking a role in its development. The expanding bureaucracies and political power struggles of the mid-1920s created an atmosphere wherein uncertainty and suspicion were allowed to grow. Competition and rivalries between ministries, organizations, institutions, and individuals seeking power, promotion, and prestige often obscured loftier ideological goals. Despite the Bolshevik obsession with statistics and mass support, attempts to convert the masses proved fruitless for much of the 1920s mainly because the state, despite supporting physical culture in theory, was not unreservedly behind it in terms of financial and material support. It was only during the course of the Five Year Plan that physical culture and sport began to receive additional state support and attention, thus leading to a general improvement in conditions and participation. In the 1930s structural and organizational changes, increased funding following the first Plan, expansion of the cities, the introduction of the GTO, and the establishment of the voluntary sports societies all contributed to raising the public profile of physical culture and sport. There were still many problems afflicting the successful implementation of physical culture objectives, however, problems which even increased centralization failed to resolve (and in many ways precipitated or exacerbated).

Targeting young people, women and peasants through physical culture and sport was a means of intercepting their traditional, "backward" mode of life and introducing these groups to the new, modern, Soviet way of life. For different reasons each of these groups were considered potential impediments to the progress of socialism. Young people, the vanguard of the revolution, were also thought to be untrustworthy with their pliable nature just as much a problem than an advantage. They were equally liable to fall prey to bourgeois tendencies as to socialist enlightenment and the rise in cases of hooliganism, alcoholism, and suicide confirmed state fears surrounding young people. Similar doubts were expressed about women, peasants, and national minorities who supposedly symbolized backward Russia and the ignorance which the Soviet state so loathed. The primary means through which these groups were directed towards active physical culture was agitprop. Although these groups might very well have been already engaged in physical culture and sport of some description, whether playing football, skiing, or playing games, this was not *organized* or sufficiently *sovietized*. The propaganda directed at young people, women and peasants thus tried to lure them towards participation in the *kruzhok* or club where they would be under party guidance. Agitation aimed to show these groups that physical culture and even the Soviet regime itself was to be embraced. All purportedly offered a sense of belonging to a greater whole, a welcoming collective with everyone's interests and needs its primary concern.

By the late 1920s and 1930s leisure and cultured activities were widely promoted, and the visual imagery associated with this, when juxtaposed to the Terror, depicts the extremity of the contrasts and contradictions within Soviet society. Spartakiads and parades reflected such contradictions. The first Spartakiad, held in 1928, was still very much a celebration of physical culture, with just as much emphasis on dance and demonstration than on competition. Parades in the 1920s and even the early 1930s were modest affairs. It was only towards the mid-1930s that they became the visual and organizational extravaganzas that came to symbolize Soviet sport. By the end of the decade, physical culture and sport had in many ways come full circle, with health, hygiene, and labour still an issue but relegated behind defence and military needs, which were receiving mounting attention. In spite of the purported goals of socialism, life in the Soviet Union was highly stratified and the emergence of heroes and stars only served to cement the divisions even further. Compromises had been made in physical culture. Earlier conceptions of a proletarian physical culture had proven unrealizable and so sport, with all its traditional connotations and associations, received official sanction. The GTO initiated this move towards competitive sport, while the regulation of the football league and establishment of the sports societies increased elements of professionalism within sport.

Further evidence of changes in the approach to physical culture and sport came in 1938 when "pointless and useless" *kruzhki* in the Central Asian region were subject to reorganization by the Red Army with help from Osoaviakhim and young local workers.[2] The militarization of physical culture had become the priority. Regular physical culture clubs began to be replaced by military units based on those used by the Red Army.[3] Both Osoaviakhim and the Red Army partook in military training and education. The "troops" undertook training under extreme geographical and climatic conditions (mountain terrain, heat, and dust) over the course of five to seven days during which they showed "high political consciousness and physical perseverance".[4] Further preparations were planned for the *sovkhozy* and *kolkhozy*. Those involved in physical culture *kruzhki* had been increasingly encouraged to join Osoaviakhim and sports such as parachuting had become popular amongst workers. Physical culture was an easily transferable term, at one time meaning sanitation and at another standing for sniper training. The militaristic discourse of the early revolutionary years had returned as "troops" and "regiments" formed of ordinary citizens prepared for attack. In just a few years time—1941—Vsevobuch would again be established and the Soviet Union would be at war.

The one overarching concept that emerges from this study is transformation. Societies are constantly in transition, but Soviet society in the 1920s and 1930s underwent revolutionary transitions. Physical culture played its own important role during these revolutionary years. It presented individuals with an opportunity to transform themselves—unlike many other areas however, physical culture entailed both physical *and* mental transformation. It fed into the visual image of what a good communist, a politically conscious worker, or a Soviet woman should look like, how they should act and even think. Muscular, toned, and tanned with a clean and tidy appearance, reading politically prescribed literature, attending club meetings, and going to the stadium or sports square—these were the criteria for the New Soviet Person. Yet this was the end product (and the New Person was anyhow engaged in an ongoing process of self-betterment and acculturation). A means to achieve this was physical culture. Physical culture offered one of the most straightforward routes to transformation. Of course it was not always applied as an explicit attempt to "transform", but it nonetheless had the intended effect of producing such a result through its function as a programme for identity. Young people, women, peasants, workers—all were encouraged to embrace physical culture to better and improve themselves, to use it to transform their lives and play an active role in socialist life.

I set out to demonstrate the vast array of meanings bound up in the concept of "physical culture", each chapter adding a new shade to its already colourful spectrum. These were all linked by a common thread—the desire to develop, change and acculturate. Physical culture has been shown to have been an intrinsic part of the Bolshevik plan to modernize the Soviet Union and help construct the New Soviet Person. It has come to light that although physical culture was a political tool of the party, one that was used in numerous ways, it was also been shown that physical culture held important and different meanings for ordinary people who were not the monolithic "masses" which physical culture agitprop targeted. Rather, they had their own lives and their own personal concerns, which physical culture may or may not have impacted upon. For these ordinary people state calls for participation in physical culture in many cases meant embracing, rejecting, or tolerating its associated ideology and propaganda. As for the Soviet state, having recognized the potential of physical culture from early on it was able to filter its preoccupation with *vospitanie*, *kul'turnost'*, the New Soviet Person—the general desire to assert a system of values on a society—through physical culture and urge people to participate in a new form of socialist lifestyle. The emotive qualities of physical culture, its collective and individual nature, and its potential to shape the body and the mind were recognized and harnessed by the Bolsheviks who were keen to implement it as an essential component in the development and modernization of the young communist state. While reflecting wider international and European trends the Soviet Union at the same time tread its own course in its approach to physical culture and sport, laying the foundations for what was to become the powerful Soviet sports system that emerged in later years.

Appendix A
Biographical Index

NIKOLAI KIRILLOVICH ANTIPOV

Born in Novgorod province, Antipov (1894–1938) was a party member since 1912. From 1920 he was involved in trade union work, becoming a member of the VTsSPS presidium. From 1923 to 1924 he was Moscow Party Committee Secretary and by 1925 was the First Secretary of the Urals provincial committee. In 1925 he was Second Secretary of the Leningrad district committee and secretary of the North-Western Party bureau. From 1928 to 1931 he held the position of People's Commissar for Post and Telegraph and afterwards became Commissar for the Worker-Peasant Inspectorate. It was also from 1931 (until 1933) that he was Chairman of the All-Union Council of Physical Culture. At the 1937 June Plenum he was expelled from the Central Committee and the Party and was soon arrested. He was shot in July of that year and rehabilitated in 1956.

DR. ARON GRIGOR'EVICH ITTIN

Ittin (1896–1937) was the Komsomol representative in the Supreme Council. Editor of *Fizkul'tura i Sport*, he was an influential but sometimes controversial figure. He was arrested in Moscow for anti-Soviet terrorist involvement and was shot in September 1937. He was later rehabilitated in 1956. Ittin was the principal advocate of a more active Komsomol role in physical culture. He referred to the absence of a truly united organization in physical culture and stated the need for the Komsomol and trade unions to work together. According to Ittin, the Supreme Council was obstructing the work of the Komsomol in the creation of its own organization of sports committees and provincial offices.[1] Ittin averred that the Komsomol had to influence the Supreme Council and through it had to serve the factory clubs and societies (*kruzhki* and *yacheiki*). He attested that the Komsomol was the core organization which supported every physical culture club. At some point in the mid-1920s Ittin switched his loyalties to the trade unions and in 1928 was referred to as a "former Komsomolite" by Podvoisky.[2] When the Supreme Council was initially established, Ittin was the Komsomol representative. However, aside from Podvoisky's remark, there was also a list of those in the Supreme Council of Physical Culture in 1925 where Ittin appears (along with Seniushkin and Isaev) as a trade union representative (the Komsomol representatives at this point were Sorokin and Seredkin.)[3]

BORIS ALEKSEEVICH KAL'PUS

Kal'pus (1895–1938) was a member of the VKP (b) and physical culture and sport representative. He was a member of the organizational committee of the First All-Union Spartakiad in 1928 and was secretary of the Supreme Council of Physical Culture. Kal'pus also played an important role in the *fizkul'tura* discussions of the 1920s but was arrested in January 1938 on charges of participating in a counter-revolutionary terrorist organization and was shot in August 1938. He was later rehabilitated in 1956.

KONSTANTIN ALEKSANDROVICH MEKHONOSHIN

Mekhonoshin (1889–1938) was an important figure in the world of physical culture and was second to Semashko in the Supreme Council of Physical Culture. Holding such a senior role, he had a good deal of influence in physical culture affairs.[4] The son of a teacher, Mekhonoshin studied at St. Petersburg University but never graduated. In 1906 he was attracted towards the revolutionary movement and in 1913 joined the RSDRP (b). After February 1917 Mekhonoshin became a member of the Petrograd Soviet and a member of the Petrograd committee of the RSDRP (b). In June 1917 he was arrested but was freed in October. From November 1920 Mekhonoshin held a position in the People's Commissariat for Military Affairs. In 1918 during the civil war he allegedly became close to Trotsky. There are in fact two different versions of Mekhonoshin's biography, one which can be found in a military encyclopaedia that omits several key details, one being his links to Trotsky.[5] From 1927 to 1931 Mekhonoshin worked in Osoaviakhim.[6] He also worked in Gosplan during these years, was involved in Vsevobuch from 1921 to 1926 and was the military representative in the Supreme Council of Physical Culture. Mekhonoshin was arrested in 1937, interned in a death camp, and shot.

NIKOLAI IL'ICH PODVOISKY

Podvoisky had joined the Russian Democratic Workers Party in 1901 and was a long-term revolutionary who stormed the Winter Palace in 1917. He was also chairman of Vsevobuch. According to Boris Bazhanov, in "government circles his name was usually accompanied by the epithet 'old fool'" and that because of his "stupidity and incapacity to do the slightest useful work, the authorities had always had a hard time finding a proper slot for him".[7] He was thus, according to Bazhanov, given the "sinecure" of Vsevobuch leader. On being appointed Vsevobuch leader, Podvoisky was allegedly "mortified and offended". When the Sportintern was created he became its head, a move which, in Bazhanov's view, made some strides in satisfying his vanity. In spite of Bazahnov's criticisms, Podvoisky's name is still synonymous with Vsevobuch.[8]

NIKOLAI ALEKSANDROVICH SEMASHKO

Nikolai Aleksandrovich Semashko was the People's Commissar of Health (1918–1930) and Chairman of the Supreme Council of Physical Culture. A doctor who had been with Lenin in emigration and participated in the Paris Party Conference in 1912, Semashko was a leading figure in Soviet health in the first two decades of its existence. He was also a central figure in the early years of physical culture in his role as Chairperson of the Supreme Council of Physical Culture and was a major advocate of medical control and supervision, viewing physical culture as the ideal means of developing youth. He argued that through its work, the Supreme Council could help improve the health of the young and generations to follow.[9] He was the author of myriad influential texts on health, hygiene, and physical culture, and was often cited as compulsory reading for budding *fizkul'turniki*. Perhaps his most important work on physical culture was *Puti sovetskoi fizkul'tury* in 1926, where he outlined the poor state of Soviet health.[10] He estimated that over 3 million people each year died as a result of typhus, cholera, tuberculosis, and other diseases. In his view, one of the best ways of combating this problem was introducing hygiene and physical culture to the nation.

F. SENIUSHKIN

Seniushkin was the trade union representative in the Supreme Council of Physical Culture. In the trade unions he was responsible for cultural and educational affairs. Not as outspoken as the other representatives, Seniushkin nonetheless made a contribution to the literature on physical culture.

A. A. ZIKMUND

The person primarily associated with the ideology of physical culture was A. A. Zikmund.[11] Zikmund, as rector of the State Institute of Physical

Culture in Moscow and chairman of the NTK,[12] was another significant and controversial figure in physical culture.[13] Representing the *Hygienist* position, he advocated the banning of competitive sports, including football among others. In terms of the scientific organization of physical culture A. A. Zikmund called for a single system of Soviet physical culture.[14] In his view work had to be based on an ideology that was directly related to daily life. Physical culture had to develop the body and prepare it for work and defence. The correct organization of physical culture would improve the workers' and peasants' quality of life, help them resist illness and disease, educate them in the principles of collectivism, and raise their work capacity and military preparation. Under his reign, both the Moscow and Leningrad institutes of physical culture adopted a profoundly *Hygienist* stance, overlooking sports and games to focus instead on medical subjects. Following accusations of links to Trotsky, Zikmund disappeared in the purges.

Appendix B
Organizational and Institutional Index

DINAMO

Oldest and most prominent, the Proletarian Sports Society Dinamo was the physical culture organization attached to the security and military organ GPU.[1] Dinamo was set up in 1923 by a group of workers from the Cheka and Moscow factory Dinamo. It came to be associated with Cheka leader Felix Dzerzhinsky and soon had "clubs in almost every city" growing more effective "as a sport power . . . with each succeeding year".[2] The first Dinamo society was in Moscow, followed by Penza and numerous other towns and cities. Its rapid rise is evident in the statistics—by October 1923 it had thirty-six sections and over 3,000 members in Moscow alone.[3] Its aim was to improve physical development and education and its task was military preparation.[4] Consequently much emphasis was placed on shooting-related sports. Dinamo claimed to have the best stadiums, though with the support of the security services, this was unsurprising. The club boasted fine stadiums in Moscow, Kiev, Leningrad, Khar'kov, Gor'ky (Nizhnii Novgorod), Voronezh, and elsewhere. It was also involved in sponsoring physical culture work on *kolkhozy*, *sovkhozy*, and enterprises. Following the dissolution of Vsevobuch, Dinamo became a legitimate contender for a leadership role in physical culture but was too closely associated with the work of the security organs to become a real threat. It commanded more power as it was, without becoming embroiled in the protracted organizational disputes between the unions and Komsomol.

OSOAVIAKHIM

Osoaviakhim, associated with defence and the military, was advanced as playing an important role in sports such as shooting, horse-riding and aviation. General Secretary of Osoaviakhim, L. Malinovskii, declared that every *fizkul'turnik* had to join the society and become an "active Osoaviakhimets".[5] In 1929 Chernyak, an inspector with Osoaviakhim, proposed introducing a medal "for excellence in physical preparedness" with the aim of encouraging membership and participation.[6] He also suggested awarding certain privileges to those who were successful in military service or in the VUZy. Membership of the society eventually became a hallmark of prestige and success and a symbol of exceptional ability in and service to physical culture and sport. Testament to this, its membership grew substantially. In 1929 it had 2,950,000 members and this increased to number 5,100,000 in 1930, with 34 per cent workers and 32 per cent peasants.[7] During the Five Year Plan its goal was to incorporate 75 per cent of all workers, 50 per cent of students, 100 per cent of the Komsomol, 80 per cent of the RKKA and 6 per cent of the peasant population.[8] Osoaviakhim also organized physical culture camps where groups of up to 400 people would spend around ten days engaged in organized physical culture of a predominantly military nature and political education.[9]

THE STATE INSTITUTE OF PHYSICAL CULTURE

The State Institute of Physical Culture in Moscow had been established in 1918 in order to train physical culture instructors and teachers. It was not attached to the Supreme Council of Physical Culture, actually falling under the direction of the Commissariat for Health. Not only did the Institute cater for individual sports (athletics, boxing, wrestling, fencing, and other sports) but it also offered courses in psychology, hygiene, anatomy, biology, chemistry, the history and organization of physical culture, as well as the ubiquitous Marxist-Leninist courses and the theory and practice of physical culture.[10] The structure included departments and laboratories for social science, gynaecology, haematology, and experimental psychology as well as psychological techniques.[11] By 1928 the Institute had its own stadium, sports and gymnastics squares, tennis and basketball courts, athletics track, as well as swimming and rowing centres. It could also boast of specialist halls for physical exercise, a library, and a museum. Although the institute was attached to the Commissariat of Health, it maintained links with a whole host of other departments and organizations, including the Commissariats of Education and Military/Navy, Osoaviakhim, the Supreme Council of Physical Culture, the various trade union organizations, the Komsomol and others. With Zikmund at its head the Institute was very much under the influence of the Hygienists in the 1920s, with myriad articles appearing in publications of the 1920s championing various systems of callisthenics or the affect of exercise on one's health. It was not really until the fall of the Hygienist school that the Institute became more closely associated with the specialist training of athletes. Since it first opened it doors, the Institute had produced over 1,500 physical culture graduates by 1929.[12]

VSEVOBUCH

Vsevobuch (*Vseobshchee Voennoe Obuchenie* or the Central Agency for Universal Military Training)—was the state response to the acute military needs of the civil war. It was set up by a 7 May 1918 decree of the All-Russia Central Executive Committee of the Soviets of Workers', Soldiers' and Peasants' Deputies, and its aim was the compulsory military training of Russian men, youth pre-conscription military training, and the physical mobilization of the population through sport. All organized sport, all existing clubs, and societies came under the jurisdiction of Vsevobuch. Its programmes operated on county, district, and provincial level, and committees were set up wherever the Bolsheviks were in control. Vsevobuch, along with the active participation of the Komsomol, created local military-sports clubs, establishing a new type of physical culture organization—the physical culture *kruzhok* of the factory, plant, and institute. As a response, Vsevobuch effectively usurped the positions of the bourgeois clubs, appropriating whatever equipment and supplies they found. The Sokol, Maccabee, and other organizations were now targeted as bourgeois centres of resistance. Any remaining vestiges of bourgeois sports activity were to be hunted and expunged.

Glossary

agitprop	*agit*ation and *prop*aganda
aktiv	activists, most active body in and organization or factory
batrak	(pl. *batraki*) lowly peasant farm labourer(s)
bedniak	(pl. *bedniaki*) poor peasant(s)
byt	everyday life
chastushka	folk song or poem
chistka	(pl. *chistki*) purge(s)
Dinamo	sports society, set up in 1923
Five Year Plan	programme for industrialization and collectivization
fizkul'tura	*fizicheskaya **kul'tura**/*physical culture
fizkul'turnik(i)	a male physical culturist(s); here refers to male and female
fizkul'turnitsa	female physical culturist
fizkul'turnitsy	female physical culturists
gorodki	a Russian folk sport, similar to bowling, which was very popular amongst both rural and city dwellers. The rules were extremely varied but were worked out by the Supreme Council of Physical Culture to include a stick/bat (*palka* or *bit*) and wooden stumps or skittles (*churki*), usually fashioned out of wood. The skittles themselves were called "gorodki" and the area where they were arranged was called the "gorod"
GTO	*Gotov k Trudu i Oborone*/Get Ready for Labour and Defence
guberniya	(pl. *gubernii*) large territorial and administrative region(s) (until 1929)
kegli	traditional Russian game similar to bowling
kolkhoz	(pl. *Kolkhozy*) Soviet collective farm(s)

Komsomol	*Kommunisticheskii Soiuz Molodezhi*/Communist Youth League
Komsomol ('ka)	Male (female) member of the Komsomol
krai	(pl. *kraia*) large territorial and administrative region(s) (until 1929)
kruzhok/kruzhki	circle/circles
kul'turnost'	level of culture
lapta	traditional Russian game similar to baseball or rounders with 5–15 players on each team on field of 70–80m in length and 30–40m in width. The bat was called the *lapta*
MGSFK	Moscow City Council of Physical Culture
MOSFK	Moscow Region Council of Physical Culture
MGSPS	Moscow City Council of Trade Unions
MOSPS	Moscow Region Council of Trade Unions
Narkomfin	People's Commissariat for Finance
Narkompros	Peoples' Commissariat for Education and Enlightenment
Narkomtrud	Peoples' Commissariat for Labour
Narkomzdrav	Peoples' Commissariat for Public Health
NEP	New Economic Policy 1921–1928
NTK	*Nauchnyi Tekhnicheskii Komitet*/Scientific Technical Committee
oblas't	(pl. *oblasti*) province(s) (similar to *krai*)
OGPU, GPU	Soviet secret police
okrug	(*pl. okruga*) large territorial and administrative region(s)
OSOAVIAKhIM (*Obshchestvo sodeistviya oborone, aviatsionnomu i khimicheskomu stroitel'stvu*)	Union of Societies of Assistance to Defence and Aviation-Chemical Construction of the USSR, amalgamated in 1927
Proletkul't	Proletarian Culture
promfinplan	industrial financial plan
rabfak	(pl. *rabfaki*) *rabochii fakul'tet*/ university preparatory course(s) for workers
raion	(pl. *raiony*) district(s) (formerly *uezd*)
rekordmenstvo	breaking sports records
Serp i Molot	Sickle and Hammer factory

ShKM	*Shkoly Kolkhoznoi Molodezhi*/ schools for *kolkhoz* youth
shock-workers	highly efficient and diligent workers (precursor to *Stakhanovism*)
sovkhoz	(pl. *sovkhozy*) Soviet state farm(s) following collectivization
Sovnarkom	Council of People's Commissars
Spartakiad	Soviet equivalent to the Olympics
Sportintern	Red Sport International/ Communist sports movement
Stakhanovism/ *Stakhanovite*	Aleksei Stakhanov was a miner who in 1935 exceeded his work quota by fourteen times. Subsequently, all workers who exceeded their norms were heralded as *Stakhanovites* and often rewarded for their efforts
VSFK	Supreme Council of Physical Culture (later All-Union)
VTsSPS	*Vsesoiuznyi Tsentral'nyi Sovet Professional'nyi Soiuzov*/ All-Union Central Council of Trade Unions
vospitanie	translated as upbringing and education, but also incorporating manners and tastes
Vsevobuch	*Vseobshchee Voennoe Obuchenie*/ Central Agency for Universal Military Training, 1918–1923
VUZ(y)	*Vysshie Uchebnye Zavedanie*/ higher educational institute(s)
yacheika	(pl. *yacheiki*) cell(s)
Young Pioneers	organization for youth between the ages of 10-15, established in 1922
zavkom	trade union committee
Zhenotdel	Women's Department

Notes

NOTES TO THE INTRODUCTION

1. Jennifer Hargreaves (ed), *Sport, Culture and Ideology* (London: Routledge & Kegan Paul, 1982), 4.
2. Jeffrey Hill, *Sport, Leisure and Culture in Twentieth Century Britain* (London; New York: Palgrave Macmillan, 2002); Barbara Keys, *Globalizing Sport: National Rivalry and International Community in the 1930s* (Cambridge, MA: Harvard University Press, 2006).
3. These are too numerous to list here. Broad or general histories include Geoffrey Hosking, *Rulers and Victims: The Russians in the Soviet Union* (Cambridge, MA: Belknap Press of Harvard University Press, 2006), David L. Hoffmann, *Stalinist Values: The Cultural Norms of Soviet Modernity, 1917–1941* (Ithaca, NY; London: Cornell University Press, 2003); *Cultivating the Masses: Modern State Practices and Soviet Socialism, 1914–1939* (Ithaca, NY; London: Cornell University Press, 2011), and Catriona Kelly and David Shepherd (eds), *Constructing Russian Culture in the age of Revolution 1881–1940* (Oxford: Oxford University Press, 1998). Work has also been undertaken by various groups and networks, most notably by the past and ongoing projects of Professor Nikolaus Katzer and Anke Hilbrenner in Germany. Other studies are discussed in the historiography below.
4. For more on social hygiene see Susan Gross Solomon, "Social Hygiene and Soviet Public Health, 1921–1930" in Solomon, Susan Gross, and Hutchinson, John F., *Health And Society in Revolutionary Russia* (Bloomington and Indianapolis: Indiana University Press, 1990), 175–199.
5. Sheila Fitzpatrick, *Tear Off the Masks! Identity and Imposture in Twentieth Century Russia* (Princeton, NJ: Princeton University Press, 2005), 5.
6. Focusing on such issues from the outset can be problematic and one should bear in mind the caution of Rogers Brubaker and Frederick Cooper, who argue that using identity as a category of analysis or even assuming that "all people have, seek, construct, and negotiate" identities is restrictive and limiting, and moreover, that it is a contradictory and ambiguous concept. Brubaker and Cooper, "Beyond 'Identity'", *Theory and Society* 29 (2000): 2.
7. Kelly and Shepherd, *Constructing Russian Culture*, 5.
8. These two terms can be translated most directly as "education/upbringing" and "level of culture". In the 1920s the term *vospitanie* was frequently used in the physical culture discourse when discussing young people. *Kul'turnost'* was a more general term that included adult education and all-round personal development and self-betterment, especially in the 1930s.

9. Régine Robin, "Stalinism and Popular Culture", in Hans Günther (ed), *The Culture of the Stalin Period* (London: Macmillan, 1990), 21–22. Lewis Siegelbaum too notes the importance of these "levels" as a means of acculturation with regard to clubs. Siegelbaum, "The Shaping of Soviet Workers' Leisure: Worker's Clubs and Palaces of Culture in the 1930s", *International Labor and Working-Class History* 56 (1999): 85.
10. Robin, "Stalinism and Popular Culture", 22.
11. Vitalii Vasil'evich Stolbov, *Istorii fizicheskoi istorii i sporta* (Moscow: Fizkultura i sport, 2000); F. I. Samoukov (ed), *Istoriya fizicheskoi kul'tury* (Moscow: Fizkul'tura i sport, 1956); D. Sinitsyn (ed), *Istoriya fizicheskoi kul'tury narodov SSSR*, (Moscow: Fizkul'tura i sport, 1953); Aksel'rod, *Fizicheskaya kul'tura i sport v SSSR. Sbornik materialov v pomoshch' propaganda* (Moscow: Fizkul'tura i sport, 1954).
12. Aksel'rod, *Istoriya fizicheskoi kul'tury*, 7.
13. I. G. Chudinov, *Osnovnye postanovleniya, prikazy i instruktsii po voprosam sovetskoi fizicheskoi kul'tury i sporta 1917–1957* (Moscow: Fizkul'tura i sport, 1959).
14. See *Bibliograficheskii ukazatel' nauchno-issledovatel'skikh i nauchno-metodicheskikh trudov professorov i prepodavatelei instituta (1920–1961)*, Moscow, 1964. In relation to the "accepted" history, see Chapter 1.
15. B. P. Goloshchapov, *Istoriya fizicheskoi kul'tury i sporta* (Moscow: Izdatel'skii tsentr "Akademiya", 2008).
16. James Riordan, *Sport in Soviet Society: Development of Sport and Physical Education in Russia and the USSR* (Cambridge; New York: Cambridge University Press, 1977); Riordan (ed), *Sport in Soviet Society, Sport under Communism: The USSR, Czechoslovakia, the GDR, China, Cuba* (London: C Hurst, 1978); and with Pierre Arnaud (eds), *Sport and International Politics: The Impact of Fascism and Communism on Sport* (London: New York: E & FN Spon, 1998).
17. Henry W. Morton, *Soviet Sport: Mirror of Soviet Society* (New York: Collier Books, 1963).
18. Mike O'Mahony, *Sport in the USSR. Physical Culture—Visual Culture* (London: Reaktion Books, 2006).
19. Barbara Keys, *Globalizing Sport* and Keys, "Soviet Sport and Transnational Mass Culture in the 1930s", *Journal of Contemporary History* 38, no. 3 (July 2003): 413–434.
20. Robert Edelman, *Serious Fun: A History of Spectator Sports in the USSR.* (New York; Oxford: Oxford University Press, 1993). Edelman's *Spartak Moscow: History of the People's Team in the Worker's State* (Ithaca, NY; London: Cornell University Press, 2009) offers an excellent analysis of the development of Soviet football and history of Spartak.
21. R. Edelman, *Serious Fun*, 21.
22. Stefan Plaggenborg, *Revoliutsia i kul'tura. Kul'turnye orientiry v period mezhdu oktyabr'skoi revoliutsiei epochoi stalinizma*, (Sankt Peterburg: Zhurnal Neva, 2000) Originally published in German,1996.
23. Nikolaus Katzer et al, *Euphoria and Exhaustion. Modern Sport in Soviet Culture and Society* (Frankfurt; New York: Campus/Verlag, 2010).
24. Katzer, *Euphoria and Exhaustion*, 11.
25. Karen Petrone, *Life Has Become More Joyous, Comrades: Celebrations in the Time of Stalin* (Bloomington: Indiana University Press, 2000); Frances Lee Bernstein, *The Dictatorship of Sex: Lifestyle Advice for the Soviet Masses* (DeKalb: Northern Illinois University Press, 2007); Tricia Starks, *The Body Soviet: Propaganda, Hygiene, and the Revolutionary State* (Madison: Wisconsin University Press, 2008).

26. Petrone, *Life has Become More Joyous, Comrades*, 30–31.
27. These groups were obviously not mutually exclusive or homogenous (and this is part of the reason for overlap within chapters) but this categorization reflects the general trend of physical culture propaganda and how it was directed at certain groups within Soviet society.
28. Aaron B. Retish, *Russia's Peasants in Revolution and Civil War: Citizenship, Identity, and the Creation of the Soviet State, 1914–1922* (Cambridge: Cambridge University Press, 2008), 213.
29. The Department of Agitation and Propaganda under the Central Committee oversaw the conduct of agitprop. As Vladimir Brovkin notes, during NEP this institution "grew into an elaborate bureaucratic structure of more then thirty sub-departments on the press, publishing houses, science, schools, cadres, training, cinema, the arts, radio, and literature, to name only a few". Vladimir Brovkin, *Russia after Lenin: Politics, Culture and Society, 1921–1929* (London: Routledge, 1998), 81.
30. V. I. Lenin, *Collected Works*, vol. 5 (Moscow, 1961) and G. V. Plekhanov, *O zadachakh sotsialistov v bor'be s golodom v Rossii* (Geneva, 1982) in Richard Taylor, *Film Propaganda: Soviet Russia and Nazi Germany* (London: I. B. Tauris, 1998), 29.
31. Anatoly Lunacharsky, "Revolution and Art, 1920–1922" in *Russian Art of the Avant-Garde: Theory and Criticism*, edited by John E. Bowlt (London; New York: Thames and Hudson, 1988), 191–192.
32. Kenez, *Birth of the Propaganda State*, 2.
33. Matthew Lenoe, *Closer to the Masses: Stalinist Culture, Social Revolution and Soviet Newspapers* (Cambridge, MA; London: Harvard University Press, 2004), 27.
34. Keys, *Globalizing Sports*, 244. A list of the destroyed files can be found in GARF, f. 7576, op.29, d.2 (Keys, *Globalizing Sports*, 244).

NOTES TO CHAPTER 1

1. Arnd Krüger, "Germany", in James Riordan and Arnd Krüger (eds), *European Cultures in Sport: Examining the Nations and Regions* (Bristol; Portland, OR: Intellect Books, 2003), 68. See Krüger, 67–70 for more information on the *Turners* and Jahn.
2. Michael Anton Budd, *The Sculpture Machine: Physical Culture and Body Politics in the Age of Empire* (New York: New York University Press, 1997), 16. Budd provides an excellent account of the early growth of physical culture, especially in Britain.
3. For more on these aspects of body culture in inter-war Europe see Anton Kaes (ed), *The Weimar Republic Sourcebook* (Berkeley; London: University of California Press, 1994), 673–692. These German movements had a longer life span than those in other countries, surviving until about 1933 when they became subsumed to Nazi ideology and its version of body culture.
4. Budd, *Sculpture Machine*, 17.
5. Budd, *Sculpture Machine*, 17.
6. For example K. Alekseev of the Bogatyr Society for Physical Education, founded in St. Petersburg in 1904. Louise McReynolds, *Russia at Play: Leisure Activities at the End of the Tsarist Era* (Ithaca, NY; London: Cornell University Press, 2003), 94. For more on clubs and societies in Tsarist Russia, see Joseph Bradley, *Voluntary Associations in Tsarist Russia: Science, Patriotism and Civil Society* (Cambridge, MA; London: Harvard University Press, 2009).

7. McReynolds, *Russia at Play*, 96.
8. Marc Keech, "England and Wales", in *European Cultures*, 9.
9. Budd, *Sculpture Machine*, 43 and 152.
10. Else Trangbaek, "Denmark", in *European Cultures*, 47.
11. Thierry Terret, "France", in *European Cultures*, 107.
12. This was a sports and gymnastic organization for youth founded in 1862 in Prague. It was a pan-Slavic organization that sought to develop physical, moral, and intellectual capacities of its members.
13. James Riordan, *Sport in Soviet Society*, 55. For good discussion of the influence of Lesgaft, Pavlov and others see Riordan, Chapter 2 on "The ideological roots of Soviet physical education and sport", 42–67.
14. McReynolds, *Russia at Play*, 91. McReynolds discusses one of the first of these clubs and societies, the Petersburg Athletics Circle, organized in 1895 which set out to improve the physical health of young people and offered group and individual sports such as bicycling and shot-put, McReynolds, *Russia at Play*, 92.
15. McReynolds, *Russia at Play*, 87. Debate on sport and physical culture was rife in other countries too. For example in Germany disdain for competition was expressed by Hans Surén, who, in his 1925 work *Der Mensch und die Sonne* noted that young people "should not regard their goal to be breaking records but the power of the health and beauty of their own fully trained bodies". Kaes (ed), *Weimar Republic Sourcebook*, 678. Fritz Wildung was also opposed to the "sport as a battle" view, expressed earlier by the "bourgeois" Dr. Carl Diem, see *Weimar Republic Sourcebook*, 674, 681.
16. McReynolds, *Russia at Play*, 91. In spite of this there was still no proper organizational structure (this did not come until the 1930s). Rather, sport continued to be ad hoc in nature, with a "wild *kruzhki*" approach—just like mushrooms, clubs would "appear after the rain in summer and disappear again in the autumn", with football and tennis popular in dacha (country house) neighbourhoods where there were young people, workers, and railroads. GARF, f.7576, op.24, d.7, l.10.
17. Peter Frykholm, "Soccer and Social Identity in Pre-Revolutionary Moscow", *Journal of Sport History* 24, no 2 (1997): 143–154.
18. Edelman, *Spartak Moscow*, 11. Edelman adds that there were class differences, with bourgeois and proletarian men using their bodies in different ways, generating "different versions of manhood". *Spartak Moscow*, 12.
19. McReynolds, *Russia at Play*, 131.
20. Budd, *Sculpture Machine*, 82.
21. Budd, *Sculpture Machine*, 99.
22. In 1915 *Russkii sport* reported on and published the pictures of successful sportsman who had volunteered to go to the front, some of whom had already perished. See *Russkii sport* nos. 9 and 10.
23. GARF, f.7576, op.24, d.7, l.10.
24. Aaron B. Retish, *Russia's Peasants*, 29.
25. Peter Gatrell, *Russia's First World War: A Social and Economic History* (Edinburgh: Pearson Longman, 2005), 1.
26. Riordan, *Sport in Soviet Society*, 37.
27. Peter Holquist, *Making War, Forging Revolution: Russia's Continuum of Crisis, 1914–1921* (Cambridge, MA; London: Harvard University Press, 2002), 286.
28. Joshua A. Sanborn, *Drafting the Russian Nation: Military Conscription, Total War, and Mass Politics, 1905–1925* (DeKalb: Northern Illinois University Press, 2003); Holquist, *Making War*. Also, for good discussion of the

military and physical culture during this period see Sanborn, *Drafting the Russian Nation*, 133–146.

29. Holquist, *Making War*, 1, 3. Discussing the revolution as part of an even longer continuum was also proposed by Beatrice Farnsworth and Lynne Viola in *Russian Peasant Women* (Oxford: Oxford University Press, 1992), 3–4.
30. Budd, *Sculpture Machine*, 124.
31. Mary Lynn Stewart, *For Health and Beauty. Physical Culture for Frenchwomen, 1880s-1930s*, (Baltimore, MD; London, Johns Hopkins University Press, 2001), 1.
32. Ina Zweiniger-Bargielowska, "Building a British Superman: Physical Culture in Interwar Britain", in *Journal of Contemporary History* 41, no. 4 (2006): 601.
33. Budd, *Sculpture Machine*, 125.
34. Wolfgang Graeser, *Gymnastik, Tanz, Sport* (Munich, 1927) in Kaes, *Weimar Republic Sourcebook*, 683–685.
35. For more discussion see Michael Geyer, "The Stigma of Violence, Nationalism and War in Twentieth Century Germany", *German Studies Review*, special issue (1992): 75–110.
36. See Gertrud Pfister, "The Medical Discourse on Female Physical Culture in Germany in the 19th and Early 20th Centuries", in *Journal of Sport History* 17, no. 2 (1990): 191.
37. Retish, *Russia's Peasants*, 203.
38. Elizabeth A. Wood, *The Baba and the Comrade: Gender and Politics in Revolutionary Russia* (Bloomington: Indiana University Press, 1997), 123.
39. There are exceptions. In the case of Japan Irie Katsumi in *Nihon fashizumu to no taiikushisô* has argued that the strong paramilitary influence within Japanese sport began in the nineteenth century rather than during the Shôwra era (1926–1937). See Allen Guttmann, "Sport, Politics and the Engaged Historian", in *Journal of Contemporary History* 38, no. 3 (2003): 365.
40. Burcu Dogramaci, "Heading into Modernity: Sporting Culture, Architecture and Photography in the Early Turkish Republic" in Nikolaus Katzer et al. (eds), *Euphoria and Exhaustion: Modern Sport in Soviet Culture and Society* (Frankfurt; New York: Campus Verlag, 2010), 114.
41. Andrew D. Morris, *Marrow of the Nation: A History of Sport and Physical Culture in Republican China* (Berkeley: University of California Press, 2004), 4.
42. Gerard Taylor, *Capoeira: The Jogo de Angola from Luanda to Cyberspace* (Berkeley, CA: North Atlantic Books, 2007), 20–21.
43. Taylor, *Capoeira*, 21.
44. See for examples Taylor, *Capoeira*, 22 and Zweiniger-Bargielowska, "Building a British Superman", 606–608.
45. Stephen Jones argued that, though not on a par with Germany, Italy, the Soviet Union, or even France, "sport and leisure were an important part of political culture" in Britain, with elements of state control present. Jones, "State Intervention and Leisure in Britain between the Wars", *Journal of Contemporary History* 22, no. 1 (1987): 165.
46. For further discussion on the "totalitarian" debate, see *Beyond Totalitarianism: Stalinism and Nazism Compared*, edited by Michael Geyer and Sheila Fitzpatrick (Cambridge: Cambridge University Press, 2009), 3–13. For a more detailed comparison, see Barbara Keys, "The Body as a Political Space: Comparing Physical Education under Nazism and Stalinism", *German History* 27 no. 3 (2009): 395–413.
47. For more on this see Detlev Peukert, *Inside Nazi Germany: Conformity, Opposition, and Racism in Everyday Life*, trans. Richard Deveson, (New Haven, CT: Yale University Press, 1982), 154–169.

48. H. W. Koch, *The Hitler Youth: Origins and Development 1922–1945* (New York: Cooper Square Press, 2000) [1975].
49. A. Hitler, *Mein Kampf*, in H. W. Koch, *Hitler Youth*, 163.
50. Jeremy Noakes and Geoffrey Pridham, *A Documentary Reader. Volume 2, Nazism: State, Economy, and Society 1933–1939* (Exeter: University of Exeter, 1984): 423.
51. Detlev Peukert and Zygmunt Bauman, *Modernity and Ambivalence*, cited in Daniel Beer, *Renovating Russia: The Human Sciences and the Fate of Liberal Modernity, 1880–1930* (Ithaca, NY: Cornell University Press, 2008), 202. For more discussion see Peter Fritsche and Jochen Hellbeck, "The New Man in Stalinist Russia and Nazi Germany", in *Beyond Totalitarianism*, 302–341.
52. Gigliola Gori, *Italian Fascism and the Female Body: Sport, Submissive Women and Strong Mothers* (London; New York: Routledge, 2004), 10.
53. Victoria De Grazia, *The Culture of Consent: Mass Organization of Leisure in Fascist Italy* (Cambridge: Cambridge University Press, 1981).
54. For more on this see Gori, *Italian Fascism*.
55. The *Dopolavoro* (*Opera Nazionale Dopolavoro*) was the Italian Fascist leisure and recreational organization.
56. Achille Starace, *L'Opera Nazionale Dopolavoro. Panorami do vita fascista, collana edita sotto gli auspice del PNF, 11 Rome, 1933*, cited in De Grazia, *Culture of Consent*, 173.
57. Margaret A. Lowe, *Looking Good: College Women and Body Image 1875–1930* (Baltimore, MD; London: The Johns Hopkins University Press, 2003), 12. The psychologist Paul Schilder, according to Lowe, was the first to explore the term in 1934 and the first to attempt to "distinguish the physical from the psychological". Noting how psychoanalysis dealt with individual experience, it failed to examine how people actually experienced their bodies. See Lowe, *Looking Good*, 155.
58. Lowe, *Looking Good*, 12.
59. Lowe, *Looking Good*, 119.
60. Lowe, *Looking Good*, 111–115.
61. Tammy M. Proctor, "Scouts, Guides, and the Fashioning of Empire, 1919–1939" in Wendy Parkins (ed), *Fashioning the Body Politic* (Oxford; New York: Berg, 2002), 131.
62. Simonette Falasca-Zamponi, "Peeking Under the Black Shirt: Italian Fascism's Disembodied Bodies", in Parkins, *Fashioning the Body Politic*, 146.
63. Christine Ruane, "Clothing in Imperial Russia", in Wendy Parkins (ed), *Fashioning the Body Politic: Dress, Gender and Citizenship* (Oxford; New York: Oxford University Press, 2002), 63. Aaron Retish and Jeffrey Burds argue that a consumer culture had already developed under Tsarism, see Retish, *Russia's Peasants*, 5.
64. N. N. Kozlova, *Gorizonty povsednevnosti sovetskoi epokhi (golosa iz khora)* (Institut Filosofii RAN, Moscow, 1996) in Lebina, Romanov, Yarskaya-Smirnova, "Care and Control: Social Policy in Soviet Reality, 1917–1930s", in *Soviet Social Policy in the 1920s–1930s*, 46.
65. Kozlova, *Gorizonty povsednevnosti*, 46.
66. Guttmann, "Sport, Politics and the Engaged Historian", 369.
67. GARF, f.7576, op.4, d.3, l.58. For example in the mid-1930s local physical culture organizations were urged to combat hostile elements among native women in Dagestan and were told to concentrate on winning over mountain-dwelling women.
68. Jennifer Hargreaves, *Heroines of Sport: The Politics of Difference and Identity* (London; New York: Routledge, 2000), 53.

69. Terry Martin defines this term, emerging after 1923, as a policy to promote national languages and national elites, with the effect of making Soviet power seem "native". Martin, *The Affirmative Action Empire: Nations and Nationalism in the Soviet Union, 1923–1939* (Ithaca, NY; London: Cornell University Press, 2001), 11–12.

70. GARF, f.7576, op.1, d.54a, l.76. Adzharistan was an autonomous republic in Transcaucasia, see Chapter 5.

71. Martin Conway and Robert Gerwarth, "Revolution and Counter-Revolution", in Donald Bloxham and Robert Gerwarth (eds), *Political Violence in Twentieth Century Europe* (Cambridge: Cambridge University Press, 2011), 172.

72. Frances L. Bernstein, Christopher Burton, and Dan Healey (eds), *Soviet Medicine: Culture, Practice and Science* (DeKalb: Northern Illinois University Press, 2010), 8.

73. Bernstein et al., *Soviet Medicine*, 6.

74. Alexander Genis, "The View from the Window" in *Red Bread* (Birmingham; Moscow: Glas New Russian Writing, 2000), 23, 18.

75. Alexander Etkind, *Eros of the Impossible: The History of Psychoanalysis in Russia*, translated by Noah and Maria Rubens (Boulder, CO; Oxford: Westview Press, 1997), 41. For more on pedagogy, see Chapter 8 in Etkind.

76. Pat Simpson, "Imag(in)ing Post-Revolutionary Evolution: The Taylorized Proletarian, 'Conditioning', and Soviet Darwinism in the 1920s", in Barbara Larson and Fae Brauer (eds), *The Art of Evolution: Darwin, Darwinsims, and Visual Culture* (Hanover, NH; London: University Press of New England, 2009), 234.

77. From the journal *Iunii kommunist*, nos. 89 (1922) in *Bolshevik Visions: First Phase of the Cultural Revolution in Soviet Russia*, edited by William G Rosenberg (Ann Arbor: University of Michigan Press, 1990), 26.

78. As Simpson notes, in the term *"novyi chelovek"* or "New Person", *chelovek* is gender neutral and treated as masculine. For further discussion of this, see Simpson, "Imag(in)ing Post-Revolutionary Evolution", 248.

79. That many did idolize those who had adopted the lifestyle of the "New Soviet Person" is undisputed. Admiration and awe for these new Soviet warriors and bureaucrats have been recounted, predominantly among the young and impressionable. See for example N. K. Novak-Deker, *Soviet Youth: Twelve Komsomol Histories* (Munich: Institute for the Study of the USSR, 1959), especially 53–54.

80. Nikolai Chernyshevsky, *What Is to Be Done?*, translated by Michael R. Katz and annotated by William G. Wagner (Ithaca, NY; London: Cornell University Press, 1989), 281.

81. Chernyshevsky, *What is to Be Done?*, 278–279.

82. See John E. Bowlt, "Body Beautiful: The Artistic Search for the Perfect Physique" in John E. Bowlt and Olga Matich (eds), *Laboratory of Dreams: The Russian Avant-Garde and Cultural Experiment* (Stanford, CA: Stanford University Press, 1996), 37–58.

83. Pat Simpson, "Imag(in)ing Post-Revolutionary Evolution: The Taylorized Proletarian, 'Conditioning', and Soviet Darwinism in the 1920s", in *The Art of Evolution*, 236.

84. "Rech' na s''ezde sovetov fizkul'tury 19 Aprelya 1924g", in *Trotsky L. Sochineniya kul'tura perekhodnogo perioda* (Moscow-Leningrad: Gosizdat, 1927), 103.

85. Simpson, "Imag(in)ing Post-Revolutionary Evolution", 241–242.

86. These "experiments" were no more than different types of rhythmic movements and exercises designed to extract maximum efficiency with minimum

energy. For more on Gastev and the Central Labour Institute see Simpson,
"Imag(in)ing Post-Revolutionary Evolution", Bowlt, "Body Beautiful", 57,
and Kendall E. Bailes, "Alexei Gastev and the Soviet Controversy over Taylorism, 1918–24", *Soviet Studies* 29, no. 3 (July 1977): 373–394.
87. David L. Hoffmann, "Bodies of Knowledge: Physical Culture and the New
Soviet Man", 269–270 in Igal Halfin, *Language and Revolution*, 69–85.
88. Vsevolod Meyerhold, "The Actor of the Future and Biomechanics", in
Edward Braun, *Meyerhold on Theatre*, cited in Hoffman, "Bodies of Knowledge", 73.
89. Simpson, "Imag(in)ing Post-Revolutionary Evolution", 252.
90. Gastev's methods accounted for the training of hundreds of workers, with
over 800 cells for the "scientific organization of labour", see Simpson,
"Imag(in)ing Post-Revolutionary Evolution", 245.
91. Hellbeck, "The New Man in Stalinist Russia and Nazi Germany", in *Beyond
Totalitarianism*, 307.
92. RGASPI, f.537, op.1, d.15, l.189. From the theses of the Third Congress of
the Red Sport International on questions of scientific method and technique
of physical culture for the proletariat.
93. Richard Stites argued that the Soviet cult of the machine had its origins as
far back as the seventeenth century, but particularly with the eighteenth and
nineteenth century administrative utopia ("the 'mechanization' of society")
and the early twentieth century urbanized utopia. Stites, *Revolutionary
Dreams: Utopian Vision and Experimental Life in the Russian Revolution*
(New York; Oxford: Oxford University Press, 1989), 145.
94. GARF, f.7576, op.1, d.68, l.81. Zasedanie v gosplane SSSR po voprosu
"fizkul'tura na proizvodstve". 5/V/1932. VSFK.
95. GARF, f.7576, op.3, d.60, l.188. NMK VSFK. NKTrudu SSSR—Dubnovu.
Oblastnogo Otdela Truda Dmitrievu LOSFK. This trial took place between
March and July 1932.
96. GARF, f.7576, op.1, d.60, l.183.
97. Physical culture work here was reportedly very strong with all shop workers
involved in the GTO. The factory had come first in Leningrad for the best
physical culture collective. GARF, f.7576, op.1, d.60, l.182. Another factory
involved in this "scientific research" was the Molotov *Avtozavod* factory in
Nizhnii Novgorod. The factory had organized physical culture brigades in
every shop and introduced physical culture exercises during work to help
increase productivity, improve the "social health of workers", and to help the
scientific research brigade in industrial physical culture. GARF, op.1, d.68,
l.99. Polozhenie o tsekovoi fizkul'turnoi brigade Nizhegorodskogo avtoza-
voda im Molotova.
98. GARF, f.7576, op.1, d.68, l.51.
99. GARF, f.7576, op.3, d.91, l.97. 1933. Such work was continued in 1935
by the Central Scientific-Research Institute of Physical Culture, which not
only monitored physical culture work in factory and laboratory environ-
ments, but also examined how physical culture could assist in the recovery
of patients from certain illnesses and physical culture exercises for military
personnel such as pilots, snipers, parachutists etc. See GARF, f.7576, op.24,
d.1g, l.51.
100. "Brigada 'FiS' prodolzhaet smotr. Na ocheredi—zavod 'Serp i Molot'", *FiS*,
no.26 (1931): 2
101. Hellbeck, "The New Man in Stalinist Russia and Nazi Germany", 309.
102. See Straus, *Factory and Community*, 327. In the major factories where
the project work was undertaken massive agitprop and political education
campaigns were conducted. The overall effect was that the research for

the project was carried out in an unnatural environment. Moreover, these workers' recollections were used uncritically and purposefully designed to impress. Questions were asked but not all of these had to be answered and respondents could expand on the subjects. Respondents were also asked to speak on whatever they considered to be interesting and significant in the history of the factory. Often raised in these instances were issues concerning *byt* and social psychology. These memories would then become the basis for further evening talks and invitations. S. V. Shuravlev, *Fenomen "isto-riya fabrikov". Gor'kovskoe nachinanie v kontekste 1930-x godov* (Moscow: RAN, 1997), 92–93. The most intensive evening remembrances were conducted during spring 1932–1933 and in *Serp i Molot* during this time nineteen such meetings were held. These were mainly limited to shop meetings but general factory meetings also took place, sometimes with over a thousand workers in attendance.

103. The files that form the basis of the physical culture collection in the Gorky project were primarily workers' recollections that had been gathered by teams of writers, worker-correspondents, and journalists. These recollections were usually accumulated during "evening remembrances", where workers would recall and discuss different subjects. Many problems existed—for example, there were difficulties experienced between workers and editors in the office, with the latter too busy and the former (mainly peasant workers) not strong enough. Shuravlev, *Fenomen*, especially 16–17, 58–59.

104. GARF, f.7952, op.3, d.323, l.17. Shipilin, "Fizkul'tura v boyakh za metall'" 1928–1932, by Nikolai Mikhailov, *Serp i Molot* worker and sportsman.

105. For more detailed discussion of *kul'turnost'* and its associated advice literature in Soviet society, see Catriona Kelly, *Refining Russia: Advice Literature, Polite Culture, and Gender from Catherine to Yeltsin* (Oxford: Oxford University Press, 2001), 230–311.

106. Raymond A. Bauer, *The New Man in Soviet Psychology* (Cambridge: Cambridge University Press, 1952), 168.

107. Riordan, "Soviet Physical Education", in Tomiak, *Soviet Education*, 173–174.

108. Vera Dunham, *In Stalin's Time: Middleclass Values in Soviet fiction* (Cambridge; New York: Cambridge University Press, 1976).

109. Chris Shilling, *The Body and Social Theory* (London: Sage Publications, 2004), 111 [1994].

110. Hellbeck, *Revolution on My Mind*, 234–235.

111. Hellbeck, *Revolution on My Mind*, 234–235.

112. See *spravka* in the personal fond of Platon A. Ippolitov, GARF, f. A-654.

113. GARF, f. A-654, op.1, d.27, l.115.

NOTES TO CHAPTER 2

1. RGASPI, f.17, op.10, d.25, l.24. During the civil war women were also to participate in Vsevobuch training and activities. For more on this see Wood, *The Baba and the Comrade*, 52–57. See also Sanborn, *Drafting the Russian Nation*, Chapter 4. It should be noted here that other groups such as the Scouts remained in existence during this period and were gradually taken over by the Bolsheviks (see Sanborn, 138–139).

2. Commissar for Health, Nikolai Aleksandrovich Semashko (1874–1949) became the Supreme Council's chairperson. Other key personalities represented in the Supreme Council were Stalin's secretary B. Bazhanov (Party Central Committee), G. Yagoda (GPU), K. Mekhonoshin (Military

Department), A. Ittin (Komsomol Central Committee), and F. Seniushkin (trade unions).

3. In October 1919 the "original" Supreme Council of Physical Culture was established. This was the main central inter-departmental organ which was to coordinate the activities of all of the other departments and institutes in the development and organization of physical culture. GARF, f.A-2306, op.1, d.286, l.1.

4. These included the party, Vsevobuch, Dinamo sports society and the Commissariats for Health and Education. By 1925 there were a total of about nine different organizations with roles in overseeing the implementation of physical culture in their respective areas. These included the military, the ministry for health, the ministry for education, the trade unions, the Komsomol, the party, the ministry for labour, the Moscow Council of Physical Culture, and the GPU (*Gosudarstvennoe Politicheskoe upravlenie pri NKVD* or State Political Directorate).

5. For more on the important debate between the trade unions and Komsomol, see my article "The Politics of Physical Culture in the 1920s", *Slavonic and East European Review* 89, no. 3 (2011): 494–515.

6. Nikolai Aleksandrovich Semashko was the People's Commissar of Health (1918–1930) and Chairman of the Supreme Council of Physical Culture. Konstantin Aleksandrovich Mekhonoshin (1889–1938) was an important figure in physical culture and was second to Semashko in the Supreme Council of Physical Culture. Holding such a senior role, he had a good deal of influence in physical culture affairs. See appendix for full biographical notes. "Pervoe vsesoyuznoe sovshchanie sovetov fizicheskoi kul'tury", *Izvestiya fizicheskoi kul'tury*, no. 8 (1924): 10–12.

7. *Kruzhki* (plural) in this analysis of physical culture are best defined as "circles" (literal translation) of enthusiasts, normally comprising at least three members. It was possible for one *kruzhok* to expand and merge with other *kruzhki*. There were many types of *kruzhok* besides physical culture, for example there were musical, choir, dance or drama *kruzhki*. For more on *kruzhki* and the local organization of physical culture, see my article "'The Collective Agitation of Arms and Legs': Revolutionizing Physical Culture Organization, 1924–1934". *Revolutionary Russia* 23 (2010): 93–113.

8. "Pervoe vsesoyuznoe", 10–12.

9. Rezoliutsiya TsK RKP (b) Utverzhdena Orgbiuro TsK ot 13 Iiulya 1925, cited in Semashko, *Puti sovetskoi fizkul'tury* (Moscow, 1926), 106.

10. Narodnyi komissariat zdravookhraneniya—Commissariat for Health; Narodnyi komissariat prosveshcheniya—Commissariat for Education. Otdel po rabote sredi zhenshchin—this was the Party's "Women's Section" which existed from 1919 to 1930 (when the "woman question" was deemed to have been solved). RGASPI, f.17, op.68, d.424, l.9. Glebova. April 1925.

11. RGASPI, f.17, op.68, d.424, l.36. Matveev. 1925.

12. RGASPI, f.17, op.68, d.424, l.14. Semashko.

13. The *Proletkul't* (Proletarian Culture), according to Lynn Mally, "viewed culture broadly as a combination of art, ideology, and daily life", but in the 1920s "debates about its significance and place in Soviet cultural life continued unabated". For quotation see Lynn Mally, *Culture of the Future* (Berkeley: University of California Press, 1990), 230–231. For a comprehensive discussion of Proletkul't and Hygienist policies in physical culture see Riordan, *Sport in Soviet Society*, 95–104. For how the Proletkul't under the Bolsheviks diverged from the original ideas of Bogdanov, see James D. White, "Alexander Bogdanov's Conception of the Proletkul't", paper presented at the Study Group for the Russian Revolution, Glasgow, January 2011.

14. For the Proletkul't in general, see Gabriele Gorzka, *A. Bogdanov und der russische Proletkul't: Theorie und Praxis Einer sozialismus* (Campus: Verlag, 1980).
15. See B. Kalpus, *Krasnyi sport*, no.1 (1924): 10.
16. Nikolai Il'ich Podvoisky joined the Russian Democratic Workers Party in 1901 and was a long-term revolutionary who stormed the Winter Palace in 1917. He was also chairman of Vsevobuch and head of the Sportintern.
17. The Red Sport International, also known as the Sportintern or officially the International Association of Red Sports and Gymnastics Organizations was a Moscow-based Comintern supported organization established at the First International Congress of Representatives of Revolutionary Workers' Sports Organizations in July 1921. Its first president was Nikolai Podvoisky. It had in part been set up as a rival to the Lucerne-based Workers' Sport International which had been set up in 1920 by French, German and Belgian social democrats. There was constant feuding between the two organizations and in April 1937 the Sportintern was disbanded by the Comintern.
18. RGASPI, f.17, op.68, d.424, ll.7, 10, 50. This file contains discussions by the commission created by the Orgburo to investigate physical culture leadership and work. It involved representatives of the Supreme Council of Physical Culture including Semashko, Mekhonshin, Seniushkin, Podvoisky, Mil'chakov (Komsomol), Rogov (Komsomol), Maria Glebova (Zhenotdel) and Genrikh Yagoda (GPU) as well as the representative, Nikolai Antipov, from the Moscow City Committee (and later chairperson of the All-Union Council of Physical Culture).
19. See Orgburo discussions 16 April 1925, RGASPI, f.17, op.68, d.424, l.23.
20. RGASPI, f.146, op.1, d.62, l.329.
21. This transliteration does not quite make sense in Russian and could be the result of a typing error in the original document.
22. In 1924 Podvoisky claimed to have attracted up to 35,000 to one mass workers' festival and proudly stated that "no other country conducted such festivals" with such active participation. RGASPI, f.146. op.1, d.325.
23. RGASPI, f.146, 1, d.62, ll.329–330.
24. RGASPI, f.17, op.68, d.424, l.70. Semashko. For more on the personal struggle between Semashko and Podvoisky, see Stefan Plaggenborg, *Revoliutsiya i kul'tura. Kulturniye orientiry v period mezhdu oktyabr'skoi revoliutsiei i epokhoi stalinizma* (Saint Petersburg: Neva, 2000), 105.
25. L. T. Lih et al. (eds), *Stalin's Letters to Molotov 1925–1936* (New Haven, CT; London: Yale University Press, 1995) in Chris Ward, *Stalin's Russia* (London; New York: Edward Arnold, 1993), 12.
26. In his study of the Red Army, Mark Von Hagen pointed to the NEP, nervous exhaustion and the imminent downfall of Trotsky as reasons behind the suicides. On Trotskyites, he noted, "[i]n 1923 and 1924 members of the Trotskyist opposition were reported to be killing themselves or resigning after they sensed that the Revolution was veering toward reaction in the hands of Trotsky's political opponents". In Von Hagen, *Soldiers in the Proletarian Dictatorship: The Red Army and the Soviet Socialist State, 1917–1930* (Ithaca, NY; London: Cornell University Press, 1990), 306n.
27. For example Dr. Zikmund, a leading theoretician on Soviet physical culture as well as rector of the State Institute of Physical Culture, was removed from his post and eventually disappeared in the purges. For more on this, see Riordan, *Soviet Sport in Society*, 92.
28. Resolution of the Central Committee of the Russian Communist Party, ratified by the Orgburo Central Committee from 13 June, "Zadachi partii

v oblasti fizicheskoi kul'tury", *Izvestiya fizicheskoi kul'tury* (hereafter *IFK*), nos. 13–14 (1925): 2.
29. "Zadachi Partii", *IFK*, 2.
30. "Zadachi Partii", *IFK*, 2.
31. "O fizkul'turnom dvizhenii. Postanovlenie TsK VKP (b)", *V pomoshch' fizkul'taktivistu*, no.19–20 (1929): 3–4. This resolution foreshadowed the 1930 decision to establish the All-Union Council of Physical Culture.
32. "O fizkul'turnom dvizhenii", 3–4.
33. "O fizkul'turnom dvizhenii", 3–4.
34. M. Kalinin and A. Yenukidze, "Postanovlenie Presidiuma Tsentral'nogo Ispolnitel'nogo Komiteta Soyuza SSR" (3 April 1930), *Fizkul'taktivist*, no. 7 (1930): 1–4.
35. Associated with "championism", record-breaking was considered a bourgeois feature and indicative of capitalism's drive for its athletes to achieve records to the detriment of their health. It was an individualistic approach to sport and was considered contrary to the collectivist proletarian approach. Parallelism was an increasingly salient feature within the Soviet system and the physical culture press often referred to it as a negative consequence of the hyper-bureaucratized system. It effectively meant the existence of two departments performing the same functions (a sign of disorganization and misunderstanding—anathema to the Soviet ideal of order yet inherent to the system it spawned).
36. Kalinin, Lezhava, Kiselev, "Postanovlenie Vserossiiskogo Tsentral'nogo Ispolnitel'nogo Komiteta i Sovieta Narodnykh Komissarov RSFSR", *Fizkul'taktivist*, nos. 23–24 (1930): 52–55.
37. Kalinin et al., "Postanovlenie", 52–55.
38. Kalinin et al., "Postanovlenie", 52–55.
39. These included six representatives from the RSFSR, four from the Ukraine, one from Belarus, three from the Trans Caucasian Federation (Azerbaijan, Armenia and Georgia), one from Turkmenistan, and one from the Uzbek and one from the Tadjik republics.
40. Kalinin et al., "Postanovlenie", 52–55.
41. At the first plenum of the All-Union Council of Physical Culture, the following were elected to its presidium and to the Soviet delegation in the KSI: Yenukidze, Antipov, Kamenev, Kal'pus (RV Soviet), Kosarev, Yanov (TsK VLKSM), Yagoda, Messing (TsK Dinamo), Zholdak (IKKSI), Abolin, Belitskii (VTsSPS), Grigor'ev (VSFK secretary), Yeshchin, Giber (Moscow regional secretary), Kondpat'ev (Leningrad), Kurts (NKP), Semashko (Osoaviakhim), Vasilenko (Ukrainian Republic), Pronina ('Trekhgornaya Manufaktura'), Kulov (Leningrad). Candidate Members to the Presidium included Zubov (VTsSPS), Lev (Belorussian Republic), Mantsev, Kogan (NKZdrav), Bespalova (Sormovo), and representatives from the Ukraine and Transcausus. "Pervyi Plenum Vsesoiuznogo Sovieta Fizkul'tury", *Fizkul'tura i sport*, no. 29 (1930): 2 (hereafter *FiS*).
42. Morton, *Soviet Sport*, 172.
43. Morton, *Soviet Sport*, 172.
44. GARF, f.7576, op.1, d.111, l.21. Stenogramma Zasedaniya Prezidiuma VSFK. 26/I/1932.
45. "Gotov k trudu i oborone", *FiS*, no. 7 (1931): 1.
46. Antipov and Grigor'ev, "O provedenii ispytanii po znachku 'Gotov k trudu i oborone'. Rezoliutsia prezidiuma Vsesoiuznogo sovieta fizicheskoi kul'tury pri TsIK SSSR ot 10 Maya t.g. po dokladam Moskovskogo i Leningradskogo obl. Sovietov fizkul'tury i VSFK", *Fizkul'taktivist*, no. 7 (1931): 46.
47. P. M. Petukhov, "Znachok 'Gotov k trudu i oborone', kak osnove Sovietskoi sistemy fizkul'tury", *Teoria i praktika fizicheskoi kul'tury*, no. 6 (1931): 7.

48. GARF, f.7576, op.9, d.5, l.54–54ob. Protokol zasedanii komissii po proektu novogo kompleksa GTO, 1939. Geography and climate were important considerations for GTO organizers, as those living in certain regions, for example in the northeast or far south, would naturally struggle to fulfil certain norms in relation to skiing or swimming. See GARF, f.7576, op.9, d.4, l.105.
49. For some examples, see GARF f.7576, op.9, d.16, l.34; d.18, l.45; d.20, l.205 (1932); d.21, l.32 (1938), l.37 (1936), l.101, l.173; d.25, l.123. All of these provide instances where instructors cheated and undermined the GTO system.
50. GARF, f.7710, op.6, d.37, l.14.
51. "Mastera—organizatory massovoi ucheby", *FiS*, nos. 28–30 (1932): 9.
52. "Mastera", 9.
53. See for example Edelman, *Serious Fun*, 53–56.
54. Gosudarstvennyi Arkhiv Penzenskogo Oblast' (hereafter GAPO), f. R.349, op.1, d.42, l.97–103ob. Protocol from 25 August 1927.
55. Keys, *Globalizing Sport*, 65.
56. Keys, *Globalizing Sport*, 70.
57. "Gotov k trudu i oborone", *FiS*, no. 7 (1931): 1. This is discussed more fully in Chapter 7.
58. "Masterov-spetsialistov na massovuiu uchobu. Beseda predsedatelya VSFK SSSR tov. Antipova s moskovskimu masterami i spetsialistami", *FiS*, nos. 14–15 (1931): 5.
59. At the 1930 First All-Union Trade Union Conference on Physical Culture a decision was passed on the transfer of physical culture and sports organization from the club principle to the production principle. This meant that the physical culture *kruzhki* were overtaken by the physical culture collectives based in the workplace, school, or institute. Goloshchapov, *Istoriya fizicheskoi kul'tury i sporta*, 173.
60. Antipov (excerpts from the trade union conference), "Kak luchshe i pravil'nee organizovat'", *Fizkul'tura Zakavkaz'ya*, 2–3.
61. TsGAMO, f. 7227, op.1, d. 5, ll.14–16. Protokol zasedanii prezidiuma Mosobkoma soiuza VMP sovmestno s predsedatelyami zavkomov. 9 Oktyabrya 1935.
62. TsGAMO, f. 7227, op.1, d. 5, l.17.
63. TsGAMO, f. 7227, op.1, d. 5, l.18.
64. Although officially called "voluntary" societies, mass membership was encouraged.
65. See Antipov (excerpts from the trade union conference), "Kak luchshe i pravil'nee organizovat'", *Fizkul'tura Zakavkaz'ya*, 2–3.
66. See Fisher, *Pattern for Soviet Youth* (New York: Columbia University Press, 1959), 180–181. The Komsomol was still criticized, for example by physical culture leader Kharchenko, who co-wrote an article (for *Komsomolskaya Pravda*) in relation to the Komsomol's "silent" presence in physical culture organization. See for example GARF f.7576, op.24, d.1g, l.38–32 (pages in reverse order), 1935, where the Komsomol is fiercely defended against such accusations, showing that some residual tensions between the leaders of various organizations in physical culture most definitely remained.
67. I. Tsalkin, "K itogam Vsesoiuznoi konferentsii po fizkul'ture", *Fizkul'taktivist*, nos. 21–22 (1930), 1–7.
68. This was the Moscow Region Council Voluntary Sports' Society "Zenit", as opposed to the Zenit club associated with St. Petersburg, originally called the Stalin Leningrad metal factory, and only renamed "Zenit" in 1939.
69. TsGAMO, f.7227, op. 1, d. 20, ll.5, 7, 64. Stenogramma. Pervaya konferentsiya dobrovolnogo obshchestva fizkul'tury 'Zenit', Tula. 10/III/1936.

70. TsGAMO, f.7227, op. 1, d. 20, ll.5, 64. See also reports in *Krasnyi sport* 6 (1936).
71. TsGAMO, f.7227, op. 1, d. 20, l.64.
72. TsGAMO, f.7227, op.1, d.3, ll.1–13, 15. O provedenii zimnikh fabrivno zavodskikh spartakiadu kollektivov fizkul'tury profsoiuzov gorod Moskvy i oblasti. Stenogramma o khode fizkul'traboty v usloviiakh zimy. 23 December 1934. Berdnikov.
73. TsGAMO, f.7227, op.1, d.3, l.22. Chubukin.
74. TsGAMO, f.7227, op.1, d.3, l. 27. Ovyasnnikov from Warehouse No.37.
75. Matthias Neumann has noted too the lack of interest in physical culture by young people in Komsomol clubs, who often found it "spiritless". Neumann, *The Communist Youth League and the Transformation of the Soviet Union, 1917–1932* (London; New York: Routledge, 2011), 131.
76. TsGAMO, f.7227, op.1, d.9, l.22. Protokol. Sobranie chlenov and kandidatov obshchestva "Zenit" zavoda No. 58 ot 18/IX/1936. Nikolaev.
77. TsGAMO, f.7227, op.1, d.9, l.22.
78. TsGAMO, f.7227, op.1, d.20, l.41. Stenogramma. Pervaya oblastnaya konferentsia dobrovol'nogo obshchestva fizkul'tury "Zenit". 10/III/1936. Dokhman, factory No. 37.
79. TsGAMO, f.7227, op.1, d.20, l.44. Rodionov, factory No. 67.
80. RGASPI, f.82, op.2, d.970. ll.2–14. 8/V/1936. Zapiska TsK VLKSM (A. Kosareva, I. Kharchenko)—S prilozheniem proektov postanovleniya SNK SSSR I TsK VKP (b) "Ob obrazovaniya Vsesoiuznoi Komiteta po delam fizicheskoi kul'tury i sporta pri SNK SSSR", postanovleniya TsIK SSSR "O likvidatsii VSFK pri TsIK SSSR i TsIK RFSFR".
81. RGASPI, f.82, op.2, d.970. ll.3, 5.
82. RGASPI, f.82, op.2, d.970. ll.7, point 12.
83. GARF, f.7576, op.1, d.253, l.15. Pis'mo Vsesoiuznogo Komiteta Fizicheskoi Kul'tury i Sporta pri SNK SSSR. Kharchenko. 31/VII/1937.
84. GARF, f.7576, op.1, d.253, ll.15–16.
85. For an explanation of the term and its usage, see John Arch Getty, *Origins of the Great Purges*, 38–57.
86. Getty, *Origins of the Great Purges*, 202. Again, to ascertain a good understanding of the nature of the purges and indeed the *Yezhovshchina*, including the variation between centre and periphery, see Getty, 202–203.
87. Getty, *Origins of the Great Purges*, 206.
88. Nikolai Petrovich Starostin (1902–1996) was the eldest brother in this family of football stars. The brothers were all associated with Spartak and Nikolai, as the most famous, was closely associated with the establishment of the club. Following his release from prison Nikolai was appointed national coach of the Soviet football team and was president of Spartak from 1955 to 1992. The Starostin affair has been covered in works by inter alia Edelman, Keys and Riordan.
89. *Pravda*, 3/IX/1937, in RGASPI, f.1-M, op.23, d.1268, l.9. Published version in *Russkoe i sovetskoe molodezhnoe dvizhenie v dokumentakh 1905–37* (Moscow: Russkii mir, OMP-press, 2002), 236.
90. RGASPI, f.1-M, op.23, d.1268, l.9. *Russkoe*, 236.
91. RGASPI, f.1-M, op.23, d.1268, l.10–11, 1/IX/1937.*Russkoe*, 237.
92. RGASPI, f.1-M, op.23, d.1268, l.10–11. *Russkoe*, 237.
93. Following the purge of Ivan Kharchenko, Knopova was temporarily in charge of the Committee of Physical Culture and Sports Affairs, until she was purged after just three months and arrested in September 1938. She was executed on 16 January 1940, see AP RF, op.24, d.377, l.133, http://stalin.memo.ru/spiski/pg12133.htm, accessed 7 May 2009.

94. RGASPI, f.1-M, op.23, d.1268, l.10–11. *Russkoe*, 237.
95. RGASPI, f.1-M, op.23, d.1268, l.12–17, 3/IX/1937.*Russkoe*, 238.
96. RGASPI, f.1-M, op.23, d.1268, l.12–17, 3/IX/1937. *Russkoe*, 238.
97. RGASPI, f.1-M, op.23, d.1268, l.12–17. *Russkoe*, 240.
98. J. Arch Getty and Oleg Naumov, *The Road to Terror: Stalin and the Self-Destruction of the Bolsheviks, 1932–1939* (New Haven, CT; London: Yale University Press, 1999), 1.
99. Both Znamenskii brothers (Georgii and Serafim) secretly denounced the Starostins to Elena Knopova. Georgii Znamenskii claimed Nikolai Starostin asked him to defend him against the Paris reports, told him how he should behave before the investigative commissions, and accused him of "entre-preneurial" activities in regard to Spartak. He also mentioned how Nikolai flaunted his big name contacts and exploited his powerful position within the club. RGASPI, f.1-M, op.23, d.1268, l.22–23. *Russkoe*, 240–243.
100. Getty, Naumov, *The Road to Terror*, xiv.
101. The reason for their arrest and exile in 1942 was their "anti-Soviet state-ments" and "doubts about Soviet victory in the war" amongst other charges yet it remains unclear why they were not arrested in 1937. In his memoirs Starostin suggested that the friendship between his and Malenkov's daughter may have had some influence but this does not seem entirely feasible. For more on this argument see Edelman, "A Small Way of Saying 'No', and N. Starostin, *Futbol skvoz' gody*, 63–64. For more on the Starostin's and the Spartak/ Dinamo rivalry see Jim Riordan, "The Strange Story of Nikolai Starostin, Football and Lavrentii Beria", *Europe-Asia Studies* 46, no.4, Soviet and East European History (1994), 681–690.

NOTES TO CHAPTER 3

1. Gregory Carleton, *Sexual Revolution in Bolshevik Russia* (Pittsburgh, PA: Pittsburgh University Press, 2005), 109.
2. Natalia Lebina, Pavel Romanov, and Elena Yarskaya-Smirnova, "Zabota i kontrol: sotsial'naya politika v sovetskoi deistvitel'nposti, 1917–1930e gody", in *Sovetskaya sotsial'naya politika 1920kh–1930kh. Ideologiya i povsednevnost'* (Moscow: Variant, TsSPGI, 2007), 37. Hooliganism (*khuliganstvo*) was popularly used to describe anti-social behaviour but as Matthias Neumann notes, it became a "catch-all term in the 1920s that included fighting, card-playing, swearing, and also often drunkenness", Neumann, *Communist Youth*, 108.
3. Lebina, *Povsednevnaya zhizn' sovetskogo goroda: normy i anomaly. 1920-e–1930-e gg* (St. Petersburg: Neva, 1999): 57 in Lebina et al, *Sovetskaya sotsial'naya politika*, 37.
4. Eric Naiman, *Sex in Public. The Incarnation of Early Soviet Ideology* (Princeton, NJ: Princeton University Press, 1997), 6.
5. For discussion of unemployment and its concomitant effects on youth, see Anne E. Gorsuch, *Youth in Revolutionary Russia: Enthusiasts, Bohemians, Delinquents* (Bloomington; Indianapolis: Indiana University Press, 2000), 36–40.
6. Sheila Fitzpatrick, "Sex and Revolution: An Examination of Literary and Statistical Data on the Mores of Soviet Students in the 1920s", in *The Journal of Modern History* 50, no. 2 (June 1978): 252–278 (256).
7. Carleton, *Sexual Revolution*, 109.
8. Vasili Alekseevich Giliarovskii, professor of psychiatry at Moscow State University, cited in Pinnow, Kenneth Martin, *Making Suicide Soviet: Medicine,*

Moral Statistics, and the Politics of Social Science in Bolshevik Russia,
1920–1930 (New York: Columbia University [dissertation], 1998), 22.

9. Cited in Pinnow, *Making Suicide Soviet*, 22.

10. I use the term *"vospitanie"* throughout because there is no direct English
translation of the word. It is not strictly education (*obrazovanie*) but is rather
a wide-ranging hybrid of education, nurture and upbringing which extended
to include the development of values and manners.

11. In *The State and Revolution* Lenin argued that the achievement of socialism
would witness the "withering away of the state": "Socialism will shorten
the working day, raise the *people* to a new life, create such conditions for
the *majority* of population as will enable *everybody*, without exception, to
perform state functions, and this will lead to the *complete withering away* of
the state in general". V. I. Lenin, "State and Revolution", in *Lenin, Selected
Works*, Vol. 2 (Moscow, 1963), 397, cited in Riordan, *Sport in Soviet Society*, 65.

12. With regard to the radical policies associated with education and children,
see Lisa A. Kirschenbaum, *Small Comrades: Revolutionizing Childhood
Soviet Russia, 1917–1932*, (New York; London: RoutledgeFalmer, 2001).
For discussion of pedagogy, Aron Zalkind and Soviet youth see Etkind, *Eros
of the Impossible*, especially Chapter 8.

13. Kirschenbaum, *Small Comrades*, 105, 107.

14. Nicholas Timasheff, *The Great Retreat* (New York: Dutton, 1946). This
referred to the period around 1934 and after when Stalinist policies returned
in many ways to pre-revolutionary values and conventions. There still exists
debate as to the extent to which this "retreat" represented a departure from
socialism.

15. Gerasimov, "Fizkul'tura—faktor polovogo vospitaniya", *Fizkul'tura v shkole*,
8 (1931): 12. The "correct socialist way" was of course a much contested territory in the 1920s. The considerable amount of material written on this
subject reflects the overall concern with the development of youth. Prominent
figures such as Semashko and Vladimir Gorinevsky (State Institute of Physical Culture) also wrote on the subject. See for example, Semashko, *Novyi
byt i polovoi vopros* (Moscow-Leningrad: Gosizdat, 1926); *Puti sovetskoi
fizkul'tury*, (Moscow: Fizkul'tizdat, 1926) or Gorinevsky, V. V., *Fizicheskoi
vospitanie detei i podrostkov* (Moscow: Tsent. Nauych-issl. In-t okhrany
zdorov'ya detei i podrostkov NKZ RSFSR, 1935).

16. Gorsuch, *Youth in Revolutionary Russia*, 29.

17. Semashko, *Puti*, 53.

18. Gerasimov, "Fizkul'tura-faktor", 14. See also Nikolai Semashko, *Puti*, 56 or
Dr. Pinkus, *The First All-Union Conference of Scientific Workers in Physical Culture* (Moscow: VSFK, 1926), 80. Gregory Carleton has written about
how similar suggestions had already been raised in the late 1920s by a group
of doctors concerned with the sexual lives of young people, as cited in Carleton, *Sexual Revolution*, 71.

19. Semashko, "Puti", 56. This message was heeded by some doctors. For
instance, concerning onanism Dr. V. N. Voskresenskii in 1926 replied in
his newspaper column to Ryazan peasants that: "This is a great strain on
the nervous system and the heart. The consequences of masturbation are
extremely serious and often lead to impotence—that is, the inability to have
normal sexual relations". Stephen P. Frank. "'Ask the Doctor!' Peasants and
Medical-Sexual Advice in Riazan Province, 1925–1928", in William B. Husband (ed), *The Human Tradition in Modern Russia* (Wilmington, DE: SR
Books, 2000): 102–103. Onanism is also discussed in Frances L. Bernstein,
"Panic, Potency, and the Crisis of Nervousness in the 1920s", in Kiaer and

Naiman, *Everyday Life in Early Soviet Russia: Taking the Revolution Inside* (Bloomington; Indianapolis: Indiana University Press, 2006), 163.

20. Gerasimov, "Fizkul'tura ", 14. It was also stated that many authorities on hygiene cautioned against pockets or zips in trousers, as these could lead to cases of sexual encounters. See also Semashko, *Novyi byt i polovoi vopros*; E. P. Radin, "Okhrany zdorov'ya detei i podrostkov i fizkul'tura", in Radin, Zikmund, Neniukov, *Fizicheskaya kul'tura v nauchnom osveshchenim. Sbornik trudov* (Moscow, 1924), 14.

21. Gerasimov, "Fizkul'tura", 13.

22. Semashko, *Puti*, 52.

23. The publication, although shortlived, was primarily aimed at physical culture readers and enthusiasts. It had a circulation of 10,000 which was a reasonable figure (*Fizkul'taktivist* also had a *tirazh* of 10,000, while the major publications were higher, with *Fizicheskaya kul'tura* at 35,000 and *Fizkul'tura i sport* at 75,000). Ushakov, "Udarnym tempami", *Fizkul'taktivist*, no. 4 (1931): 21. It was however more expensive than the popular physical culture publications, costing fifty kopecks, as opposed to fifteen for *Fizkul'tura i sport* or *Fizkul'taktivist'*. Advertisement featured in *Teoriia i praktika fizicheskoi kul'tury*, no. 11 (1930): 27.

24. Kenez, *Birth of the Propaganda State*, 111. Slogans, posters and music were considered an important part of physical culture education in school. This was outlined in the first programme published in 1927/1928. See I. M. Koryakovskii, M. V. Leikinoi, and L. D. Shtakel'berg, *Metodika fizicheskogo vospitaniya v srednei i vyshei shkole* (Moscow, 1938). Sometimes music had to accompany almost all games as the movement and rhythm of the body received most attention. National songs were sometimes used. *Voprosi fizicheskogo vospitaniya i fizicheskogo obrazovaniya* (Leningrad, 1928).

25. V. Yakovlev, "Shkol'nyi fizkul'tplakat", *Fizkul'tura v shkole*, no. 3 (1930): 28–29.

26. Yakovlev, "Shkol'nyi fizkul'tplakat", 28.

27. Starks, *The Body Soviet*, 181.

28. GAPO, f. R-349, op.1, d.49, l.23. Saransk USFK 13 November 1926.

29. GAPO, f. R-349, op.1, d.49, l.23ob.

30. GAPO, f. R-349, op.1, d.42, l.154. Bedno-Demyansk USFK, copy of letter from Gorbsevsk GSFK instructor of physical culture, Nikitin, 16 September 1927.

31. City Conference on Physical Culture, "Fizkul'tura", *Trudovaya Pravda* no. 83/43 (1930): 6.

32. For more on young people and the "macho subculture" see Neumann, *Communist Youth*, 105–113.

33. GARF, f.7576, op.24, d.4, l.4.

34. GARF, f.7576, op.24, d.4, l.8.

35. These were short, satirical Russian folk songs, poems or plays. In the Soviet era, they assumed a new, more political dimension.

36. RGASPI, f.1-M, op.23, d.800, ll.67–68, 1927.

37. See Lynn Mally, *Revolutionary Acts*, 36–38. Mally draws very plausible comparisons between these *agitki* and Victoria Bonnell's examination of Soviet poster art.

38. Lynn Mally, *Revolutionary Acts*, 48.

39. *Materialy dlya klubnoi tseny*, no. 1 (1928): 2.

40. Neumann, *Communist Young Communists*, 44–45.

41. Lynn Mally, *Revolutionary Acts*, 5.

42. Evgenii Pavlov, "Konkurs na luchshego strelka", *Materialy dlya klubnoi tseny*, no. 6 (1929): 27–35.

43. TRAM (*Teatr Rabochei Molodezhi*) was an acronym for the Theatre of Working-Class Youth, a very popular theatre group among young people. Begun in Leningrad in the 1920s, it abandoned traditional methods and used a "collective creative process" in order to "illuminate concrete political and social problems". See Lynn Mally, "The Rise and Fall of the Soviet Youth Theatre *TRAM*", *Slavic Review* 51, no. 3 (Autumn 1992), 411–430 (411). According to Mally TRAM members were "not actors but rather activists who drew their material from the streets, factories and dormitories" and their "aim was to influence the behaviour of viewers". Mally, *Revolutionary Acts*, 12.

44. TRAM, N. "Klesh zadumchivyii", *Materialy dlya klubnoi tseny*, nos. 7–8 (1929): 11.

45. "Orgsoveshchanie TRAM'ov: Utrennee zasedanii 7/VII/31", RGALI, f.2723, op.1, d.536, l.21 in Mally, *Revolutionary Acts*, 139.

46. A. Larskii, "Bumazhka", *Materialy dlya klubnoi tseny*, no. 1 (1928): 11–19.

47. Larskii, "Bumazhka", 14.

48. A. Kasatkina, "Problemy klubnogo repertuara", *Teatr i dramaturgiya* 8 (1933): 52, in Mally, *Revolutionary Acts*, 5. For quotation, see Mally, 5. For more on cases of "imposture" and portrayals of "confidence men" such as Kuritsyn and Khlestakov, see Fitzpatrick, *Tear off the Masks!*, 20.

49. Gr. Gradov, "V poryadke samokritikii", *Materialy dlya klubnoi tseny*, no.1 (1928): 20–25.

50. Gradov, "V poryadke samokritikii", 23.

51. Victoria Bonnell, *Iconography of Power: Soviet Political Posters under Lenin and Stalin*, (Berkeley; London: University of California Press, 1997), 123.

52. For more on patriarchal behaviour in the home and the physical abuse of women and children by their husbands/fathers see GARF A-2313, op.9, d.2, l.23, "Sostoyanie i perspektivy klubnoi raboty".

53. See figures from the 1926 census in E. Z. Volkov, *Dinamika naseleniya SSSR za vosem'desyat let* (1930) and F. Lorimer, *The Population of the Soviet Union: History and Prospects* (1946), cited in Fitzpatrick, Rabinowitch and Stites (eds), *Russia in the Era of NEP*, 4–5.

54. See Isabel Tirado, "The Village Voice: Women's Views of Themselves and their World in Russian Chastushki of the 1920s", The Carl Beck Papers, CREES, Pittsburgh, December 1993, 1.

55. Tirado, "Village Voice", 52.

56. Tirado, "Village Voice", 2.

57. "Fizkul'turnyi raek", (letnii). RGASPI, f. 1-M, op.23, d.800, ll. 64–66.

58. Mally, *Revolutionary Acts*, 147.

59. Mally, *Revolutionary Acts*, 146.

60. Mally, *Revolutionary Acts*, 155.

61. James Riordan, "Soviet Physical Education" in Tomiak (ed), *Soviet Education in the 1980s* (New York, 1983), 178–179.

62. Riordan, *Sport in Soviet Society*, 115.

63. B. P. Goloshchapov, *Istoriya fizicheskoi kul'tury i sporta* (5th ed.) (Moscow: Izdatel'skii tsentr "Akademiya", 2008). See also N. A. Karpushko, *Istoriko-teoreticheskoi analiz shkol'nykh programm po fizicheskoi kul'ture* (Moscow, 1992), 17–32.

64. A. A. Zikmund, G. Bezak, and V. Stasenkov, "Pedagogicheskaya praktika po normal'nym urokam sovfizkul'tury", in Zikmund, Gorinevsky (eds), *Fizkul'tura v nauchno-prakticheskom osveshchenii. II Sbornik trudov* (Leningrad, 1925), 178.

65. The programmes were classified into age groups with different sports and exercises outlined for each group. The age groups were 7–9, 9–12, 12–15,

and 15–18. At the first physical culture All-Union meeting in 1924, where Zikmund had recommended that physical education be compulsory for all students, he paid particular attention to older age groups (12–18) as these were "not emotionally developed, inclined towards nervous disorders and egocentrism". They were also prone to "overvalue their own strength" and sought opportunities to display heroism. RGASPI, f.17, op.68, d.424, l.214.

66. GARF, f.7576, op.3, d.60, l.82–82ob. Tezisy dokladi sostoyaniya i perspektivy fizicheskoi kul'tury v pedagogicheskikh VUZ"akh, Tekhnikumakh i rabfakakh. USSR 1/II/1932.
67. GARF, f.7576, op.3, d.60, l.82–82ob.
68. GARF, f.7576, op.3, d.60, l.82ob.
69. GARF, f.7576, op.3, d.60, l.111. V Narkomfin T. Mantsevu, ot Antipova. 28/1/1932 and l.115, V VSNKh T. Moskbinu, from Antipov, 28/I/1932.
70. RGASPI, f.537, op.1, d.116, ll. 167–171 (1926).
71. RGASPI, f.17, op.68, d.424, l.29. Orgburo discussions 1925. See also f.537, op.1, d.116, ll. 167.
72. For a comprehensive account of school education during this period see Larry E. Holmes, *The Kremlin and the Schoolhouse: Reforming Education in Soviet Russia, 1917–1931* (Bloomington; Indianapolis: Indiana University Press, 1991).
73. GARF, f.7576, op.12, d.11, l.1. 15 June 1932 (Rabishcheva school)
74. GARF, f.7576, op.12, d.11a, l.15.
75. GARF, f.7576, op.12, d.11a, l.10. (1935)
76. GARF, f.7576, op.12, d.11a, l.11.
77. GARF, f.7576, op.12, d.1a, l.8.
78. GARF, f.7576, op.6, d.11, l.2. Many of these reports were filed by Kvedorelis on the orders of the Moscow Committee (MK VKP/b/).
79. GARF, f.7576, op.6, d.11, l.2. According to the questionnaires, 14,647 out of 30,000 students in the Vologarskii district were provided for in this regard.
80. GARF, f.7576, op.6, d.11, l.39.
81. GARF, f.7576, op.6, d.11, l.2.
82. GARF, f.7576, op.3, d.100, l.13. Nauchnyi-metodicheskii komitet. Stenogramma soveshchaniya po fizkul'turoi rabote sredi detei. 20/IV—24 / IV/1933. A file dated 1932 noted that of the twenty-five schools in the Stalinskii district, there were seventeen physical culture teachers of whom seven had higher level education, three mid-level education, and the rest (seven) course preparation. GARF, f.7576, op.11, d.12, l.39.
83. GARF, f.7576, op.6, d.11, l.39.
84. GARF, f.7576, op.12, d.13, l.26. (1939)
85. GARF, f.7576, op.6, d.11, l.2. For more on the nationalities question, see Chapter 4.
86. GAPO, f. R-349, op.1, d.42, l.9. (21 January 1927). Befani (Penza GSFK). Physical culture in relation to the national minorities is discussed in more detail in Chapter 4.
87. GARF, f.7576, op.1, d.253, l.54. Sovnarkom. Postanovlenie "O fizicheskom vospitanie shkolnikov". 1937.
88. GARF, f.7576, op.12, d.13, l.21. 1939.
89. While architecturally striking and innovative clubs such as the Zuev Workers' Club (Ilya Golosov, Moscow, 1926) or the Rusakov Worker's Club (Konstantin Melnikov, Moscow, 1927) grabbed headlines, clubs that could cater for physical culture activities were not that widespread and were modest in size and design.
90. GARF, f.7576, op.12, d.13, l.156.
91. GARF, f.7576, op.12, d.13, l.156.

92. Larry E. Holmes, *Kirov's School No.9: Power, Privilege, and Excellence in the Provinces, 1933–1945* (Kirov: "Loban", 2008), 19, 29, 88. Physical education seemed to be the subject most frequently skipped by students.
93. GARF, f.7576, op.12, d.13, l.155.
94. GARF, f.7576, op.12, d.13,l.155.
95. GARF, f.7576, op.12, d.14, l.171. (1939)
96. GARF, f.7576, op.12, d.15, l.11. (1940) According to the All-Union Committee for Physical Culture and Sport's education section inspector's report the kitchen was small but the rooms there were generally clean and tidy. There were however no bedside lockers in the bedrooms and one girl had no mattress so had to share a bed with her friend. The inspector here was Konstantinov, 21 June 1940.
97. GARF, f.7576, op.12, d.15, l.11. The students interviewed were Volkov and Shalina.
98. GARF, f.7576, op.12, d.15, l.11.
99. GARF, f.7576, op.12, d.15, l.11.
100. For more on the education versus entertainment debate in clubs and *kruzhki* see my article, "'The Collective Agitation of Arms and Legs": Revolutionizing Physical Culture Organization, 1924–1934', *Revolutionary Russia* (2010): 93–113.
101. GARF, f.7576, op.12, d.14a, l.3. 4 December 1935, as reported by the club representative Kalognomos. The gymnastics section had already had to double its size and even the enlarged capacity was not big enough so the club had to "temporarily stop taking people."
102. In response the club sent a "little library", instructions on how to organize physical culture, and also conducted *shefstvo* (patronage) activities with this school. GARF, f.7576, op.12, d.14a, l.3. There is detailed discussion of *shefstvo* in Chapter 4.
103. Fitzpatrick, "Sex and Revolution".
104. Fitzpatrick, "Sex and Revolution", 255. The latter signal, advocating sexual restraint "came in the form of advice from party authorities to Communist youth" and was represented mainly by the Old Bolsheviks, who campaigned for "self-discipline, abstinence, fidelity to one partner, and sublimation of sexual energies in work". Fitzpatrick, "Sex and Revolution", 255–256.
105. Alexandra Mikhailovna Kollontai, (1872–1952) was one of the most prominent figures in the sexuality debate and played an important role in the movement for female emancipation, publishing widely on these topics. She advocated marriages based on love and which freed women from the traditional confines of marriage, motherhood and family life. However, her ideas were often misinterpreted and understood to endorse "free love".
106. Ivanovsky was a *"privat dotsent"* or lecturer in the Institute of Physical Culture. He also contributed articles on various medical issues to other physical culture publications, such as *Teoriya i praktika fizicheskoi kul'tury.*
107. B. Ivanovsky, "Polovaya zhizn'" i fizkul'tura", *FiS*, no. 16 (1929): 4–5.
108. Ivanovsky, "Polovaya zhizn'", 4. This echoed Lenin's stance, who considered that promiscuity was degenerate and bourgeois. He regarded the sexual licentiousness which followed the revolution as a waste of young people's health and energy; they should pursue a more "healthy sport". K. Tsetkin, "Lenin o morale i voprosakh", in *Komsomol'skii byt: Sbornik*, ed. O. Razin (1927) cited in David L. Hoffmann, *Stalinist Values: The Cultural Norms of Soviet Modernity, 1917–1941* (Ithaca, NY; London: Cornell University Press, 2003), 92.

109. Ivanovsky, "Polovaya zhizn'", 4. For more on this debate see Carleton, *Sexual Revolution*, 70–71.
110. Dr. Iu. I. Pinus was on the Stalingrad *Gubzdrav* (Provincial Health Board) and was a contributor at the First All-Union Conference of Scientific Workers in Physical Culture, 1925 where he would have come into contact with others such as Kradman and Dr. N. D. Korolev (who is discussed in the next chapter).
111. Dr. Iu. I. Pinus, "Polovaya zhizn' i fizkul'tura", *The First All-Union Conference of Scientific Workers in Physical Culture* (Moscow, 1926), 78–79.
112. Ivanovsky, "Polovaya zhizn'", 4–5.
113. Many of those visiting the clinics were young students or party activists. Bernstein noted the comments of one doctor: "And so to the surprise of medicine, which usually has no clients from the proletarian sphere, proletarian students get for themselves before their Party card and their professional card a 'psychocard' [*psikhbilet*] . . . these neuropathic dysfunctions never befell the proletariat before in such a quantity. But since we have before us an entire class generation of the Revolution . . . this statistic becomes extremely alarming". Gannushkin, "Ob okhrana zdorov'ia partaktiva", cited in Bernstein, "Panic", 163. Even Vladimir Mayakovsky, one of the most prolific and talented poets of the 1920s, was diagnosed with "nervous exhaustion" and temporarily hospitalized in early April 1930. He committed suicide later that month.
114. For examples, see the diaries examined in Jochen Hellbeck, *Revolution on my Mind*.
115. Markoosha Fisher, *My Lives in Russia* (New York: Harper & Brothers, 1944), 11, cited in Gorsuch, *Youth in Revolutionary Russia*, 81. It should be noted that, while there was an increase during the NEP years, suicide in Russia was not a new problem. Following the 1905 revolution the problem was widely discussed. See Pinnow, *Making Suicide Soviet*.
116. Pinnow, *Making Suicide Soviet*, 24.
117. Leon Trotsky, *The Revolution Betrayed* cited in Mark Von Hagen, "Soldiers in the Proletarian Dictatorship", in Fitzpatrick, Rabinowitch, and Stites, *Russia in the Era of NEP*, 157.
118. Suicide statistics in the Red Army and Navy from 1924 and 1925. (RGVA, f.9, op. 13, d.512, l. 1 ob) These statistics were taken from PUR, OGPU, GURKKA and the military procurator.
119. RGVA, f.9, op.13, d.512, l.2 ob.
120. RGVA, f.9, op.13, d.512, l.7.
121. RGVA, f. 9, op. 13, d. 512, l. 7.
122. RGVA, f.9. op.13, d.512, l. 7 ob, l.8. In 1912 the number of suicides stood at 761, compared to 307 in 1903, 349 in 1905, 462 in 1906, 426 in 1908 and then 520 in 1924, l.7ob.
123. Von Hagen, *Soldiers*, 305.
124. Von Hagen, *Soldiers*, 305.
125. Von Hagen, *Soldiers*, 307.
126. Von Hagen, *Soldiers*, 195.
127. NACHINFSTATOTDEL (Head of the Information and Statistics Department) of PUR, Chernevskii. RGVA, f.9. op.13, d.512, l. 7 ob, l.8.
128. Gorsuch, *Youth in Revolutionary Russia*, 7.
129. Derek Sayer, "Everyday Forms of State Formation: Dissident Remarks on Hegemony", in *Everyday Forms of State Formation: Revolution and the Negotiation of Rule in Modern Mexico*, ed. Gilbert Joseph and Daniel Nugent (Durham, NC: Duke University Press, 1994), 371, cited in Gorsuch, *Youth in Revolutionary Russia*, 62.

NOTES TO CHAPTER 4

1. This was later revised in 1927 when the marriage age was raised to eighteen for women. For more on the medical and legal debates surrounding abortion (in the Soviet Union and Germany) see Susan Gross Solomon, "The Soviet Legalization of Abortion in German Medical Discourse: A Study of the Use of Selective Perceptions in Cross-Cultural Scientific Relations", *Social Studies of Science* 22 (1992): 455–485.

2. See Wendy Goldman, "Women, Abortion, and the State, 1917–36", in Barbara Evans Clements, Barbara Alpern Engel, and Christine Worobec (eds), *Russia's Women: Accommodation, Resistance, Transformation* (Berkeley; Oxford: University of California Press, c1991), 245. According to Goldman, women who most frequently resorted to abortion were aged between twenty and twenty-nine (60 per cent), with a tiny percentage aged under eighteen (less than 1 per cent). Goldman, "Women, Abortion, and the State", in *Russia's Women*, 254, 259–260.

3. It was reported that every year about 50,000 women in Russia died from "birthing fever", an illness which included high temperature, stomach cramps, loss of consciousness, weight loss, and eventual death after five to seven days. Vrach. Gofmekler, "Boleznei posle rodov ne dolzhna byt", *Krest'yanka*, no. 6 (1925): 19.

4. Buckley, *Women and Ideology in the Soviet Union* (New York; London: Harvester Wheatsheaf, 1989), 90.

5. RGASPI, f. 1-M, op.23, d.477. The equivalent statistics for men were 422,226 (67 per cent) participating in 1924 with an increase of 454,141 to 876,367 (67 per cent) in 1925. The figure of 33 per cent was considered inflated by Zhenotdel member Glebova. RGASPI, f.17, op.68, d.424, ll7, 9, 23, 43, 60.

6. GARF, f.7576, op.3, d.1, l.51. This was in relation to collective competition in the second All-Union Festival of Physical Culture, 1924.

7. D. Yeshchin, "Vovlechem v fizkul'turu trudyashchuiusya zhenshchinu", *FiS*, no. 15 (1929): 2.

8. RGASPI, f.17, op.68, d.424, ll.7, 9, 23, 43, 60.

9. RGASPI, f.17, op.68, d.424, ll.7, 9, 23, 43, 60.

10. Irina Pellinger, "K voprosu o fizicheskoi kul'ture zhenshchiny", *IFK*, no. 9 (1927): 2. According to Pellinger, the only three authorities on physical culture and women were herself, Dr. Korolev and Dr. Gorinevskaya.

11. Dr. Veronika Gorinevskaya, *Fizkul'tura rabotnitsy* (Moscow: MGSPS, 1925), 11.

12. Prof. Aron Zalkind's "Twelve Commandments" of sexual behaviour is an example. For discussion of Anton Nemilov's *The Biological Tragedy of Women*, see Pat Simpson, "Bolshevism and 'Sexual Revolution': Visualizing New Soviet Woman as the Eugenic Ideal" in Fae Brauer and Anthea Callen (eds), *Art, Sex and Eugenics, Corpus Delecti* (Aldershot: Asgate, 2008), 229. Examples are also found in Frances Bernstein, "Science and Gender in Revolutionary Russia", in David Hoffmann and Yanni Kotsonis (eds), *Russian Modernity. Politics, Knowledge, Practices* (London; New York: Macmillan, 2000), 142–143.

13. Dr. N. D. Korolev wrote also on the physical upbringing of girls aged between fifteen and seventeen years, dealing especially with gynaecological issues and their psychological effects and how *fizkul'tura* could be used to overcome some of these problems. GARF, f.7576, op.28, d.29, ll.1 13. During the interwar period the study of women and the body was not uncommon, see David G. Horn, *Social Bodies: Science, Reproduction, and Italian Modernity* (Princeton, NJ: Princeton University Press, 1994), 7–18. Yet, as Horn noted,

in spite of the commonality of ideas, the "Italians didn't carry them through as feverishly as in Russia", whether by the state or individuals. Horn, *Social Bodies*, 44.

14. Dr. N. D. Korolev, "Etiudy po fizicheskomu vospitaniiu zhenshchiny", *IFK*, nos. 5–6 (1924): 10–11.
15. Korolev, "Etiudy", 4–6.
16. Korolev, "Etiudy", 5.
17. Pellinger, "K voprosu", 2.
18. Dr. N. Korolev, "Fizkul'turnye zhenskie tipy", *IFK*, no. 1 (1926): 2–3.
19. This limited view of women was also reflected in attitudes towards sexuality, where female orgasm and satisfaction were considered only as relative to their male partners. Failure in this area was deemed a result of male dysfunction, in which case *he* had to consult a doctor. The problem was out of the control of the woman—she was a silent and passive observer. Bernstein, "Panic", 166–169. For similar, peasant views of women see Rose L. Glickman, "Peasant Women and their Work", in Beatrice Farnsworth and Lynne Viola (eds), *Russian Peasant Women*, 69.
20. These include *Nauchnyi kontrol' i uchet rezul'tatov po fizicheskomy vospitaniiu* (Leningrad: 1924), *Kratkoe rukovodstvo po fizicheskoi kul'ture zhenshchiny* (Leningrad: 1925), *Osnovy fizicheskoi kul'tury muzhiny i zhenshchiny* (Leningrad: LGSPS, 1925), *Fizicheskaya kul'tura v povsednevnoi zhizni trudyashchegosya* (Leningrad: 1926), *Fizicheskoe ukreplenie i zakalivanie zhenshchiny* (Leningrad: 1927).
21. *Pervaya vsesoiuznaya konferentsiya nauchnykh rabotnikov po fizicheskoi kul'ture, 10–15 noyabrya 1925 v Mockve (otchet)* (Moscow: VSFK, 1926). The two other participants on Korolev's panel were Dr. L. P. Kuzovkovoi-Aryamovoi of the State Institute of Physical Culture (gynaecological control, exercise and women) and a paper delivered by Smolyanrov, Kornil'evoi, and Rozenberg (on the Young Pioneers)
22. *Fizkul'tura v nauchno-prakticheskom osveshchenii* (Leningrad: GTsIFK, 1925).
23. Camogie is an Irish stick-and-ball game played by women. Agnes O' Farrelly was an Irish academic who promoted the Irish language and women's issues in Ireland. She was a member of the Gaelic League, a founding member of Cumann na mBan and president of the Camogie Association. Ríona Nic Congáil, *Úna Ní Fhaircheallaigh agus an Fhís Útóipeach Ghaelach* (Gaillimh: Arlen House, 2010), 320–344.
24. Nic Congáil, *Úna Ní Fhaircheallaigh*, 320–344.
25. Hugo Sellheim, "Auswertung der Gymnastik der Frau fur die arztliche Praxis", *Medizinische Klinik* 27 (1931) in Gertrud Pfister, "The Medical Discourse on Female Physical Culture in Germany in the 19th and Early 20th Centuries", in *Journal of Sport History* 17, no. 2 (1990): 193.
26. Mary Lynn Stewart, *For Health and Beauty. Physical Culture for Frenchwomen, 1880s–1930s*, (Baltimore, MD; London: Johns Hopkins University Press, 2001), 158.
27. Gigliola Gori, *Italian Fascism and the Female Body: Sport, Submissive Women and Strong Mothers* (London; New York: Routledge, 2004), 54.
28. As Stewart notes in relation to women after the war, "[f]ilms, plays, and posters encouraged Frenchwomen to take up sports in order to bring them up to the physical standards of English and American women". *For Health and Beauty*, 166. See also Zweiniger-Bargielowska, "Building a British Superman", 602, and Lowe, *Looking Good*.
29. GARF, f.7576, op.9, d.2, l.129. Zasedanie plenarnoi kommissii po okonchatel'noi redaktsii novogo proekta kompleksa GTO, 1938. This age

versus maturity debate in Central Asia, albeit in relation to marriage, is discussed in Douglas Northrop, *Veiled Empire: Gender and Power in Stalinist Central Asia* (Ithaca, NY; London: Cornell University Press, 2004), 41, 245–256.

30. GARF, f.7576, op.9, d.2, l.130. (Novikov)
31. GARF, f.7576, op.9, d.2, l.130.
32. GARF, f.7576, op.9, d.2, l.130. (Starikov) Starikov, disagreed with Novikov and wanted one single union age for the norm with local republican committees having the right to diverge from All-Union Committee sanctions.
33. See for example "Irina", "Okhrana zdorov'ya", *Rabotnitsa*, no. 18 (1925): 21–22; "Na zametky rabotnitsy", no. 19 (1925): 6, 10; no. 12 (1927): 13–14; no. 23 (1927): 17; no. 26 (1927): 15.
34. Isabel Tirado, "The Village Voice. Women's Views of Themselves and their World in Russian Chastushki of the 1920s", (Pittsburgh: The Carl Beck Papers, CREES, December 1993), 1.
35. Demyan Bednyi (1883–1945) was the pen name of the Soviet poet Yefim Aleksandrovich Pridvorov. Bednyi was a close friend of Lenin's and was a popular poet and satirist, managing to stay on the "right" side of the Soviet authorities until in 1938. Then he was stripped of Communist Party membership and membership of the Union of Soviet Writers. He slowly regained acceptance during the Second World War. In 1923 he had been awarded the Order of the Red Banner and in 1933 received the Order of Lenin. He wrote anti-religious works in the 1920s and wrote verse in support of Stalinist policies, including the purges.
36. RGASPI, f.M-1, op. 23, d. 800, ll. 62–64. February—November 1927. *"Fizkul'turnye chastushki"*.
37. Farnsworth, "Village Women Experience the Revolution", in *Russian Peasant Women*, 145. Sarah Badcock also provides insightful discussion of how peasants were viewed by the political elites, see Badcock, *Politics and People in Revolutionary Russia* (Cambridge: Cambridge University Press, 2007), Chapter 5.
38. These are *On the Construction of the New Factory Halls*, 1926, and *Conductor*, 1928, examined in Nina Sobol Levent, *Healthy Spirit in a Healthy Body: Representations of the Sports Body in Soviet Art of the 1920s and 1930s* (Frankfurt am Main: Peter Lang, 2004), 90–91.
39. In 1930, 430,000 women entered industry, four times higher than the number of new women entering industry in 1929. In 1931, 587,000 more entered. Between 1929 and 1935 there were almost 4 million women working for wages, 1.7 million of whom worked in industry. By 1935, 45 per cent of all industrial workers were women, and in 1932 and 1933 women represented the only new source of labour. *Trud v SSSR. Statisticheskii spravochnik*, (1936), cited in Wendy Goldman, *Women at the Gates: Gender and Industry in Stalin's Russia* (Cambridge: Cambridge University Press, 2002), 1.
40. Barbara Engels Clement, "Later Developments: Trends in Soviet Women's History, 1930 to the Present", in *Russia's Women*, 268.
41. Clement, "Later Developments", 268. See also S. Fitzpatrick, *Education and Social Mobility in the Soviet Union 1921–1934* (Cambridge: Cambridge University Press, 2002).
42. Attwood, *Creating the New Soviet Woman*, 71. On images of women and clothing see also Pat Simpson, "Bolshevism and 'Sexual Revolution', 217–221.
43. As Turner stressed, dress and manner had serious connotations in a general context, with cosmetics and corsets signifying the "absence of work and the ability to consume conspicuously". Bryan S. Turner, *The Body and Society: Explorations in Social Theory* (Oxford: Blackwell, 1984), 173.

44. "I–go–go" (a peasant physical culture ditty performed in the sport *yacheika*, sung by a man and woman and accompanied by the harmonica or the balalaika). RGASPI, f.1-M, op.23, d.800, ll.67–68.
45. "Slovo predostavlyaetsya fizkul'turnitsam", *FiS*, no. 16 (1930): 4–5. Lipstick was a controversial subject, with advocates arguing it was attractive and protected lips, to other arguing that it was unnecessary and a waste of time and money. "Fizkul'turnitsy, borites' za novyi byt!", *FiS*, no. 13 (1930): 10.
46. Brovkin, *Russian after Lenin: Politics, Culture and Society, 1921–1929*, (London: Routledge, 1988), 149.
47. Bonnell, *Iconography of Power: Soviet Political Posters under Lenin and Stalin* (Berkeley; London: University of California Press, c1997), 101–123. For discussion of the changing visual representations of the female body see also Levent, *Healthy Spirit*, 90–99.
48. Lynne Attwood (ed), *Red Women on the Silver Screen: Soviet Women and Cinema from the Beginning to the End of the Communist Era* (London: Pandora, 1993), 162.
49. O'Mahony, *Sport in the USSR*, 54–56. These include Samokhvalov's *Woman with a File* (1929), *Butter Maker Golubeva* (1931/1932), and later *Girl Wearing a Football Jersey* (1932), *Girl with a Shot Put* (1933). See also Levent, *Healthy Spirit in a Healthy Body*.
50. Christina Kiaer, "The Swimming Vtorova Sisters: The Representation and Experience of Sport in the 1930s", in Katzer, *Euphoria*, 89.
51. Petrone, *Life Has Become More Joyous, Comrades*, 34.
52. GARF, f.7576, op.54a, l.13, 26, 163.
53. Semashko even published on this topic, see *Iskusstvo odevat'sya* (Moscow; Leningrad: Gosizdat, 1927) especially 17–23.
54. GARF, f.7576, op.14, d.2, l. 10. Stenogramma soveshchanii po uluchshennogo fizkul'turoi raboty sredi zhenshchin. 16/II/36.
55. GARF, f.7576, op.14, d.2, l. 10.
56. GARF, f.7576, op.14, d.2, l. 10.
57. Turner, *Social Bodies*, 197.
58. Kiaer, "Vtorova Sisters", 90.
59. Between 1935 and 1937 there was an increase but this fell again in 1938. See Hoffmann, *Stalinist Values*, 109–117. It should be noted that the Soviet attitude to the birth rate and the desire to attract more women to the role of mother was not unique in inter-war Europe as other states also sought to increase the declining birth rates.
60. Hoffmann, *Stalinist Values*, 109–117.
61. Emma Widdis, "The Cinematic Pastoral of the 1930s", in Valerie A. Kivelson and Joan Neuberger (eds), *Picturing Russia: Explorations in Visual Culture* (New Haven, CT; London: Yale University Press, 2008), 176.
62. Alison Rowley, "Sport in the Service of the State: Images of Physical Culture and Soviet Women, 1917–1941", *The International Journal for the History of Sport* 23, no. 8 (2006): 1334.
63. Rowley, "Sport in the Service of the State", 1334. Pat Simpson discusses the popular image of motherhood, see Simpson, "Bolshevism and 'Sexual Revolution'", 221–229.
64. Galina Tusova, "Privetstvuiu zakonoproekt", *Krasnyi sport*, no. 73 (1936): 1.
65. Maria Shamanova, *Krasnyi sport*, no. 77 (1936): 2.
66. Zinaida Shumova, "Nauchit' uvazhat' sovetskie zakony", *Krasnyi sport*, no. 74 (1936): 1.
67. A. Kudrevtsev, "Kak byt' materi-studenke", *Krasnyi sport*, no. 74 (1936): 2. Sympathetic fathers were probably the exception rather than the rule. For more on personal and family difficulties experienced by female high achievers

(especially those living in rural areas), see Roberta Manning, "Women in the Soviet Countryside on the Eve of World War II", in *Russia's Peasant Women*, 219–223.

68. Kiaer, "Vtorova Sisters", 100.
69. Kiaer, "Vtorova Sisters", 100.
70. L. Barkhasha, "Fizkul'turnitsy sovetskoi strany", *Smena*, no. 5 (1929): 6–7.
71. This figure of Barkhasha's is roughly supported by statistics provided by V. V. Sokolov, *Prava zhenshchini po sovetskim zakonom* (Moscow, 1928), 16 cited in Wendy Goldman, *Women, the State and Revolution: Soviet Family Policy and Social Life, 1917–1936* (Cambridge: Cambridge University Press, 1993), 130.
72. This was often even more emphatic in the national republics, when girls were expected to marry from a young age. As one Soviet writer informed readers, having been "sold like goods" and forced to perform very difficult work, the "young girl turns into an old woman". An example of one such girl was, Ziul'ne Islamova, a fifteen year old from Turkmenistan who had to marry "an old man", was provided. *Krest'yanka*, no. 4 (1925): 17. See again Northrop's discussion of marriage in Central Asia.
73. Barkhasha, "Fizkul'turnitsy sovetskoi strany", 6–7.
74. Barkhasha, "Fizkul'turnitsy sovetskoi strany", 6–7. Similar concerns were also expressed by Gorinevskaya in *Fizkul'tura rabotnitsy*, 11.
75. It is difficult to know whether or not these and other accounts are genuine. Letters to periodicals were sometimes dictated (mainly to *Bednota* or *Krest'yanka*) and in other cases writers and respondents might have "spoken Bolshevik", writing what they assumed officials wanted to hear. See Beatrice Farnsworth, "Peasant Women after the Revolution", in *Russian Peasant Women*, 178, and Stephen Kotkin, *Magnetic Mountain*.
76. This account appears as part of a larger project where the trade union workers of ten factories asked female workers about how they related to physical culture, P. Surozhskii, "Chem interesuiutsia rabochie v fizkul'ture", *FiS*, no. 26 (1929): 4.
77. Some women found the training difficult, as one woman's experience in Penza Guberniya shows. Maria Mikhailovna Troshina was enrolled in a course for instructors but for the entire duration of her course (February to June) she washed the floors, cleaned the clothes of the other course attendees, and made the tea—hardly adequate training for a physical culture instructor, GAPO, f. R.349, op.1, d.17, l.452 (1925). Befani.
78. GAPO, f. R.349, op.1, d.37, l.45 (1927). In Penza the negligence of an instructor combined with a lack of interest by women led to all *kruzhok* classes being terminated. There was "dissidence" reported among *kruzhok* members regarding the instructor but it was claimed that the "Komsomol *yacheika* and physical culture *kruzhok* do not enforce their directives when it comes to the removal of instructors", l.46.
79. G. Plecheva, "Vsroslaya Rabotnitsa, idi v kruzhok fizkul'tury!", *FiS*, no. 7 (1930): 3.
80. E. Bol'shakova, "Vne fizkul'turnykh ryadov!", *FiS*, no. 31 (1931): 9.
81. This would seem to be a valid point. In Gomel', Belorussia, for instance, women's groups were formed separately (for the collectives, events, competitions, the GTO) and this seemed to work well, with increasing numbers becoming involved in physical culture activities. GARF, f.7576, op.6, d.7, l.1 (1935).
82. These accounts were part of an article that investigated why women who had been active in physical culture until a year or two ago had now stopped going to classes. "V XX godovshchinu mezhdunarodnogo kommunisticheskogo

zhenskogo dnya shlem plamennyi privet trudyashchimsya zhenshchinam! (Chto govoryat rabotnitsy o fizkul'ture)", *FiS*, no. 13 (1930): 4–5.

83. N. Slivina, "Mastera—organizatory massovoi ucheby", *FiS*, no. 26–27 (1932): 7.

84. Stephen Kotkin, *Magnetic Mountain. Stalinism as a Civilization* (Berkeley: University of California Press, 1997), 190.

85. Christina Kiaer also makes this argument. Kiaer, "Vtorova Sisters", 98.

86. "V XX godovshchinu" , 5.

87. Workers did not work a typical five day week. For example, they could work eight days in a row and receive seven days off. This varied according to factory and workplace. The upshot of this system was that workers had quite substantial periods of leisure time (in theory at least).

88. "V XX godovshchinu", 5.

89. GARF, f.7576, op.4, d.4, l.159, "O sostoyanii fizkul'turnoi raboty sredi zhenskoi chast' molodezhi goroda Ivanovo" (1935). The two women were Prokhorova and Lebedeva. The same statistics on women in Ivanovo factories reappeared in the trade union files on physical culture, GARF, f.7710, op,6, d.36, l.23 in a Komsomol decision on attracting young women towards physical culture, 5 September 1935.

90. GARF, f.7576, op.4, d.4, l.159.

91. GARF, f.7576, op.4, d.4, l.159.

92. GARF, f.7576, op.4, d.4, l.160

93. GARF, f.7576, op.4, d.4, l.160.

94. Kiaer, "Vtorova Sisters", 107. This was not always the case though and some heroes, even famous ones such as Pasha Angelina, were considered outcasts by their local communities.

NOTES TO CHAPTER 5

1. Retish, *Russia's Peasants*, 9. I use both the terms peasants and national minorities throughout, even though the former can arguably carry negative connotations. There is also overlap, as "peasants" were majority and minority populations. In some instances the catch-all terms "rural" or "countryside" are used, though again this is less than perfect and naturally excludes national minorities living in towns and cities.

2. Northrop, *Veiled Empire*, 8.

3. Recent studies of the national minorities have made the case for a policy of Soviet imperialism, with the national republics in Central Asia in particular treated as "colonies", see Paula A. Michaels, *Curative Powers: Medicine and Empire in Stalin's Central Asia* (Pittsburgh, PA: University of Pittsburgh Press, 2003), Francine Hirsch, *Empire of Nations: Ethnographic Knowledge & the Making of the Soviet Union* (Ithaca, NY; London: Cornell University Press, 2005), Northrop, *Veiled Empire*, and Yuri Slezkine, "Imperialism as the Highest Stage of Capitalism", *Russian Review* 59, no. 2 (2000): 227–234. In terms of physical culture, many of the campaigns directed at the peasants and national minorities were similar in tone and content, aimed at reforming "backward" ways irrespective of geographical or ethnic provenance.

4. GARF, f.7576, op.1, d.54a, l.9.

5. "Rezoliutsii 1-go Vserossiiskogo Soveshchaniya po fizkul'trabote v nats respublikakh oblastyakh", no. 11 (1927): 5.

6. Northrop, *Veiled Empire*, 60.

7. Sheila Fitzpatrick, *Stalin's Peasants: Resistance and Survival in the Russian Village after Collectivization* (London; New York: Oxford University Press,

1994), 13. On the collectivization debate see Christopher Read, *The Making and Breaking of the Soviet System* (Basingstoke, Hampshire; New York: Palgrave Macmillan, 2001), 96–98.

8. Part of the Five Year Plan, collectivization was an attempt to address the disequilibrium that had arisen in grain distribution. Individual peasant holdings were to be amalgamated into larger state collective farms called *kolkhozy* and *sovkhozy*. Peasants who resisted collectivization (most often accused of being kulaks) were frequently arrested, deported or executed.

9. RGASPI, f.17, op.68, d.424, ll7, 9, 23, 43, 60. Glebova in Orgburo discussions.

10. RGASPI, f.17, op.68, d.424, ll7, 9, 23, 43, 29. Yagoda in Orgburo discussions.

11. RGASPI, f.17, op.68, d.424, ll7, 9, 23, 43, 29–30.

12. RGASPI, f.17, op.68, d.424, ll7, 9, 23, 43, 29–30.

13. GARF, f.7576, op.1, d.54a, l.3. Stenogramma zasedaniya fraktsii zakavkazkogo VFSK ot 27/vii-1930.

14. GARF, f.7576, op.1, d.54a, l.59.

15. RGASPI, f.1-M, op.23, d.944, l.70 (1929).

16. *Dzhigitovka* is an equestrian sport popular in the Caucasus traditionally associated with Russian Cossacks. It involves galloping at speed, standing on horseback, shooting targets, and other feats. *Bol'shaya Sovetskaya Entstiklopediya*.

17. RGASPI, f.1-M, op.23, d.944, l.72 (1929).

18. Kh. Fatkullin, "Medlenno, no uverenno idem vpered", *FiS*, no. 13 (1929): 8.

19. Lebedeva, using peasant questionnaires from the archives, found that *lapta* was most popular amongst children (33 per cent) and teenagers (17 per cent) and that adults preferred card games (14 per cent) but also enjoyed *gorodki* (8 per cent) and *lapta* (6 per cent). Penza State Regional Museum (PGKM) n. A. No.88. Podschety avtora. l.49, l.198, in Larissa V. Lebedeva, *Povsednevnaya zhizn' Penzenskoi derevni v 1920-e gody: traditsii i peremeny* (Moscow: ROSSPEN, 2009), 118. These games were also a feature of urban life and no doubt played a role in peasant assimilation into the cities. For explanations of *lapta* (similar to baseball or rounders) and *gorodki* (similar to bowling), see Glossary.

20. Lebedeva, *Povsednevnaya zhizn'*, 118.

21. For discussion of these farming methods as well as general living and working conditions, see Moshe Lewin, *Russian Peasants*, 28–32.

22. Lebedeva, *Povsednevnaya zhizn'*, 123.

23. Lebedeva, *Povsednevnaya zhizn'*, 118.

24. See Lebedeva, *Povsednevnaya zhizn'*, 122–123. As the provincial party commission disapprovingly observed, the winner appeared the next day with a bruised and swollen face.

25. GARF, f.7576, op.3, d.90, ll.49–53.

26. Victor and Jennifer Louis, *Sport in the Soviet Union* (Oxford: Oxford University Press, 1980), 39.

27. N. Semashko, "Fizicheskaya kul'tura, a ne tol'ko fizicheskie uprazhnenye", *IFK*, no. 2 (1924): 2. In 1924 Semashko was also on the Committee for the Assistance to the Peoples of the Northern Borderlands, so had an added interest in minority groups. See Yuri Slezkine, *Arctic Mirrors: Russian and the Small Peoples of the North* (Ithaca, NY; London: Cornell University Press, 1994), 152.

28. GAPO, f.R-349, op.1, d.15, l.279, "Towards the Question of Dance as a Means of Physical Development", NTK VSFK (Filitis). Traditional dances were viewed as preferable to new western dances such as the foxtrot.

29. GAPO, f.R-349, op.1, d.15, l.221 (1925).
30. L. Petrov, "Pervye shagi fizkul'turnoi raboty v kolkhozakh", *Fizkul'taktivist*, no. 7 (1930): 10–12.
31. Saroyan, "Beyond the Nation-State: Culture and Ethnic Politics in Soviet Transcaucasia", in R. Suny (ed), *Nationalism and Social Change* (Ann Arbor: University of Michigan Press, 1996), 405–406.
32. For more on holidays and ritual see Christel Lane, *The Rites of Rulers* (Cambridge: Cambridge University Press, 1981). See also http://www.gov. tatarstan.ru, accessed 29 April 2008. These traditionally religious celebrations often remained but were incorporated into Soviet festivals, and physical culture authorities took a particular interest in developing them. See for example correspondence between the Soviet Supreme Council of Physical Culture and the Bashkir Supreme Council of Physical culture on *Sabantui* and other national games, GARF, f.7576, op.3, d.90, l.78 (May 1932). See also "Peredoviki bol'shevistkoi rabotoi na polyakh", *Rabotnitsa*, no. 16 (1933): 11–12.
33. Christel Lane suggests claims that *Sabantui* was never ethnically exclusive with all local nationalities welcome to participate and that this, along with its "folk" nature allowed it to survive the Soviet period with most traditional elements intact. Lane *Rites of Rulers*, 125.
34. http://www.gov.tatarstan.ru.
35. Malte Rolf, "A Hall of Mirrors: Sovietizing Culture under Stalinism", *Slavic Review* 68, no. 3 (2009): 616.
36. GARF, f.7576, op.3, d.36, l.34 (1929).
37. GARF, f.7576, op.3, d.36, l.34 (1929).
38. GARF, f.7576, op.3, d.55a. These were resolutions from the first all-union meeting on physical culture in the national republics that aimed to attract the indigenous populations and to set up a one-year course in physical culture technical colleges in Kazan for the training of national minorities from the eastern parts of the RSFSR. Statistics also show a rise in numbers participating in physical culture in the 1930s, though this was on a much smaller scale in the Central Asian republics, see GARF f.7576, op.4, d.4, l.37.
39. GARF, f.7576, op.24, d.1v, l.13.
40. GARF, f.7576, op.24, d.1v, l.13.
41. Kenez, *The Birth of the Propaganda State: Soviet Methods of Mass Mobilization, 1917–1929* (Cambridge: Cambridge University Press, 1985), 138. The village reading-room was under local control of the political education committees (*Politprosvet*) and the overall control of *Glavpolitprosvet*.
42. In Imperial Russia peasants had expressed an interest in improving literacy levels while under the Bolsheviks peasants in Viatka requested a reading hut so as to bring "enlightenment to the darkened masses of the village". See for Retish, *Russia's Peasants*, 222, and for citation, 224. For more on peasant reading-rooms in Viatka see Retish, 222–226. On the trope of peasant "darkness" see also Badcock, *Politics and the People*, 133–134.
43. *Pedagogicheskaya entsiklopediya*, vol. 3 (1927–1930) in Kenez, *Propaganda State*, 137.
44. Retish, *Russia's Peasants*, 223.
45. L. Petrov, "Pervye shagi", 10.
46. Petrov, "Pervye shagi", *Fizkul'taktivist*, 10. There was no specific explanation of what these old materials actually were. By 1930 many of the "old materials" were outdated because debates from the 1920s such as those between the Proletkul't or Hygienists had been relegated and no longer discussed in the current literature.
47. GARF, f.7576, op.1, d.54a, l.137.

48. Isabel Tirado, "Peasants into Soviets: Reconstructing Komsomol Identity in the Russian Countryside of the 1920s", *Acta Slavica Iaponica*, 18 (2001): 45. By the mid 1920s the Komsomol could count approximately 9 per cent of young peasants within its ranks.
49. Poster by Griffel', *Shkoly kolkhoznikh molodezh*, no. 18 (1928): 1.
50. Tirado, "Peasants into Soviets", 50.
51. A.Gubarev, "Fizkul'tura—v derevnyu!", *FiS*, no. 13, (1928): 1.
52. Gubarev, "Fizkul'tura", 1.
53. For discussion of some of the problems faced by the Komsomol in the countryside, see Tirado, "Peasants in to Soviets", 54. For problems with structure and communication see Neumann, *Communist Youth*, 159–160.
54. On the disappearance of traditional peasant crafts and clothing during collectivization see Fitzpatrick, *Stalin's Peasants*, 214–218. The preservation and promotion of peasant dance was supported by the central authorities, as evidenced by discussions by the NTK in 1925 (GAPO, f.R-349, op.1, d.8, l.111; d.15, l.221, 279).
55. GARF, f.7576, op.1, d.54a, l.107.
56. Meshcherskii "O tantsakh i igrakh v izbe-chital'nye", *Izba-chital'nya*, no. 7–8 (1924): 107.
57. Meshcherskii, "O tantsakh",107.
58. Meshcherskii, "O tantsakh", 107.
59. Kenez, *Propaganda State*, 142. Komsomol members were often the worst offenders and unpopular. See Brovkin, *Russia after Lenin*, 108–113.
60. Tirado, "Peasants into Soviets", 50.
61. For more on these peasant schools and Soviet education in general, see Fitzpatrick, *Education and Social Mobility in the Soviet Union 1921–1934* (New York; Oxford: Oxford University Press, 1994). Rural children usually attended the *Shkoly Kolkhoznoi Molodezhi* (ShKM) or schools for *kolkhoz* youth, which were the schools established to educate and train Soviet peasant youth. Between 1928–1929 and 1932–1933 the number of pupils in rural primary schools rose from 8 to 14 million while in secondary schools (grades 5–7) the number of pupils was estimated to be just over 2 million. Fitzpatrick, *Stalin's Peasants*, 225. See also Holmes, *The Kremlin and the Schoolhouse*, 86.
62. See for example GARF, f.7576, op.9, d.16, l.7.
63. For excellent discussion of schools in the North, see Slezkine, *Arctic Mirrors: Russia and the Small Peoples of the North* (Ithaca, NY; London: Cornell University Press, 1994), 236–246.
64. GARF, f.7576, op.1, d.54a. (1930). Adzharistan was an autonomous republic in Transcaucasia, although in the 1926 census Adzhars were considered a sub-group of Georgians. For more on the issue of nationality in Transcaucasia, see Hirsch, *Empire of Nations*, 132–138.
65. Slezkine, *Arctic Mirrors*, 238–239.
66. Petrov, "Pervye shagi", 11.
67. Petrov, "Pervye shagi", 11.
68. Class stratification among the peasantry began to increase after 1924, which, as Moshe Lewin noted, "was causing widespread disillusion amongst the *batraks* and the *bednyaks*". *Russian Peasants*, 42. See Chapters 2 and 3 for discussion of peasant class stratification. For more analysis of class and youth see Neumann, *Communist Youth*, Chapters 4 and 8.
69. The propaganda at times misled these groups too, who also felt discriminated against. See Tirado, "Peasants into Soviets", 54–61.
70. GAPO, f.R-2024, op.1, d.2, l.97. Instructor's report. Of the 3,000 participants, 500 were rural children.

71. GARF, f.7576, op.1, d.54a, l.76. From 27/8/1930.
72. GARF, f.7576, op.1, d.54a, l.76.
73. GARF, f.7576, op.3, d.56, l.9.
74. GARF, f.7576, op.3, d.56, l.9.
75. In disseminating propaganda, the authorities had an uphill battle. The 1926 census put the rural illiteracy figure at approximately 50 per cent. There were just 170,900 professional schoolteachers, one for every 705 rural inhabitants. TsU, *Vsesoiuznaya perepis'*, vol. 34, 160–161, cited in Sheila Fitzpatrick, Alexander Rabinowitch, and Richard Stites (eds), *Russia in the Era of NEP: Explorations in Soviet Society and Culture* (Bloomington; Indianapolis: Indiana University Press, 1991), 6. As a more effective form of propaganda books and journals sent to the reading-rooms should have contained interesting illustrations, diagrams, and charts. L. Petrov, "Pervye shagi", 11–12.
76. Petrov, "Pervye shagi", 11–12.
77. Lynne Viola, *The Best Sons of the Fatherland: Workers in the Vanguard of Soviet Collectivization* (Oxford; New York: Oxford University Press, 1987), 23.
78. G. Shibailo, "Kul'turnaya rol' shefov v derevne", *Kom. Rev.*, cited in Kenez, *Propaganda State*, 143.
79. Viola, *The Best Sons*, 32. Viola notes that the state put an end to these mobilizations in spring 1931.
80. Viola, *The Best Sons*, 33.
81. Zabolotniev, "Pered derevenskim soveshchaniem po fizkul'ture v derevne (formy organizatsii fizkul'traboty)", *Fizkul'taktivist*, no. 10 (1930): 4–9.
82. Kenez, *Propaganda State*, 144.
83. Lynn Mally, *Revolutionary Acts*, 158.
84. V. Mel'nikov, "Opyt Suvorovskogo zernosovkhoza (Severnyi Kazakstan)", *Fizkul'taktivist*, no. 10 (1930): 9–10. For similar campaigns in the 1930s see also GARF, f.7576, op.4, d.2.
85. It was proposed that the SKhLR along with the other unions organize special physical culture courses for workers in the *sovkhozy*, forestry industry, MTS (machine and tractor stations) and others. "Perenesti opyt predpriyatii v sovkhozy i kolkhozy. Po sodokladu VTsSPS "Zadachi proforganizatsii v fizkul'turnoi rabote sotsialisticheskogo sektora derevni", *Fizkul'taktivist*, no. 12 (1930): 10–12.
86. It was a tendency of those sent to outlying regions, such as Kazakhstan, to harbour such views. As Paula Michaels observes, the Soviet view of Kazakh nomads as backward was one originally shared by missionaries and ethnographers. See *Curative Powers*, especially Chapter 6. The same could be argued in relation to peasants in general, with the political and social elites viewing them as backward. See Retish, *Russia's Peasants*, 9, and on official views of the Udmurt population, 36–37.
87. Mel'nikov, "Opyt", 9.
88. Mel'nikov, "Opyt", 9.
89. In many parts of the Soviet Union, for example in Siberia or in parts of the Urals or Caucasus, skiing in winter was often the only form of transport.
90. Mel'nikov, "Opyt", 9. Apparent success stories could be compared to the argument made by Paula Michaels in relation to biomedicine in Kazakhstan, where she concludes that many Kazakhs, once they witnessed the benefits of Soviet biomedicine, accepted it and used it instead of or alongside traditional forms of Kazakh medicine, Michaels, *Curative Powers*.
91. Michaels, *Curative Powers*, 154–155. For red yurts in general, see 154–164. See also Slezkine on the *kul'tbaza* of the North, *Arctic Mirrors*, 150–163, 229–230. The physical culture campaigns could also be compared to the type

of mobilization that occurred towards the end of the civil war, as described by Aaron Retish, where Bolsheviks descended on villages in an effort to educate peasants. These types of campaigns could be considered to be earlier forms of *shefstvo*, where it seemed every other week was the "week of the peasant", the "week of sanitation" or the "week of physical culture" etc. See Retish, *Russia's Peasants*, 216–222. It is important to bear in mind that lack of success did not equate with misunderstanding, see Badcock, *Politics and the People*, 236.

92. GARF, f.7576, op.24, d.7, l.48. 1933. The main period of *shefstvo* work was here reported to have taken place between 1933 and 1935.
93. RGASPI, f. M-6, op.7, d.33, ll.63–64. Raporty i privetstviya IX S'ezdy VLKSM ot komsomolskikh organizatsii Krasnoi Armii. Fizkul'turnykh, turistskikh organizatsii. Yanvar' 1931. "The Eighth Anniversary of the October Revolution". Physical culture instructors Gryazinsky and Androsov.
94. RGASPI, f. M-6, op.9, d.33, ll.66–67. Raport. Kozlov, City Council of Physical Culture.
95. Similar reports can be found in GARF, f.7576, op.3, d.64, ll.30–31, 37–38, 56, 62, 104–107, 114–116.
96. For more on the Potemkin village, see Fitzpatrick, *Stalin's Peasants*, 16–18.
97. "Nashi devushki-strelki/Ochen; ochen' lovkie; Pishet vnuk pis'mo dedu:/V otpusk skoro ya priedu./Nachnu ya deda vraz/Kak nosit' protivogaze"; "Ne liubliu ya bol'she fediu/On plokhoi u nas strlok". Iu. Subotin, "Pesni kolkhoznoi molodezhi", *Krasnyi sport*, 1. For more on elements of Soviet Potemkinism in physical culture propaganda see films such as *Sluchainaya Vstrecha* or *Vratar'*.
98. A competition for the best rural or regional physical culture group was launched in 1936 as an incentive and the results seemed impressive. At the start of the competition there had been 2,000 *kruzhki* with 60,000 members whereas when the competition ended it was claimed that there were 12,660 *kruzhki* with 315,000 members. *Krasnyi sport*, no. 1 (1936): 2.
99. *Esli nasidelsya mnogo poraznyat' zakhochesh' nogi. Povozit' chasok s futbolom stanesh' dobrym veselym. Shagai, fizkul'turnym derevnya!* M. Mikhailov and A. Ryzhanov, *Krasnyi sport*, no. 1 (1936): 2.
100. Petrov, "Pervye shagi", 10–13.
101. *Krasnyi sport*, no.1 (1936): 2–3.
102. *Krasnyi sport*, no.1 (1936): 2.
103. *Krasnyi sport*, no.9 (1936): 1.
104. GARF, f.7576, op.3, d.63, l.86. Those nationalities involved in the competition included 113 Armenians, 59 Greeks, 4 Russians, 27 Persians, and 2 Georgians.
105. Dzhumbaeva—Komsomol and party member—was a Kirghiz girl who had been married at thirteen but ran away to the city to work in the factory. She returned to her "childhood passion" of physical culture when she enrolled in one of the two month courses for training instructors from the national republics. M. Krasnostavskii, "Shari Dzhumbaeva i ee podrugi", *Krasnyi sport*, no. 99, (1936): 2.
106. GARF, f.7576, op.1, d.336, l.14 (1937). This was based on information furnished by thirty-three republican, regional, and provincial committees, December 1936. According to these statistics, there were 23,773 physical culture *kruzhki* in the *kolkhozy* with 557,735 *fizkul'turniki*.
107. GARF, f.7576, op.1, d.336, l.15.
108. GARF, f.7576, op.3, d.36, l.32 (1929).
109. GARF, f.7576, op.6, d.2, l.30. Svodka by Piskunov 22/5/1935.
110. GARF, f.7576, op.1, d.336, l.15.

111. For more on the debate concerning collectivization, see Stephen Wheatcroft, "More light on the Scale of Repression and Excess Mortality in the Soviet Union in the 1930s", in John Arch Getty and Roberta T. Manning (eds), *Stalinist Terror: New Perspectives* (Cambridge: Cambridge University Press, 1993), 275–290. For collectivization more generally see also Slezkine, *Arctic Mirrors*, 187–217 and *The War Against the Peasantry, 1927–1930: The Tragedy of the Russian Countryside*, edited by Lynne Viola, V. P. Danilov, N. A. Ivnitski, and Denis Kozlov, translated by Steven Shabad (New Haven, CT; London: Yale University Press, 2005).
112. GARF, f.7576, op.3, d.56, l.72. 29/ix/1931 (Zagorskii).
113. GARF, f.7576, op.3, d.56, l.73. (Zagorskii).
114. GARF, f.7576, op.3, d.56, l.75ob.
115. GARF, f.7576, op.3, d.56, l.81.
116. GARF, f.7576, op.3, d.56, l.97ob.
117. GARF, f.7576, op.3, d.64, l.28.
118. GARF, f.7576, op.1, d.336, l.12. This statement to Kharchenko, written by A. Ryzhmanov, was not the first. He had previously pleaded with Kharchenko regarding the continued existence of the physical culture section. He complained that when he was there work would begin to get done but then he would be sent away on some duty (*komandirovka*) and work would be put on hold again. In the end Ryzhmanov requested that, if the section was to be liquidated, he be released from the village section and transferred to another area of work.
119. TsGAMO, f.4045, op.1, d.4. l.3. Kolomenskoe Remontno-Traktirovnogo i Arman. Zavoda, Shumilina. 28/VII/1937.
120. See "V otvet kolkhoznitsam georgievskogo raiona. Strana trebuet myla. Dadim mylo", *Rabotnitsa*, no. 33 (1933): 6.
121. GARF, f.7576, op.1, d.266, l.4. Stenogramma soveshchaniya po voprosu o raspredenii sportinventarya pri Komitete ot 7/VIII/1936.
122. GARF, f.7576, op.1, d. 266, ll.15ob- 16.
123. GARF, f.7576, op.1, d. 266, ll.15ob- 16.
124. TsGAMO, f.4045, op.1, d.10, l.6. "Avtobiografiya".
125. Hellbeck, *Revolution on My Mind*.
126. Brovkin, *Russia after Lenin*, 216–217.

NOTES TO CHAPTER 6

1. "March of the Physical Culturists," 1936. Refrain and verse.
2. For more on these see Mike O' Mahony, *Sport in the USSR* and for *The Goalkeeper*, see John Haynes, "Film as Political Football: *The Goalkeeper*", *Studies in Russian and Soviet Cinema* 1, no. 3 (2007): 283–297.
3. Edwin Redslob in Nadine Rossol, *Performing the Nation in Interwar Germany: Sport, Spectacle and Political Symbolism, 1926–1936* (Basingstoke, Hampshire; New York: Palgrave Macmillan, 2010), 51.
4. Mary Douglas, *Natural Symbols: Explorations in Cosmology* (London: Routledge, 1996) [1976], 69.
5. Douglas, *Natural Symbols*, 74.
6. Lane, *Rites of Rulers: Ritual in Industrial Society—the Soviet Case* (Cambridge: Cambridge University Press, 1981).
7. Lane, *Rites of Rulers*, 4.
8. Lane, *Rites of Rulers*, 11.
9. Lane, *Rites of Rulers*, 224.
10. See Mikhail Bakhtin, *Rabelais and His World*, trans. Helene Iswolsky (Cambridge, MA; London: MIT Press, 1968), 10, and Helmut Altrichter,

"Insoluble Conflicts Village Life between Revolution and Collectivization", in Fitzpatrick, Rabinowitch, and Stites (eds), *Russia in the Era of
NEP*, 198.

11. Andrei Arzhilovskii, "Dnevnik 36–37-ogo godov", *Ural*, no. 3 (1992): 142–
143, in Hoffmann, *Stalinist Values*, 131.
12. Rosalinde Sartorti, "Stalinism and Carnival", in Hans Günther (ed), *The
Culture of the Stalin Period* (London: Macmillan, 1990), 44.
13. Rolf, "A Hall of Mirrors", 602.
14. Edelman, *Serious Fun*, 37.
15. In 1926 Ittin had maintained that the collectives and teams, from all the
unions, had to organize their own festivals, for example, a USSR championship of metal-workers, railway workers, and other shop- and union-based
competition. He devised a sample timetable whereby the International
Spartakiad would be held every four years, in different cities with national,
regional, and trade union spartakiads held in the intervening years. Aron
Ittin, "Planovost' v provedenii Sorevnovanii", *IFK*, no. 1 (1926): 5. Spartakiads were not always held successfully, however, and there were none in the
early 1930s.
16. Edelman, *Serious Fun*, 41.
17. Spartakiad is spelled in higher case when referring to a specific International
Spartakiad; lower case in all other instances.
18. Even before the 1928 International Spartakiad had begun, the organizing
committee had set about "investigating the psychology of the masses on the
forthcoming Spartakiad". GARF, f.7576, op.1, d.43, l.82.
19. "Spartakiada Profsoiuzov", *FiS*, nos. 16–17 (1932): 13. In relation to national
dance, Turkmenistan wanted to send its own delegation to provide dramati-
zations of "The Theft of Turkmen Women" and "A Turkmenistan Wedding".
GARF f.7576, op.1, d.46, l.36.
20. Edelman, *Serious Fun*, 38.
21. *Bol'shaya Sovetskaya Entsiklopediya*, no. 40 (1957): 247. This figure seems
inflated. Files in GARF suggest a lower turn out from the republics. For
example, Uzbekistan had a total of 196 participants, Turkmenistan 100,
Ukraine 425, and Zakavkaz 457. See GARF, f.7576, op.1, d.40, l.22.
22. Edelman, *Serious Fun*, 38. For more on the history of the spartakiad and the
individual sports involved, see Edelman, 37–41.
23. *Spartakiada* correspondent, "Okolo Amsterdamskoi olimpiady", *Spartakiada*, no. 2, (1928): 7.
24. For instance, in the United States 280,739 dollars had been amassed. A.
Kulagin, "Vsesoiuznaya spartakiada 1928 goda", *IFK*, nos. 16–17 (1927): 2.
In England, the government had set aside 200,000 pounds for the preparation of their athletes and a further thirty state institutes had agreed to provide financial support. The same was mirrored throughout other capitalist
countries, such as Finland, Switzerland, Holland, and others. It was argued
that the Soviet sports authorities were not in a position to request such vast
sums from the government as it had other, more immediate concerns.
25. Kulagin, "Vsesoiuznaya spartakiada", 2. Overlooked was that the Soviet
authorities did expend considerable time and funding in the preparation and
organization of its physical culture events, perhaps even more so than its
western counterparts. As well as that, Soviet sport was not dependent on
state funding alone and those involved in physical culture could expect some
kind of funding from various institutes and organizations.
26. All of the republics and provinces across the Soviet Union (as well as international delegations) were to compete in the event. By far the largest number
of participants, unsurprisingly, came from Moscow (663 in total, with 523

male and 140 female), followed by Transcaucasia (457 in total, with 355 male and 102 female). The smallest number of participants came from Northern Manchuria (25 in total). Slightly better was the Far East (97 in total, 83 men and 14 women) and then Turkmenistan with a total of 100 participants (80 men and 20 women).

27. GARF, f.7576, op.24, d.1v, l.10. April 1932.
28. GARF, f.7576, op.24, d.1v, l.9.
29. GARF, f.7576, op.24, d.1v, l.10.
30. Lynne Attwood and Catriona Kelly, "Programmes for Identity: The 'New Man' and 'New Woman'" in Kelly and Shepherd, *Constructing Russian Culture*, 285.
31. GARF, f.7576, op.1, d.44, l.76ob.
32. "O massovyikh deistviakh na Spartakiade", *Spartakiada*, no. 2 (1928): 12.
33. "O massovyikh deistviakh", 12.
34. GARF, f.7576, op.1, d.42, l.104.
35. GARF, f.7576, op.1, d.44, l.97. The issue of national dance was much debated and it was decided to incorporate national dance into the festival on Lenin Hills rather than into the more educational exhibition of physical culture. Zikmund in particular was against national dance taking up too much of the exhibition, arguing that the exhibition should only showcase "that which we would recommend". GARF, f.7576, op.1, d.44, l.77.
36. James Van Geldern, "The Centre and Periphery: Culture and Social Geography in the Mass Culture of the 1930s", in Stephen White (ed), *New Directions in Soviet History* (Cambridge: Cambridge University Press, 1992), 68.
37. This was especially portrayed in films such as *Vratar'* and *Sluchainaya Vstrecha*.
38. N. Znamenskii, "Navstrechu zriteliu," *Spartakiada*, no. 3 (1928): 4.
39. GARF, f.7576, op.1, d.42, l.93.
40. Znamenskii, "Navstrechu zriteliu", 4. This attitude repeated itself on other levels, as the example of the Tambov city children from Chapter 3 illustrated.
41. "Prodazha sportivnoi literatury vo vremya spartakiady", *Spartakiada*, no. 3 (1928): 15.
42. "Vokrug spartakiady", *Spartakiada*, no. 3 (1928): 14.
43. TsAOPIM, f.4, op.1, d.38, l.183. Protokol No.13, Zasedaniya Sekretariata Gorkoma VKP(b) ot 5-go iiunya 1931g.
44. "Fabrichno-zavodskie i sovkhozho-kolkhoznye spartakiady ispol'zuem sorevnovatel'nyi metod dlya vovlecheniya v fizkul'tury novykh kadrov trudyashchikhsya aktiviziruem fizkul'tury na predpriyatii, v sovkhozakh i kolkhozakh", *FiS*, no. 42 (1929): 2.
45. GARF, f. 7576, op.1, d.80, l.8ob. Stenogramma zasedaniya Prezidiumaot 30 sentyabrya 1931 o postanovke fizkul'tury raboty sredi shkolnikov. Patysh.
46. GARF, f. 7576, op.1, d.80, l.8ob.
47. "Spartakiada Profsoiuzov", *FiS*, nos. 16–17 (1932): 13.
48. Keys, "Soviet Sport", 417.
49. "Spartakiada Profsoiuzov", 13. For discussion of international aspects of physical culture see in particular Edelman, *Serious Fun* and Keys, *Globalizing Sport* and "Soviet Sport".
50. "Spartakiada Profsoiuzov", 13.
51. "Spartakiada Profsoiuzov", 13.
52. Rossol, *Performing the Nation*, 101.
53. Sandra Budy, "Changing Images of Sport in the Early Soviet Press", in Katzer et al., *Euphoria and Exhaustion*, 81.
54. GARF, f.7710, 6, d.53, l.13.

55. "Gotovtes' k fabrichno-zavodskoi spartakiade!", *FiS*, nos. 9–10 (1933): 3
56. "Gotovtes' k fabrichno-zavodskoi spartakiade!", 3. This had been received from the physical culture bureau of the MGSPS (Moscow City Trade Union Council).
57. "V Moskve nachinaiutsya. Fabrichno-zavodskie spartakiady", *FiS*, nos. 11–12 (1933): 5.
58. RATAP: *Raboty Avtotraktornoi i Aviatsionnoi promyshlennosty* or the Tractor and Aviation industry's workers' union (officially organized in 1934 but founded in 1931 following the VTsSPS resolution "*O razukrupnenii provsoiuzov*", dividing the already existing trade union structure into smaller units. Instead of the twenty-two unions, there were now forty-four. Prior to this, RATAP workers had been represented by the metallists union, which numbered about half a million. http://www.profavia.ru/about/history.shtml, accessed 7 July 2008.
59. GARF, f.7710, op.6, d.88, l.69. The spartakiad was to include dances (including national dances), wrestling, exercises, pyramids and games and a jury would rate contestants on a ten-point system.
60. "Gotovtes' k fabrichno-zavodskoi spartakiade!", 3.
61. "V Moskve nachinaiutsya. Fabrichno-zavodskie spartakiady", *FiS*, nos. 11–12 (1933): 5.
62. "V Moskve nachinaiutsya", 5. Khorosheva's estimation of 30 per cent female workers in her factory was not too inaccurate and corresponds to other factory statistics found in the research findings of Kenneth Straus, Straus, *Factory and Community*, 70.
63. GARF, f.7576, op.14, d.2, l.22.
64. Sportsman's March, from Semyon Timoshenko's *The Goalkeeper*. Vasily Lebedev-Kumach and Isaac Dunaevsky (1936) in James Van Geldern and Richard Stites (eds), *Mass Culture in Soviet Russia: Tales, Poems, Songs, Movies, Plays and Folklore 1917–1953* (Bloomington: Indiana University Press, 1995), 236.
65. Evgenii Riumin. "Fizkul'turnaya organizatsiya prazdnestv", *IFK*, no. 3 (1927): 4. The artistic element was developed even further in the 1930s, when artists were called upon to assist choreograph and "design" the parades, TsGAMO, f.2180, op.1, d.930, l.5.
66. The creation of "living pictures" or "living images" was also a feature of German festivities during and even before the Weimar Republic. See Rossol, *Performing the Nation*, 64.
67. For detailed discussion of the role of the national republics in the physical culture parades, see Petrone, "Parading the Nation: Physical Culture Celebrations and the Construction of Soviet Identities in the 1930s", *Michigan Discussions in Anthropology, Post-Soviet Eurasia* 12 (1996): 25–35.
68. The immense surge in the relevance and popularity of the parades is evidenced by the statistics of those involved. For instance, prior to 1927 (excluding the Vsevobuch parade of 1919), the International Youth Day parade in 1924 included 4,000 athletes from Moscow's trade union clubs. In 1934, there were 120,000 Moscow *fizkul'turniki*. Petrone, "Parading the Nation", 25. The Second All-Union parade in 1924 was by all accounts a fairly dismal affair, not helped by the torrential rain which was one of the cited reasons for the low turnout of both participants and spectators. GARF, f.7576, op.3, d.1, l.50.
69. As noted by the Moscow Party City Committee, see TsAOPIM, f.4, op.2, d.48, l.29.
70. TsAOPIM, f.3, d.31, l.65. Protokol No.66. Moskovskii Gorodskii Komitet VKP (b). Sekretariat. Protokol nn.65–70. Zasedanii Sek-a MGK VKP (b). Spravochniki, tom III. 8/V/1933.

71. Dm. Ya-ea, "Parad Semidesyati tysyach", *FiS*, no. 9 (1932): 5–6.
72. Ya-ea, "Parad Semidesyati tysyach", 5–6.
73. TsAOPIM, f.4, op.4, d.6, l.179.
74. TsAOPIM, f.4, op.2, d.48, l.29. The 1927 parade had 12,000 participants; 1928 witnessed a rise to 18,000; this dropped to 15,000 in 1931; while in 1932 there was a massive surge to 65,000 participants (10,000 below the figure requested by the Moscow city committee). The 1933 parade in Leningrad saw 96,000 participants and was outdone by Moscow, whose participants numbered 106,000. "Parad 12 Iiunya", *FiS*, no. 13 (1933): 4.
75. TsAOPIM, f.4, op.3, d.31, l.65.
76. TsAOPIM, f.4, op.2, d.48, l.29. Protocol No. 19. Moskovskii Gorodskoi Komitet VKP (b) Sekretariat Protokol nn19–22. Zasedanii Sekretariata MGK VKP (b)/ spravochniki. 8 Maya 1932.
77. Thomas Alkemeyer, "Images and Politics of the Body in the National Socialist Era", paraphrased in Keys, "The Body as a Political Space", 399.
78. TsASPIM, f.3, op.49, d.67. Report from department of party cadres of Moscow city committee to the Moscow city committee party secretariat (Khrushchev on 28 April 1935). My thanks to Judith Devlin for this reference.
79. TsASPIM, f.3, op.49, d.67. ll.80–81. The absence of basic necessities, such as bread, unsurprisingly aroused worker discontent. Matthias Neumann has discussed this in relation to the commitment of *komsomol'tsy* to the communist cause and Stalin. See *Communist Youth*, 185–187.
80. TsASPIM, f.3, op.49, d.67. l.108.
81. TsASPIM, f.3, op.49, d.23, l.58. Oruzhzavod, tsekh no. 8. Again, with thanks to Judith Devlin for this reference.
82. Nikita S. Khrushchev (ed), *Memoirs of Nikita Khrushchev. Volume 1: Commissar, 1918–1945* (University Park, PA: Pennsylvania State University Press, 2004), 54.
83. TsASPIM, f.3, op.49, d.67. l.71.
84. TsASPIM, f.3, op.49, d.23, l.58ob.
85. TsASPIM, f.3, op.49, d.67. l.71.
86. L. Shalova ."Pyat' paradov", *Krasnyi sport*, no. 93 (1936): 4. Shalova was a Komsomol member and leader of the Stakhanovite section of the "Tekhnik" shop, thus she was predictably (when being interviewed at least) a firm supporter of the parade.
87. Ya-ea, "Parad Semidesyati tysyach", 5–6.
88. "Parad 12 Iiunya", *FiS*, no. 13 (1933): 4.
89. "Parad 12 Iiunya", 4.
90. TsAOPIM, f.4, op.5, d.10, l.43. O parade moskovskikh fizkul'turnikov.
91. TsAOPIM, f. 4, op.5, d.10, l.43.
92. TsAOPIM, f. 4, op.5, d.10, l.43. Of all the districts, the Stalinskii, Oktyabr'skii, Krasno-Presnenskii (a "Red" working class district and leading district party organization in Moscow of which Khrushchev was elected secretary in 1931) and Baumanskii (home to Elektrazavod and other important factories) districts were to have the highest number of participants (6,000), followed by the Leninskii, Proletarskii and Dzerzhinskii districts (5,000 each).
93. There were to be 60,000 in total from all the districts of Moscow. The column of trade unions was to number 12,500 and include footballers, chess players, swimmers, wrestlers, athletes, hunters, and tourists. Of the other columns involved in the parade, there were to be 12,000 from Dinamo, 10,000 from Spartak, 6,000 from the Red Army, 5,000 Pioneers, 5,000 railway workers, 5,000 cyclists, and 3,000 from Osoaviakhim. Once again, it was stated that these had to be the "most devoted, cultured and physically developed" *fizkul'turniki*, as well as medallists. TsAOPIM, f. 4, op.5, d.10, l.43–44.

94. GARF, f.7710, op.6, d.35, l.83–84. Popov, 17 June 1935.
95. TsAOPIM, f. 4, op.5, d.10, l.44.
96. TsAOPIM, f. 4, op.5, d.10, l.44.
97. Petrone, "Parading the Nation", 28.
98. GARF, f.7576, op.10, d.1, l.65–69.
99. GARF, f.7576, op.24, d.3, l.46. Yuri Pimenov's painting *Fizkul'turnyi parad* covered the back wall of the pavilion, see Rolf, "A Hall of Mirrors", 601–602.
100. GARF, f.7576, op.24, d.3, l.39.
101. GARF, f.7576, op.10, d.1, .69ob.
102. TsAOPIM, f.4, op.3, d.31, l.65.
103. "Torzhestvennyi marsh sta pyati tysyach!", *FiS*, no. 13 (1933): 9.
104. "Torzhestvennyi marsh", 9.
105. TsGAMO, f. 2180, op.1, d.930, l.20, in Petrone, *Life Has Become More Joyous*, 31.
106. Petrone, *Life Has Become More Joyous*, 31.
107. TsAOPIM, f.4, op.4, d.6, l.179. Predlozheniya komissii po voprosu fizkul'tury i provedeniiu parada fizkul'turnikov.(Bulganin)
108. TsAOPIM, f.4, op.4, d.6, l.179.
109. TsGAMO, f. 2180, op.1, d.930, l.22, in Petrone, *Life Has Become More Joyous*, 31.
110. Shura Kirchenko, "Pyat' paradov", *Krasnyi sport*, no. 93 (1936): 4.
111. At a MOSPS meeting to discuss the 1936 physical culture parade, it was mentioned that despite uniforms looking well in the factory, when it rained at the parade in May the colours faded. TsGAMO, f.2180, op. 1, d.930, l.9. See also ll.12–14.
112. TsGAMO, f.2180, op.1, d.930, l.15. Fainshtein.
113. TsGAMO, f.2180, op.1, d.930, l.15. Fainshtein.
114. GARF, f.7576, op.1, d.266, l.28. Basson from *Vympel*.
115. GARF, f.7576, op.1, d.266, l.26. Medovarov from *Kauchuk*.
116. For further argument on the material used see GARF, f.7576, op.1, d.266, l.27.
117. See TsGAMO, f.7227, op.1, d.54, l.26ob. Gurev.
118. TsGAMO, f.7227, op.1, d.54, l.26.
119. TsGAMO, f.7227, op.1, d.54, ll.26–27. Discussions included the type of material it should be written on, how the word order should be arranged, where the flowers should be placed and other questions.
120. TsGAMO, f.2180, op.1, d.930, l.5. For the physical culture parade in 1936 the organizing committee went to extreme lengths to find the best artist, calling special meetings of leading artists in Moscow to discuss the matter and at the same time including union artists so as to appear "impartial". Only after two days of such discussions would an artist be chosen to lead the design of the parade. Fore more on the socialist realist dialogue between cultural and political worlds see Rolf, "A Hall of Mirrors", 621–622.
121. TsAOPIM, f.4, op.3, d.31, l.65.
122. Rolf, "A Hall of Mirrors", 618.
123. RGASPI, f.558, op.11, d.829, l.46. My thanks again to Judith Devlin for these references.
124. RGASPI, f.558, op.11, d.829, l.47.
125. RGASPI, f.558, op.11, d.829, l.40. The reasons for these suggestions are unclear.
126. O'Mahony, *Sport in the USSR*, 89.
127. Petrone, *Life has Become More Joyous, Comrades*, 35.
128. Hellbeck, *Revolution on My Mind*, 156.

129. Hellbeck, *Revolution on My Mind*, 156.
130. Hellbeck, *Revolution on My Mind*, 157. Yevgeny Zamyatin, *We*. Translated by Clarence Brown (New York, 1993) [1924], 124.
131. Hellbeck, *Revolution on My Mind*, 6.
132. Pierre Bourdieu, "Program for a Sociology of Sport", *Sociology of Sport Journal*, no. 5 (1988): 161.
133. Criticisms of the totalitarian model have not been confined to studies of the Soviet Union. Analyzing Nazi Germany from a totalitarian perspective has also been deemed problematical. Geyer and Fitzpatrick, *Beyond Totalitarianism*, 3–13. For related discussion see Keys, "The Body as a Political Space".

NOTES TO CHAPTER 7

1. Stakhanovite workers could officially enjoy up to a month's holiday in the summer and spent their free time cycling, swimming, or skating; Bertha Malnick, *Everyday Life in Russia* (London: G. G. Harrap & Co., 1938), 146–147.
2. *Park of Culture and Rest*, Intourist brochure, 1928.
3. Vonzblein, "Vospitaem novogo cheloveka", *FiS*, no. 13 (1933): 5–7. This figure is probably inflated, given the propensity for GTO statistics to exist on paper only.
4. "Tezisy po dokladu T. Oktyabr'skogo na soveshchanii sektretarei kraevykh, oblastnykh i respublikanskikh sovetov fizkul'tury RSFSR. O fizkul'turnoi rabote na novostroikakh", *Fizkul'taktivist*, no. 8 (1931): 81.
5. GARF, f. A-2313, op.9, d.2, l.9. This figure was no doubt an average and actual numbers varied considerably across the Soviet Union.
6. Katharina Kucher, *Der Gorki-Park. Freizeitkultur im Stalinismus 1928–1941* (Köln; Weimar; Wien: Beiträge für Geschichte Osteuropas, 2007), 258.
7. Kucher, *Der Gorki-Park*, 259.
8. Kucher, *Der Gorki-Park*, 257. Statistics date to August 1929.
9. O' Mahony, *Sport in the USSR*, 114.
10. N. N. Znamenskii, "Navstrechu zriteliu", *Spartakiada*, no. 3 (1928): 5, and O' Mahony, *Sport in the USSR* 114.
11. GARF, f.7576, op.23, dd.1–3.
12. TsAOPIM, f.4, op.5, d.10, l.44.
13. GARF, f.7576, op1, d.54a, l.11.
14. Claire Shaw, "A Fairground for 'Building the New Man': Gorky Park as a Site of Soviet Acculturation", *Urban History* 38, no. 2 (2011): 335.
15. N. N. Znamenskii, "Sotsialisticheskoe planirovanie fizicheskoi kul'tury", *Teoria i praktika fizicheskoi kul'tury*, no. 6 (1931): 20.
16. Kucher, *Der Gorki-Park*, 259.
17. GARF, f.7576, op.12, d.11, l4, 15/11/1932.
18. GARF, f. 7576, op.1, d.190, l.121.
19. GARF, f.7576, op.9, d.16, l.92. It was further noted that in 1938 Armenia did not have "one kopeck" for physical culture construction work and so had to appeal to Sovnarkom for financial assistance.
20. Znamenskii, "Sotsialisticheskoe planirovanie", 19.
21. As reported in the decision of the III Plenum of the VSFK VTsIK in *Fizkul'tura i sotsialisticheskoe stroitel'stvo*, no. 6 (1933): 2.
22. Grigory Fedorovich Grin'ko was Soviet Commissar for Finance from 1930 to 1937. Accused of being a Right Oppositionist, he was shot in 1938.

23. GARF, f. 7576, op.1, d.195, ll.1–2.
24. A. Poroshin, "V poiskakh standardnikh inventarya", *Krasnyi sport*, no. 122 (1936): 2.
25. GARF, f.7576, op.14, d.1, l.4.
26. GARF, f.7576, op.14, d.1, l.4.
27. Edelman, *Serious Fun*, 48. That is not to say that there was a complete absence of stadium building in the 1920s. There was stadium construction and this was often celebrated in the press, whether physical culture or otherwise. See, for example, *Trud*, 2 September 1925, where a German delegation attended the opening ceremony of the Red Stadium of Workers. GARF, f. 5451, op.13a, d. 47, l. 41ob. My thanks to Gleb Albert for this reference.
28. TsAOPIM, f.4, op.3, d.31, l.189. Reshennye putem voprosa Sekretarei MGK VKP (b). Ot 21 Iiunya 1933 goda. O letnii ozdorovitel'nyi i kul'turno-mass-ovoi rabote s det'mi v gorode.
29. TsAOPIM, f.4, op.3, d.31, l.189. Malnick asserts that, in the mid-1930s under Khrushchev's instigation, every district in Moscow was to have a children's park. Malnick, *Everyday Life*, 83.
30. TsAOPIM, f.4, op.3, d.31, l.190.
31. TsAOPIM, f.4, op.3, d.31, l.190.
32. Shaw, "A Fairground", 333.
33. TsAOPIM, f.4, op.3, d.31, l.190.
34. TsAOPIM, f.4, op.3, d.31, l.191.
35. GARF, f.7576, op.12, d.11, l4, 15/11/1932.
36. GARF, f.7576, op.12, d.11, l.14.
37. GARF, f.7576, op.12, d.11, l.14.
38. GARF, f.7576, op.12, d.11, l.30.
39. GARF, f.7576, op.12, d.15, l.5. This was reported by the inspector of the Sport's Council Konstantinov.
40. GARF, f.7576, op.12, d.15, l.5.
41. This occurred in spite of efforts not to sell alcohol in clubs and social venues. For discussion of this problem see Neumann, *Communist Youth*, 112–113.
42. See John McCannon, *Red Arctic: Polar Exploration and the Myth of the North in the Soviet Union, 1932–1939* (New York; Oxford: Oxford University Press, 1998), 108–109; Katerina Clark, *The Soviet Novel: History as Ritual* (Bloomington: Indiana University Press, 2000 [1981]), 36–41.
43. GAPO, f. R-349, op.1, d.35, l.6. Protocol from the Mokshan VolKom, RLKSM 6 February 1926 (Sarasov).
44. GARF, f. A-2313, op.9, d.2, l. 24.
45. Although provisions might have been lacking the ideal expressed through propaganda did encourage older people to become active too (no doubt to help contribute to society, such as in the *chastushka* with the old man and youth). It should not be forgotten that older people—like everyone else—"want to live to the fullest physically, mentally, emotionally and spiritually". Susan Feldman, "Please Don't Call Me 'Dear': Older Women's Narratives of Health Care", *Nursing Inquiry* 6 (1999): 270. Feldman's argument reminds us that as we grow older the maintenance of physical health and well-being becomes critical to one's ability to remain independent and in control of one's body and mind.
46. GARF, f. A-482, op.25, d.980, l.6. Gorinevsky.
47. GARF, f.7576, op.14, d.2, l.42.
48. GARF, f.7576, op.14, d.2, l.42. Gabarevich.
49. GARF, f. A-482, op.25, d.980, ll.5–6.
50. GARF, f. A-482, op.25, d.980, l.24.

51. GARF, f. A-482, op.25, d.980, l.27.
52. GARF, f.7710, op.6, d.43, 15.
53. GARF, f.7576, op.1, d.297, l.12. Postanovlenie Vsesoiuznogo Komiteta po Delam Fizkul'tury i Sporta, 14 Iiulya 1937.
54. A Park of Culture and Rest for the Deaf had also been touted in 1935 by the textile union (this had the largest number of deaf, numbering some 17,000 workers and 40,000 residents). A stadium had been built and over the next three years it was hoped that a theatre, physical culture pavilion, parachute tower, solarium etc. would be constructed. GARF, f.7710, op.6, d.56, l.1.
55. TsGAMO, f.7227, op.1, d.13, ll.27–28. Protokol No.2 obshchego sobranie studentov Tul'skogo Mekhanicheskogo Instituta. 1935.
56. GARF, f.7576, op.14, d.3a, l.111. 30/III/1936.
57. See *Krasnyi sport*, no. 44 (1936): 3.
58. See *Krasnyi sport*, no. 90 (1936): 4.
59. Valery Chkalov, lauded for his aviation exploits, died during a test flight in December 1938. Other martyred heroes included the young Pavlik Morozov and later during the war the partisan Zoya Kosmodemyanskaya.
60. GAPO, f. R-340, op.1, d.47, l.250b. Protocol 13, 18 January 1927, OZO. The official was here defending doctors who had been criticized for having a "devil-may-care attitude" to physical culture.
61. GARF, f.7576, op.1, d.111, l.28. 1932.
62. GARF, f. 7576, op.9, d.16, l.13, 60.
63. GARF, f.7576, op.1, d.297, ll.24–25. 19 May 1937. "O smerti fizkul'turnoi-boksera T. Govyashova".
64. Edelman, *Serious Fun*, 57.
65. Edelman, *Serious Fun*, 67.
66. RGASPI, f. M-1, op.23, d.1316, l.2. Letter from Beria to Stalin, 16 August 1938. My thanks to Steven Jug for this reference.
67. *Krasnyi sport*, 1926 cited in Edelman, *Serious Fun*, 52.
68. RGASPI, f.17, op.68, d.424, l.37. Matveev in Orgburo discussions.
69. Some of the most obvious consequences of the loss of key players for clubs included poor league results, low morale as well financial and administrative repercussions.
70. GARF, f. 7576, op.14, d. 3a, l.44. Postanovlenie Presidium VSFK 8/XII/1934. Ob uporyadochenii perekhoda fizkul'turnikov iz odnoi fizkul'turnoi organi-zatsii v drugoi.
71. GARF, f. 7576, op.14, d. 3a, l.44.
72. The letter can be found in GARF, f.7576, op.14, d.3a, ll.109–109ob.
73. Another high profile transgression of 1936 occurred within the ranks of the Bolshevik sports society, with the poaching of the swimmer Petigorskaya-Moskatel'nikova by the physical culture organization Moscow Metro. During a period of competition towards the end of May she had been "enticed" (*peremanit'*) by "Metro". The Bolshevik society representative requested that this transfer be cancelled and that those held responsible for poaching sportspersons be held to account for their actions. In this case the Moscow City Council of the Physical Culture Presidium, following communications with the Committee for Physical Culture and Sport, disallowed the transfer of Petigorskaya. Action was taken in this case but this did seem to be the exception. GARF, f.7576, op.14, d. 3a, l.135, l.137. Letter from representative Evdokimov, 29/VI/1936.
74. GARF, f.7576, op.14, d. 3a, l.1.
75. GARF, f.7576, op.14, d. 3a, l.1.
76. GARF, f.7576, op.14, d. 3a, l.1.

77. GARF, f.7576, op.14, d. 3a, l.1.
78. The factory director, Likhachev, wrote not only to the Moscow city and regional physical culture council representatives (Luk'yanov and Korolev), but also to the VTsSPS representative Vasil'ev and Mantsev of the All-Union Physical Council Bureau. This letter was then passed on to Kharchenko. GARF, f.7576, op.14, d. 3a, l.115.
79. GARF, f.7576, op.14, d. 3a, l.115.
80. GARF, f.7576, op.14, d. 3a, l.115ob.
81. GARF, f.7576, op.14, d. 3a, l.115ob.
82. For discussion of player transfers and misbehaving players see Edelman, *Serious Fun*, 51–56.
83. GARF, f.7576, op.14, d. 3a, l.97. The transfer was ratified by Starostin. Many sportspersons, such as Artem'ov, played two sports. Ippolitiov was also a successful speed-skater and cyclist. The Russian climate facilitated those interested in sports to play different sports in the off-season.
84. Attwood and Kelly, "Programmes for Identity", in Kelly and Shepherd (eds), *Constructing Russian Culture*, 290.
85. TsGAMO, f.7227, op.1, d.20, l. 19. Stenogramma pervoi oblast'noi-konferentsii obshchestva "Zenit". 10–11/III/1936.
86. TsGAMO, f.7227, op.1, d.20, l.19.
87. TsGAMO, f.7227, op.1, d.20, l.23.
88. TsGAMO, f.7227, op.1, d.20, l.44.
89. Other masters the Kalinin factory could claim were N. Starostin (football), Bykova (athletics), Agurenkov (boxing), Vasileva (skiing), Mel'nikov (skating) and Riumen (chess). TsGAMO, f.7227, op.1, d.3, ll.34–36.
90. TsGAMO, f.7227, op.1, d.20, l.30. Nartov.
91. TsGAMO, f.7227, op.1, d.20, l.30. Nartov.
92. TsGAMO, f.7227, op.1, d.20, l.76. Sugrovov.
93. It should be remembered that although heroes and stars were admired, they did not receive the same level of fame as western stars and were as far as possible always subject and subordinate to the highest authority, that is, Stalin and the party (my thanks to Malcolm McLean for drawing my attention to this issue). Barbara Keys also notes this, "Soviet Sport", 433.
94. TsGAMO, f.6835, op.1, d.14, l.14.
95. TsGAMO, f.6835, op.1, d.14, l.14. Unnamed representative; not dated.
96. GARF, f.7710, op.6, d.35, l.50. 1935.
97. Edelman, *Serious Fun*, 53 and 67.
98. TsGAMO, f.6835, op.1, d.22, l.1. From 1 December 1935, by MGSFK representative Penkin.
99. TsGAMO, f.6835, op.1, d.22, l.1.
100. TsGAMO, f.6835, op.1, d.22, l.1.
101. TsGAMO, f.6835, op.1, d.22, l.1.
102. TsGAMO, f.6835, op.1, d.22, l.1ob.
103. GARF, f.7576, op.1, d.238, l.23. Polozhenie o komissii po ulucheniiu byta masterov sporta pri prezidiuma VSFK SSSR. 14/II/1936.
104. GARF, f.7576, op.1, d.297, l.43. Ratified by Kharchenko 22/V/1937.
105. GARF, f.7576, op.1, d.297, l.43.
106. GARF, f.7576, op.1, d.297, l.70. Postanovlenie "O poryadke perekhoda fizkul'turnikov iz odnoi fizkul'turnoi organizatsii v druguiu", 20/IV/1937. Kharchenko.
107. GARF, f.7576, op.1, d.297, l.61. Postanovlenie "O premirovanii uchastnikov sportivnikh sorevnovanii", 10/V/1937. Kharchenko.
108 GARF, f.7576, op.1, d.297, l.61.

NOTES TO THE CONCLUSION

1. Igal Halfin, *Terror in My Soul: Communist Autobiographies on Trial* (Cambridge MA: Harvard University Press, 2003), 27.
2. RGASPI, f.1-M, op.2, d.1316, l.61. To Kosarev from the Military Commander of Sabo-Komkor Ananasenko, member of the Military Council of Sabo's Commissar Division Pantas and head of Kombrig headquarters Kazakov. My thanks to Steven Jug for this reference.
3. In Tashkent, for example, a mountain shooting division with three regiments had been established with 4,500 members; more regiments had been formed in Samarkand, Fergana and Termez (all Uzbekistan). In Turkmenistan, Tadjikistan, and Kazakhstan there were similar developments. RGASPI, f.1-M, op.2, d.1316, l.62.
4. RGASPI, f.1-M, op.2, d.1316, l.62. Furthermore, in all of the major Central Asian cities, workers were preparing and "raising their response level to 'aerial attack'" and "with great enthusiasm were carrying out work in how to 'deal with the consequences of a chemical attack'".

NOTES TO APPENDIX A

1. A. Ittin, "Blizhaishie zadachi Komsomola v stroitel'stve fizkul'tury", *IFK*, no. 4, (1924): 3.
2. RGASPI (Komsomol), f.M-6, op. 8, d. 7, l.49. Stenogramma soveshchaniya delegatov VIII S"ezda VLKSM, "O sostoyanii i ocherednyikh zadachakh voennoi raboty Komsomola; Rezoliutsiya soveshchaniya; teksty vystuplenyi po voprosam fizkul'tury". May 1928
3. RGASPI, f.17, op.60, d.811, l.52.
4. He argued that *fizkul'tura* was often misunderstood and misidentified, in that "sometimes other methods and meanings were substituted for the actual understanding of physical culture, for example, where sport was understood to denote physical culture as a whole, or where physical exercises assumed the label 'physical culture'". RGASPI, f.537, op.1, d.10, l.9. On competition and individual achievement, he observed that through individual competition a higher level of competency could be achieved. However, "individual competition had to be strictly monitored and kept under strict leadership and control. All forms of narrow sports had to be absolutely rejected as it went against the basic ideology of the workers organization". RGASPI, f.537, op.1, d.10, l.17.
5. *Sovetskaya voennaya entsiklopaediya v 8—i tomakh, t. 5,* www.hronos.ru/biograf/mehonosh.html, accessed 20 July 2008.
6. The information found in the other version was taken from a book by K. A. Zalesskii, *Imperiya Stalina. Biograficheskii entsiklopedicheskii slovar'* (Moscow, 2000); available at www.hronos.ru/biograf/mehonosh.html, accessed 20 July 2008.
7. Boris Bazhanov, *Bazhanov and the Damnation of Stalin*, 167.
8. Bazhanov, *Bazhanov*, 167.
9. Decree No. 119441 of 27 June 1923 issued by the Presidium, *IFK*, no. 20 (1924): 2–3.
10. Semashko, *Puti sovetskoi fizkul'tury* .
11. As one of the leading theoreticians, Zikmund's writings were widely promoted. This was even the case in the military. For example, *VTOPAS (Vserossiiskoe tovarishchestvo obrazovatel'no-proizvodstvennykh assotsiatsii*

doprizyvnikov) [The All-Russian Society of Educational-Production Associations of Youth in Pre-Conscription Military Training] in existence from 1923–1925 ordered repeated copies of Ziikmund's books as part of its quota for physical culture literature. TsAGM (*Tsentral'nyi Arkhiv Gorod Moskvy*) [Central Archive of Moscow City], f.1791, op.1, d.20, ll.193–241.

12. The NTK or Scientific Technical Committee was responsible for physical education syllabuses in both primary and secondary schools and thus commanded considerable influence. Riordan, *Sport in Soviet Society*, 91.

13. Zikmund was later discredited. In 1930 Novikov and Osipov criticized Zikmund's book on the *Soviet system of Physical Culture* (*Osnovy sovietskoi sistemy fizicheskoi kul'tury*), which was used as one of the leading guides to physical culture, particularly in the provinces. They stated that it confused and misled the masses regarding the political tasks of physical culture and that the theoretical basis of physical culture should not be taken as dogma. A. Novikov and L. Osipov, "Razrabotka marksistsko-leninskoi metodologii v oblasti fizkul'tury—boevaya zadacha dnya", *Fizkul'taktivist*, no. 14 (1930): 5–7.

14. A. A. Zikmund, "Zadachi nauchno-metodicheskoi raboty po fizkul'ture", *Teoria i praktika fizicheskoi kul'tury*, no. 2 (1927): 7–10.

NOTES TO APPENDIX B

1. After the revolution the state security organ was the *Cheka*, which was established on 20 December 1917. In February 1922 this was reorganized into the *GPU (Gosudarstvennoe Politicheskoe Upravlenie NKVD RSFSR)*. This was the State Political Directorate or the secret police. On 15 November 1923 this was renamed OGPU (*Ob'edinennoe Gosudarstvennoe Politicheskoe Upravlenie*), also known as the Joint State Political Directorate or the All-Union State Political Administration.

2. Morton, *Soviet Sport*, 166.

3. Riordan, *Sport in Soviet Society*, 94.

4. "Vsesoiuznyi prazdnik *Dinamo*", *FiS*, no. 31 (1929): 1.

5. L. Malinovskii, "Fizkul'turniki—v pervye ryady Osoaviakhima", *FiS*, no. 36 (1929): 1.

6. E. Chernyak, "Nashi zadachi v dele oborony", *FiS*, no. 45 (1929): 5.

7. "Privet II Vsesoiuznomu S'ezdu Osoaviakhima", *FiS*, no. 8 (1930): 1.

8. "Privet II Vsesoiuznomu S'ezdu", 1.

9. "Privet II Vsesoiuznomu S'ezdu", 1.

10. *Bibliograficheskii ukazatel' nauchno-issledovatelskikh i nauchno-metodicheskakh trudov professorov i prepodavatelei instituta* (1920–1961) (Moscow, 1964).

11. GARF, f.A-482, op.2, d.1496, l.53. 1929. Godovoi otchet. O deyatel'nosti Gosudarstvennogo Tsentral'nogo Instituta Fizicheskoi Kul'tury za 1928.

12. GARF, f.A-482, op.2, d.1496, l.63.

Bibliography

PRIMARY LITERATURE

Archives

Gosudarstvennyi Arkhiv Rossisskoi Federatsii (GARF)

f. 814 All-Russian Union of Red Organizations of Physical Culture (VSOFK) (1922–1923)
f. 5469 Central Committee of the All-Union Trade Union of Metal-Workers (1917–1931)
f. 7576 Committee of Physical Culture and Sport of the Soviet Union (GOSSPORT SSSR) (1920–1959)
f. 7709 Central Trade Union Committee of Workers from State Institutes (1931–)
f. 7710 Central Bureau of Physical Culture of the Trade Unions (1929–1937)
f. 7952 State publication of "The History of Plants and Factories" (1931–1938)
f. 8410 Central Council of Sports Societies and the Council of the Moscow proletarian sports society *Dinamo* (1923–1936)

GARF (Malyi)

f. A-482 Ministry of Health of the RFSFR (Minzdrav RSFSR) 1918–1991
f. A-654 Ippolitov, Platon Afanas'evich, sportsman, Honoured Master of Sports
f. A-2306 Ministry of Education of the RSFSR (Minpros RSFSR) 1917–1988
f. A-2313 Main Political-Education Committee (Glavpolitprosvet) under the People's Commissariat (Narkom) of Education RSFSR 1920–1930

Rossisskii Gosudarstvennyi Arkhiv Sotsial'no-Politicheskoi Istorii (RGASPI)

f. 17 Central Committee of the Communist Party of the Soviet Union (TsK KPSS) (1898, 1903–1991)
f. 45 Tenth party congress (1921)
f. 48 Eleventh party congress (1922)
f. 50 Twelfth party congress (1923)
f. 52 Thirteenth party congress (1924)
f. 54 Fourteenth party congress (1925)
f. 55 Fifteenth party congress (1926)
f. 58 Sixteenth party congress (1930)
f. 82 Molotov Vyacheslav Mikhailovich (1890–1986)
f. 146 Podvoiskii Nikolai Il'ich (personal fond)

f. 537 Red Sport International (Sportintern) (1921–1937)

RGASPI (M)

f. 1M Komsomol Central Committee (1918–1991)
f. 6M All-Russian and All-Union Komsomol Congresses (1918–1991)

Rossisskii Gosudarstvennyi Voennyi Arkhiv (RGVA)

f. 9 Political Administration of the Red Army

Tsentral'nyi Arkhiv Obshchestvenno-Politicheskoi Istorii Moskvy (TsAOPIM)

f. 3 Moscow Party Committee (Secretariat).
f. 4 Moscow City Committee.
f. 429 *Serp i Molot*

Tsentral'nyi Gosudarstvennyi Arkhiv Moskovskoi Oblasti (TsGAMO)

f. 2180 Moscow Province Council of Trade Unions
f. 4045 Kolos Sports Society (1936–1939)
f. 6835 Spartak (1934–1937, 1939)
f. 7227 Zenit (1933–1938)

Tsentral'nyi Arkhiv Goroda Moskvy (TsAGM)

f. 1791 Factory sports inventory of "VTOPAS" (1923–1926)

Gosudarstvennyi Arkhiv Penzenskogo Oblast' (GAPO)

f. R-349 Penza Guberniya Council of Physical Culture (1923–1927)
f. R-2143 Spartak (1939–1940)
f. R-1189 Serdobskyi Uezd (1925)

Magazines, Journals, and Newspapers

Fizicheskaya kul'tura
Fizkul'taktivist
Fizkul'tura i sotsialisticheskoe stroitel'stvo
Fizkul'tura i sport
Fizkul'tura v shkole
Fizkul'tura Turkestana
Fizkul'tura Zakazvkaz'ya
Izba chital'nya
Izvestnyi sport
Izvestiya sporta
Izvestiya fizicheskoi kul'tury
Klubnaya stena
Krasnyi sport
Krest'yanka

Krokodil
Kul'turnaya rabota profsoiuzov
Muravei
Na susha i na more
Proletarskii sport
Rabotnitsa
Smena
Sovetskaya fizkul'tura
Sovetskii sport
Spartakiada
Sport
Teoria i praktika fizicheskoi kul'tury
Trudovaya pravda
Turist aktivist
V pomoshch' fizkul'taktivist
Zhurnal krest'yanskoi molodezhi

Selected Books and Collections

Aleksandrov, A. D. *Fizkul'tura, podvizhnye igry, shakhmaty. Sistematicheskii ukazatel' literatury, vyshedshei za gody revoliutsii.* Leningrad: Nachatki znanii, 1925.

Antipov, Nikolai Kirillovich. *Sostoyanie i zadachi fizkul'turnogo dvizheniya.* Moscow: Fizkul'tura i sport, 1930.

Bednyi, Demyan. *P'yasanka.* Moscow; Leningrad: Gosizdat, 1926.

Benak, F. *Zadachi Sportinterna i proletkul'tury. Predislovie K. Mekhonoshina.* Moscow: Gosizdat, 1924.

Biulleten' Moskovskogo Oblsoveta Osoaviakhima. Moscow: Mosoaviakhim, 1932.

Biulleten' 6 s'ezd profsoiuzov SSSR. Moscow: VTsSPS, 1924.

Bol'shaya Sovetskaya Entsiklopediya. Moscow: Gosizdat, 1930, 1953.

Chernyshevsky, Nikolai. *What Is to Be Done?* Translated by Michael R. Katz and annotated by William G. Wagner. Ithaca, NY; London: Cornell University Press, 1989.

Chesnokov, B. *Fizkul'turnaya Moskva: Spravochnyi putevoditel'.* Moscow: Leningrad: Fizkul'tura i Sport, 1930.

Dobin, E. S. *Il'ich i fizkul'tura. Po perepiske Vladimira Il'icha i vospomimaniyam o nem.* Moscow; Leningrad: Fizkul'tura i turizm, 1931.

Doklad nachal'nika Glavnogo Upravlenii Vsevobuch, terrkadrov i kommunisticheskikh chastei. T. Podvoiskogo na soveshchanii nachal'nikov polkovnykh okrugov. Moscow: 1920.

Eber, Zhorzh. *Sport protiv fizkul'tury.* Leningrad: 1925.

Eigera, Ya. B. and Simonova, I. S. *Voprosy fizicheskoi kul'tury.* Leningrad: 1925.

Fizicheskaya kul'tura proletarista v SSSR. Petrograd: Fizkul'tura i sport, 1923.

Fizicheskoe vospitanie. Moscow: Fizkul'tura i sport, 1925.

Fizkul'tura v nauchno-prakticheskoi osveshchenii. IV Sornik trudov. Leningrad: GTsIFK, 1928.

Fülöp-Miller, René. *The Mind and Face of Bolshevism.* Translated from the German by F. S. Flint and D. F. Tait. London: G.P. Putnam, 1927.

Glan, Betty. *Moskaus Kulturpark.* Moscow; Leningrad: Verlagsgenosseschaft Ausländischer arbeiter in der USSR, 1934.

Gol'tsman, A. *Reorganizatsiya cheloveka.* Leningrad: Gosizdat, 1925.

Gorinevskaya, Dr. Veronika. *Fizkul'tura Rabotnitsy*. Moscow: MGSPS, 1925.

Gorinevskaya, Veronika Valentinovna. *Moskovskii Institut Sanitarnoi Kul'tury. Park Kul'tury Otdykha*. Moscow; Leningrad: 1930.

Gorinevsky, V. V. *Fizicheskaya kul'tura zhenshchin*. Moscow; Leningrad: 1931.

Gorinevsky, V. V. *Fizicheskoe vospitanie detei i podrostkov*. Moscow: Tsent. Nauych-issl. In-t okhrany zdorov'ya detei i podrostkov NKZ RSFSR,1935.

Gorinevsky, V. V. *Zdorov'ye fizkul'turnitsa*. Moscow: OGIZ, Fizkul'tura i turizm, 1938.

Gorinevsky, V. V. *Zdorov'ye fizkul'tury*. Moscow: 1938.

Griffith, Hubert (various authors). *Playtime in Russia*. London: Metheun, 1935.

Ignatiev, V. E. *Osnovy fizku'turnye gody*. Moscow: Fizkul'tura i sport, 1925.

Institut Fizicheskoi Kul'tury im P. F. Lesgafta. Sbornik trudov, 1924–1926. Leningrad: Fizkul'tura i sport, 1926.

Itogi devyatogo s'ezda VLKSM. Materialy dlya dokladchikov. Moscow: Molodaya gvardiya, 1931.

Itogi deyatel'nostiya sovetskoi vlasti v tsifrakh 1917–1927. Moscow: 1927.

Itogi IX Vsesoiuznoo s'ezda professional'nykh soiuzov. Moscow: VTsSPS, 1932.

Ittin, A.G. *Soiuzy i blizhaishie zadachi fizkul'tury*. Moscow: VTsSPS, 1926.

Ivan Shagin (fotograficheskoe nasledie). Moscow: Art-Rodnik, 2007.

K itogam IX Vsesoiuznogo s'ezda profsoiuzov. Material dlya dokladchikov i propagandistov. Moscow: Profizdat, 1932.

Kalinin, M. I. *O voprosakh sotsialisticheskoi kul'tury. Sbornik state ii rechei 1925–1938gg*. Moscow: Gos. Izd. Polit. Lit.,1938.

Kedrov, M. S. *Raskol'nicheskaya deyatel'nost' sotsial-demokratov v rabochem sporte*. Leningrad: Krasnaya gazeta, 1929.

Kharchenko, I. *Sovetskii sport na pod'eme*. Moscow: Fizkul'tura i sport,1936.

Khrushchev, Sergei (ed.). *Memoirs of Nikita Khrushchev. Volume 1: Commissar, 1918–1945*. University Park, PA: Pennsylvania State University, 2004.

Korolev, N. D. *Nauchnyi kontrol' i uchet rezul'tatov po fizicheskomy vospitaniiu*. Petrograd: Izd Petrogr. Otd. Glaz. Kontory "Izvestiya TsIK SSSR i VTsIK",1924.

Korolev, N. D. *Kratkoe rukovodstvo po fizicheskoi kul'ture zhenshchiny*. Leningrad: SOO "Izvestnii TsIK SSSR i VtsIK", 1925.

Korolev, N. D. *Osnovy fizicheskoi kul'tury muzhiny i zhenshchiny*. Leningrad: LGSPS, 1925.

Korolev, N. D. *Fizicheskaya kul'tura v povsednevnoi zhizni trudyashchegosya*. Leningrad: LGSPS, 1926.

Korolev, N. D. *Fizicheskoe ukreplenie i zakalivanie zhenshchiny*. Leningrad: Izd. Leningr. Gubprofsoveta, tip. OKO Leningr. Gubprofsoveta, 1927.

Kradman, D. A. *Fizkul'tura kak chast' kul'turno-prosvetitel'noi raboty*. Leningrad: Kn. Sector Leningr. Gubono, 1924.

Kurkin, P. I. *Moskovskaya rabochaya molodezh'. Fizicheskoe razvitie, zdorov'e, usloviya, truda i byta*. Moscow: Glavlit, 1924.

Lenin, Vladimir I. *The Tasks of the Youth Leagues: Speech Delivered at the Third All-Russia Congress of the Russian Young Communist League October 2 1920*. Moscow: 1976.

Lenin, Vladimir I. *On Youth*. Moscow: Progress Publishers, 1977.

Malnick, Bertha. *Everyday Life in Russia*. London: George C Harrap & Co Ltd, 1938.

Mandelshtam, Nadezhda. *Hope Against Hope. A Memoir*. Translated by Max Hayward. London: Collins, Harvill Press, 1991 [1971].

Mayakovsky, Vladimir. *The Bedbug and Selected Poetry*. Edited with an introduction by Patricia Blake and translated by Max Hayward and George Reavey. Bloomington: Indiana University Press, 1975.

Mehnert, Klaus. *Youth in Soviet Russia*. Translated by Michael Davidson. New York: Harcourt, Brace and Company, 1933.

Metodika fizicheskogo vospitaniya v srednei i vysshei shkole. Moscow: Fizkul'tura i sport, 1938.

Mikhailov, V. M. *Ocherednye zadachi i perspektivy sovetskoi fizkul'tury*. Moscow: MGSPS, 1927.

Mil'chakov, A. *K itogam VII s'ezda VLKSM*. Moscow; Leningrad: Molodaya Gvardiya, 1928.

Nechaev, A. P. *Psikhologiya fizicheskoi kul'tury*. Moscow: Gosizdat, 1927.

Neronov, M. *Fizkul'tura v detskom dome*. Moscow: 1931.

Olesha, Yuri. *Envy*. Translated from the Russian by Marian Schwartz; introduction by Ken Kalfus; illustrations by Natan Altman. New York: New York Review Books, 2004. [1927]

Orlova, Raisa. *Memoirs*. New York: Random House, 1983.

Park of Culture and Rest. Moscow: Intourist, 1928.

Pervaya Plenuma Moskovskogo oblastnogo soveta fizicheskoi kul'tury. Moscow: Mosoblispolkoma, 1931.

Pervaya Vsesoiuznaya konferentsiya nauchnykh rabotnikov po fizicheskoi kul'ture, 10–15 Noyabrya 1925 v Mockve (otchet). Moscow: VSFK, 1926.

Pervaya Vsesoiuznaya spartakiada. Moskva-1928. Moscow: 1928.

Pervyi Plenum Vsesoiuznogo Soveta Fizicheskoi Kul'tury. 6 Aprelya 1930. Moskva-Kreml' (stenograficheskoi otchet). Moscow: Fizkul'tura i sport, 1930.

Rezolutsii i postanovleniya VI-go s'ezda profsoiuzov SSSR. Moscow: VTsSPS, 1924.

Rezoliutsii VII Vsesoiuznogo S'ezda professional'nikh soiuzov 6–18 Dekabrya 1926. Moscow: VTsSPS 1927.

Revolution in Photography. Alexander Rodchenko. Moscow: Mul'timedinyj kompleks aktual'nyh iskusstv, 2008.

Schvarts, G. I. and Zaitsev, V. *Molodezh' SSSR v tsifrakh*. Moscow: Voprosy truda, 1924.

Semashko, Nikolai Aleksandrovich. Za ukreplenie agitatsionno-propagandistskoi raboty Osoaviakhima. Moscow: Izd-vo "Osoaviakhim", 1930.

Semashko, Nikolai Aleksandrovich. *Novyi byt' i polovoi vopros*. Moscow; Leningrad: Gosizdat, 1926.

Semashko, Nikolai Aleksandrovich. *Okhrana zdorov'ya rabochikh krest'yan i krest'anok za desyat' let*. Moscow: Narkomzdrav RSFSR, 1927.

Semashko, Nikolai Aleksandrovich. *Puti sovetskoi fizkul'tury*. Moscow: Fizkul'tizdat, 1926.

Semashko, Nikolai Aleksandrovich. *Fizicheskaya kul'tura v derevne. Sbornik statei*. Moscow: Fizkul'tizdat, 1925.

Semashko, Nikolai Aleksandrovich. *The Right to Rest and Leisure*. Moscow: Fizkul'tizdat, 1937.

Starikov, V. *Fizicheskaya kul'tura trudyashchikhsya*. Moscow: Fizkul'tura i sport, 1925.

Starostin, Nikolai Petrovich. *Futbol skvoz' gody*. Moscow: Sovetskaya Rossiya, 1989.

Starostin, Nikolai Petrovich. *Moi futbol'nye gody*. Moscow: 1986.

Tomsky, M. *Nashi dostizheniya i nedostatki: doklad i zakliuchenoe slovo na VII Vsesoiuznyi s'ezd profsoiuzov*. Moscow: VTsSPS, 1927.

Tomsky, M. *Vsegda s massami, v glave mass: rech' pri otkrytii VII*. Moscow: VTsSPS, 1929.

Tomsky, M. *Itogi VI s'ezda professional'nykh soiuz v SSSR. 11–18 Noyabr' 1924*. Moscow: VTsSPS, 1924.

Trotsky, Lev. *Sochineniya kul'tura perekhodnogo perioda*. Moscow; Leningrad: Gosizdat, 1927.

Vasilevskii, L. M. *Molodezh, bud' chista!* Moscow: Novaya Moskva, 1925.
Vasilevskii, L. M. *Gigiena molodoi devushki.* Moscow: Novaya Moskva, 1926.
Vasserman, L. M. *Trud, zdorov'ya, byt' Leningradskoi rabochie molodezhi.* Leningrad: Izdanie Sanprosveta Leningradskogo Gubzdravotdela, 1925.
Voprosi fizicheskogo vospitaniya i fizicheskogo obrazovaniya. Leningrad: Isdatel'stvo Leningradskogo Meditsinskogo Zhurnala, 1928.
Yevseev, G. *Fizkul'turnoe dvizhenie v SSSR.* Khar'kov: Gos. Institut Fizicheskoi Kul'tury Ukrainy. Kafedra istorii fizkul'tury, 1940.
Za sotsialisticheskii park. Moscow: 1932.
Zamyatin, Yevgeny. *We.* Translated by Clarence Brown. New York, 1993 [1924].
Zikmund, A. A. *Fizkul'tura i byt.* Moscow: Vseros. Proletkul't, 1925.
Zikmund, A. A. *Osnovy sovetskoi sistemy fizkul'tury.* Moscow: Novaya Moskva,1926.
Zikmund, A. A. *Sovetskaya fizkul'tura: tsel', sredstva, metodike.* Moscow: Novaya Moskva, 1924.
Zikmund, A. A. *Itogi deyatel'nosti Gosudarstvennogo Tsentral'nogo Instituta Fizicheskoi Kul'tury Harkomzdrava.*
Zikmund A. A. and Ivanovsky, B. A. *Fizicheskoe vospitanie v shkole, 1 stupeni po metody Gosudarstvennogo tsentral'nogo institute fizicheskoi kul'tury.* Moscow: VSFK, 1926.
1 Plenum Moskovskogo Oblastnogo Soveta Fizicheskoi Kul'tury 7–10 Yanvarya 1931 goda. Moscow: Mosoblispolkoma, 1931.
10 let stroitel'stva. Moscow: Vestnik fizicheskoi kul'tury, 1928.
VIII Vsesoiuznyi S'ezd professional'nikh soiuzov (stenograficheskii otchet). Moscow: VTsSPS, 1928.

SELECTED SECONDARY MATERIAL

Books

Adas, Michael. *Machines as the Measure of Man: Science, Technology and Ideologies of Western Dominance.* Ithaca, NY; London: Cornell University Press, 1989.
Aksel'rod. *Fizicheskaya kul'tura i sport v SSSR. Sbornik materialov v pomoshch' propaganda.* Moscow: Fizkul'tura i sport, 1954.
Attwood, Lynne. *Creating the New Soviet Woman: Women's Magazines as Engineers of Female Identity, 1922–53.* Basingstoke, Hampshire; Macmillan; New York: St. Martin's Press, in association with Centre for Russian and East European Studies, 1999.
Attwood, Lynne. *The New Soviet Man and Woman: Sex-Role Socialization in the USSR.* Basingstoke, Hampshire: Macmillan, in association with the Centre for Russian and East European Studies, University of Birmingham, 1990.
Attwood, Lynne. *Red Women on the Silver Screen: Soviet Women and Cinema from the Beginning to the End of the Communist Era.* London: Pandora, 1993.
Badcock, Sarah. *Politics and People in Revolutionary Russia.* Cambridge: Cambridge University Press, 2007.
Batyrev, P. V., Vasil'ev N. M., D'yakov, M. I. *Rasskazy starykh sportssmenov.* Moscow: Fizkul'tura i sport, 1951.
Bauer, Raymond. A. *The New Man in Soviet Psychology.* Cambridge, MA: Harvard University Press, 1952.

Bauer, Raymond A., Inkeles, Alex, and Kluckhohn, Clyde. *How the Soviet System Works.* Cambridge, MA: Harvard University Press, 1956.

Bazhanov, Boris. *Bazhanov and the Damnation of Stalin*, translation and commentary by David Doyle. Athens: University of Ohio Press, 1990.

Bazhanov, Boris. *Vspomimaniya byvshego sekretarya Stalina.* France: Tret'ia Volna, 1980.

Beer, Daniel. *Renovating Russia: The Human Sciences and the Fate of Liberal Modernity, 1880–1930.* Ithaca, NY: Cornell University Press, 2008.

Bernstein, Frances Lee. *The Dictatorship of Sex: Lifestyle Advice for the Soviet Masses.* DeKalb: Northern Illinois University Press, 2007.

Bernstein, Frances Lee, Burton, Christopher, and Healey, Dan (eds). *Soviet Medicine: Culture, Practice and Science.* DeKalb: Northern Illinois University Press, 2010.

Bloxham, Donald and Gerwarth, Robert (eds). *Political Violence in Twentieth Century Europe.* Cambridge: Cambridge University Press, 2011.

Bock, Gisela and Thane, Pat. *Maternity and Gender Policies: Women and the Rise of the European Welfare States, 1880s–1950s.* London; New York: Routledge, 1991.

Bonnell, Victoria E. *Iconography of Power: Soviet Political Posters under Lenin and Stalin.* Berkeley; London: University of California Press, 1997.

Bowlt, John E (ed). *Russian Art of the Avant-Garde: Theory and Criticism.* London; New York: Thames and Hudson, 1988.

Bowlt, John E. and Matich, Olga. *Laboratory of Dreams: The Russian Avant-Garde and Cultural Experiment.* Stanford, CA: Stanford University Press, 1996.

Brandenburger, David. *National Bolshevism: Stalinist Mass Culture and the Formation of Modern Russian National Identity 1931–1956.* Cambridge, MA; London: Harvard University Press, 2002.

Brooks, Jeffrey. *Thank You Comrade Stalin! From Revolution to Cold War.* Princeton, NJ: Princeton University Press, 2000.

Brovkin, Vladimir. *Russia after Lenin: Politics, Culture and Society 1921–1929.* London: Routledge, 1998.

Brunton, Deborah (ed). *Medicine Transformed: Health, Disease and Society in Europe 1800–1930.* Manchester: Manchester University Press in association with Open University, 2004.

Buckley, Mary. *Women and Ideology in the Soviet Union.* New York: Harvester Wheatsheaf, 1989.

Budd, Michael Anton. *The Sculpture Machine: Physical Culture and Body Politics in the Age of Empire.* New York: New York University Press, 1997.

Carleton, Gregory. *Sexual Revolution in Bolshevik Russia.* Pittsburgh, PA: University of Pittsburgh Press, 2005.

Chudinov, I. G. *Osnovnye postanovleniya, prikazy i instruktsii po voprosam sovetskoi fizicheskoi kul'tury i sporta 1917–1957.* Moscow: Fizkul'tura i sport, 1959.

Clark, Katerina. *The Soviet Novel: History as Ritual.* Bloomington: Indiana University Press, 2000.

Clements, Barbara Evans. *Bolshevik Feminist: The Life and Work of Aleksandra Kollontai.* Bloomington: Indiana University Press, 1979.

Clements, Barbara Evans, Engel, Barbara Engel, and Worobec, Christine D. (eds). *Russia's Women: Accommodation, Resistance, Transformation.* Berkeley; Oxford: University of California Press, c1991.

Coakley, Jan and Dunning, Eric (eds). *Handbook of Sports Studies.* London; Thousand Oaks, CA: SAGE Publications, 2000.

Conquest, Robert. *The Harvest of Sorrow.* New York: Oxford University Press, 1987.

Costlow, Jane, Sandler, Stephanie, and Vowles, Judith (eds). *Sexuality and the Body in Russian Culture*. Stanford, CA: Stanford University Press, 1993.

Cullerne Brown, Matthew and Taylor, Brandon (eds). *Art of the Soviets: Painting, Sculpture and Architecture in a One-Party State 1917–1992*. Manchester: Manchester University Press; New York: Distributed exclusively in the USA and Canada by St. Martin's Press, 1993.

David-Fox, Michael. *Revolution of the Mind: Higher Learning among the Bolsheviks, 1918–1929*. Ithaca, NY: Cornell University Press, 1997.

Davies, Sarah. *Popular Opinion in Stalin's Russia*. Cambridge: Cambridge University Press, 1997.

Davies, R. W., Harrison, Mark, and Wheatcroft, S. G. *The Economic Transformation of the Soviet Union 1913–1945*. Cambridge; New York: Cambridge University Press, 1994.

DeGrazia, Victoria. *The Culture of Consent: Mass Organization of Leisure in Fascist Italy*. Cambridge: Cambridge University Press, 1981.

Demeter, G. S. *Lenin ob okhrana zdorov'ya trudyashchikhsya i fizicheskoi kul'ture*. Moscow: Fizkul'tura i sport, 1965.

Demeter, G. S. and Gorbunov, V. V. *70 let sovetskogo sporta: liudi, sobytiya, fakty*. Moscow: Fizkul'tura i sport, 1987.

Dobrenko, Evgenny and Naiman, Eric (eds). *The Landscape of Stalinism: The Art and Ideology of Soviet Space*. Seattle: University of Washington Press, 2003.

Douglas, Mary. *Natural Symbols: Explorations in Cosmology*. London; New York: Routledge, 1996.

Dunham, Vera S. *In Stalin's Time: Middleclass Values in Soviet Fiction*. Cambridge; New York: Cambridge University Press, 1990 [1976].

Dunning, Eric. *Sport Matters: Sociological Studies of Sport, Violence, and Civilization*. London; New York: Routledge, 2001.

Edelman, Robert. *Serious Fun: A History of Spectator Sports in the USSR*. New York; Oxford: Oxford University Press, 1993.

Engel, Barbara Alpern and Vanderbeck, Anastasia Posadkaya. *A Revolution of Their Own: Voices of Women in Soviet History*, translated by Sona Hoisington. Boulder, CO: Westview Press, 1998.

Eremeeva, O. I. *Uchastie molodezhi v obshchestvennoi i kul'turnoi zhizni severa (1920–1932gg)*. Omsk: 2001.

Etkind, Alexander. *Eros of the Impossible: The History of Psychoanalysis in Russia*, translated by Noah and Maria Rubins. Boulder, CO: Westview Press, 1997.

Evseev, G. *Fizkul'turnoe dvizhenie v SSSR*. Kharkov: Gosudarstvennyi Institut Fizicheskoi Kul'tury Ukrainy, 1940.

Ewing, Thomas. *The Teachers of Stalinism: Policy, Practice and Power in Soviet Schools of the 1930s*. New York: P. Lang, 2002.

Fainsod, Merle. *How Russia Is Ruled*. Cambridge, MA: Harvard University Press, 1993.

Farnsworth, Beatrice and Viola, Lynne. *Russian Peasant Women*. New York: Oxford University Press, 1992.

Filatov, N. N. *Politika Sovetskogo gosudarstva v sfere zdravookhraneniya rabochie molodezi (1921–1925)*. Saratov: 1992.

Fisher, Ralph T. *Pattern for Soviet Youth: A Study of the Congresses of the Komsomol 1918–1954*. New York: Columbia University Press, 1959.

Fitzpatrick, Sheila. *The Commissariat of Enlightenment: Soviet Organization of Education and the Arts under Lunacharsky*. Cambridge: Cambridge University Press, 1970.

Fitzpatrick, Sheila. *The Cultural Front: Power and Culture in Revolutionary Russia*. Ithaca, NY: Cornell University Press, 1992.

Fitzpatrick, Sheila. *Cultural Revolution in Russia 1928–1931*. Bloomington: Indiana University Press, 1978.

Fitzpatrick, Sheila. *Education and Social Mobility in the Soviet Union 1921–1934*. Cambridge: Cambridge University Press, 1979.

Fitzpatrick, Sheila. *Everyday Stalinism: Soviet Russia in the 1930s: Ordinary Life in Extraordinary Times*. New York: Oxford University Press, 1999.

Fitzpatrick, Sheila. *Stalin's Peasants: Resistance and Survival in the Russian Village After Collectivisation*. New York: Oxford University Press, 1994.

Fitzpatrick, Sheila. *Tear off the Masks! Identity and Imposture in Twentieth Century Russia*. Princeton, NJ: Princeton University Press, 2005.

Fitzpatrick, Sheila and Slezkine, Yuri. *In the Shadow of Revolution: Life Stories of Russian Women from 1917 to the Second World War*. Princeton, NJ: Princeton University Press 2000.

Fitzpatrick, Sheila, Rabinowitch, Alexander, and Stites, Richard (eds). *Russia in the era of NEP: Explorations in Soviet Society and Culture*. Bloomington: Indiana University Press, 1991.

Galagan, A. A. *Istoricheskii opyt KPSS i VLKSM po formirovanniu sistemy komsomol'skoi periodicheskoi pechati 1918–1928gg*. Moscow: 1990.

Garros, Veronique, Korenevskaya, Natalia, and Lahusen, Thomas. *Intimacy and Terror: Soviet Diaries of the 1930s*, translated by Carol A. Flath. New York: New Press, 1995.

Gatrell, Peter. *Russia's First World War: A Social and Economic History*. Edinburgh: Pearson Longman, 2005.

Getty, John Arch. *Origins of the Great Purges*. Cambridge: Cambridge University Press, 1985.

Getty, John Arch and Manning, Roberta (eds). *Stalinist Terror: New Perspectives*. Cambridge: Cambridge University Press, 1993.

Getty, John Arch and Naumov, Oleg. *The Road to Terror: Stalin and the Self-Destruction of the Bolsheviks, 1932–1939*, translations by Benjamin Sher. New Haven, CT: Yale University Press, 1999.

Geyer, Michael and Fitzpatrick, Sheila (eds). *Beyond Totalitarianism: Stalinism and Nazism Compared*. Cambridge: Cambridge University Press, 2009.

Gleason, A., Kenez, P., and Stites, R. (eds). *Bolshevik Culture: Experiment and Order in the Russian Revolution*. Bloomington: Indiana University Press, 1985.

Goldman, Wendy Z. *Terror and Democracy in the Age of Stalin: The Social Dynamics of Repression*. Cambridge: Cambridge University Press, 2007.

Goldman, Wendy Z. *Women at the Gates: Gender and Industry in Stalin's Russia*. Cambridge; New York: Cambridge University Press, 2002.

Goldman, Wendy Z. *Women, the State and Revolution: Soviet Family Policy and Social Life, 1917–1936*. Cambridge; New York: Cambridge University Press, 1993. Moscow: Izdatel'skii tsentr "Akademiya"

Goloshchapov, B. P. *Istoriya fizicheskoi kul'tury i sporta* (Moscow: Izdatel'skii tsentr "Akademiya", 2008).

Gorelov, Iurii Pavlovich. *Istoriya fizicheskoi kul'tury i sporta*. Kemerovo: Kuzbassvuzizdat,1997.

Gori, Gigliola. *Italian Fascism and the Female Body: Sport, Submissive Women, and Strong Mothers*. London; New York: Routledge, 2004.

Gorsuch, Anne E. *Youth in Revolutionary Russia: Enthusiasts, Bohemians, Delinquents*. Bloomington: Indiana University Press, 2000.

Gorzka, Gabrielle. *A. Bogdanov und der russische Proletkul't. Theorie und Praxis Einer Sozialismus*. Campus: Verlag, 1980.

Günther, Hans (ed). *The Culture of the Soviet Period*. New York: St. Martin's Press, 1990.

Halfin, Igal (ed). *Language and Revolution: Making Modern Political Identities.* London; Portland, OR: Frand Cass, 2002.

Halfin, Igal. *Terror in My Soul: Communist Autobiographies on Trial.* Cambridge, MA: Harvard University Press, 2003.

Hargreaves, Jennifer. *Heroines of Sport: The Politics of Difference and Identity.* London; New York: Routledge, 2000.

Hargreaves, Jennifer (ed). *Sport, Culture and Ideology.* London: Routledge and Kegan Paul, 1982.

Hargreaves, John. *Sport, Power and Culture: A Social and Historical Analysis of Popular Sports in Britain.* Oxford: Oxford University Press, 1986.

Harré, Rom. *Physical Body.* Oxford: Oxford University Press, 1991.

Harris, James R. *The Great Urals: Regionalism and the Evolution of the Soviet System.* Ithaca, NY: Cornell University Press, 1999.

Haynes, Deborah. *Bakhtin and the Visual Arts.* Cambridge: Cambridge University Press, 1995.

Haynes, John. *New Soviet Man: Gender and Masculinity in Stalinist Soviet Cinema.* Manchester: Manchester University Press; New York: Distributed exclusively in the USA by Palgrave, 2003.

Healey, Dan. *Homosexual Desire in Revolutionary Russia: The Regulation of Sexual and Gender Dissent.* Chicago: University of Chicago Press, 2001.

Hellbeck, Jochen. *Revolution on My Mind: Writing a Diary under Stalin.* Cambridge, MA: Harvard University Press, 2006.

Hill, Jeffrey. *Sport, Leisure and Culture in Twentieth Century Britain.* London; New York: Palgrave Macmillan, 2002.

Hirsch, Francine. *Empire of Nations: Ethnographic Knowledge and the Making of the Soviet Union.* Ithaca, NY; London: Cornell University Press, 2005.

Hoffmann, David L. *Peasant Metropolis: Social Identities in Moscow, 1929–1941.* Ithaca, NY: Cornell University Press, 1994.

Hoffmann, David L. *Stalinist Values: The Cultural Norms of Soviet Modernity, 1917–1941.* Ithaca, NY: Cornell University Press, 2003.

Hoffmann, David L. and Kotsonis, Yanni (eds). *Russian Modernity: Politics, Knowledge, Practices.* London; New York: Palgrave Macmillan, 2000.

Holmes, Larry E. *Kirov's School No.9: Power, Privilege, and Excellence in the Provinces, 1933–1945.* Kirov: "Loban", 2008.

Holmes, Larry E. *The Kremlin and the Schoolhouse. Reforming Education in Soviet Russia, 1917–1931.* Bloomington: Indiana University Press, 1991.

Holquist, Peter. *Making War, Forging Revolution: Russia's Continuum of Crisis, 1914–1921.* Cambridge, MA; London: Harvard University Press, 2002.

Horn, David G. *Social Bodies: Science, Reproduction and Italian Modernity.* Princeton, NJ: Princeton University Press, 1994.

Hosking, Geoffrey. *Rulers and Victims: The Russians in the Soviet Union.* Cambridge, MA: Belknap Press of Harvard University Press, 2006.

Husband, William E. *The Human Tradition in Modern Russia.* Wilmington, DE: SR Books, 2000.

Ilic, Melanie. *Women Workers in the Soviet Interwar Economy: From "Protection" to "Equality".* Basingstoke, Hampshire: Macmillan in association with Centre for Russian and East European Studies, University of Birmingham, 1999.

Istoriya fizicheskoi kul'tury i organisatsiya fizicheskoi kul'tury i sporta v SSSR (Metodicheskoe posobie dlya studentov otdeleniya zaochnogo obucheniya institutov fiziceskoi kul'tury). Moscow: Leningrad: Fizkul'tura i sport, 1949.

Kaes, Anton (ed). *The Weimar Republic Sourcebook.* Berkeley; London: University of California Press, 1994.

Kassatov, Alexander Anatol'vich. *Deyatel'nost' VLKSM po osushchestvlenniu politiki Kommunisticheskii partii v oblasti fizicheskoi kul'tury i sporta v period stroitel'stvo osnov sotsializma v SSSR, 1921–1932.* Moscow: 1985.

Katzer, Nikolaus (ed). *Euphoria and Exhaustion: Modern Sport in Soviet Culture and Society.* Frankfurt; New York: Campus/Verlag, 2010.

Kelly, Catriona. *Refining Russia: Advice Literature, Polite Culture, and Gender from Catherine to Yeltsin.* Oxford: Oxford University Press, 2001.

Kelly, Catriona and Shepherd, David (eds). *Constructing Russian Culture in the Age of Revolution 1881–1940.* Oxford: Oxford University Press, 1998.

Kenez, Peter. *Cinema and Soviet Society 1917–1953.* Cambridge: Cambridge University Press, 1992.

Kenez, Peter. *The Birth of the Propaganda State: Soviet Methods of Mass Mobilization, 1917–1929.* Cambridge: Cambridge University Press, 1985.

Keys, Barbara J. *Globalizing Sport: National Rivalry and International Community in the 1930s.* Cambridge, MA: Cambridge University Press, 2006.

Kiaer, Christina and Naiman, Eric (eds). *Everyday Life in Early Soviet Russia: Taking the Revolution Inside.* Bloomington: Indiana University Press, 2006.

Kirschenbaum, Lisa A. *Small Comrades: Revolutionizing Childhood in Soviet Russia 1917–1932.* London: Routledge Falmer, 2001.

Koch, H. W. *The Hitler Youth. Origins and Development 1922–1945.* New York: Stein and Day, 1975.

Kotkin, Stephen. *Magnetic Mountain: Stalinism as a Civilization.* Berkeley: University of California Press, 1995.

Kryachko, I. A. *Fizcheskaya kul'tura.* Moscow; Leningrad: Gosudarstvennoe izdatel'stvo Fizkul'tura i sport, 1948.

Kucher, Katharina. *Der Gorki-Park. Freizeitkultur im Stalinismus 1928–1941.* Köln Weimar Wien, 2007.

Kuhr-Korolev, Corinna. *Gezähmte Helden: die Formierung der Sowjetjugend 1917–1932.* Essen, Klartext Verlag, 2005.

Kuhr-Korolev, Corinna, Plaggenborg, Stefan, and Wellman, Monica. *Sowjetjugend 1917–1941. Generation zwischen Revolution und Resignation.* Essen: Klartext Verlag, 2001.

Kulinkovich, Konstantin Antonovich. *Istoriya fizicheskoi kul'tury i sporta v SSSR 1923–1982.* Minsk: Polymya, 1984.

Lahusen, Thomas and Dobrenko, Evgeny. *Socialist Realism without Shores.* Durham, NC: Duke University Press, 1997.

Lane, Christel. *The Rites of Rulers: Ritual in Industrial Society: The Soviet Case.* Cambridge: Cambridge University Press, 1981.

Lebedeva, L. V. *Povsednevnaya zhizn' Penzenskoi derevni v 1920-e gody: traditsii i peremeny.* Moscow: ROSSPEN, 2009.

Lebina, N. B. *Fabrichno-zavodskaya molodezh' Petrograda v 1921–1923gg.* Leningrad: 1975.

Lebina, N. B. and Chistikov, A. N. *Obyvatel' i reformy. Kartiny povsednevnoi zhizni gorozhan v gody NEPa i khrushchevskogo desyatiletiya.* St. Peterburg: Dmitrii Bulanin, 2003.

Lebina, Natalia, Romanov, Pavel and Yarskaya-Smirnova, Elena. *Sovetskaya sotsial'naya politika 1920-kh—1930-kh. Ideologiya i povsednevnost'.* Moscow: Variant, TsPGI, 2007.

Lekareva, Vera Aleksandrovna. *Rol' fizicheskoi kul'tury v ukreplenii sotsial'noi stabil'nosti gosudarstva 1917–1928.* Samara: 1998.

Levent, Nina Sobol. *Healthy Spirit in a Healthy Body: Representations of the Sports Body in Soviet Art of the 1920s and 1930s.* Frankfurt am Main: Peter Lang, 2004.

Lewin, Moshe. *The Making of the Soviet System: Essays in the Social History of Inter-War Russia.* New York: Pantheon Books, 1985.

Lewin, Moshe. *Russian Peasants and Soviet Power: A Study of Collectivization*, translated by Irene Nove; with a preface by Alec Nove. New York: Norton, 1975.

Louis, Victor. *Sport in the Soviet Union*. Oxford: Oxford University Press, 1964.

Louis, Victor and Louis, Jennifer M. *Sport in the Soviet Union*. Oxford: Oxford University Press, 1980.

Lowe, Margaret. *Looking Good: College Women and Body Image 1875–1930*. Baltimore, MD; London: The Johns Hopkins University Press, 2003.

Makovskii, Iu. V. *Vlyanie natsionalizma i militarizma v burzhuaznom molodezhnom dvizhenii Germanii v gody Beimarskoi Respubliki (1919–1933)*. Tomsk: 1987.

Mally, Lynn. *The Culture of the Future: The Proletkul't Movement in Revolutionary Russia*. Berkeley: University of California Press, 1990.

Mally, Lynn. *Revolutionary Acts: Amateur Theatre and the Soviet State, 1917–1938*. Ithaca, NY: Cornell University Press, 2000.

Markevich, Andrei and Sokolov, Andrei. *Magnita bliz sadovogo kol'tso. Stimuly k rabote na Moskovskom zavode 'Serp i Molot' 1883–2001*. Moscow: ROSSPEN, 2005.

Martin, Terry. *The Affirmative Action Empire: Nations and Nationalism in the Soviet Union, 1923–1939*. Ithaca, NY; London: Cornell University Press, 2001.

McCannon, John. *Red Arctic: Polar Exploration and the Myth of the North in the Soviet Union, 1932–1939*. New York; Oxford: Oxford University Press, 1998.

McReynolds, Louise. *Russia at Play. Activities at the end of the Tsarist Era*. Ithaca, NY; London: Cornell University Press, 2003.

Michaels, Paula A. *Curative Powers: Medicine and Empire in Stalin's Central Asia*. Pittsburgh, PA: University of Pittsburgh Press, 2003.

Michelson, Annette (ed). *Kino-Eye: The Writings of Dziga Vertov*, translated by Kevin O'Brien. Berkeley: University of California Press, 1984.

Moroz, Leonid Abramovich. *Fizicheskaya kul'tura i sport kak oblast' ideologicheskoi bor'by*. Moscow: 1984.

Morris, Andrew D. *Marrow of the Nation: A History of Sport and Physical Culture in Republican China*. Berkeley: University of California Press, 2004.

Morton, Henry. *Soviet Sport: Mirror of Soviet Society*. New York: Collier Books, 1963.

Naiman, E. *Sex in Public: The Incarnation of Early Soviet Ideology*. Princeton, NJ: Princeton University Press, 1997.

Neumann, Matthias. *The Communist Youth League and the Transformation of the Soviet Union, 1917–1932*. London; New York: Routledge, 2011.

Neustatz, Dietmar. *Die Moskauer Metro. Von den ersten Planen bis zur Grossbaustelle des Stalinismus (1897–1935)*. Köln: Böhlau Verlag, 2001.

Nic Congáil, Ríona. *Úna Ní Fhaircheallaigh agus an Fhís Útóipeach Ghaelach*. Gaillimh: Arlen House, 2010.

Noakes, J. and Pridham, G. *A Documentary Reader. Volume 2. Nazism: State, Economy, and Society 1933–1939*. Exeter: University of Exeter, 1984.

Northrop, Douglas. *Veiled Empire: Gender and Power in Stalinist Central Asia*. Ithaca, NY; London: Cornell University Press, 2004.

O'Mahony, Mike. *Sport in the USSR: Physical Culture—Visual Culture*. London: Reaktion Books, 2006.

Outram, Dorinda. *The Body and the French Revolution*. New Haven, CT: Yale University Press, 1989.

Parkins, Wendy (ed). *Fashioning the Body Politic*. Oxford; New York: Berg, 2002.

Peppard, Victor and Riordan, James. *Playing Politics: Soviet Sport Diplomacy to 1992*. Greenwich, CT; London: JAI Press, 1993.

Pethybridge, Roger. *The Social Prelude to Stalinism*. London: Macmillan, 1974.

Petrone, Karen. *Life Has Become More Joyous, Comrades: Celebrations in the Time of Stalin*. Bloomington: Indiana University Press, 2000.

Peukart, Detlef. *Inside Nazi Germany: Conformity, Opposition, and Racism in Everyday Life*, translated by Richard Deveson. New Haven, CT: Yale University Press, 1982.

Pine, Lisa. *Nazi Family Policy, 1933–1945*. Oxford; New York: Berg, 1997.

Plaggenborg, Stefan. *Revoliutsiya i kultura. Kulturniye orientiry v period meshdu oktyabr'skoi revoliutsiei i epokhoi stalinizma*. Saint Petersburg: Zhurnal Neva, 2000.

Platt, Kevin M. F. and David Brandeburger (eds). *Epic Revisionism: Russian History and Literature as Stalinist Propaganda*. Madison: University of Wisconsin Press, 2006.

Popov, Sergei. *Soviet Sports: Questions and Answers*. Moscow: Novosti, 1971.

Potulov, B. M. *N. A. Semashko. Vrach i revolutsioner*. Moscow: Meditsina, 1986.

Razzkazov, F. I. *Zvezdnye tragedii: zagadki, sud'by i gibel'*. Moscow: Eksmo Press, 2000.

Read, Christopher. *The Making and Breaking of the Soviet System*. Basingstoke, Hampshire; New York: Palgrave Macmillan, 2001.

Retish, Aaron B. *Russia's Peasants in Revolution and Civil War: Citizenship, Identity, and the Creation of the Soviet State, 1914–1922*. Cambridge: Cambridge University Press, 2008.

Riordan, James (ed). *Soviet Youth Culture*. Bloomington: Indiana University Press, 1989.

Riordan, James. *Sport in Soviet Society: Development of Sport and Physical Education in Russia and the USSR*. Cambridge; New York: Cambridge University Press, 1977.

Riordan, James. *Sport, Politics and Communism*. Manchester: Manchester University Press; New York: Distributed exclusively in the USA and Canada by St. Martin's Press, 1991.

Riordan, James (ed). *Sport under Communism: The USSR, Czechoslovakia, the GDR, China, Cuba*. London: C Hurst, 1978.

Riordan, James and Arnaud, P. (eds). *Sport and International Politics: The Impact of Facism and Communism on Sport*. London; New York: E & FN Spon, 1998.

Riordan, James and Krüger, A (eds). *European Cultures of Sport: Examining the Nations and Regions*. Bristol, UK: Portland, OR: Intellect, 2003.

Roberts, Graham. *Forward Soviet! History and Non-Fiction Film in the USSR*. London; New York: I. B. Tauris, 1999.

Rosenberg, W. G. (ed). *Bolshevik Visions: First Phase of the Cultural Revolution in Soviet Russia*. Ann Arbor, MI: Ardis, 1984.

Rossol, Nadine. *Performing the Nation in Interwar Germany: Sport, Spectacle and Political Symbolism, 1926–1936*. Basingstoke, Hampshire; New York: Palgrave Macmillan, 2010.

Russkoe i sovetskoe molodezhnoe dvizhenie v dokumentakh, 1905–1937. Moscow: Russkii mir, OMP Press, 2002.

Samoukov, F. I. (ed.) *Istoriya fizicheskoi kul'tury*. Moscow: Fizkul'tura i sport, 1956.

Samosudov, V. M. *Vospitanie molodezhi 30-x godov zhestokostye stalinskogo rezhima*. Omsk: Izd-vo Omskogo ped. Un-ta, 1997.

Sanborn, Joshua. A. *Drafting the Russian Nation: Military Conscription, Total War, and Mass Politics, 1905–1925*. DeKalb: Northern Illinois University Press, 2003.

Schneidman, Norman N. *The Soviet Road to Olympus: Theory and Practice of Soviet Physical Culture and Sport*. Toronto: Ontario Institute for Studies in Education, 1978.

Schteinbakh, V and Gerlitsyn, V. (compilers). *Soviet Sport: The Success Story.* Moscow: Raduga, 1987.

Scott, Sue and Morgan, David (eds). *Body Matters: Essays on the Sociology of the Body.* London; Washington, DC: Falmer Press, 1993.

Shilling, Chris. *The Body and Social Theory* (2nd ed.). London: SAGE Publications, 2003.

Siegelbaum, Lewis and Sokolov, Andrei. *Stalinism as a Way of Life.* New Haven, CT; London: Yale University Press, 2000.

Sinitsyn, D (eds). *Istoriya fizicheskoi kul'tury narodov SSSR.* Moscow: Fizkul'tura i sport, 1953.

Slezkine, Yuri. *Arctic Mirrors: Russia and the Small Peoples of the North.* Ithaca, NY; London: Cornell University Press, 1994.

Sokolov, V. I. *Istoriya molodezhnogo dvizheniya Rossii.* Ryazn': Uzoroch'e, 2002.

Solomon, Susan Gross and Hutchinson, John F. (eds). *Health and Society in Revolutionary Russia.* Bloomington: Indiana University Press, 1990.

Starks, Tricia. *The Body Soviet: Propaganda, Hygiene, and the Revolutionary State.* Madison: Wisconsin University Press, 2008.

Starovoitova, Z. A. *Fizkul'turnoe dvizhenie v pervye gody sovetskoi vlasti i rol' N. I. Podvoiskogo v ego razvitii (1918–1920gg).* (Avtoreferat) Moscow: 1968.

Steinberg, Mark D. *Proletarian Imagination: Self, Modernity and the Sacred in Russia, 1910–1925.* Ithaca, NY: Cornell University Press, 2002.

Stetsura, Iu. A. *Revoliutsionnyi pafos i tragizm pokoleniya 20–30-kh godov.* Ekaterinburg; Perm': RAN Ural. Otd-nie Institut istorii i archeologii, Kom. Po delam molodezhi adm. Perm. Obl., 1995.

Stewart, Mary Lynn. *For Health and Beauty: Physical Culture for Frenchwomen, 1880s–1930s.* Baltimore, MD; London: Johns Hopkins University Press, 2001.

Stites, Richard. *Revolutionary Dreams, Utopian Visions: Experimental Life in the Russian Revolution.* Oxford: Oxford University Press, 1989.

Stites, Richard. *Russian Popular Culture Entertainment and Society since 1900.* Cambridge: Cambridge University Press, 1992.

Stites, Richard. *The Women's Liberation Movement in Russia: Feminism, Nihilism and Bolshevism, 1860–1936.* Princeton, NJ: Princeton University Press, 1978.

Stolbov, Vitalii Vasil'evich. *Istorii fizicheskoi istorii i sporta.* Moscow: Fizkul'tura i sport, 2000.

Tamashin, L. *Sovetskaya dramaturgiya v gody grazhdanskoi voiny.* Moscow: Iskusstvo, 1961.

Taylor, Charles. *Sources of the Self: The Making of Modern Identity.* Cambridge: Cambridge University Press, 1989.

Taylor, Richard. *The Film Factory: Russian and Soviet Cinema in Documents 1896–1939,* co-edited with an introduction by Ian Christie. London: Routledge & Kegan Paul, 1988.

Taylor, Richard. *Film Propaganda: Soviet Russia and Nazi Germany.* London: I. B. Tauris, 1979.

Taylor, Richard and Derek Spring (eds). *Stalinism and Soviet Cinema.* London; New York: Routledge, 1993.

Timasheff, Nicholas. *The Great Retreat.* New York: Dutton, 1946.

Tirado, Isabel. *Young Guard! The Communist Youth League Petrograd 1917–1920.* Westport, CT: Greenwood Press, 1989.

Turner, Bryan S. *The Body and Society: Explorations in Social Theory.* Oxford: Oxford University Press, 1984.

Turner, Victor (ed). *Celebration: Studies in Festivity and Ritual.* Washington, DC: Smithsonian Institution Press, 1982.

Van Geldern, James and Stites, R. *Mass Culture in Soviet Russia: Tales, Poems, Songs, Movies, Plays, and Folklore, 1917–1953.* Bloomington: Indiana University Press, 1995.

Viola, Lynne. *Peasant Rebels Under Stalin: Collectivization and the Culture of Peasant Resistance.* New York: Oxford University Press, 1996.

Von Hagen, Mark. *Soldiers in the Proletarian Dictatorship: The Red Army and the Soviet Socialist State, 1917–1930.* Ithaca, NY; London: Cornell University Press, 1990.

Ward, Chris. *Stalin's Russia.* London: Edward Arnold; New York: Distributed in the USA by Routledge, Chapman and Hall, 1993.

White, Stephen. *The Bolshevik Poster.* New Haven, CT: Yale University Press, 1988.

White, Stephen (ed). *New Directions in Soviet History.* Cambridge; New York: Cambridge University Press, 1992.

White, Stephen. *Political Culture and Soviet Politics.* New York: St. Martin's Press, 1979.

Wood, Elizabeth. *The Baba and the Comrade: Gender and Politics in Revolutionary Russia.* Bloomington: Indiana University Press, 1997.

Youngblood, D. *Movies for the Masses: Popular Cinema and Soviet Society in the 1920s.* Cambridge; New York: Cambridge University Press, 1992.

Zhuravlev, S. V. *Fenomen 'Istoria fabrikov'. Gor'kovskoe nachinanie v kontekste 1930-x godov.* Moscow: RAN, 1997.

Zuzanek, Jiri. *Work and Leisure in the Soviet Union: A Time-Budget Analysis.* New York: Praeger, 1980.

Articles, Collections, Dissertations

Bergman, Jay. "Valerii Chkalov: Soviet Pilot as New Soviet Man". *Journal of Contemporary History* 33, no. 1 (1998): 135–152.

Bernstein, Frances L. "Envisioning Health in Revolutionary Russia: The Politics of Gender in Sexual-Enlightenment Posters of the 1920s". *Russian Review* 57, no. 2 (1998): 191–217.

Bourdieu, Pierre. "Program for a Sociology of Sport". *Sociology of Sport Journal*, no. 5 (1988): 154–169.

Brubaker, Rogers and Cooper, Frederick. "Beyond 'Identity'", *Theory and Society* 29 (2000): 1–47 .

Chanysheva, T. "Kul'tshefskaya deyatel'nost' gorodskikh rabochikh v derevne v gody pervoi pyatiletki". In *Sovetskaya kul'tura: 70 let Razvitiya*, edited by V. V. Piotrovskii and M. Nauka, 138–148. Moscow: Nauka, 1987.

Danilov, V. P. "O Russkoi chastushke kak istochnike po istorii derevni". In *Sovetskaya kul'tura: 70 let razvitiya*, edited by V. V. Piotrovskii, 376–392. Moscow: Nauka, 1987.

David-Fox, Michael. "What is Cultural Revolution?" *Russian Review* 58, no. 2, (1999): 181–201.

Edele, Mark. "Soviet Society, Social Structure, and Everyday Life. Major Frameworks Reconsidered". *Kritika: Explorations in Russian and Eurasian History* 8, no. 2 (2007): 349–373.

Edelman, Robert. "A Small Way of Saying 'No': Moscow Working Men, Spartak Soccer, and the Communist Party, 1900–1945". *The American Historical Review* 107, no. 5 (2002): 1441–1474.

Entsiklopedicheskii slovar' po fizicheskoi kul'ture i sportu. Tom 1. Absoliutnyi rekord-klinch. Ed. by G. I. Kukushkin. Moscow: Fizkul'tura i sport,1961.

Fizicheskaya kul'tura i sport, Moskva. 50 let izdatel'stvu. 1923–73. Bibliograficheskii ukazatel'. Moscow: Fizkul'tura i sport,1973.

Fizicheskaya kul'tura i sport v SSSR v tsifrakh i faktakh, 1917–1961gg. Moscow: Fizkul'tura i sport, 1962.

Fizicheskaya kul'tura i sport v SSSR, 40 let 1917–1957. Moscow: Fizkul'tura i sport, 1957.

Fitzpatrick, Sheila. "Cultural Revolution in Russia 1928–1932". *Journal of Contemporary History* 9 (1974): 1–40.

Fitzpatrick, Sheila. "Cultural Revolution Revisited". *Russian Review* 58, no. 2 (1999): 202–209.

Fitzpatrick, Sheila. "Happiness and Toska: A Study of Emotions in 1930s Russia". *Australian Journal of Politics and History* 50, no. 3 (2004): 357–371.

Fitzpatrick, Sheila. "Sex and Revolution: An Examination of Literary and Statistical Data on the Mores of Soviet Students in the 1920s". *The Journal of Modern History* 50 (1978): 252–278.

Fitzpatrick, Sheila. "The 'Soft Line' on Culture and Its Enemies: Soviet Cultural Policy, 1922–1929". *Slavic Review* 33, no. 2 (1974): 268–287.

Fox, Michael S. "Glavlit, Censorship and the Problem of Party Policy in Cultural Affairs, 1922–1928". *Soviet Studies* 44, no. 6 (1992): 1045–1068.

Frykholm, Peter. "Soccer and Social Identity in Pre-Revolutionary Moscow". *Journal of Sport History* 24, no. 2 (1997): 143–154.

Fürst, Juliane. "Prisoners of the Soviet Self? Political Youth Opposition in Late Stalinism". *Europe-Asia Studies* 54, no. 3 (2002): 353–375.

Geiger, Kent. "Changing Political Attitudes in Totalitarian Society: A Case Study of the Role of the Family". *World Politics* 8, no. 2 (1956): 187–205.

Geyer, Michael. "The Stigma of Violence, Nationalism and War in Twentieth Century Germany". *German Studies Review*, special issue (1992): 75–110.

Gorsuch, Anne E. "NEP Be Damned! Young Militants in the 1920s and the Culture of Civil War". *Russian Review* 56, no. 4 (1997): 564–580.

Gorsuch, Anne E. "'A Woman is Not a Man': The Culture of Gender and Generation in Soviet Russia, 1921–1928". *Slavic Review* 55, no. 3 (1996): 636–660.

Graham, Loren R. "Science and Values: The Eugenics Movement in Germany and Russia in the 1920s". *American Historical Review* 82, no. 5 (1977): 1133–1164.

Grant, Susan. "The Collective Agitation of Arms and Legs: Revolutionizing Physical Culture Organization, 1924–1934". *Revolutionary Russia* (2010): 93–113.

Grant, Susan. "The Politics of Physical Culture in the 1920s". *Slavonic and East European Review* 89, no. 3 (2011): 494–515.

Guttmann, Allen. "Sport, Politics and the Engaged Historian". *Journal of Contemporary History* 38, no. 3 (2003): 363–375.

Harman, Dilshat. "The New Man and the New Way of Life: Who Built 1920s Moscow and for Whom?" Paper presented at the Study Group on the Russian Revolution January 2009.

Hatch, John B. "Hangouts and Hangovers: State, Class and Culture in Moscow's Workers' Club Movement, 1925–1928". *Russian Review* 53, no. 1 (1994): 97–117.

Hatch, John B. "Working Class Politics in Moscow during the Early NEP: Mensheviks and Workers' Organisations, 1921–1922". *Europe-Asia Studies* 39, no. 4 (1987): 555–574.

Ilic, Melanie. "Soviet Women and Civil Defense Training in the 1930s". *Minerva Journal of Women and War* 2, no. 1 (2008): 100–113.

Institut Fizicheskoi Kul'tury. Moskva. Bibliograichaskii ukazatel' nauchno-issledovatelei (1920–1961). Moscow: Fizkul'tura i sport,1964.

Jones, Stephen. "State Intervention and Leisure in Britain between the Wars". *Journal of Contemporary History* 22, no. 1 (1987): 163–185.

Keys, Barbara J. "The Body as a Political Space: Comparing Physical Education under Nazism and Stalinism". *German History* 27, no. 3 (2009): 395–413.

Keys, Barbara J. "Soviet Sport and Transnational Mass Culture in the 1930s". *Journal of Contemporary History* 38, no. 3 (2003): 413–434.

Livers, Keith A. "The Soccer Match as Stalinist Ritual: Constructing the Body Social in Lev Kassil's *The Goalkeeper of the Republic*". *Russian Review* 60, no. 4 (2001): 592–613.

Mally, Lynn. "The Rise and Fall of the Soviet Youth Theater TRAM". *Slavic Review* 51, no. 3 (1992): 411–430.

Miller, James W. "Youth in the Dictatorships". *The American Political Science Review* 32, no. 5 (1938): 965–970.

Murphy, Kevin. "Opposition at the Local Level: A Case Study of the Hammer and Sickle Factory". *Europe-Asia Studies* 53, no. 2 (2001): 329–350.

Osnovnye postanovlenie, prikazy i instruktsii po voprosam sovetskoi fizkul'tury i sporta 1917–1957. Moscow: Fizkul'tura i sport, 1953.

Petrone, Karen. "Parading the Nation: Physical Culture Celebrations and the Construction of Soviet Identities in the 1930s". *Michigan Discussions in Anthropology, Post-Soviet Eurasia* 12 (1996): 25–32.

Pfister, Gertrud. "The Medical Discourse on Female Physical Culture in Germany in the 19th and Early 20th Centuries". *Journal of Sport History*, 17, no. 2 (1990): 183–198.

Philips, Laura. "In Defence of Their Families: Working-Class Women, Alcohol, and Politics in Revolutionary Russia". *Journal of Women's History* 11, no. 1 (1999): 97–120.

Pinnow, Kenneth Martin. "Making Suicide Soviet: Medicine, Moral Statistics, and the Politics of Social Science in Bolshevik Russia, 1920–1930". Columbia University dissertation, 1998.

Riordan, James. "The Rise, Fall and Rebirth of Sporting Women in Russia and the USSR". *Journal of Sport History* 18, no. 1 (1991): 183–199.

Riordan, James. "Sidney Jackson: An American in Russia's Boxing Hall of Fame". *Journal of Sport History* 20, no. 1 (1993): 49–56.

Riordan, Jim. "Soviet Youth: Pioneers of Change". *Soviet Studies* 15, no. 4 (1988): 556–572.

Rolf, Malte. "Constructing a Soviet Time: Bolshevik Festivals and Their Rivals during the First Five-Year Plan. A Study of the Central Black Earth Region". *Kritika: Exploration in Russian and Eurasian History* 1, no. 3 (2000): 447–473.

Rolf, Malte. "A Hall of Mirrors: Sovietizing Culture under Stalinism". *Slavic Review* 68, no. 3 (2009): 601–630.

Rowley, Alison. "Sport in the Service of the State: Images of Physical Culture and Soviet Women, 1917–1941". *The International Journal for the History of Sport* 23, no. 8 (2006): 1314–1314.

Saroyan, Mark. "Beyond the Nation-State: Culture and Ethnic Politics in Soviet Transcaucasia" in *Transcaucasia, Nationalism, and Social Change: Essays in the History of Armenia, Azerbaijan, and Georgia*, 401–426, edited by R. Suny. Ann Arbor: University of Michigan Press, 1996.

Shaw, Claire. "A Fairground for 'Building the New Man': Gorky Park as a Site of Soviet acculturation". *Urban History* 38, 2 (2011): 324–244.

Siegelbaum, Lewis. "The Shaping of Soviet Workers' Leisure: Worker's Clubs and Palaces of Culture in the 1930s". *International Labor and Working-Class History* 56 (1999): 78–95.

Simpson, Pat. "Bolshevism and 'Sexual Revolution': Visualizing New Soviet Woman as the Eugenic Ideal", in *Art, Sex and Eugenics, Corpus Delecti*, edited by Fae Brauer and Anthea Callen, 209–238. Aldershot: Ashgate, 2008.

Simpson, Pat. "Imag(in)ing Post-Revolutionary Evolution. The Taylorized Pro-letarian, 'Conditioning', and Soviet Darwinism in the 1920s", in *The Art of Evolution: Darwin, Darwinisms, and Visual Culture*, edited by Barbara Larson and Fae Brauer, 226–261. Hanover, NH; London: University Press of New England, 2009.

Slezkine, Yuri. "Imperialism as the Highest Stage of Capitalism", *Russian Review* 59, no. 2 (2000): 227–234.

Solomon, Susan Gross. "The Soviet Legalization of Abortion in German Medical Discourse: A Study of the Use of Selective Perceptions in Cross-Cultural Scientific Relations". *Social Studie of Science* 22 (1992): 455–485.

Solomon, Susan Gross. "The Demographic Argument in Soviet Debates over the Legalization of Abortion in the 1920's". *Cahiers du Monde Russe et Soviétique* 33, no. 1 (1992): 59–81.

Starks, Tricia. "A Revolutionary Home: Housekeeping and Social Duty in the 1920s". *Revolutionary Russia*, 17, no. 1 (1994): 69–104.

Stolee, Margaret K. "Homeless Children in the USSR, 1917–1957". *Soviet Studies* 40, no. 1 (1988): 64–83.

Tirado, Isabel. "Peasants into Soviets: Reconstructing Komsomol Identity in the Russian Countryside of the 1920s", *Acta Slavica Iaponica* 18 (2001): 42–63.

Tirado, Isabel. "The Village Voice. Women's Views of Themselves and their World in Russian Chastushki of the 1920s". The Carl Beck Papers, CREES, Pittsburgh, PA, December 1993.

Tovarishch Komsomol. Dokumenty s'ezdov, konferentsii i TsK VLKSM 1918–1968. Tom 1. Moscow, 1969.

White, James D. "Alexander Bogdanov's Conception of the Proletkul't". Paper presented at the Study Group on the Russian Revolution, January 2011.

Widdis, Emma. "The Cinematic Pastoral of the 1930s", in *Picturing Russia. Explorations in Visual Culture*, edited by Valerie A. Kivelson and Joan Neuberger, 175–180. New Haven, CT; London: Yale University Press, 2008.

Zweiniger-Bargielowska, Ina. "Building a British Superman: Physical Culture in Interwar Britain". *Journal of Contemporary History* 41, no. 4 (2006): 595–610.

Electronic Resources

Archinform lists of constructivist architecture in Moscow, including clubs; available at http://eng.archinform.net/projekte/8736.htm, accessed 3 September 2009.

Khronos i sodruzhestvo literaturnykh proektov, Biograficheskii ukazatel'; available at http://www.hronos.info/biograf/antipov.html, accessed 10 and 20 July 2008.

The main archive administration attached to KMRT. E. Tagirov and d. Sharafutdinov "Sabantui in Local and Global Civilizational Space" available at http://www.archive.gov.tatarstan.ru/_go/anonymous/main/?path=/pages/ru/1gau/901sborniki/izdatelskay/Sabantuy/4Glava_3, accessed 28 April 2008.

Pervye ustavy RKKA, istochnik "Voenno-istoricheskii zhurnal" (Red Army regulations available from the "Military history journal"); available at http://rkka.ru/history/ustav/main.htm, accessed 27 July 2009.

Rossiisskii profsoiuz trudyashchikhsya aviatsionnoi promyshlennosty (The trade union for workers of the aviation industry); available at http://www.profavia.ru/about/history.shtml, accessed 7 July 2008.

"Stalinskie spiski" ("Stalin's lists"), compiled by "Memorial" and the Archive of the President of the Russian Federation. APRF , op.24, d. 377, l.133; available at http://stalin.memo.ru/spiski/pg12133.htm, accessed 7 May 2009.

Filmography

Dziga Vertov, 1929. *Chelovek s kinoapparatom*
Grigory Aleksandrov, 1934. *Veselye Rebyata*
Grigory Aleksandrov, 1936. *Tsirk*
Igor Savchenko, 1936. *Sluchainaya Vstrecha*
Leni Riefenstahl, 1937. *Triumph des Willens*
Nikita Mikhalkov, 1994. *Utomlennoe Sontse*
Semyon Timoshenko, 1936. *Vratar'*

Index

T

Tambov, 64, 111–112
"Tasks, Plans, Programmes and Norms
of Women's Physical Culture,
The" (Korolev), 76
Taylor, Gerard, 16
Taylorism, 24
teachers of physical culture. *See*
instructors and teachers of
physical culture
Timasheff, Nicholas, 50
Timoshenko, Semyon, 125
Tirado, Isabel, 60, 107, 109
Tishchenko, Pavel Alekseevich, 122,
133
Tomsky, Mikhail, 31, 34
Torpedo (automobile workers),
160
tractor and combine drivers, 117–118,
121
trade unions: the deaf, 156–157;
funding physical culture, 152;
genesis and organizational
conflict, 31, 32, 33, 34–35,
36–37; GTO, 38–39, 42–44;
Italian, 18; parks and stadiums,
152; resources and funding,
150, 151–152; spartakiads
and parades, 126–127,
130–132, 136, 139–140;
voluntary sports societies,
41–44
TRAM (Theatre of Working Class
Youth), 58, 204n43
Transcaucasia, 102, 109, 112
transformation, society, 7, 51,
173–174
Trekin, 162
Trotsky, Lev, 23, 31, 34, 176
TsDKA (Central House of the Red
Army), 42, 136, 139, 161,
162
Tsirk, 147
Turkey, 16
Turnen gymnastics, 10
Tusova, Galina, 90
25,000ers, 114

U

Ukraine, 42, 63, 119, 128, 144, 158
Union of Economic Workers,
167–168
United States, 4, 18–19, 40, 52, 78
Uzbekistan, 128, 144, 220n21

V

"V poryadke samokritiki" (Gradov),
59–60
Van Geldern, James, 129
Vasil'eva, A.P., 94
Vertov, Dziga, 83, 125
village reading rooms, 79, 100,
106–109, 123
Viola, Lynne, 113–114
visual culture, 4, 146
Voitkovskaya, 158
voluntary sports societies, 41–44, 48.
See also specific societies
von Hagen, Mark, 69–70
vospitanie, 3, 31, 50–52, 64–65, 174,
187n8, 202n10
Vratar', 83, 125
Vsevobuch (Central Agency for
Universal Military Training),
14, 30–31, 173, 176–177, 181,
195n1
VSFK. *See* Supreme Council of Physical
Culture
Vtorova sisters, 91, 97
VTsSPS, 37, 41, 130, 151
VUZy, 63, 136, 180

W

Wandervogel, 10
war communism, 53–54
What Is to Be Done? (Chernyshevsky),
22–23
Widdis, Emma, 86
women: background and overview,
72–73, 97–98; body, 18–20,
67, 72, 74–76, 85–86; education, 79–81; Germany and
Italy, 17–18; medical and
scientific views, 74–79; older,
93–94, 154–156; participation,
93–97; post-war attitudes,
14–16; propaganda, 6,
110–111, 172; spartakiads,
134; sport, 20, 91–92,
192n67; in workforce, 82,
210n39
worker discontent, 137–138

Y

Yagoda, Genrikh, 101
Yarskaya-Smirnova, Elena, 49
Yenukidze, A., 31
Yeshchin, Dmitri, 73
Yesinin, Sergei, 50